NEW PLAYWRIGHTS

The Best Plays of 2007

D1196034

NEW PLAYWRIGHTS

The Best Plays
of 2007

Edited by Lawrence Harbison

CONTEMPORARY PLAYWRIGHTS
SERIES

A Smith and Kraus Book
Hanover, New Hampshire

A Smith and Kraus Book
Published by Smith and Kraus, Inc.
177 Lyme Road, Hanover, NH 03755
www.SmithandKraus.com

Manufactured in the United States of America
Cover and text design by Julia Gignoux, Freedom Hill Design, Cavendish, Vermont
Composition by Jenna Dixon, Bookbuilder, jdbb.net
photo of Bathsheba Doran by Gavin Gould.

First Edition: June 2008
10 9 8 7 6 5 4 3 2 1

Library of Congress Control Number: 2008923279
ISBN-13 978-1-57525-591-0 / ISBN-10 1-57525-591-X

CONTENTS

FOREWORD

For the past seven years the esteemed D. L. Lepidus has done an admirable job of editing this important series for Smith and Kraus. It is my intention to carry on his tradition of making this anthology a comprehensive and varied collection of new writing for the theater — in style, in subject, and in genre. In making my choices I have seen at least 200 plays and read easily that many. Making my final selections was not an easy task, for in this new golden age of playwriting there are many new plays by new playwrights worthy of selection. The hardest part was cutting plays I loved that for one reason or another seemed less important than the ones I finally chose.

I have started off the book with Anna Ziegler's *BFF*, a tale of undying friendship between two teenaged girls, one of whom is determined to carry on the memory of her friend into adulthood by literally becoming her. *dark play or stories for boys* by Carlos Murillo is written in the new faux-free-verse style that is becoming all the rage. This provocative play focuses on a teenaged computer whiz who invents an alter ego in order to lure another boy into his fantasy world. Like D. L. Lepidus, I think this anthology should contain at least one out-and-out comedy, and this year's selection is Scott Sickles' *Intellectuals*, a very amusing play about a psychologist who decides to take a "sabbatical" from her marriage to pursue her untapped potential as a lesbian. *Living Room in Africa* by Bathsheba Doran is an intense drama about a couple who have moved to a small village in Africa to set up a museum there with money donated from the West, only to learn that they are living in an area devastated by AIDS. *No Child . . .* by Nilaja Sun is an acclaimed long-running Off- Broadway hit that subsequently toured all over the U.S. and abroad. In it, Ms. Sun played a beleaguered substitute teacher in the inner city high school from hell. She was hired to work with this problem school's most incorrigible students to present a play. She played all the roles — from herself to students to parents to other teachers to the principal to a veteran, much-beloved janitor — in this insightful look at life in a hellish American high school. Bruce Norris' terrific dark satire *The Pain and the Itch* achieved Off-Broadway acclaim and went on the London, where it was equally sensationally received. It's a hilarious social satire about liberal hypocrisy, focusing on an American family who want it all: moral superiority and a wide-screen TV. Finally, there is Kathryn Walat's delightfully brash coming-of-age comedy *Victoria Martin: Math Team Queen.* Victoria wants to be Most Popular, but she also wants to be known for her brains. She becomes the first girl ever on her high school's math team — which scrambles the team's all-male dynamic.

I am absolutely convinced that every one of these wonderful new playwrights will go on to join the A-List within the next few years.

I hope you enjoy these wonderful new plays.

—Lawrence Harbison

BFF

Anna Ziegler

PLAYWRIGHT'S BIOGRAPHY

Anna Ziegler's plays include: *BFF* (produced by W.E.T. at the DR2 Theatre, 2007), *Novel* (SPF, 2007), *Life Science* (produced by Bulldog Theatrical, 2007), Photograph 51 (produced and commissioned by Active Cultures, February–March 2008), *Dov and Ali* (to be produced June–July 2008, Theatre 503, UK)*, In the Same Room, The Minotaur, Variations on a Theme, To Be Fair,* and *Everything You Have.*

Ziegler's plays have been developed by: The Sundance Theatre Lab, The Old Vic New Voices program, Primary Stages, The Geva Theatre Center, The Lark Theatre, Ars Nova, The Kennedy Center, Theater J, New Georges (where she is an Affiliated Artist), The New Harmony Project, The hotINK Festival, The Icicle Creek Theatre Festival, Catalyst Theater, The Playwright's Center PlayLabs Festival, Short + Sweet Festival (Melbourne, Australia), The Fireraisers Theatre Company at the Hampstead Theatre (London) and The Birmingham Rep, and by Company B at the Belvoir St. Theatre in Sydney, Australia. She was a Dramatist's Guild Fellow for 2004–2005 and a member of the 2005 Soho Rep Writer/Director Lab. She has been published in *Ten-Minute Plays for 2 Actors: The Best of 2004* (Smith and Kraus, Inc.) and in *New American Short Plays 2005* (Backstage Books, ed. Craig Lucas). *BFF* and *Life Science* will be published by Dramatists Play Service. A graduate of Yale, she holds an M.F.A. from Tisch.

Anna Ziegler's poetry has appeared in *The Best American Poetry 2003, The Threepenny Review, The Michigan Quarterly Review, Reactions, The Mississippi Review, Arts and Letters, Mid-American Review, Smartish Pace, The Saint Ann's Review,* and many other journals.

For more information, please see www.annabziegler.com.

ORIGINAL PRODUCTION

BFF was given its World Premiere by W.E.T. (Women's Expressive Theater, Inc.), Executive Producers Sasha Eden and Victoria Pettibone. BFF opened Off-Broadway in New York City on February 24, 2007, and ran at The DR2 Theatre, where W.E.T. was a theater-in-residence.

CAST

LAUREN	Sasha Eden
ELIZA	Laura Heisler
SETH	Jeremy Webb

Director .... Josh Hecht
Set Designer .... Robin Vest
Costume Designer .... Sara Jean Tosetti
Lighting Designer .... Clifton Taylor
Sound Designer and Original Music .... David Stephen Baker
Video Projection Designer .... Kevin R. Frech
Production Manager .... David Nelson
Production Stage Manager .... Ashley B. Delegal
Casting Director .... Jack Doulin
Assistant Producer .... Ashley Eichhorn

BFF has been developed at the Soho Rep Theatre, The Lark Play Development Center, Ars Nova, and The Sundance Theatre Lab. It was produced by W.E.T. (February 17–March 31, 2007) at the DR2 Theatre in New York.

CHARACTERS
ELIZA: late twenties, early thirties
LAUREN: late twenties, early thirties
SETH: late twenties, early thirties

SETTINGS
1991 in upstate New York and 2005 in New York City

BFF

SCENE 1

Lauren, twelve, is swimming in a pool. She gets out and dries herself off. Eliza, twelve, is lying on a towel, reading a magazine. It's summer; the sun is bright. Lauren is in a bikini. Eliza wears a t-shirt and eats, intermittently, from a box of cereal. Lauren lies down, her head on Eliza's stomach. They lie in this position for a little while before speaking.

LAUREN: Liza, what do you think it'll be like to be grown up?

ELIZA: I don't know.

LAUREN: I mean, do you think it feels different than this?

   (Eliza thinks about it.)

ELIZA: No. Probably not.

LAUREN: Right. Probably not.

ELIZA: Why do you ask?

LAUREN: I don't know.

ELIZA: OK.

LAUREN: No, I mean, I just got this feeling, while I was swimming, that the years are gonna pass so quickly.

ELIZA: Oh . . . I don't want them to.

LAUREN: This feeling that everything happens at once, you know? That we're already grown up and walking around somewhere and doing some job and we just don't know it.

ELIZA: You're not making sense, Lauren.

LAUREN: I am.

ELIZA: OK.

LAUREN: Let's make something up.

ELIZA: OK.

LAUREN: Let's tell the future.

ELIZA: I don't want to think about the future.

LAUREN: Like, where are we gonna live in the year 2000?

ELIZA: I don't know —

LAUREN: New York City?

ELIZA: Yeah, I guess.

LAUREN: We could have, like, apartments next to each other.

ELIZA: *(Finally getting into it a little.)* We could live in the same apartment.

LAUREN: Absolutely.

> *(Beat.)*

Will we get married?

ELIZA: To each other?

LAUREN: No! I meant, in general.

ELIZA: I think we will. When we want to.

LAUREN: How will we know when we want to?

ELIZA: I don't know. I guess when the right person comes along.

LAUREN: But who will the right person be?

ELIZA: Really nice.

LAUREN: Eliza.

ELIZA: What?

LAUREN: He's gotta be hot.

ELIZA: Of course hot. I meant hot too. Nice and hot.

LAUREN: And funny.

ELIZA: It would be great if he were funny. *(Beat.)* And he should have a secret.

LAUREN: What do you mean?

ELIZA: Something he only tells you.

LAUREN: I guess. Yeah.

ELIZA: He'll be shy but also open. A little awkward but in a sweet way.

LAUREN: If you say so.

ELIZA: Will you rub my back?

> *(Lauren does.)*

Isn't this is a great day, Lauren?

LAUREN: It is.

ELIZA: I feel really happy right now.

LAUREN: You do?

ELIZA: I sort of wish we could just stay here forever.

LAUREN: We have til four, right? I mean, that's still a couple hours —

ELIZA: But I can feel it becoming a memory even as it's happening.

LAUREN: Don't say that.

ELIZA: But it's how I feel.

LAUREN: Hey, did you know that Jason Priestly lost twenty-five pounds?

ELIZA: I didn't.

LAUREN: Jason Priestly's so hot.

ELIZA: I know. Totally hot.

> *(Long beat.)*

ELIZA: But do you ever get the feeling of missing someone even when you're sitting right next to them?

LAUREN: Liza —
ELIZA: I miss you.
    (Beat.)
LAUREN: I'm sorry.
ELIZA: About what?
LAUREN: I don't know.

SCENE 2

Lauren, now in her late twenties, is doing yoga on a mat in a large empty room. Seth enters and stares at her for a few moments. He coughs. Lauren turns around abruptly. The two make eye contact for a long moment. Then Lauren begins to gather her things.

SETH: You don't have to go.
LAUREN: Oh no, I was leaving anyway.
SETH: I think I'm just early for the next class.
LAUREN: I didn't know there was another class in here.
SETH: Yeah, there is.
    (Beat.)
    It has to do with finding your inner voice in a post 9/11 landscape.
LAUREN: Right.
SETH: I lost a bet.
LAUREN: *(Turning to leave.)* OK.
SETH: But I figured maybe, well . . . given the way my life is now, it wouldn't be bad to try some new things. Why not try to find my inner voice? Find out if that sort of thing is possible.
LAUREN: What's the way your life is now?
SETH: I mean, maybe if more people had inner voices, the world would be in better shape.
LAUREN: I don't know.
SETH: *(Awkwardly.)* You look like you're in pretty good shape.
LAUREN: I have work.
SETH: My life now is a little monotonous. A little bit the same all the time.
LAUREN: I think that's what life's like.
SETH: I don't think it has to be.
LAUREN: You don't?
SETH: No.

(Beat.)

LAUREN: Well. I better —

SETH: Right.

(Lauren stands, packs up and heads for the door. Eliza's in the doorway.)

Um . . . what's your name?

(Eliza takes Lauren's hand and pulls her into the next scene. Seth doesn't see Eliza and watches Lauren go.)

SCENE 3

Lauren and Eliza, the teenagers, are singing along to a cassette in Lauren's bedroom. They're holding hands and dancing. The song is the Divinyls "I Touch Myself." They're hamming it up. The song ends; they collapse on the floor.

LAUREN: I think Mrs. Linklater should touch herself. She's so totally repressed.

ELIZA: Maybe all math teachers are.

LAUREN: Why, because numbers are like a language for people who don't want to use words?

ELIZA: No, because they all look totally repressed.

LAUREN: I bet Mrs. Linklater's a virgin.

ELIZA: I bet she is.

LAUREN: I bet she's never kissed anyone. I bet she lives alone and she's never smoked a cigarette. I bet she's having a very lonely summer.

ELIZA: Yeah, I bet.

LAUREN: Maybe she's an orphan and never knew any love and everything follows from that.

ELIZA: That's awful! . . . But yeah, maybe. I could see that.

LAUREN: I think my mom never slept with anyone but my dad. I asked her once . . . She told me it was none of my business. That's why I think it's true.

(Long beat.)

Oh, I'm sorry, Liza — I didn't mean to bring anything up —

ELIZA: No — it's fine.

LAUREN: I think you're doing so well these days. My mom says you seem to be doing really well and I think so too.

ELIZA: Sure, yeah.

(Long beat.)

LAUREN: Anyway, sometimes I think my mom's shy and, like, modest, because her name is Sarah. I mean, isn't that a shy kind of name?

ELIZA: I don't know. Is my name shy?

LAUREN: No way. It's loud. It, like, has a voice. Eliza. I mean, say it.

ELIZA: Um, no.

LAUREN: Come on, say it . . . Eliza . . .

ELIZA: No.

LAUREN: Just say it. *(Then more dramatically.)* Eliza . . . *(Low and sexy.)* Eliza. Say it.

ELIZA: *(Snapping, angry.)* No!

LAUREN: *(Hurt.)* OK. Sorry.
   (Beat.)

ELIZA: *(Quietly.)* You dweeb.

LAUREN: Lauren's quiet. I don't think she's shy but she's quiet. She slips along.

ELIZA: I think it's the other way around.

LAUREN: No. You're brave.

ELIZA: Right.

LAUREN: Your pick this time.
   (Eliza leafs through the albums. She puts one on. It's slower and mellow. Her dad's favorite song. She stands, begins to sway.)
   That's like . . . I don't know . . . I feel like my mom likes that song.

ELIZA: Right. No — I think I put it on by mistake.
   (She stops it abruptly. She sits down. Beat.)
   Lauren, do you ever feel like the hardest thing in the world is just waking up?

LAUREN: Wow, um . . . Liza?

ELIZA: What?

LAUREN: You know, the thing is, these days I'm never sure what you're going to say.

ELIZA: I surprise you?

LAUREN: Yeah, I mean. You do.

ELIZA: *(Thoughtfully.)* Good.

SCENE 4

Lauren, the adult, is back on the yoga mat. Seth watches her again from the doorway.

SETH: You must do this every Tuesday.

(Lauren turns around.)

LAUREN: I guess that's the nature of a weekly class.

SETH: But you stay after.

LAUREN: I like quiet.

SETH: Me too.

LAUREN: *(Standing.)* So, did you find it?

SETH: What?

LAUREN: Your inner voice?

SETH: Oh. No. But I did learn some ways to begin to understand what an inner voice is. See, first you have to understand it, then you can begin to try to locate it. You can't try to find something when you don't know what you're looking for. It's all very . . .

LAUREN: What?

SETH: Well, I don't know you so I'm not sure how you feel about things like this. I could say "deep" with a sort of sarcastic edge or I could say it's all very zen and try to take it seriously. I don't want to offend you.

LAUREN: You're not offending me —

SETH: I don't want to make you late for work.

LAUREN: I'm always late.

SETH: What do you do?

LAUREN: I work with aquatic animals.

SETH: What, like at an aquarium?

LAUREN: No.

(Long beat.)

SETH: OK.

(Beat.)

I like your bracelets.

LAUREN: Thanks.

SETH: They caught my eye.

LAUREN: They were cheap.

SETH: Most people don't wear jewelry to work out, do they?

LAUREN: Right so what do you do?

SETH: Oh it's hard to explain. Very serious business. Lots of abstract thinking and late nights.

LAUREN: Oh.

SETH: No — I'm kidding. I'm a banker. I mean, I work at a bank.

LAUREN: Are you married?

SETH: No.

(Beat.)

Are you?

LAUREN: I only asked because —

SETH: You think I'm coming on to you?

LAUREN: No, I . . . I don't know. Are you?

SETH: Can I?

LAUREN: I don't know, um —

SETH: Seth.

LAUREN: Right, Seth. I don't like invasions, you know.

SETH: Am I being invasive?

LAUREN: No, I'm just letting you know.

SETH: What's your name?

LAUREN: Eliza.

SETH: Eliza. I like it.

LAUREN: Did I say Eliza? I meant —

SETH: Eliza — like the song.

(Beat.)

LAUREN: Is there a song?

SETH: I assume there are songs for most names.

(Long beat.)

LAUREN: Well I don't think there's one for me.

SETH: Not yet, maybe. But these things get written every day, don't they?

LAUREN: I guess so.

SCENE 5

Lauren and Eliza are on swings that have dropped down; the girls are too big for them, but they don't care. They hold hands.

ELIZA: 1991. It doesn't sound like much, does it?

LAUREN: No.

ELIZA: No.

LAUREN: I wonder if we'll ever be a part of history, like real history. Like a war or a . . . revolution.

ELIZA: Maybe we don't want to be. My mom says things are better this way. Like you don't know to appreciate something until it's gone.

LAUREN: She's talking about your dad dying, right?

ELIZA: *(After a beat.)* I guess so, yeah.

LAUREN: But you appreciated him.

ELIZA: I don't know.

LAUREN: Liza, you did, you —

ELIZA: Anyway, the sixties would have been fun, right?

LAUREN: Totally fun.

ELIZA: Like, rad.

> *(Beat.)*
>
> Lauren?

LAUREN: Yeah?

> *(Beat.)*

ELIZA: Isn't this breeze great? Like peaceful?

LAUREN: Yeah.

ELIZA: Like we could be in the middle of nowhere at any point in history. Like people have been feeling this breeze for all of eternity. Like this could be August in 1891 or 1691 and we have no idea what's coming next even though it's all bound to happen; it'll happen no matter what, like space travel or women's rights; we're just, well, we're just in the middle of all this wind.

LAUREN: It's a really good breeze.

ELIZA: Sort of like we're outside of time.

LAUREN: I guess so.

> *(Beat. Lauren drops Eliza's hand.)*

LAUREN: So I got my period.

ELIZA: What?

LAUREN: Yeah.

ELIZA: When?

LAUREN: Three days ago.

ELIZA: Oh.

LAUREN: It was annoying.

ELIZA: Oh.

LAUREN: My mom made me learn to use a tampon. Right away. She said there was no reason not to. But that was gross.

ELIZA: I can see why.

LAUREN: Can you?

ELIZA: Yeah.

LAUREN: I'm not sure it's something you can understand until you do it.

ELIZA: Well, I'm not sure if it's something I want to understand.

LAUREN: You don't even want to wear a bra yet.

ELIZA: Why should I?

LAUREN: Why not?

ELIZA: *(After a beat.)* So . . . you still have it?

LAUREN: Yeah.

ELIZA: Like right now?

LAUREN: Yeah.

ELIZA: Gross.

LAUREN: Yeah.

SCENE 6

Lauren and Seth are at a restaurant. They are silent and awkward for a few moments before speaking.

SETH: So, I've heard it's not uncommon for soldiers in the heat of battle to become paralyzed with fear. Many get shot because they can't move. They're sitting ducks.

LAUREN: Gosh.

SETH: Right and the awful thing is, a lot of them, well, shit themselves as they're dying. Right when they're dying.

LAUREN: That is awful.

SETH: I know. *(Beat, then trying to be funny:)* Death, right? It's just no fun. *(Awkward beat.)*
But war's really just survival of the fittest. And the thing is there's no way to train for it. You just get into the situation and then you react that way or you don't. You can't simulate war.

LAUREN: No.
(Beat.)

SETH: So do you have to be like a really good swimmer to be a marine biologist?

LAUREN: Decent, I guess.

SETH: Uh-huh.

LAUREN: I mean, you have to like the water.

SETH: Right.
(Beat.)

LAUREN: Do you like your wine?

SETH: It's good.

LAUREN: Good.

SETH: *(Referring to her teacup.)* Do you like your — ?

LAUREN: Yeah.

SETH: Good.

LAUREN: So —

SETH: Right, I mean, my dad — my father — was drafted for Vietnam. He got a bad number in the lottery — twenty-two — and he was drafted. But he never saw action. He was sent to type code in a dark room in the jungle. Once he heard gun shots, but that was all.

LAUREN: So he was lucky.

SETH: I guess so.

LAUREN: I could never go to war.

SETH: Neither could I. But you never know. I mean, the way we're living, you think nothing will happen but then the next moment, it does. It will . . . Like, my buddy Trevor was in Tower Two on 9/11 for a meeting; I mean he's all right; he wasn't very high up, but . . . things just, they don't wait for you. They happen anyway. They creep up on you and take over your life so that you don't ever, well, fully recover.

(Beat.)

LAUREN: What happened?

SETH: To Trevor? He was OK — he just, well, got down in time.

LAUREN: No, to you.

SETH: What do you mean?

LAUREN: You don't have to talk about it.

SETH: Did I . . . Was I suggesting something?

LAUREN: I think so.

SETH: It must be unconscious.

LAUREN: OK.

SETH: No, it's just that . . . well, my dad died.

LAUREN: Oh.

SETH: I mean, it's nothing. It was a year ago. It was a long time ago now.

LAUREN: That's not a long time.

SETH: Let's just . . . let's change the subject. Ask me something. Anything.

LAUREN: Are you sure?

SETH: I'm totally not hung up on it, just so you know. I'm not one of those —

LAUREN: Seth —

SETH: Like self-pitying, moaning, "oh I have dreams and they torment me," analysis every afternoon kind of . . . well, that's just not me.

LAUREN: I didn't think it was.

(Lauren reaches out without meaning to and touches his hair. Seth is shocked. She pulls her hand back. Beat.)

SETH: Well, he died of lung cancer. Never even smoked a cigarette.

LAUREN: Wow.

SETH: I'm ruining this, aren't I? Am I ruining this?

LAUREN: No.

SETH: Anyway, I'm totally not . . . I mean I barely ever think of it anymore.

LAUREN: It would be normal if you did —

SETH: So, ask me something — just ask me about something else.

LAUREN: What should I ask?

SETH: My dad had a mustache. In the past year, I've tried growing them, but on me, they don't look right, like I'm impersonating a much older or much different man.

LAUREN: Tell me.

SETH: What?

LAUREN: Did you think of me at all today? At work?

SETH: Wow. That's quite a question . . . Wow. But since you asked . . . I mean that is quite a question. But I guess . . . yes. Yes I did.

LAUREN: In what way?

SETH: Well, I was nervous about tonight.

LAUREN: You were nervous?

SETH: I worried. I'm a worrier. I try to plan what to say and then it never comes out right. I've learned to stop writing out conversations though and focus on topics, ad lib from there.

LAUREN: So your story about working at that animal shelter?

SETH: Vaguely planned.

LAUREN: And your mother becoming a dentist?

SETH: Definitely planned. You don't see many women making mid-career moves into dental hygiene.

LAUREN: You said you like to walk in the rain.

SETH: I do. But I knew I'd talk about it. It makes women think I'm serious and potentially romantic.

LAUREN: What else do you worry about?

SETH: I worry I might clam up at any moment around you.

LAUREN: I *am* very intimidating.

SETH: Yes, Eliza, you are.

(Beat.)

But do you think —

LAUREN: What?

SETH: I wouldn't usually ask this kind of question. I mean, usually I'd wait to see if it would happen organically.

LAUREN: What?

SETH: I was wondering if . . . Eliza . . . do you think I could take you home tonight?

(Long beat.)

LAUREN: I don't think so.

SETH: Why not?

LAUREN: It's a story.

SETH: You don't like me. I knew it.

LAUREN: No, it's just — I should tell you —

SETH: Well, do you like me?

LAUREN: I don't think I know you yet.

SETH: But you must have a sense. You must know whether you might.

LAUREN: I might.

SCENE 7

Lauren and Eliza sit on a dock by a lake. Summer's ending; school's about to begin.

ELIZA: I think he's kind of goofy-looking.

LAUREN: Are you serious?

ELIZA: I mean, isn't his new haircut kind of . . . weird? Is it supposed to stick up like that?

LAUREN: I think so.

ELIZA: Well, I think it's weird. Like an alien.

LAUREN: He's not like an alien.

ELIZA: No, just his hair.

LAUREN: Well, I like it.

ELIZA: I know.

(Beat. Lauren dips her toes in the water.)

LAUREN: Remember when I went with Julie and Jason to that field up near her dad's place?

ELIZA: Where was I?

LAUREN: You didn't want to come that day.

ELIZA: I don't remember that.

LAUREN: And we saw this cow but Julie thought it might be a bull and we didn't know what to do so we all just walked really slowly toward the fence, hoping it wouldn't follow us.

ELIZA: Julie's a cow.

LAUREN: The whole time I was staring at it and it was staring at me and I couldn't look away, Liza. I couldn't look away.

ELIZA: Wasn't Julie just jabbering away? She never stops talking.

LAUREN: I mean, in the end, it *was* just a cow. It was fine. Jason laughed at me because I was so scared. But seriously, I thought I might die and I think he did too.

ELIZA: Once I thought I might —

LAUREN: It felt like it would never let me go but I also didn't want it to. Like, I could have stared into its eyes forever.

ELIZA: When my mom left me at home at Halloween last year and the intercom light kept flashing as though someone was in another room of the house, I was pretty terrified.

LAUREN: But it's not the same. I'm talking about something primal. Like . . . lust.

ELIZA: *(Not understanding.)* OK.

LAUREN: I mean, I know you were scared.

ELIZA: I don't like staying alone to begin with. I mean, when I'm alone it feels like there's no one else and there's nothing to come. Does that ever happen to you?

LAUREN: Not really, no.

ELIZA: Oh, well, I think I'm exaggerating. And I mean, anyway, I can just stay with you. It's easier and I'm not scared that way . . . BFF, right?

LAUREN: *(They pinky swear.)* BFF. But I do really think he's cute. I like his hair now.

(Beat.)

And I think Ben's cute too. Do you think Ben's cute?

ELIZA: No.

LAUREN: I think so. And I thought when we ran into them he was looking at you.

ELIZA: He wasn't.

LAUREN: He was. I noticed.

ELIZA: He had something stuck between his teeth, like a seed or something. I noticed that.

LAUREN: That's not the point.

ELIZA: Is there a point here?

LAUREN: The point is, you should go for him.

ELIZA: Well that would imply that I want to go for someone.

LAUREN: Don't you?

ELIZA: No!

LAUREN: OK, OK . . .

ELIZA: I just think it's gross . . . I think we're too young to be thinking of stuff like that. That's what my mom says!

LAUREN: Don't get worked up, Liza.

ELIZA: I'm not worked up.

LAUREN: But you think there's something wrong with my liking Jason?

ELIZA: Just do what you want.

LAUREN: Well, I will.

(Beat.)

ELIZA: So what do you want to do now?

LAUREN: I don't know. I think I'm gonna go for a swim.

ELIZA: You want me to just sit here and watch you swim?

LAUREN: You could swim with me.

ELIZA: Ha ha.

LAUREN: It's really not scary, Liza. I mean, I love it. It, like, takes you away from everything.

ELIZA: Really?

LAUREN: Someday you'll try it.

ELIZA: I don't think so.

SCENE 8

Lauren and Seth are at a dance lesson. They're dancing in each other's arms.

SETH: I knew you'd be good at this and I'd be awful.

LAUREN: You're not awful.

SETH: I guess I had this optimistic idea that we'd, like, learn something together, at the same pace, but . . .

LAUREN: I used to take lessons. All the kids took ballroom dance one winter. This old man taught it and he was traditional, like he made the men ask the women to dance with them. We were twelve. It was horrific.

SETH: I bet you were always asked.

LAUREN: No.

SETH: I don't believe it.

LAUREN: How about you? What were you like?

SETH: What do you mean?

LAUREN: I mean, did people find you attractive, when you were young?

SETH: Oh. I don't know. I guess I was average.

LAUREN: You weren't average.

SETH: I wasn't?

LAUREN: No.

SETH: Thanks. *(Beat.)* Or did you mean I was below average?
   (Lauren slaps him playfully.)

LAUREN: So when was the first time you —

SETH: What?

LAUREN: Like, went out with someone.

SETH: I went out with Hannah Carerra in sixth grade but I don't think that
   counts.

LAUREN: Why not?

SETH: Well . . . it was a yearlong relationship and in that year we went out
   three times. Once to Burger King, where my older brother chaperoned
   and made fun of us at the same time. Once for breakfast where we ran
   into my mom's friend and she sat with us. And once to a dance, where
   we never even touched.

LAUREN: I think that counts.
   (Beat.)

SETH: So what about you? When was the first time you went out with someone?

LAUREN: Oh. Um. I guess there was this guy Jason.

SETH: Jason, huh? And what was he like?

LAUREN: Short. I guess. His voice cracked all the time so it sounded like he
   was making fun of himself.

SETH: Yeah, I matured late too. My voice didn't change til like twelfth grade.

LAUREN: It still cracks a little every now and then.

SETH: Because I'm not entirely grown up, right? I like to think the kid I was
   still creeps in sometimes.

LAUREN: That's a sweet idea.
   (Beat.)

SETH: So tell me something about you. Something I don't know.

LAUREN: Like what?

SETH: I know you don't want me to pry. But give me something.

LAUREN: Um.

SETH: You can do it.

LAUREN: I'm embarrassed.

SETH: Choose not to be embarrassed . . . It's just me, after all.

LAUREN: It's you.

SETH: Right.

LAUREN: Well . . . I love to swim.

SETH: Why?

LAUREN: Because it's like you're on another planet where the things that were once useful don't matter anymore — doing math, or making friends, or getting to work on time. You just have to focus on being. Because it feels like time isn't passing.

SETH: That's nice.

LAUREN: It is?

SETH: I think we all look for ways to escape it. Time, I mean.

LAUREN: We do?

SETH: Yeah. Some people sleep too much, or drink. I daydream, pretend I'm a kid again.

LAUREN: Me too!

SETH: I picture me and my brother and my dad in the car, just driving. We're not going anywhere, we're just driving. And the radio's on and time is . . . well, it's . . . it hasn't gotten to us yet. And there's the open road and my brother complains about the radio station and I don't care. I just let him change it.

LAUREN: It's so sad.

SETH: What?

LAUREN: That you can't just stay in the car.

SETH: I don't think so.

(Seth kisses Lauren. It's quick and Lauren pulls away. Eliza appears. They keep dancing for a while before Lauren notices Eliza; when she does, she's shocked.)

Oh, you're stepping on my feet!

LAUREN: Sorry!

SETH: I didn't mean we had to stop.

LAUREN: I hate dancing.

SETH: You OK, Liza?

LAUREN: Oh God.

SETH: Liza?

(She stares at Eliza and Eliza stares at her.)

SCENE 9

Lauren and Eliza. After a school dance.

LAUREN: And then he tongue-kissed me.

ELIZA: Really?

LAUREN: And it felt . . . strange and wet and slimy . . . but nice.

ELIZA: Then what happened?

LAUREN: Well, that's it.

ELIZA: That's it?

LAUREN: We did that for a while and then he kind of patted my shoulder, maybe he was aiming for my arm, and went back on the dance floor.

ELIZA: So you'll see him again?

LAUREN: I don't know. I guess so.

ELIZA: He didn't say, like, "let's do this again"?

LAUREN: No.

ELIZA: Jerk. I mean that's really unimpressive.

LAUREN: I think he's shy.

ELIZA: Not too shy to stick his tongue down your throat.

LAUREN: Eliza!

ELIZA: What?

LAUREN: Don't be vulgar.

ELIZA: So now you're mad at me?

LAUREN: Maybe, I don't know. I wanted to tell you and you —

ELIZA: What? What did I do?

LAUREN: You didn't understand. *(Beat.)* I mean, why didn't you dance with Ben when he asked you?

ELIZA: Ew. How can you even ask that?

LAUREN: I mean, he's cute —

ELIZA: No he's not!

LAUREN: And he likes you.

ELIZA: I hate the kind of dancing everyone does, the kind you do with Jason. It's way too, like, close.

LAUREN: Why don't you just dance with him next time? I bet he'll still ask you. Julie doesn't think he'll hold a grudge.

ELIZA: I don't care what Julie thinks.

LAUREN: You can dance with him in any way you want.

ELIZA: Um, no thank you.

LAUREN: But why not, Liza?

(*Eliza stands and dances.*)

What are you doing?

ELIZA: I'm dancing to my own beat.

LAUREN: I don't get it.

ELIZA: There's nothing to get.

LAUREN: You're kind of exasperating, you know that?

ELIZA: Thanks.

LAUREN: No, I mean, I just think you could try a little harder to understand what I'm dealing with right now.

ELIZA: Maybe you could try to understand what I'm dealing with.

LAUREN: What's that?

ELIZA: Exactly.

LAUREN: Liza —

ELIZA: You want me to dance with Ben and then let him do things to me so that I'll understand what you're dealing with?

LAUREN: I mean, is this about your dad, Liza?

ELIZA: I'm sorry?

LAUREN: My mom says it might take a long time for you to, like, fully recover. So now you're just still really upset about it, right?

ELIZA: I don't know what you're talking about.

LAUREN: I'm just saying maybe you have a thing about guys because you don't have a dad.

ELIZA: That's an awful thing to say.

LAUREN: But is it true?

ELIZA: No.

LAUREN: I've heard that girls who grow up without fathers can be really repressed when it comes to sexuality.

ELIZA: I'm not repressed.

LAUREN: Yes, you are.

ELIZA: What makes you think that?

LAUREN: Everything.

ELIZA: Look, I don't want to talk about my dad.

LAUREN: I'm talking about you.

ELIZA: Well, what do I have to do to prove to you that I'm not repressed, huh? Bring my dad back to life?

LAUREN: No.

ELIZA: Fuck some guy?

LAUREN: Eliza! No.

ELIZA: Lose twenty pounds and waltz around in miniskirts and halter tops like some sluts I know?

LAUREN: Are you talking about me?

ELIZA: Ding ding, Einstein. You know, you're lucky you're pretty because intelligence really isn't your strong suit.

(Eliza storms out.)

SCENE 10

Lauren paces in front of a park bench. She's waiting. She's been waiting for a long time. Seth appears.

LAUREN: Seth!

SETH: I'm so sorry. I have a tremendous excuse — the trains and the — I got lost; it took longer than I thought; there were delays —

LAUREN: What kind of delays? I mean, it's been half an hour . . . I thought —

SETH: I'm sorry —

LAUREN: I thought you'd been hit by a bus . . . I thought a building had blown up. I thought some awful disease had been released in the subways and you were coughing up blood crouched in some sad little corner!

SETH: No . . . I just . . .

LAUREN: What?

SETH: I lost track of time.

LAUREN: You forgot about me?

SETH: No. I mean . . . I didn't. I had this all planned out. Look —
(He holds up a basket.)
Wine, and cheese and crackers and grapes. I mean, I brought grapes! We can feed each other grapes!

LAUREN: I thought you were gone.

SETH: I'm right here.

LAUREN: This is ridiculous.

SETH: What is?

LAUREN: Worrying. Thinking you were gone. It's ridiculous.

SETH: No — it's OK to worry. It's fine. It's like my middle name. It's like home to me. Like the living-room couch.

LAUREN: I don't like it.

SETH: It's normal. It means you like me. *(Beat.)* I'm sorry. I didn't mean to make you wait. It was the last thing I wanted.

LAUREN: I was thinking.

SETH: About me? About us? Because I don't want this minor, this — I'm not usually late. It won't become a pattern —

LAUREN: No, about other things. Like, life.

SETH: Oh.

LAUREN: How predictable it is.

SETH: You mean, you knew I'd be late? *I* didn't know I'd be late —

LAUREN: I just . . . I never thought I'd . . . be in this kind of situation.

SETH: What kind of situation?

LAUREN: You know. Like, with you. I mean, I never honestly thought I'd be, like . . . seriously into —

SETH: What are you trying to tell me?

LAUREN: It's such a beautiful day, isn't it? This breeze, and . . . I mean, I feel like I could be sitting here at any time in the history of the world.

SETH: Eliza —

LAUREN: Don't you ever feel that we're just on the edge of our lives? That they're happening but we're outside of them and nothing we can do will stop anything?

SETH: Like fate.

LAUREN: Like being stuck. Even if we know what the right thing to do is, we still won't do it. There's something we can't define holding us back.

SETH: That's a pretty negative outlook.

LAUREN: Sometimes I can be negative. You do know that, right? That I can be negative? I'm not as easygoing as you are.

SETH: I'm not easygoing.

LAUREN: You seem it. Easy to get to know.

SETH: Those aren't the same thing.

LAUREN: It's just that . . . I don't think I'm as simple as I've seemed. Or something like that. I mean, we've just been having a good time together and I'm not like that. I don't just have a good time. There are consequences.

SETH: Are the consequences bad? You make them sound bad.

LAUREN: Yes. They're bad.

SETH: I don't know what you're talking about. I think you're great and that's all that matters.

LAUREN: Don't say that.

SETH: Listen, we don't have to do the grapes and the . . . maybe . . . do you want a hot dog? There's a Gray's Papaya not too far from the park and I love their hot dogs . . . something about them. I don't know what it is —

LAUREN: No, I don't want a hot dog.

SETH: OK.

> (Beat.)

It was just an idea.

LAUREN: I'm just feeling so . . .

SETH: Frustrated?

LAUREN: No! Not frustrated. Aren't you listening to me? I'm trying to express something to you.

SETH: I'm sorry, I'm —

LAUREN: Yeah, well I'm sorry too. I'm sorry too.

SETH: What do you want me to say?

LAUREN: I don't know. I think I want to be alone.

SETH: Well, maybe you should be alone.

LAUREN: Right. Maybe I should be.

SCENE 11

> *Lauren and Eliza sit on the floor; it's raining out. Autumn and boredom.*

ELIZA: We could play cards.

LAUREN: No.

ELIZA: Prank phone calls?

LAUREN: No.

ELIZA: Monopoly?

LAUREN: Ew. No.

ELIZA: I'd like to take a walk in the rain.

LAUREN: I know. You and your walks.

ELIZA: I get thinking done in the rain.

LAUREN: Why won't he call?

ELIZA: When I say thinking I don't mean like concrete thoughts. I mean, it's totally abstract. Like I'll just picture things, scenes from my life. I just replay scenes from my life.

LAUREN: I left a message over fourteen hours ago.

ELIZA: I think it's fifteen by now.

LAUREN: Great. Fifteen.

ELIZA: Lauren I'm sorry I called you a slut.

LAUREN: It's OK.

ELIZA: It is?

LAUREN: I'm more focused on other things right now anyway.

ELIZA: Oh. Well, I think we should try to get your mind off —

LAUREN: I don't want to get my mind off it. I want him to call.

ELIZA: Lauren.

LAUREN: What?

ELIZA: Lauren.

(Eliza puts her hand on Lauren's shoulder.)

LAUREN: What?

(Eliza puts her arms around Lauren's shoulders — maternal.)

What are you doing?

ELIZA: I'm giving you a hug.

LAUREN: Why?

ELIZA: You seem to need some consolation. I'm doing my best.

(Lauren wriggles away.)

LAUREN: I'm fine.

ELIZA: You're not acting fine.

LAUREN: I'm not?

ELIZA: No.

(Beat.)

LAUREN: Last night I had a dream that my boobs grew and I was like a 38 double D.

ELIZA: Was that a nightmare?

LAUREN: No! . . . I was so happy.

(Beat.)

And what if I told you I've been . . . fantasizing.

ELIZA: Fantasizing about what?

LAUREN: You know.

ELIZA: No.

LAUREN: About Jason, about . . .

ELIZA: Oh no, ew. Don't tell me.

LAUREN: Yeah. I feel . . . kind of awful. Like, dirty.

ELIZA: That is *not* normal.

LAUREN: It isn't?

ELIZA: No.

LAUREN: It's like, when I see him, I want things. And when I go to sleep at night, I want the same things only . . . they're more intense then, when I'm on my own.

ELIZA: I think you should try to stop thinking.

LAUREN: How?

ELIZA: Think about other stuff. Think about . . . me. Like, my mom's driving to the mall tomorrow and we could go with her.

LAUREN: To do what? Buy towels?

ELIZA: Faucets. I think. For the kitchen sink.

LAUREN: Why won't he call??

ELIZA: But we could hang out. We could see a movie. While she shops. You know she takes forever.

LAUREN: Maybe I didn't adopt the right tone. "Just give me a call when you have a chance" could sound a little like it doesn't expect a response. Is that true? Or?

ELIZA: When you call me and say that I call you back.

LAUREN: But that's you.

ELIZA: I know.

LAUREN: I mean, he's probably busy. Maybe his dad like took him out of town or something.

ELIZA: Or maybe he doesn't like you.

LAUREN: What?

ELIZA: It is possible.

LAUREN: What do you mean?

ELIZA: That he's not interested in you. It does happen.

LAUREN: But I've put so much time into liking him.

ELIZA: I know.

LAUREN: He likes me. Come on . . . doesn't he?

ELIZA: I don't know. I can't say for sure. It's not like he's called you back.

LAUREN: You know, Julie Miller says you're a prude.

ELIZA: What?

LAUREN: Yeah.

ELIZA: Why would she say that? I don't even know her.

LAUREN: Because I told her you are. I told her you don't like anyone.
(Beat.)

ELIZA: You did that?

LAUREN: I just wanted another opinion. I can't do everything on my own.

ELIZA: You told her? You went behind my back?

LAUREN: I guess I did. Sorry.

ELIZA: Sorry? No, I mean . . . why?

LAUREN: Now everyone kind of knows. I guess Julie has a big mouth.

ELIZA: She's known for that.

LAUREN: I guess so. So now you kind of like have to prove that you're not.

ELIZA: Are you making this up?

LAUREN: Come on. I don't lie.

ELIZA: Well, I'm not proving anything.

LAUREN: It's just that . . . Julie thinks you might be holding me back.

ELIZA: If holding you back means keeping you sane.

LAUREN: To be honest, she doesn't know why we're friends.

ELIZA: Well, did you tell her?

LAUREN: No.

ELIZA: Why not?

LAUREN: Why are we friends? I mean . . .

  (Beat.)

ELIZA: Did you hear what you just said?

LAUREN: I didn't mean it.

ELIZA: You're sorry?

LAUREN: I'm sorry.

  (The phone rings.)

SCENE 12

Seth holds a guitar. He begins to play; he's teaching himself. He has a "How To Play the Guitar" manual on his lap. He tries different chords. He suddenly reaches for the phone and dials. Lauren's phone rings.

SETH: Eliza, please pick up the phone. Please. I'm sorry I left you alone. I guess when people say they want to be alone what they really mean is they want to be with other people and I read that all wrong. Please pick up. I mean, I went out with some friends last night and Trevor told this story about a date he had. He met this girl online. Apparently they match perfectly in terms of goals and lifestyle, whatever that means. He says I should go online too, Liza. Meet someone. I say I'm already taken. At that point, my friends all laugh. They shoot each other knowing glances. They say, "Seth, you're a real romantic, aren't you"; they say I went on a few dates and now I think I'm married. And considering the fact that I haven't heard from you, maybe they're right that I thought we were . . . closer than we were. So given all that I've made a sort of promise to myself. I say sort of because it might be hard to stick to but I think I should and so does Nancy — my therapist, I mean. She thinks, and I mean, I agree, that this should be the last message I leave you. It's a very one-sided relationship I'm engaged in, she says, and I guess she's right. So when I hang up I'm not calling back. I mean, I'll call back if you call me first and leave a message. I'm just not going to leave any more of these . . .

whatever these are. But before I go . . . I just want to say . . . well, maybe this is my last chance, so why the hell not, right? I mean, I think I was starting to . . . I mean, you might not know it, but I'm not a real hotshot with women; I don't date that much. But I've dated enough . . . I mean, I've met enough women to know that you're really very . . . I mean, I think you're something. Really something. And for what it's worth, whatever it is you're going through right now . . . we can get through it. It'll be OK. I mean I *know* in my gut that if we're together, we can . . . But anyway I guess I'll leave it there. So, well, good-bye. I'm hanging up now. And I won't beg you to call me back . . . but why not just call me back? *(He hangs up and sits with the guitar without playing.)*

SCENE 13

Lauren is applying makeup in front of a mirror while Eliza watches, eating carrots.

LAUREN: I mean, it's not like he could expect me to buy a new dress, right? My mom was like if you really need one Lauren but it'll be an early birthday present and do you really want that? And I don't want that. I don't want to cut into my birthday present. It's just that, well, Julie thinks I look fat in pink and I should really have a cute little black dress. She says everyone should have a little black cocktail dress. It says so in *Mademoiselle*, so it must be true. On the other hand, why not be a little different, right? I'm torn. I mean, I don't want to just blend in. Hey, can you give me a hand here?
(Eliza stands and helps Lauren with her mascara.)
Thanks. I mean, do you think my lashes are too long? I want it to look like I'm wearing makeup but not nearly as much as I'm actually wearing. On the other hand, should it look like I'm wearing it at all? Jason went out with Maggie before me and she never wore any makeup because she has like perfect skin. What a whore.
(Eliza eats carrots.)
Aren't you going to say anything?
ELIZA: No.
LAUREN: When are you going to get ready?
ELIZA: Do you think carrots are kind of phallic?
LAUREN: I think everything's kind of phallic; now shouldn't you get ready?

We're leaving in two hours.

ELIZA: I'm well-acquainted with the time.

LAUREN: There's no need to be snide.

ELIZA: I don't think I'm going.

LAUREN: Oh perfume! We need perfume!

(She runs around frantically looking for some.)

Do you know where it is?

ELIZA: Did you hear me? I said I'm not going.

LAUREN: I heard you.

ELIZA: OK then.

LAUREN: The thing is, I don't really believe you. I'm sure you'll change your mind. I think this is some ploy either to make me feel sorry for you or stay home with you and you know what? I'm not your babysitter, Liza. I'm just not.

ELIZA: Wow.

(She stands, she claps.)

LAUREN: What are you doing?

ELIZA: Are you sure you don't have anything to add?

LAUREN: What do you mean?

ELIZA: Cuz I'd love to hear more.

LAUREN: Look, Liza — I think maybe . . . I mean, I've been thinking about it, and maybe it's true what Julie says.

ELIZA: What does Julie say now?

LAUREN: She thinks maybe we need some time apart.

ELIZA: Excuse me?

LAUREN: Like this whole thing about your not coming tonight. Maybe you shouldn't come. You don't like these things anyway. I could go without you.

ELIZA: You could?

LAUREN: Yeah. I think so. Yeah. And like, what if I smoke a cigarette or something? Or God forbid have a drink? You'll go apeshit and I don't want to risk offending you. I understand your point of view but you should understand mine and maybe just politely back out. No one will judge you.

ELIZA: Are you kidding? Everyone will judge me!

LAUREN: No — no, I don't think so.

ELIZA: What are you saying?

LAUREN: I'm just saying I don't think you should come tonight . . . and maybe later this week we should skip certain things.

ELIZA: Like what?

LAUREN: Like . . . everything. Like maybe I do want some time alone.

ELIZA: Not alone. With Julie. And with Jason.

(Beat, then putting down the carrots, and quietly:)

Don't do this, OK.

LAUREN: What? I didn't quite hear you.

ELIZA: I said, don't do this.

LAUREN: Do what?

ELIZA: Abandon me.

LAUREN: It's not abandoning . . . it's just . . . taking a break.

(Eliza begins to cry. She tries to hide it but can't. It's been building.)

ELIZA: Don't. Please don't.

LAUREN: Why are you crying?

ELIZA: *(Her tone and volume raised.)* Why do you think?

LAUREN: Don't just yell at me like that! I mean, I'm trying to have a conversation with you!

ELIZA: I'm not yelling.

LAUREN: You were.

ELIZA: OK . . . well, what if I just go to the damn dance? Let's just do that. I don't want to go but I will — I'll go.

LAUREN: Honestly, I think it's too late for that.

ELIZA: No. I mean, I'll go. I'll get dressed. Let me get dressed right now.

(She starts taking her clothes off.)

LAUREN: Ew. What are you doing?

ELIZA: I'm getting changed. What does it look like I'm doing?

LAUREN: I don't really want to see your whole body.

ELIZA: God! What can I do? What do you want me to do?

(Beat.)

LAUREN: This is about your dad, isn't it . . .

ELIZA: What are you talking about? Lauren, please . . .

(Eliza tries to touch Lauren, to hug her.)

LAUREN: Get off me.

ELIZA: No. Lauren, please.

LAUREN: *(Getting away from her.)* I'm sorry your dad died. But . . . it's not really an excuse for . . .

ELIZA: What?

LAUREN: I mean, it's kind of obvious.

ELIZA: What?

LAUREN: I mean, you're like a lesbian, right?

(Beat. Eliza looks down at herself, half-naked and then at Lauren.)

Right? I mean, everyone says so. Julie says girls without father figures are much more likely to . . . go that route.

ELIZA: Lauren.

LAUREN: I just don't know why you didn't tell me.

ELIZA: Tell you . . .

LAUREN: So you're just gonna cry like a baby? Like a little kid?

ELIZA: *(Crumpling to her knees.)* Lauren.

LAUREN: I mean, I'm really sick of all this crying all the time. I can't take care of you anymore, Liza. I just, I have other things to do.

ELIZA: *(Still looking at Lauren.)* Lauren.

LAUREN: I mean, you just didn't understand. I'm sorry but it's not my fault that you don't like Ben. You just have to accept the fact that I do like Jason and we're together and I want certain things and —
(She begins to leave.)

ELIZA: Where are you going?

LAUREN: To the dance with my boyfriend. To have a good time for once. OK?
(Lauren looks at her and exits. Eliza holds herself.)

SCENE 14

Lauren and Seth are at a bar.

LAUREN: I'm so glad you could come out. I know it was last minute.

SETH: That's OK.

LAUREN: I mean, at least I suggested a bar near the bank, right?

SETH: I guess.

LAUREN: I'm sorry it's kind of well, seedy. That's what you get when you find a bar online, right?

SETH: Right.

LAUREN: I really wanted to see you, Seth.

SETH: Uh-huh.

LAUREN: Here, let's have a drink. Should we have a drink?

SETH: OK.

LAUREN: What do you want?

SETH: What are you having?

LAUREN: I don't know. Something strong. Absinthe? Um, is that imported here yet?

SETH: Eliza —

LAUREN: I missed you. And I wanted to see you. And I'm sorry I didn't call you back. I feel awful. I mean, I know I'm awful. I don't know what's wrong with me.

SETH: I left you five messages. Embarrassing messages.

LAUREN: I don't like when things feel inevitable. I want to see if they'll endure despite certain obstacles.

SETH: Like a week of ignoring me.

LAUREN: I guess.

SETH: I just don't know if I understand you —

(She kisses him suddenly.)

SETH: Is that an apology?

LAUREN: It's . . . Seth, I need to tell you something —

SETH: What?

LAUREN: See, I'm not —

(Before she can finish he kisses her.)

SETH: Not what? Not gonna do that to me, ever again?

LAUREN: Right. Right.

SETH: Good. It wasn't any fun. I'd say it ranks just ahead of the week I had my wisdom teeth out and just behind the week at the bank last year when they made us wear berets.

LAUREN: Berets?

SETH: Gimmicks don't generally work and that one was no exception.

LAUREN: I'm really sorry, Seth.

SETH: *(Genuinely.)* It wasn't as bad as the week when my dad died.

LAUREN: I'm sure it wasn't.

SETH: Anyway.

LAUREN: Tell me what your dad was like.

SETH: I think it's better not to talk about it, better to be distracted.

LAUREN: No! I mean . . . no. I think it's bad to keep things bottled up.

SETH: Are you sure?

LAUREN: Yeah.

SCENE 15

A couple months have passed. Lauren and Seth are in bed together. It's morning. They're reading the paper. Lauren's eating cereal from a box.

LAUREN: I can't decide if I want to read or go back to sleep.

SETH: Go back to sleep. The news'll wait.

LAUREN: I know. But it's nice, reading next to you.

SETH: It is nice.

LAUREN: Give me something to read. Something you think I'll like.

SETH: OK.

(*He leafs through the paper.*)

Here.

(*He hands a section to Lauren.*)

LAUREN: Is this some kind of joke?

SETH: Sort of.

LAUREN: Well, I don't get it. I mean, obituaries?

SETH: I want us to appreciate things.

LAUREN: Oh.

SETH: Because, I mean, I really do appreciate things, these days. I appreciate you.

LAUREN: Oh.

SETH: And it's good to remind ourselves, sometimes. That everything's transient.

LAUREN: (*Snippily.*) I don't need to be reminded of that.

SETH: You know, you never agree with me.

LAUREN: What?

SETH: I mean, why can't you ever agree with me?

LAUREN: I do agree with you. All the time.

SETH: There you go again.

LAUREN: Seth —

SETH: Sometimes it feels like you're just out to contradict me. And/or make me feel like an idiot but I like to think it's less vindictive than that.

LAUREN: You think I'm vindictive?

(*Lauren gets out of bed, paces.*)

SETH: What are you doing?

LAUREN: Torturing myself.

SETH: Why?

LAUREN: It's who I am.

SETH: Come here.

(*She doesn't go to him.*)

You know, Trevor's screensaver is this one line scrolling across. It's Shakespeare, you know: "Our remedies oft in ourselves do lie" and I was thinking about it yesterday when I should have been working, and I realized that it's true, that we do, like, have the power to make ourselves happy.

LAUREN: I don't think we do, Seth.

SETH: Of course we do.

LAUREN: No. Once I was swimming; I was in the ocean — this was during college — and I dove down so deep and the water was so clear at the bottom and so beautiful, like hauntingly beautiful, that I almost didn't go back up.

SETH: But you did go back up.

LAUREN: I mean, you feel your lungs get tight.

SETH: You saved yourself.

LAUREN: I could have not saved myself.

SETH: I'd save you, if I could.

LAUREN: You would?

SETH: Yes.

   (Beat.)

LAUREN: So maybe we'll go swimming one day? I think I'd like to swim with you.

SETH: And I'd love to see you in a bikini.

LAUREN: No —

SETH: Or we could go skinny-dipping —

LAUREN: Seth, I'm being serious.

SETH: Yes, of course we can go swimming, Liza.

LAUREN: But Eliza's scared of the water.

SETH: What?

LAUREN: I mean, when I was a baby I fell in a pool and almost drowned and ever since then —

SETH: What are you talking about? What's going on?

LAUREN: Please don't leave me.

SETH: Look at me. I'm not going anywhere.

LAUREN: Seth?

SETH: I'm not going anywhere. But can you try to explain to me what's going on with you? Because in these moments, I'm confused. I don't have a handle on . . . I worry you won't ever —

LAUREN: What?

SETH: Because it's not about meeting your parents, or seeing your office. I don't even care that you don't want to hang out with Trevor. He can be annoying sometimes.

LAUREN: I'm sorry, Seth —

SETH: It's just that . . . I want you to be happy, Liza.

LAUREN: I am happy.

SETH: No, I want you to be happy. I'm pretty sure it is possible. Otherwise, how would we get through each day?

LAUREN: I'm happy.

SETH: But not really.

LAUREN: No. Not really.

SETH: Well, at least you're agreeing with me.

(He takes her in his arms.)

SCENE 16

Lauren is sitting at a table in the school cafeteria. Eliza walks by. She's sweaty and out of breath. She's wearing shorts and a tight shirt for the first time in the play.

LAUREN: Liza —

(Eliza turns around.)

ELIZA: What?

(Beat.)

LAUREN: How are you?

(Eliza goes to Lauren's table.)

ELIZA: Great, how are you?

LAUREN: Why are you all —

ELIZA: I joined the track team.

LAUREN: You did?

ELIZA: It's amazing. I never knew my body could do stuff like that. It's all about endurance, you know? And motivation. You really can get your body to do whatever you want it to if you try hard enough.

LAUREN: Oh.

ELIZA: And anyway, running's such a high. It's like, I don't know. Amazing.

LAUREN: I'm glad you're happy.

ELIZA: Oh I'm totally happy.

(Beat.)

How are you?

LAUREN: Fine.

ELIZA: Good.

(Beat.)

I guess we haven't talked in —

LAUREN: I know. A while.

ELIZA: Midterms suck, right?

LAUREN: Right.

> *(Beat.)*
>
> You look thin, Liza.
>
> *(Beat.)*

ELIZA: I know. I had no idea my thighs were so fat before.

LAUREN: They weren't —

ELIZA: You know, I just love shopping now. My mom and I have been going on these amazing sprees. You should see some of the stuff I've gotten. I mean, if you want to.

LAUREN: I want to.

ELIZA: OK. Maybe one day you can come over and —

LAUREN: But I mean, Liza, aren't you eating anymore? People are saying —

ELIZA: It's none of your business.

LAUREN: I know.

ELIZA: OK.

LAUREN: But why? You love to eat.

ELIZA: No, I don't.

LAUREN: Yes, you do. I mean . . . you kind of look like . . .

ELIZA: What?

LAUREN: Are you starving?

ELIZA: And just so you know. I'm not a lesbian. In case you care. I mean I've been thinking about it and I'm not.

LAUREN: OK.

ELIZA: Anyway I better go. I've got study hall and you know how Jenkins gets if you're late.

LAUREN: OK.

ELIZA: OK.

LAUREN: Take care of yourself, Liza.

ELIZA: What are you, fifty?

LAUREN: No.

> *(Eliza walks away. She turns back as though to say something more but then thinks better of it and keeps going.)*

SCENE 17

Lauren watches Seth sleep.

SETH: What are you doing?

LAUREN: Don't wake up. You don't have to.

SETH: OK.

(Beat.)

LAUREN: Seth? Are you awake?

SETH: I guess so.

LAUREN: Can I tell you something?

SETH: Is everything all right?

LAUREN: I don't know.

SETH: *(Gently.)* What is it?

LAUREN: When we first met I wondered what you saw in me.

SETH: Well, you were hot.

LAUREN: I wondered why you'd want to be with someone like me. Because I know I'm not easy.

And now I'm trying to figure out what's going on —

SETH: What's going on?

LAUREN: I mean, who we are. Like, sometimes I think you're someone else. And sometimes I'm someone else and it's getting really cloudy for me, really cloudy.

SETH: Who do you think you are?

LAUREN: This girl Eliza.

SETH: But you are —

LAUREN: I know it must feel like I'm hiding something from you.

SETH: Are you?

LAUREN: I think so.

SETH: You're a private person. You're just not used to this kind of thing yet.

LAUREN: No, I mean, yes, but . . .

SETH: What are you hiding?

LAUREN: Here's a story. You might think it's stupid —

SETH: I won't.

LAUREN: But when I was kid, my best friend and I used to watch this one movie over and over again. It wasn't even a good movie and we were like, I don't know, eleven, right? She'd come over and we'd just sit there and my mom didn't get it. She'd always ask if we wanted to watch something else but she let us do it, I think because it wasn't harmful and we enjoyed it.

SETH: Was it porn?

LAUREN: No, it wasn't porn. It doesn't even matter what it was. I mean, it was *Pretty Woman*. We saw it at my birthday party one year and got a real kick out of it, but that's not what kept us watching it.

SETH: Your mom let you watch *Pretty Woman* at eleven?

LAUREN: But the point of the story is . . . it wasn't that every time the movie seemed like new, or that we kept finding fresh things in it. It was simply that this was what we did and it was comfortable and . . . my friend and I ate sandwiches my mom made for us and drank juice and the afternoon just passed watching that movie. When it was over, it was dark and she went home and by then my mom had made dinner and we'd eat and the rest of the night would go as it always did.

SETH: It sounds nice.

LAUREN: Right. But *more* than nice. And that's what I can't get out of my mind. That . . . I don't think we've found that movie yet.

SETH: What movie?

LAUREN: The one we could watch over and over.

SETH: You're not making sense. It's the middle of the night.

LAUREN: I am making sense, Seth.

SETH: Then what are you saying?

LAUREN: Don't get me wrong. I mean, I love you.

SETH: You do?

LAUREN: *(She's surprised herself.)*
Yes.

SETH: I know. I love you too.

LAUREN: But that's the problem. I mean, that's the problem.

SETH: Liza —

LAUREN: Do you know what I'm trying to tell you?

SETH: Um.

LAUREN: That I'm confused, or something? Or scared? That maybe I've gone too far down some road and I can't get off? That I can't get rid of the old movie? Are you hearing me? This is important, Seth. Please try.

SETH: OK . . . Yes, I think I've heard you. You need reassurance.

LAUREN: I do?

SETH: I can give you that. We're going to watch so many movies.

LAUREN: We are?

SETH: And we'll talk about them. And sometimes we'll agree that one was really really good, like life-changingly good, and we'll buy it and memorize all the lines and watch it whenever we can.

LAUREN: We will?

SETH: Metaphorically.

LAUREN: Is that what this is?

SETH: Isn't it?

LAUREN: I guess so . . . But —

SETH: But what?

LAUREN: I don't know . . . I'm sorry for waking you up.

SETH: It's fine. You know that.

(He kisses her on the cheek and goes back to sleep. She continues to watch him.)

SCENE 18

Eliza is in the hospital. She's knitting and barely looks up. Lauren sits beside her.

LAUREN: So, how are you doing?

(Beat.)

This is a nice room.

(Beat.)

What are you making?

ELIZA: Scarf.

LAUREN: Cool.

ELIZA: I mean, while I'm in this fucking place, I may as well get something done.

LAUREN: It's not so bad, is it?

ELIZA: Look around.

LAUREN: Well, some of the people in here do look really . . . well, not good.

ELIZA: I know. I'm like, why the fuck am I here?

LAUREN: Well, it's a nice scarf.

ELIZA: Yeah.

LAUREN: I didn't know you could knit.

ELIZA: And they won't let me exercise. Fuckers.

LAUREN: But . . . don't you think you should be resting?

ELIZA: And they want me to say things.

LAUREN: Like what?

ELIZA: They want me to say all these things that are such bullshit. Like I'm angry because my dad died. Or because my mom was too needy. I tell them they're assholes . . . But you know they say I might never get my period. And the problem is —

LAUREN: What?

ELIZA: I don't know.

LAUREN: Liza —

ELIZA: What?

(Beat.)

LAUREN: I mean, at least you have your own room, right?

ELIZA: Whatever.

LAUREN: You want to hear about school at all, or?

(Beat.)

Like, yesterday Mr. Halverson told us that if we wanted to write a long paper at the end of the semester we could skip all the reading quizzes and I thought that was a good idea and was sure we would decide to do that but then Julie Miller was like, "well, how much will the paper be worth?" and he was like, "I haven't decided yet but a fair bit of your grade" and she was like "it's not worth it, guys" and then everyone was nodding and now we have to keep taking these ridiculous reading quizzes.

(Beat.)

Yeah, and then after class she — I mean, Julie — came up to me and was like, I heard you and Jason slept together, loud enough that other people could hear — and I was like, "who are you to confront me in the hallway about something like that?"

(Beat.)

ELIZA: You slept with Jason?

LAUREN: Yeah.

(Beat.)

ELIZA: Congratulations.

LAUREN: I wanted to tell you first.

ELIZA: Thanks.

LAUREN: Yeah. So. It was two nights ago. We were going to wait for the end of the school year but, well, Jason really wanted to and I figured what's the difference between now and June, right?

ELIZA: *(Quietly.)* So how was it?

LAUREN: Oh, amazing.

ELIZA: Good.

LAUREN: I mean, well, we were in his brother's room . . . and the walls in there are brown and it's dark and it smells kind of like gym socks and some weird cologne. And then . . . afterwards there were no candles and Jason didn't say much . . .

ELIZA: Uh-huh —

LAUREN: No, I mean, it was great. It's just that, I mean, I figured . . . it would feel more different than this, not being something anymore. But really I'm just still . . . whatever I was.

ELIZA: So Julie found out about it?

LAUREN: Yeah, and I told her it was none of her business. And she said she heard it from a "confirmed" source and when I started walking away she said "Jason, Jason told me" and I turned around and slapped her. I don't know what came over me.

(Beat. She waits for Eliza to speak, but she doesn't.)

Anyway she looked so shocked. SO shocked. Like she'd just fallen down ten flights of stairs but had survived . . . But then she told me she'd slept with Jason too, before me. She told me they still hung out sometimes, which I think was supposed to mean that she still sleeps with him. She said she convinced him to go out with me because I needed some male attention. She said a lot of things . . . so I spat on her shoes. Her new shoes . . . and she kicked me. See?

(Lauren lifts her leg to show Eliza a bruise.)

ELIZA: (Seriously.) That's because Julie is a total bitch.

LAUREN: She's not a total bitch.

ELIZA: She kicked you and slept with your boyfriend.

LAUREN: I know.

ELIZA: You still like her?

LAUREN: I don't know. I guess so.

ELIZA: And Jason?

LAUREN: I'm, well, I'm meeting him later. To talk. Like maybe he'll tell me Julie was lying and —

ELIZA: Great friends.

LAUREN: Well you could be a little more sympathetic. I mean, I got suspended. And now my parents say I'm "acting out" and they think it's because of you.

(Beat.)

ELIZA: Will you just go away, Lauren. I don't know why you keep coming here.

(Beat.)

LAUREN: Because I'm worried about you.

ELIZA: Well, worry about yourself.

SCENE 19

Seth and Lauren eat by candlelight.

SETH: And I told Trev that if I went any longer without eating a burger — just a goddamned burger — I might go mad.

LAUREN: So you gave in?

SETH: I didn't give in. I surrendered. I gave myself wholeheartedly. It was the best burger I ever ate.

LAUREN: So you were a vegetarian for?

SETH: Three days freshman year. The worst three days.

LAUREN: And you didn't score a single chick?

SETH: Not a one.

LAUREN: Poor Seth.

SETH: College is tough for the heterosexual male. So much temptation everywhere. So much that's unattainable. It's cruel, really. The bank is much better. At least I'm not tempted all the time.

LAUREN: Hey!

SETH: Not that I want to be.

LAUREN: Do I still tempt you?

SETH: Yes.

LAUREN: How much?

SETH: Enough.

LAUREN: That's it.

SETH: More than enough.

LAUREN: Be careful what you say.

SETH: Why?

LAUREN: Once you say things you can't take them back.

SETH: I know.

(He leans over and kisses her. He stands. He goes offstage.)

LAUREN: What are you doing?

SETH: You'll see.

LAUREN: Seriously, what —

SETH: Hold your horses, honey.

LAUREN: You don't call me honey.

SETH: I just did.

(Seth returns with his guitar and begins to strum.)

LAUREN: What's that?

SETH: Guitar.

LAUREN: Right, I meant —
(He begins to sing.)
ELIZA ELIZA I OWE YOU A SONG
IT WON'T BE MUCH; IT WON'T TAKE LONG
BUT AS THAT BARD WAS KNOWN TO SIGH
"OUR REMEDIES OFT IN OURSELVES DO LIE"
AND ELIZA ELIZA I OWE YOU A SONG
DON'T JUDGE MY LYRICS; THEY'RE ALL WRONG
BUT OUT OF EVERYTHING I KNOW IN MY LIFE
ONE THING'S FOR SURE . . .
(He stops playing.)
Will you be my wife?
(He takes a box from his jacket and opens it for Lauren.)
I don't have a speech or anything. It's just that, I think this is the right
thing. I know we haven't known each other for like ten years the way my
parents did before they got married, but I don't think that matters. I love
you, and the strange thing is, I have this feeling that my dad would have
loved you too, which is something I haven't told you because I didn't
want to freak you out, but now I'm freaking you out anyway, so I figured
you should know.
(Beat.)
Well?
LAUREN: You've asked the wrong person.
SETH: What do you mean?
LAUREN: I mean . . . That's not my name.
SETH: What's not your name?
LAUREN: Eliza. That's not my name.
SETH: What are you talking about?
LAUREN: That. That's all. That's what I'm talking about. You've got the wrong
girl.
(Lauren has stood and put on her jacket.)
SETH: Where are you going?
LAUREN: I just have to get out of here.
SETH: Oh no. You're not leaving. Not again.
LAUREN: I am Seth. I am. I wanted to . . . do this, or something, or whatever
this is but now I'm getting out of here. I can't . . . I can't do this anymore.
I mean, I promised myself. I told myself. No one else. I told myself over
and over. All that time. All these years. I told myself.
SETH: What are you talking about? You're not making any sense.

(Seth blocks her.)

LAUREN: Seth. Get out of my way.

SETH: No.

LAUREN: The fact is, you don't love *me*. You don't even know me.

SETH: What do you mean? Of course I do.

LAUREN: No you don't. *(Beat.)* Let me go, Seth.

   (She pushes past him and leaves.)

SETH: Where are you going? I just proposed to you. Where are you going?

SCENE 20

   Eliza and Lauren. Eliza is still in the hospital. She's hooked up to a heart rate monitor.

LAUREN: I bought you these, see?

   (Eliza barely moves.)

   Here, they're fun.

   (Lauren slips a few bangle bracelets on Eliza's arm. They hang there.)

   If you move your arm, they'll sparkle.

   (Eliza doesn't move.)

   But they're nice like that too, still.

   (Beat.)

   I mean, they weren't expensive. I got them at the pharmacy. I got myself some too — in pink. You wanna see?

ELIZA: Go away. Please. I don't want you to see me this way.

   (Beat.)

LAUREN: So what should we do?

ELIZA: I'm not happy.

LAUREN: I know.

ELIZA: I just want things to be the way they were.

LAUREN: I know.

ELIZA: I never have nice dreams anymore.

LAUREN: I know.

ELIZA: You do?

LAUREN: Yeah.

ELIZA: I'm not sure it's something you can understand unless you've been through it.

LAUREN: Oh. Well, that's probably true.

(Beat.)

So, do you want to play Monopoly?

(Eliza shakes her head.)

No. Do you want to watch a movie? I rented a few, just in case . . . I even brought *Pretty Woman* . . .

(Eliza shakes her head.)

Are you tired?

(Eliza nods.)

OK.

(Eliza sleeps.)

Liza? . . . Can you hear me?

(Beat.)

Because I wanted to tell you I've been having this dream that it's like a year ago and we're just sitting on the floor of your room playing checkers and you beat me, over and over again, and then I wake up and I'm really happy.

(Beat.)

Liza . . . please don't give up. I mean, if you give up now, I'll never forgive you. Never.

(Beat.)

It'll break my heart.

SCENE 21

Lauren is all alone in the large empty yoga room. She is sitting in the middle of the floor, not moving. After a long while, a woman, played by the same actress as Eliza, enters.

MEGAN: Oh! I'm sorry. I'm interrupting —

(Beat.)

Are you OK?

(Beat. Lauren doesn't even look up.)

If you want, I can leave. There might be another open room. If you want privacy.

LAUREN: *(Quietly, meaning "please leave.")* It's fine.

MEGAN: *(Not getting it at all.)* OK!

(Megan spreads out her mat.)

I guess you're having a rough day too. I know I shouldn't say it; we've barely just met, but you'd think by my age, I'd have found a way to get over PMS, huh? But no. I'm as pissed off as ever. *(Beat.)* Now you definitely want me to leave, right? What an introduction. Megan.

LAUREN: What?

MEGAN: My name. Megan. And you? Do you have one?

LAUREN: Eliza.

MEGAN: No, you don't look like an Eliza. It's funny. I guess I knew one once.

LAUREN: *(More to herself.)* I did too.

MEGAN: I just started yoga. I find it incredibly calming. My therapist says I talk so much that I need to find something I can do in silence. So what do I do? I find you! There were other empty rooms. Don't tell.

LAUREN: OK.

MEGAN: It just seemed so much nicer than going to the gym. I hate those machines, the way you strap in and stay there for forty-five minutes. It's like your brain's on hold while your body sweats. It's unnatural.

LAUREN: *(After a breath.)* I can't stand gyms.

MEGAN: This is the closest I could come. I like to take walks, really. But my doctor doesn't think it's cardiovascular enough. *(Beat.)* Let me know if you want me to be quiet. I can do that. I am capable.
(Long beat.)
I mean, it's been such a day already. What a breath of fresh air, huh? Just chatting. I swear, if I have to look another woman in the eye and ask her whether she's menstruating. God help me.
(Beat. Lauren stares at her.)
No — I'm a nurse. A nurse. *(Beat.)* What a world, eh?

LAUREN: Yeah.

MEGAN: How about you? What do you do?

LAUREN: I work with aquatic animals.

MEGAN: You're a marine biologist?

LAUREN: That's right.

MEGAN: You like the water?

LAUREN: Yeah, I guess so.

MEGAN: I hate it. Refused to learn to swim when I was a girl. All I would do was stand on the first step of the pool or in the shallowest part of the ocean and stare out at the deep. It seemed so daunting. And to this day, I won't put my whole head in. I like being able to breathe. Without breath, how do you feel alive, right?

LAUREN: In school, senior year of high school, I won the contest for staying longest underwater.

MEGAN: How long?

LAUREN: Oh, I think I nearly died. However long is almost too long.

MEGAN: Good lord. You and I are not the same.

LAUREN: You know, a man proposed to me the other day. *(Beat.)* I don't know why I'm telling you, but —

MEGAN: No, I love this stuff. Eat it up. What'd you say?

LAUREN: Well, I took off.

MEGAN: Oh honey. You don't love him?

LAUREN: I don't know.

MEGAN: I was once in a relationship with a man, let's call him Gus. He used to take me places, to parks, to sit in the empty pews of churches at midnight, to late-night movies, to small towns upstate. He was so good to me. Romantic, you know, and like I said I'm not very . . . romantic, just a late-bloomer I guess, and after awhile I got wary of all the nice things he did. They started seeming more . . . I don't know, manipulative than they really were. I stopped sleeping with him. Soon, we didn't even kiss. He moved to Vermont, I think, or maybe Maine? And I heard recently that he got married. You know how it goes.

LAUREN: Were you sad?

MEGAN: Yes.

(Beat.)

But did I have a right to be? There I'm not so sure.

LAUREN: I think you had a right to be.

MEGAN: Yeah? Well . . . Life's so hard. One can't always blame oneself. We make so many decisions, some are bound to be wrong.

LAUREN: You know . . . you remind me of someone. It's incredible, really.

MEGAN: Is that right?

LAUREN: Like a friend I once had —

MEGAN: All my life people have told me that. That I seem like someone else.

LAUREN: I miss her.

MEGAN: Who?

LAUREN: Eliza.

MEGAN: You have the same name? Cute.

LAUREN: No — I mean, yes. The same name. Had.

MEGAN: Was she nice?

LAUREN: Of course. I mean, she was very nice.

MEGAN: No one's very nice. Some people pass themselves off as nice tolerably well but we're animals, all of us.

LAUREN: No, she was . . . she didn't have a cruel bone in her body.

MEGAN: She did. She hated people. She probably hated you for a while.

LAUREN: But I deserved it.

MEGAN: She thought you were mean.

LAUREN: And I am.

MEGAN: You were in school. You were a child . . . You know, I went into a lot of people's private yoga rooms and no one else said a word to me.

LAUREN: What are you talking about? What do you mean I was a child —

MEGAN: I sensed, even then, that . . .

LAUREN: That what?

MEGAN: You were a good person. I deal with so many people in the course of a day — people in less pain than you and they're unashamed about being malicious.

LAUREN: No. I promise you. I guarantee you. I'm not at all good —

MEGAN: You've been through the mill.

LAUREN: Who are you?

MEGAN: Who are you?

LAUREN: I'm . . .

MEGAN: You're wonderful.

LAUREN: That's what Seth says. I don't know what he sees in me.

MEGAN: He's lonely. He's reached the end of being alone. And he has nice hair — the way it sticks up a little, like an alien.

LAUREN: Eliza?

MEGAN: (Standing to leave.) Megan. I'm sorry — maybe I should go.

LAUREN: No!

MEGAN: You know, in my experience, life is what you make of it. If you decide you like gray days, then you like gray days. They're transformed.

LAUREN: But —

MEGAN: Right after my father died, when I was eleven, I told my mother that I wished she was dead too. We had a fight about R-rated movies; she didn't want me to go to a party where they would be watching *Pretty Woman* even though it was my best friend's party, and I said that awful thing and then she cried in a way she'd never cried before, not even after my father died.

LAUREN: You were upset.

MEGAN: But I said it. And at the time, I meant it.

LAUREN: Did you apologize?

MEGAN: Never. But my mother knew it wasn't how I really felt. She forgave me.

LAUREN: Oh God. Eliza?

MEGAN: No, there is no God.

LAUREN: This is a dream.

MEGAN: Then wake up.

LAUREN: What if I can't?

MEGAN: You can.

SCENE 22

Lauren stands at Seth's front door, knocking. The whole scene has a kind of fast and frantic quality; Lauren, even when she has Seth's attention, seems to be trying urgently to get it, to say something.

LAUREN: Um, Seth. Seth. It's . . . me. *(Beat.)* I know you're home because . . . well, I saw you walk home. You had a bag from Changs and I can smell your food, Peking Duck or something, so I know you're in there . . . and I feel like . . . I mean, I really need to see you. I mean, Seth, I really need to see you . . . I need to —
(Seth opens the door. Beat.)
You opened the door.
(Beat.)
So, hi.
(Beat.)
How are you?

SETH: I'm not going to talk to you.

LAUREN: But you opened the door.
(He begins to close the door.)
No! Seth.
(He opens the door a little.)

SETH: I'm not going to talk to —

LAUREN: I have to tell you something! I have to; I have to.

SETH: *(Opening the door, and angrily:)* Like what, that you're insane?

LAUREN: No, Seth. I mean, yes, I mean in a way. Yes —

SETH: Try making some sense. A coherent thought would be nice.

LAUREN: Don't get mad, please —

SETH: Don't get mad? Look, if you're crazy just tell me right now that you're crazy — because I mean, I thought . . . even though you were a little . . . mysterious . . . I thought I knew you. And it's not like I don't have my

own problems, I mean — do I need this? Do I need someone so . . .
messed up? How messed up are you exactly?

LAUREN: Eliza died.

SETH: Great.

LAUREN: No, I mean. She was my best friend. And she died. When we were fourteen.

SETH: Yup.

LAUREN: I'm not lying.

SETH: No, of course not.

LAUREN: Please, Seth.

SETH: Please, what?

LAUREN: I was just a kid.

SETH: Uh-huh.

LAUREN: And I made an awful mistake and ever since then, I've been, well, inside of it. It just goes on and on. Like I'm outside of time and I can't get back in.

SETH: You're outside of time.

LAUREN: *(Looking down and quietly.)* And the problem is, there aren't punishments!

SETH: What are you talking about?

LAUREN: For little girls who do bad things. Who are mean and selfish and trying to grow up. There are no punishments. No one blamed me even though it was my fault, Eliza dying. I just went back to school and sat at my desk and ate my lunch and did my algebra homework. I just, I mean, did my homework like anyone else.

SETH: What do you mean it was your fault?

LAUREN: I abandoned her.

SETH: Like in a sinking ship, on a desert island? What are you trying to tell me?

LAUREN: I made other friends and I left her behind.

SETH: Uh-huh.

LAUREN: It was when she needed me most.

SETH: And?

LAUREN: And then she got very thin and sort of faded away.

(Beat.)

SETH: And you think that was your fault?

LAUREN: I know it was.

SETH: When I was fourteen, my best friend was Mark Hickman. When I was fourteen and two weeks, Mark Hickman wouldn't look me in the eye, literally ran away from me down crowded hallways. I didn't kill myself.

LAUREN: No, for so long after she died, I didn't get out of bed. My parents thought I might never recover and they were right, in a way, even though I did eventually get out of bed and sort of go through the motions. That is, until I met you, when I thought, and I know this is crazy, I thought for the first time, wow, Eliza would have really liked this guy; she would have really liked him, the way he's unpretentious and open and caring and brave. That's the kind of man she would have liked. And so . . . I don't know . . . I just said her name. Because she was with me anyway. Because it just came out that way —

SETH: God.

LAUREN: And I was OK for a while because everything was new, because it hadn't gotten serious.

SETH: Uh-huh.

LAUREN: But then things got confusing because I still couldn't give her up, even when I wanted to —

SETH: Liza —

LAUREN: Seth, my name's Lauren.

(Beat.)

SETH: Lauren.

LAUREN: Lauren.

(Beat.)

And I can show you where I grew up and I can meet your friends and you can meet my parents, even though they'd be shocked that you really exist, that anyone exists who could have helped me . . . emerge. And you can call me at work even though I kind of keep to myself there and people would talk if I got a call. I mostly spend my time underwater, in the tanks, running tests. But now I don't want to. I don't want to anymore. I don't want to anymore.

SETH: Lauren.

LAUREN: I don't know. Maybe we can at least be friends? If . . .

SETH: I don't want to be your friend.

LAUREN: OK.

SETH: It's just that . . . and this is me talking and not my therapist or Trevor or anyone. It's just that, I can't keep putting myself through, well, this, or you, I mean. I can't keep putting myself through you.

LAUREN: I know.

SETH: If I could, I would.

LAUREN: I understand that.

SETH: I'm sorry.

LAUREN: I'm sorry too.

(Long beat.)

SETH: But what do you think.

LAUREN: What do you mean?

SETH: It's possible.

LAUREN: What is?

SETH: Happiness.

LAUREN: Oh. I don't know.

SETH: But take a stab at it.

(Beat.)

LAUREN: OK, I think it's possible.

SETH: You do?

LAUREN: Yes.

SETH: Why?

LAUREN: Well otherwise, how would we get through each day?

SCENE 23

A flashback. Lauren and Eliza are lying on a bed, side by side; they're eleven.

LAUREN: So, Julie Miller and I are going to go on a walk later today. She says some of the farms near her dad's house are haunted. Do you want to come?

ELIZA: I don't think this is the right time for me to be touring haunted houses.

LAUREN: Oh, right, sorry . . . But, well, I think there are some fields too. And cows. Maybe you should get some fresh air. It might be good for you. Don't people say that? Plus I don't want to be alone with Julie Miller. She talks so much.

ELIZA: Not today.

(Beat.)

LAUREN: Don't you want to talk about it, Liza?

ELIZA: No.

LAUREN: If I were you, I'd want to talk about it. I'd have to. I couldn't keep all that bottled up.

ELIZA: Well, we're not the same.

LAUREN: I'd never seen someone . . . dead before.

ELIZA: Neither had I.

LAUREN: Do you believe in heaven?

ELIZA: I don't know.

LAUREN: Did your dad?

ELIZA: I don't know.

(Beat.)

LAUREN: I'm sorry — I shouldn't have asked that.

ELIZA: No, I just wish I knew.

LAUREN: Maybe your mom knows.

ELIZA: It's not the same.

LAUREN: No.

(Beat.)

But the funeral was really nice. What your mom said. And your grandpa.

ELIZA: Yeah.

LAUREN: I mean, it was really nice. I wish someone would say such nice things about me when I die.

ELIZA: Lauren.

LAUREN: Yeah?

ELIZA: What do you think happens when we die?

LAUREN: I don't know.

ELIZA: But what do you think?

LAUREN: My mom says —

ELIZA: No, what do *you* think?

LAUREN: I don't know . . . I think . . . it's probably very quiet.

ELIZA: Yeah, I agree.

LAUREN: And probably very warm, just the right temperature.

ELIZA: Yeah, that sounds right.

LAUREN: And probably you have the wildest dreams.

ELIZA: Wow, yeah.

LAUREN: So that you're not alone.

(Eliza curls up closer to Lauren; she puts her head on her chest.)

ELIZA: I don't want my dad to be alone.

LAUREN: No, he's having wonderful dreams.

ELIZA: Do you think he's dreaming about me?

LAUREN: Oh, definitely.

ELIZA: He never got to see me graduate high school or get married or have a baby.

LAUREN: He's going to dream all those things.

ELIZA: But it's so sad.

LAUREN: It is.

ELIZA: And my mother's so sad.

LAUREN: I know. My mother said she didn't know what she'd do . . . if it happened to her.

(Eliza takes Lauren's hand and curls closer.)

I don't know what she would do. She's so reliant on my father. He's like . . . what wakes her up. Literally, I mean. Alarm clocks don't work for her anymore.

ELIZA: I'm so sad, Lauren. What if I'm sad forever?

LAUREN: (Stroking Eliza's hair.) You won't be.

ELIZA: How do you know?

LAUREN: I just do. You're very resilient.

ELIZA: What does that mean?

LAUREN: I don't know. I think I read it somewhere. But it seemed to apply to you.

ELIZA: Well, thank you.

LAUREN: Of course.

ELIZA: I'll always have you, right, Lauren?

LAUREN: Of course.

ELIZA: You promise?

LAUREN: I promise.

(They stare at each other; Lauren keeps stroking Eliza's hair. She pauses and then leans in and kisses Eliza, on the lips.)

ELIZA: (Quietly.) What are you doing?

LAUREN: I don't know.

(She kisses her again. It's very tender.)

You're my best friend, Liza.

ELIZA: I know. You're my best friend too.

END OF PLAY

dark play

or
stories for boys

Carlos Murillo

PLAYWRIGHT'S BIOGRAPHY

Carlos Murillo's *dark play or stories for boys* world premiered at the 31st Annual Humana Festival of New American Plays at Actors Theatre of Louisville in March 2007. Other plays include *Unfinished American Highwayscape #9 & 32, Mimesophobia (Or before and after), A Human Interest Story (Or The Gory Details and All), Offspring of the Cold War, The Patron Saint of the Nameless Dead, Schadenfreude, Near Death Experiences With Leni Riefenstahl, Never Whistle While You're Pissing,* and *Subterraneans.* They have been produced in New York (NYC Summer Play Festival, En Garde Arts, Soho Rep, The Hangar Theatre Lab), LA (Theatre @ Boston Court, Circle X, Son of Semele), Chicago (Walkabout Theatre, DePaul University), Minneapolis (Red Eye), Seattle (The Group), Atlanta (Actors Express) and Austin (dirigo group). His plays have been developed at The Public, NY Theatre Workshop, The Goodman, South Coast Rep, Portland Center Stage, Madison Rep, Sundance, The Playwrights' Center, Bay Area Playwrights Festival, A.S.K. Theatre Projects, Annex Theatre, U.C. Santa Barbara, and others. He was a Jerome Fellow at The Playwrights' Center in Minneapolis, and he has received grants from the Rockefeller Foundation, the Minnesota State Arts Board and is a two-time recipient of the National Latino Playwriting Award from Arizona Theatre Company.

Mr. Murillo teaches playwriting and performance at The Theatre School of DePaul University in Chicago, where he lives with his wife Lisa Portes and their two children Eva Rose and Carlos Pablo. He is a member of New Dramatists.

INTRODUCTORY STATEMENT

dark play or stories for boys was written during a residency at the 2005 U.C.S.B. Summer Theatre Lab. In January 2006, a workshop production of the play was presented at The Theatre School of DePaul University, directed by the author.

The play owes it's existence to lots of folks who offered their support along the way: Naomi Iizuka; the students at U.C.S.B.; Lisa Portes, who directed the original workshop; John Culbert (Dean of The Theatre School of DePaul); Stewart Calhoun; Melissa diLeonardo; Adam Poss; John Smythe; Andrea Tichy; Theatre @ Boston Court; Bryan Davidson; Tom Jacobsen; Michael Michetti; Jessica Kubzansky; Sherry Kramer; Henry Godinez; Tanya Palmer; The Goodman Theatre Latino Festival; Arizona Theatre Company and Elaine Romero. A very special thanks to Actors Theatre of Louisville, The Humana Foundation, Marc Masterson, Adrien-Alice Hansel, Merv Antonio,

Zan Sawyer-Dailey, Michael John Garcés, Jennifer Mendenhall, Liz Morton, Will Rogers, Matthew Stadelmann, Lou Sumrall, and Mary Resing. I would also like to thank Antje Oegel and all the good folks at Bret Adams, Ltd.

This play is dedicated to Todd.

ORIGINAL PRODUCTION

dark play or stories for boys by Carlos Murillo was presented by Actors Theatre of Louisville at the 31st Annual Humana Festival of New American Plays (made possible by a generous grant from The Humana Foundation) March 2 to 31, 2007. It was directed by Michael John Garcés.

CAST

NICK . . . . .Matthew Stadelmann
MOLLY/RACHEL . . . . .Liz Morton
ADAM . . . . .Will Rogers
MALE NETIZEN . . . . .Lou Sumrall
FEMALE NETIZEN .Jennifer Mendenhall

Scenic Designer . . . . .Michael B. Raiford
Costume Designer . . . . .Lorraine Venberg
Lighting Designer . . . . .Brian J. Lilienthal
Sound Designer . . . . .Matt Callahan
Video Designer . . . . .Jason Czaja
Properties Designer . . . . .Mark Walston
Fight Director . . . . .Drew Fracher
Stage Manager . . . . .Megan Schwarz
Dramaturg . . . . .Mary Resing
Casting . . . . .Judy Bowman Casting
Directing Assistant . . . . .Tina Sanchez

Presented by Special Arrangement with Bret Adams Ltd.

The West Coast premiere of *dark play or stories for boys* opened at Theatre @ Boston Court in Pasadena, Calif. in October 2007.

CHARACTERS

NICK

ADAM

MOLLY/RACHEL

MALE NETIZEN: (Change Hustler, Jock, Soccerdude2891, ThaibabeslonelyinUSofA@Yahoo.com, Donttreadonme76, Tony)

FEMALE NETIZEN: (Sarah, Ms. Spiegel, Mother, Olivia)

TIME

Now

PLACE

A college dorm room

An affluent town along the Southern California coast

Cyberspace

The symbol // indicates overlapping speech.

dark play or stories for boys

1

NICK: I make shit up.
    I make shit up all the time
    partly cause I like making shit up
    partly cause I'm good at it
    and partly cause
    well
    I *can.*
    Which is not to say that I'm oblivious to the consequences
    Christ, do I know there are consequences.
    You find yourself in sticky situations, painted into corners
    And it takes the dexterity of a sharp-thinking comic book hero to
    Unstick yourself, tiptoe across the wet paint
    Hoping you don't leave a trail of painted toe prints,
    Or if you do,
    that they're faint enough so no one will notice.
    I'm thinking about this right now
    'Cause
    Well
    I find myself in one of those sticky situations
    Situation I'll have to muster up the deepest wells of my superhero dexterity
    To get out of
    Or not.
    See: there's a girl lying next to me
    in my bed,
    In the dark,
    Here in my dorm room.
    She's naked. We've just had sex.
    I guess you can call her my girlfriend
    'Cause yes,
    She's naked
    She's lying next to me
    And we've just had sex?
    This is a new thing for me, this girl

so you'll understand my hesitation —
First time, you know, doing the ol'
in out in out
and stuff.
Yeah, we've been through those cagey first conversations
where you talk all over each other's sentences
But we haven't crossed that threshold,
where suddenly it's like
This one might be around for a spell, she's shared such and such
I've shared such and such
We're not talking over each other's sentences anymore
All the stuff that adds up to
Intimacy.
Nope. We haven't gotten there yet.
Nope. We're in the middle of the post-first-time-humping awkward silence.
And let me emphasize that this post-first-time silence is incredibly meaningful —
The whole future of the relationship hovers over this silence
Like a promise
Like a threat.
We could start talking and find out that we do in fact have all the things we imagined we had in common
MOLLY: My dad's a total dick.
NICK: Yours too?
MOLLY: Oh, you don't know dick until you've met my dad.
NICK: Or she could put out her cigarette,
     grab her panties off the floor,
     Slip on her jeans and T-shirt and say
MOLLY: Yeah, that was nice. Um.
     Give me a call some time — I mean I'm really busy the next month or so?
     but yeah.
     See ya.
NICK: Or she could finish up her cigarette
     And fall asleep
MOLLY: *(Yawn.)*
NICK: But she doesn't do any of those things. No.
     What she does do —

She extends her index finger,
Presses the tip of it against my Adam's Apple,
Drags it slowly down my neck
Over my ribs
Over my left nipple
And down down down
In the direction of my crotch.
When at a loss for words, why not start bumping uglies again, right?
And so her index finger is slowly making its way down towards my
Pubis,
All suggestive,
when she comes to an abrupt stop.
Just above the belly button,
Where she notices my skin
Is no longer the smooth,
Post-adolescent torso,
Where the tip of her finger finds a speed bump.
A pink strip of raised skin a few inches above my belly button
A quarter inch thick
About three and a half inches long.
Yes, her finger stops at this sudden change in the geography of my skin.
Tentatively, she traces a line along the length of it.
Then, even more hesitant, she explores the rest of my abdomen
She feels other pink speed bumps, of different sizes and angles.
Some three inches
Some an inch
Some just thin wisps.

MOLLY: What are these?

NICK: And that's when time stops
And I feel the familiar sensation —
Sweat glands juicing up,
A hardening between my legs
That low-grade migraine
When I'm like an atom in a particle accelerator
And the world around me slows like it's moving through peanut butter.

MOLLY: Come on Nick, what are these?
Nick?
Nick?

NICK: Do I tell her?

Or do I let my comic book dexterity get me out of this one.
In other words,
do I tell her the truth
Or do I do what I do so well:
Make some shit up.

2

NICK: The question the choice the question the choice the question the choice
MOLLY: What are these?
NICK: What are these?
MOLLY: Nick, can you hear me? What are these?
NICK: Do I tell the truth?
MOLLY: Nick
NICK: Or do I make shit up.
MOLLY: Nii-iick
NICK: The low-grade migraine, sweat glands juicing up, a hardening between
    my legs
MOLLY: Earth to Nick. Do you copy?
NICK: Me speeding up
MOLLY: What are these
NICK: The air taking on the consistency of peanut butter
MOLLY: NICK!
NICK: The question the choice the question the choice
    Launches me backward in time.
    To when I was fourteen
    Period in my life where I was
    living according to a theory I call
    The Universal Theory of the Gullibility Threshold —
    Or U.T.G.T., or even better, G.T. for short.
    The theory organizes the chaos of twenty-first-century life into a simple,
    manageable model:
    Everyone has a gullibility threshold,
    Everyone at some point will come to recognize
    That the wheelbarrow of caca they're being fed
    Is in fact a wheelbarrow of caca. Nothing more. Nothing less.
    The G.T. works on a scale of 1 to 10.
    At the bottom of the scale, you have your 1s.

The 1s don't even bother taking a swallow of the caca,
they know it's caca

They can smell it a hundred miles away.

Their healthy skepticism becomes a cancer:

They end up paranoid conspiracy-nut shut-ins

Thinking everything is caca.

"The world is round."

MALE NETIZEN: No it's not. You're fucking with me.

NICK: The sky is blue.

MALE NETIZEN: That's just an illusion man.

NICK: Now most people fall in the middle of the scale —

The 4s, 5s, and 6s.

They'll give the wheelbarrow of caca the benefit of the doubt,

But then they'll get wise.

But the top of the scale you have your 10s.

The suckers who'll gorge themselves on the caca

Repeat over and over,

"Yum, Yum, tastes just like chicken

can I have seconds, can I have thirds."

And when the wheelbarrow is empty,

They'll eat their own caca 'cause they're addicted.

The 10s are those girls that collect unicorns

and draw rainbows on their biology-class notebooks.

They're the ones who end the day with their wallets empty

Cause they believe every sob story they're told by every homeless person
they meet on the street.

CHANGE HUSTLER: Hey, you got a twenty? I'm not like this, I don't do this,
ever. It's just my husband? He just got back from Iraq? and he's like all
messed up in the head? He's at the VA hospital up in Sacramento. And
he spent his last disability check on crack? I don't have any money to get
on the bus to Bakersfield? to pick up our kids? Who are staying with their
grandmother who's deaf and on dialysis and can't drive 'cause the repo
man got her car? And she can't keep them for another night cause her
boyfriend is crazy and doesn't want the kids around the house no more
so I got to go get them then go get my husband so we can go find a place
to live? If you give me your phone number? I'll call you so I can pay you
back. Can you help me out?

NICK: Yes, the 10s are rare. But they do exist.

Adam fell into that category.

ADAM: I'm not gullible.

NICK: Adam was a perfect 10.

ADAM: I am not gullible.

NICK: A perfect 10. Or so he seemed.

Which was strange . . .

How do you account for a perfectly average sixteen-year-old

From southern California

Having a G.T. of 10?

You could write him off and say he was just stupid

ADAM: I'm not stupid.

NICK: But that would've been unscientific.

To get to the bottom of the mystery of Adam's existence

You gotta start with the question:

How did you get to be so gullible?

Did no one ever kick the scoop off your ice cream cone for no reason?

Was your backyard a Garden of Eden under the ever-present California sun?

Did your parents actually stay married?

Did your mother jab her nipple in your mouth any time you so much as whimpered?

Did your parents decimate nature with an overabundance of nurture?

ADAM: My parents? I dunno.

They're all right I guess. I mean they're not like

weird or anything.

They kinda keep to themselves. I don't

Hate them.

They're just . . .

Kind of there.

Dad with his book.

Mom with her puttering around.

Me in my room doing

Homework or

Surfing the net.

It's like

We each have our own little areas of the house

And like

the dining room's the one place

Where we

You know,

eat.

And I guess that's what we do when we're together. Eat.

And then when we're done eating

We like

go back to our own little areas until it's time to go to bed.

Every day it's

Pretty much the same.

NICK: So no, the Garden-of-Eden-Nipple-on-Demand model couldn't explain
Adam.

And I started thinking maybe it was something more fundamental.

ADAM: I'm not gullible.

I'm not stupid.

NICK: Maybe

In the face of knowing that Mom, Dad,

Santa Claus,

The Tooth Fairy, The Easter Bunny, The Great Pumpkin,

And God are all Dead,

You still have to believe in something.

Don't you?

ADAM: I don't know.

I guess I believe in God.

I mean,

I don't go to church or anything —

We used to but

then we moved to California and we just

you know

Stopped.

And it's like, "Yeah, maybe there is something out there."

But is it like some bearded guy with white hair up in the sky?

I have this cousin? up in Oregon?

And she's like

One of those total religious freakoids.

One day we were on the beach at sunset?

And out of the blue she said:

SARAH: What do you see Adam?

ADAM: Uhh,

Water?

SARAH: Water, yes. What else?

ADAM: Waves?

SARAH: Water, waves, yes. But what *else?*

ADAM: The sky? Some clouds? Seagulls?

Sand?

A bunch of junk on the sand?

SARAH: Yes, Adam. Yes, I see all those things too. But you know what else I see?

When you put them all together —

the water, the waves, the sky, the junk on the beach,

the little kid over there smiling at the waves with her mother —

you know what I see?

ADAM: No.

SARAH: I see God.

ADAM: Oh.

SARAH: You can see him too, Adam. If only you'd let him in your heart.

ADAM: I was like,

"Whatever."

NICK: So, Adam, like pretty much the rest of us

was a belief-starved kid hopscotching across the 500 channels of satellite TV

and wandering the infinite portals of the World Wide Web

scavenging for that morsel of diversion that would sustain you

until you found the next one.

So that couldn't explain Adam's stratospheric G.T.

otherwise

we'd all be fish hanging stupidly from hooks

ADAM: I'm not stupid

NICK: But he wasn't totally belief-starved —

I recognized this reading the first six words of Adam's online profile

ADAM: "I want to fall in love"

NICK: I read that I was like, "Whoa." Who uses that word?

Adam's like the first person I ever met my age who used that word "love"

without rolling his eyes

or making it sound like the punch line of a really stupid joke

ADAM: I want to fall in love with a girl

15-18. Would like her to have green eyes, dirty blonde hair,

she should be like 5'4", 5'6" tops,

have a good body (No fat girls, please, no offense.)

she should be smart and likes to chill out on the beach.

I'm 16. Kinda tall. I used to play soccer, but trying to expand my horizons.

E-mail me at JustWant2ChillWithU@aol.com

NICK: Now when I read that I was like:

"Duh, who doesn't want a girl like that." I can imagine all the 15-18 year old dirty blonde, green-eyed girls in the world reading that, breathing a sigh of relief saying,

MALE NETIZEN: "Finally. Finally there's someone out there who wants me!"

NICK: "I want to fall in love . . . "

Huh. "*Love*"

Did the fact he believed such a thing existed

explain why Adam's G.T. was way off the scale?

I mean, he wasn't just that rare 10,

He was like that amp in *Spinal Tap* —

His G.T. went up to 11.

Intrigued, I set out to find out.

OLIVIA: Now when you do it,

I need you to promise me that you'll tell him

That you love him.

3

NICK: The question the choice the question the choice the question the choice

MOLLY: What are these?

NICK: What are these?

MOLLY: Nick, can you hear me? What are these?

NICK: Do I tell the truth?

MOLLY: Nick

NICK: Or do I make shit up.

MOLLY: Nii-iick

NICK: The low-grade migraine, sweat glands juicing up, a hardening between my legs

MOLLY: Earth to Nick. Do you copy?

NICK: Me speeding up

MOLLY: What are these

NICK: The air taking on the consistency of peanut butter

MOLLY: NICK!

NICK: The question the choice the question the choice
    Launches me backward in time.
    Three and a half weeks before I read those
    Six
    Magic
    Totally baffling words.
ADAM: I want to fall in love
NICK: Back to a time when I
    took this Theater Arts elective
    'Cause I thought it would be a total blow off,
    Antidote to the accelerated English, Science, History, and Math classes I
    was taking.
    Teacher was this lady, Ms. Spiegel
    Who must have been like 40 or 50
    And who was a
    total
    dyke.
MS. SPIEGEL: The best theater is theater that challenges the audience.
    That provokes.
    That's *dangerous.*
NICK: That's what she used to say, she liked that word
MS. SPIEGEL: *Dangerous.*
    The best theater holds a mirror up to the audience
    And invites them —
    No,
    Demands them to look at the reflection,
    No matter how unflattering,
    No matter how *ugly* it is.
    The best theater takes the audience on a journey into the darkest,
    Most *dangerous,*
    Regions of the human soul.
    And at the end of the journey,
    The audience,
    Having faced that *darkness,*
    That
    Danger,
    Can recognize
    The darkness and danger in their own souls,
    And actively take steps to

Change

It.

NICK: Which I guess was all well and good,

Though,

I couldn't reconcile all this

MS. SPIEGEL: *darkness*

NICK: and

MS. SPIEGEL: *danger*

NICK: She was talking about with the fact that we spent the entire semester

Playing these stupid kid's games. Tag. Duck Duck Goose.

Finally one day in class,

After she practically broke down in tears

Telling us how *important*

It was to recognize the

MS. SPIEGEL: *Darkness*

NICK: And

MS. SPIEGEL: *danger*

NICK: in the human soul,

And that portraying that on the stage was one of nature's highest callings,

I raised my hand:

MS. SPIEGEL: Yes, Nick.

NICK: Um. Ms. Spiegel? I think I understand what you mean

With all this darkness and danger stuff

But

What I'm having trouble with

Is what does any of that have to do with playing

"Pussy Wants a Corner"?

There were all sorts of repressed giggles,

And a little bit of awe, I might say —

Other kids were used to not noticing me,

Flying as far under the radar as I did in school.

It took a moment to gather herself,

And improvise an answer to my question.

MS. SPIEGEL: Well . . .

Games are

Games are the essence of theater.

When you play a game

You *allow* yourself to

let go.

You *allow* yourself to
believe.
Acting in a play is kind of like
Well,
Kind of like playing in a game.
Only instead of pretending you're a pussy cat,
You're pretending to be
Hamlet.
Instead of trying to get your "corner" in the circle,
You're trying to decide whether or not to kill your stepfather.

NICK: Oh.
And then she got on a roll.
She started talking about how there are games that are really *dangerous*
for the players. That —

MS. SPIEGEL: When I was in grad school? — like a million years ago ha ha
Anyway,
We had this one professor —
A really intense guy who did all sorts of wild theater in N.Y. back in the
sixties —
He would make us play games, but the dangerous kind.
He called these kinds of games "Dark Play" —
Does anyone know what "Dark Play" is?
Does anyone want to take a stab?

NICK: Silence.

MS. SPIEGEL: Dark play is a kind of game
Where certain players know the rules,
And other players don't.
In other words — some of the players
Are fully aware that they are participating in a game,
While others are completely in the dark.
Has anyone engaged in this kind of play?

NICK: I raised my hand to "take a stab," as it were.

MS. SPIEGEL: Yes, Nick.

NICK: Is that like
When you go on the Internet,
And you go into a chat room and pretend you're someone else?

MS. SPIEGEL: Maybe. Could you unpack that for me?
I'm totally nineteenth century when it comes to technology —
I still have a hard time getting my toaster to work.

NICK: Well . . . say you're some girl
And you're kind of ugly
MS. SPIEGEL: We should avoid making those kinds of judgments
NICK: I'm just saying, so I'm sure I understand:
Say you're some girl and
You look a certain way that no one wants to "get with you."
And you go online,
And you meet a guy and he says,
MALE NETIZEN: What do u look like?
NICK: You could tell him the truth,
MALE NETIZEN: I'm overweight, I have bad acne,
I have facial hair
I don't dress cool at all.
NICK: Which would get you nowhere.
Or you could be like
MALE NETIZEN: I'm 5'7", I've got dirty blonde hair, green eyes
I wear short miniskirts. I'm totally hot.
NICK: Which would get the guy interested, right?
MS. SPIEGEL: Depends on the guy, but I think I see where you're going.
NICK: Anyway, so the guy's like
MALE NETIZEN: You sound hot
I wanna get to "know" you.
NICK: And he could be some fat pimply gay kid
Who's just bored and wants to see where the whole thing's gonna go, right?
And then they end up cybering
MS. SPIEGEL: Pardon? Cybering? Could you define that for me?
NICK: That's when one of the jocks in the class chimed in —
JOCK: That's when you get all nasty with some chick online.
MS. SPIEGEL: Oh . . .
I didn't know people did that.
NICK: Anyway,
Ms. Spiegel,
Is that what you mean by this
"Dark Play"?
MS. SPIEGEL: I suppose.
I'll have to think about that more
And get back to you.
NICK: She never did get back to me.

But I figured I was right,

And I sort of got the point she was trying to make about games,

And how theater was supposed to be like a game,

Only more

MS. SPIEGEL: *Dangerous*

NICK: But I'd been to the school plays.

They were about as "dangerous" as "Pussy Wants a Corner" —

But this "dark play" thing — that was pretty cool.

And if they did a school play that was like the Internet?

With all the "dark play" happening there . . . ?

I'd check it out.

But until they did that play

I'd get my dose of *dangerous*

and *dark* play

In the one place in the world where a kid my age

And well

Of my *demeanor*

Could escape the cruel and unusual punishments assigned you by your "peers":

The World Wide Web.

Where you could be anything.

You could enact revenge on all the shits that made your world

A miserable place to inhabit.

At first it was mostly small-potatoes stuff.

You'd pose as some girl,

Lure some dickhead soccer player into a private chat,

And you'd be all slutty

Say things like

FEMALE NETIZEN: "I wanna suck it. Put your mammoth cock in my mouth."

NICK: And you'd get the guy to say all sorts of stupid shit like

SOCCERDUDE2891: Lick it.

Lick it, bitch.

Lick it like an ice cream cone.

NICK: And you knew as you were spinning out the fantasy,

That some schmuck out in,

I don't know,

Yorba Linda,

Was upstairs in his room,

Pants rolled down to his ankles

One hand hunt and pecking on the computer keyboard

The other hand MIA deep in the jungle of his tightie whities.

And just as he was getting to the point of no return,

You'd pull the Lucy van Pelt to his Charlie Brown

Pulling the football away just as he was about to kick it:

FEMALE NETIZEN: "Oh, my cock is so hard for you! I'm gonna blow!!!!"

NICK: Then there'd be this silence.

And sometimes they'd split without typing in another word

SOCCERDUDE2891: <u>SoccerDude2891</u> has left the chat room.

NICK: Other times they'd get all threatening say shit like

SOCCERDUDE2891: "Motherfucker, I'll find out where you live and cut your fuckin' faggot dick off!"

NICK: That was fun for about two and a half minutes.

Once you exhausted all the possibilities, and there were quite a few,

It was the same old same old.

Which got me thinking about what Ms. Spiegel said about going

Deeper

Darker

more

MS. SPIEGEL: *Dangerous*

NICK: digging into the murky recesses of human nature,

See what people were really made of.

That's when the fake ads started.

THAIBABESLONELYINUSOFA@YAHOO.COM: I am Kim. I am exchange student from Thailand. I am 17 years old. My sister Kim is also exchange student. We both are in Catholic High School here in California, United States. We are both lonely, as we are only starting to learn English and our hosts are not very fun. We are looking for mature American man to show us the "American way of life." He must have car, and maybe friend who can join us on American adventure. My sister and me are looking for new experience. We want to meet someone who, as you Americans say, will "Rock our world." Respond with picture of yourself to ThaiBabesLonelyinUSofA@yahoo.com.

NICK: I posted that

Thinking

No one is going to respond to this —

But the next day

There were like

Eight.

Hundred.

E-mails.

In my Inbox.

It's like all the

Creepoids crawled out of their rocks, found that one,

Wrote back and sent pictures to prove their hideous existence.

One picture really freaked me out.

Some dude standing in front of a mirror

Shirtless,

Vienna Sausage prick sticking out of his scummy boxers,

Fat belly drooping down,

Old lady tits,

Ratty goatee

Shoulder-length greasy hair.

He was holding his digital camera up and behind his head.

The harsh light of the flash made his skin even pastier . . .

And his eyes . . .

I can't even describe what his eyes looked like.

Creeped me out.

At the same time

It triggered this

Feeling

In me.

But the fake ads too lost their charm for me.

Once you put one up the rest were the same.

Same disgusting, depraved people

Sending their disgusting, depraved responses

With accompanying disgusting and depraved pictures.

Confirmation that the world was populated by disgusting, depraved people

Who for some reason believed their beer guts and old lady tits

Would attract a pair of nubile, underage, sex-hungry Asian chicks.

At that point I was ready to pack the whole thing in —

That is

Until I stumbled on Adam's profile

And those six words

ADAM: I want to fall in love . . . .

NICK: Those words were so

Naked

Love.

What the fuck is that?

ADAM: I want to fall in love with a girl . . .

   15-18. Would like her to have green eyes, dirty blonde hair,

   she should be like 5'4", 5'6" tops,

   have a good body (No fat girls, please, no offense.)

   she should be smart and likes to chill out on the beach.

   I'm 16. Kinda tall. I used to play soccer, but trying to expand my horizons.

   E-mail me at // JustWant2ChillWithU@aol.com

NICK: JustWant2ChillWithU@aol.com

   Now:

   I couldn't just write him and say,

   "Hey, I'm Nick,

   I'm like

   Fourteen

   And I'm pretty confused about most things

   so

   What's up with this 'love' shit?"

   I might get him on the "Smart" part,

   But

   You would never mistake me for a cute

   Five foot six inch

   Dirty blonde

   Green-eyed

   Girl

ADAM: "Who likes to chill"

NICK: No, nature did not endow me with such generous gifts.

   But nature,

   With all its insurmountable obstacles,

   Doesn't really exist anymore, does it?

   Not when you have 512 megabytes of RAM,

   650 megahertz of microprocessing power

   And a high-speed Internet connection . . .

   No,

   armed with that, there is no natural boundary that once crossed over

   can't be crossed back again.

   So in spite of the physical shortcomings nature cursed me with,

   In the nature-free world I could become this girl of his dreams

I could invent Rachel.

The tricky thing about inventing Rachel was

Unlike the horny Thai exchange student,

Rachel had to be

Well

Plausible —

Which you'd know is a tall order if you ever had to invent a human being from scratch.

Especially one of the *female* species.

First and foremost

She had to fit the critera —

ADAM: What do u look like?

RACHEL: What do u think I look like?

ADAM: I dunno.

RACHEL: Wellll . . .

I have green eyes.

ADAM: Yeah?

RACHEL: Iiiiiiii

Have dirty blonde hair.

ADAM: Yeah?

RACHEL: Annnnnd

I'm about five foot five?

ADAM: Do u like to chill?

RACHEL: I loooove to chill.

NICK: Fitting the criteria was easy, cause Adam pretty much sketched her out for me

It was just a question of fleshing her out, so to speak.

She needed to be pretty,

but she couldn't be a total babe that was

Out of his league

ADAM: Describe what u look like.

RACHEL: Oh . . .

I'll try I guess . . .

I mean, I'm not good at talking about myself

ADAM: Try . . .

RACHEL: Well, OK.

People say I'm like a cross

Between Hillary Duff (but not so cutesy and annoying)

And Avril Lavigne (but not so faux edgy)

With a little bit of a Natalie Portman vibe
ADAM: Yeah, I can totally see that.

Cool.
NICK: She needed to be smart,

But not so smart that Adam would feel like an ox next to her
RACHEL: Let's see.

I got a B on my math midterm,
ADAM: Uh huh.
RACHEL: A B+ in English
ADAM: Huh.
RACHEL: I'm stuck somewhere between a B and a B+ in History
ADAM: Uh huh.
RACHEL: I totally aced French last semester
ADAM: Oh . . .
RACHEL: Chemistry totally sucks and right now my average is a C

But I think I can still pull off a B
ADAM: Cool.
NICK: I also wanted her to be quirky —

In the way that makes certain guys all smitten —

But not so quirky he'd think she was a freak.
RACHEL: I used to play practical jokes on my ex-boyfriend.

One time?

He was away on a band trip up in Sacramento?

I convinced his mom to let me and my friend Carrie into his room.

We filled his room up —

Waist high —

With foam packing peanuts.

You should have seen his face when he got back.

He opened his door and there was this tidal wave

Of packing peanuts.

He tried to get me back with a practical joke of his own

But . . .

I broke up with him 'cause

he didn't really have a good sense of humor.
NICK: Rachel also had to suggest to Adam the possibility of sex

Without coming off as a total ho
RACHEL: I read somewhere? That on average it lasts

Eleven minutes. Worldwide.
ADAM: No shit.

RACHEL: Think about it. Eleven minutes.

    You might as well spend those eleven minutes

    Writing the word "alone" over and over again on the wall.

    But to answer your question: No

    I don't have a boyfriend.

    I mean I'd like to have one —

    I'm really not into the whole hook-up thing —

    I mean I'm not against hooking up?

    In principle?

    It's just that

    There's got to be something more.

    You know?

NICK: In other words,

    For Rachel to be

    Plausible

    She had to be

    Well

    Kind of

    Average.

    That first chat online

    Was surprisingly easy

    I figured out pretty quickly that

    With every exchange,

    Adam was inventing Rachel as much as I was.

    She could say something totally generic like

RACHEL: Like, when is Ben Affleck NOT totally lame?

NICK: And that would lead Adam to construct a whole matrix of assumptions about her

    And what she thought about like

    Iraq. Religion. The last election.

    Which I guess is what people do, right?

    You really don't know anything about anyone else

    Just surfaces.

    So you have to

    Well

    Make shit up

    About what's going on underneath . . .

    That first chat between Rachel and Adam

    Time disappeared.

We'd started chatting around 7 at night.
It only seemed like maybe half an hour
But when I looked at the clock
It read
6:45 AM.
Eleven hours and forty-five minutes
Nonstop.
It kind of freaked me out,
But it also excited me,
That I could sustain Rachel for so long,
But I remembered I had a math quiz that day,
So Rachel wrote:
RACHEL: I don't want to get off
　　　But
　　　I've got a chemistry quiz tomorrow — well today.
　　　I need to catch a few Z's. Gotta get that C to a B.
ADAM: Yeah. That's cool.
NICK: I wondered,
　　　Do I just leave it at that?
　　　Or
　　　Do I keep the carrot dangling?
RACHEL: Will you be online tomorrow night?
ADAM: Yeah. Probably.
RACHEL: We shall meet again . . . .
NICK: And with that . . .
RACHEL: <u>RachelIsRoses</u> has left the chat room.
ADAM: We shall meet again.
NICK: And meet again they did.
　　　They exchanged jokes.
RACHEL: So these horny gay pirates get shipwrecked on an island?
　　　And it turns out that this island
　　　Is home to a Catholic convent . . .
NICK: They exchanged intimacies.
ADAM: u ever feel like
　　　like
　　　u r the loneliest person on earth?
NICK: They exchanged pictures.
RACHEL: Did you get the picture I e-mailed you?
ADAM: Yup.

RACHEL: Annnd?

ADAM: u r totally cute.

RACHEL: Thanks.

    Tho . . . Adam?

    "cute" isn't exactly a

    compliment

    for a girl. I mean

    Koala bears are cute.

ADAM: Sorry.

    I mean

    What do u want me 2 say?

RACHEL: A girl shouldn't have to tell a guy what she wants to hear.

ADAM: So, what? A guy has 2 be like

    Psychic?

RACHEL: No.

    Not psychic. Just

RACHEL AND NICK: Imaginative.

ADAM: OK. Ummm. How about this: u r perfect.

RACHEL: That's sweet, Adam. That's

    So sweet.

    But Adam.

    I'm not perfect. I'm far from being perfect

    I'm

ADAM: u r?

RACHEL: I'm just so afraid of disappointing you.

NICK: Yes, they laid down the groundwork

    for the inevitable face-to-face that would prove

    If their virtual world connection

    Could survive the chaotic muck of the real world.

ADAM: I want 2 meet u

NICK: And if the connection did survive

    Then they could

    You know

    Exchange bodily fluids.

ADAM: I want 2 meet u

RACHEL: I want to meet you too

ADAM: What's the problem then?

RACHEL: I can't tell you that. It's

    Complicated.

NICK: Now the weird thing:

    In spite of the impossibility of a real world face-to-face

    Between Rachel and Adam,

    Something in me

    Craved for it as much as he did.

    But I sensed Adam was on the verge of reaching his Gullibility Threshold.

ADAM: Sometimes

    I get the feeling that

RACHEL: That what?

ADAM: Never mind.

RACHEL: If we're ever going to have a relationship, Adam

    We need to be open with each other. I've been open with you.

ADAM: Yeah, until it's time 2 be like

    Hey, why don't we meet?

RACHEL: I can't begin to tell you how much I want that.

ADAM: Then what's the problem?

RACHEL: I can't tell you that Adam.

ADAM: There u go again with all your

    Mystery.

RACHEL: Be patient.

    Please. Pretty please? For my sake?

    Adam?

ADAM: It's just that

    I've never met anyone like u.

RACHEL: I feel exactly the same.

ADAM: And I've never felt

RACHEL: Felt what, sweetie?

ADAM: U r gonna think its queer for me 2 say

    But

    I've never felt like this before about anyone.

RACHEL: Adam . . .

    Oh, Adam. I don't think that's // queer.

NICK: Queer.

RACHEL: I think that's

    That's the sweetest thing anyone's ever said to me.

ADAM: Rachel . . .

    I think I luv you.

RACHEL: Adam. You don't know what that means to me.

ADAM: Why can't I meet you?

It's like

u r 2 good 2 be true.

RACHEL: I'm not good, Adam.

I'm bad.

Sometimes I think I'm the most awful person in the world.

ADAM: Why?

RACHEL: I can't tell you that.

Someday I hope that I can.

And face-to-face, not like this.

Someday I hope that I can kiss your beautiful mouth,

And cradle your beautiful head on my breast

And stroke your hair

And kiss your ears.

ADAM: I don't believe u.

RACHEL: Since things have to be this way

Let me love you the only way I can.

Will you let me do that?

ADAM: Maybe.

RACHEL: Turn on your webcam, Adam.

ADAM: I don't know if I want 2.

RACHEL: Please? Adam?

Please?

I want to love you.

I want to love you the only way I can love you right now.

Turn on your webcam.

ADAM: Fine.

I'm turning it on.

RACHEL: Show me how much you love me.

I want to see it Adam.

Show it to me.

Show it to me and show me how much you love me.

NICK: And there he was on screen.

Grainy, choppy.

Standing up from his chair.

Undoing the button and zipper of his jeans.

I urged him on.

RACHEL: I feel like you're here in my room with me.

You're so beautiful, Adam.

Show me how much you love me

Show me
Show me
Show me . . .

OLIVIA: Now when you do it,
I need you to promise me that you'll tell him
That you love him.

4

NICK: The question the choice the question the choice the question the choice

MOLLY: What are these?

NICK: What are these?

MOLLY: Nick, can you hear me? What are these?

NICK: Do I tell the truth?

MOLLY: Nick

NICK: Or do I make shit up.

MOLLY: Nii-iick

NICK: The low-grade migraine, sweat glands juicing up, a hardening between my legs

MOLLY: Earth to Nick. Do you copy?

NICK: Me speeding up

MOLLY: What are these

NICK: The air taking on the consistency of peanut butter

MOLLY: NICK!

NICK: The question the choice the question the choice

NICK: Those nightly sessions were
Whoa.
Rachel asked Adam to do things that
And he did them. I couldn't believe it.
Aside from the
Excitement of watching Adam,
The nightly sessions served their purpose:
To keep Adam hooked. To keep him from demanding
The face-to-face he wanted.
But it started to feel like a nightly tap dance to Squarepusher.
Just couldn't keep up.
So drastic measures were in order.
I had to insert myself as a character in the saga of Rachel and Adam.

MALE NETIZEN: <u>NickWillRockYou</u> has entered the chat room.

NICK: Of course I couldn't go online and seek him out —
   No, Adam had to find me.
   How I did this —
   Well, I gotta say this was clever —

ADAM: No. I'm an only child. What about u?

RACHEL: I've got a brother, Nick.

ADAM: Older or younger?

RACHEL: Younger. He's 14.

ADAM: Is he cool?

RACHEL: I guess. I mean, he's my little brother so
   How cool can he be?
   I mean he's kind of a dweeb
   Keeps to himself a lot at school
   But he's like
   The biggest brain I ever met.
   And he can be pretty funny sometimes too.

ADAM: Cool.

RACHEL: Like his screen name?
   You've got to swear to me that if you ever meet him
   You won't tell him I told you this:
   His screen name is
   <u>NickWillRockYou</u>
   I mean if you ever saw this kid?
   Last thing you'd ever imagine him doing
   Would be "rocking you."

ADAM: You should get him to change it to "DweebWillRockYou"
   LOL

RACHEL: That's my little brother you're talking about, Adam.

ADAM: Sorry.

RACHEL: Yeah, he can be a total dweeb
   But
   In some ways?
   And this is gonna sound weird
   But
   He's the only person in the world I have.

MALE NETIZEN: <u>NickWillRockYou</u> has entered the chat room.

NICK: I wish I could have seen Adam's reaction when that name popped up
   on his screen.

MALE NETIZEN: <u>NickWillRockYou</u>

NICK: I was pretty sure he'd interpret my arrival as

    Some kind of divine synchronicity.

    That's what people do when they think they're in love.

    Don't they?

    There were a few other people in the room in addition to Adam

    I steered clear of him —

    But made the point to provoke everyone else in the room

    On the one hand to make sure my screen name was visible at all times

    On the other to piss everyone off enough

    With tirades of bullshit that I'd clear the room.

    <u>Donttreadonme76</u>

    Dude, that's totaly fucked up. I hop Homland Sacuraty's monitiring this so they send your ass 2 Gwantanumo.

NICK: Did you actually read the 9/11 report, dickhead?

    Probably not, cause seeing how badly you spell you must be an illiterate fuck.

DONTTREADONME76: u r

NICK: Well if you read it — and I have from cover to cover

    You'd know there's holes in it you could fly 20 767s through.

DONTTREADONME76: You muthaf —

NICK: I'm telling you: The U.S. government orchestrated the whole thing.

DONTTREADONME76: Bullshit.

NICK: It's all over the web, dude,

    You just gotta know where to look to get the facts.

DONTTREADONME76: u r

NICK: And fuck it

    Those guys who hijacked the planes were totally right

DONTTREADONME76: u r a fucking dick!

    <u>Donttreadonme76</u> has left the chat room.

NICK: It didn't take long to clear the room

    Adam stuck out all the bullshit

    cause he recognized my screen name

ADAM: <u>NickWillRockYou</u>

    Hey.

NICK: Hey.

ADAM: All that stuff u were saying?

    Do u mean it?

NICK: No. Of course not.

ADAM: Then why'd u say it.

NICK: I like seeing how far you can push people's reactions.

ADAM: That's weird.

NICK: There was silence.

Then Adam made the first move.

It was kind of funny

And at the same time kind of

Sad

Watching *him* try to play *me*.

ADAM: Yeah. I'm just hanging. Waiting for this girl —

NICK: After a while of him getting nowhere

I decided to throw him a bone

ADAM: Wow. That's wild, see,

'Cause this girl I'm waiting for?

She lives in that neighborhood too.

NICK: What's this girl's name?

ADAM: Rachel.

NICK: Rachel.

Not

Rachel

Sutcliffe

By any chance?

ADAM: No way . . .

Dude,

u know her?!?!?!

NICK: Know her?

Dude,

She's my sister.

ADAM: No. Fucking. Way.

NICK: Once that was out in the open

The questions just poured in

ADAM: Is she as cool in person as she is online?

NICK: She's awesome.

ADAM: And is she as hot as she is in her picture?

NICK: Dude, you're asking me,

Her brother,

If I think my sister's hot.

That's gross man.

ADAM: You know what I mean.

NICK: Let me put it this way:
  If she wasn't my sister
  I'd like
  Totally wanna do her.
ADAM: That's sick dude.
NICK: Then came the plea for help . . . .
ADAM: She says she can't meet me
  'Cause
  Well
  She says
RACHEL: It's complicated.
NICK: Well,
  Dude,
  I'm sorry to say:
  It is.
ADAM: Why?
NICK AND RACHEL: I can't explain that to you right now.
ADAM: That's what she always says.
NICK: But hey — even with all the
  Complications . . . ?
  I might be able to help you.
ADAM: Really?
NICK: Sure dude.
  As they say
  Your wish is my command.
OLIVIA: Now when you do it
  I need you to promise me that you'll tell him
  That you love him.

5

NICK: The question the choice the question the choice the question the choice
MOLLY: What are these?
NICK: What are these?
MOLLY: Nick, can you hear me? What are these?
NICK: Do I tell the truth?
MOLLY: Nick
NICK: Or do I make shit up.
MOLLY: Nii-iick

NICK: The low-grade migraine, sweat glands juicing up, a hardening between
    my legs
MOLLY: Earth to Nick. Do you copy?
NICK: Me speeding up
MOLLY: What are these
NICK: The air taking on the consistency of peanut butter
MOLLY: NICK!
NICK: The question the choice the question the choice
    Adam became as addicted to me
    As he was to Rachel.
    I became his corrupt psychiatrist —
    Instead of curing him of his fixation
    I deepened it,
    Until I could make my next move.
ADAM: Friday night?
    And Rachel will be there.
NICK: I promise you.
    Thing is though
    It has to be a surprise.
    She finds out I invited you
    She'll go ballistic.
ADAM: Why?
NICK: Rachel has her reasons,
    Which my friend,
    Are sometimes a complete mystery to me.
ADAM: I'll think about it.
NICK: I didn't think about what I'd do
    if I did manage to lure Adam to my house for the "sleep over"
    I just figured I'd play it by ear. See:
    That's the thing that separates pros from the amateurs in this kind of
    game.
    Amateurs don't leave any room for uncertainty or
    improvisation.
    They try to lock in their strategy before they even start to play the game,
    Not taking into account the infinite contingencies that might come into
    play,
    Wishfully thinking that the course of the future is something within
    their control.
    But the pro,

On the other hand,
Knows that locking in too early
Is a recipe for disaster — See:
When you lock in, you cut off the possibility of re-strategizing mid-game,
Staying in the moment,
taking the unexpected wild left turn to keep your mark off balance —
And yeah, this method of playing is riskier —
Chances of making a fatal mistake are exponentially greater —
But then, that's why I'm a pro and everyone else are amateurs.
When he showed up that Friday night —
After he met my Mom (And that was really fucking awkward)
We went downstairs to my bat cave

ADAM: So where's Rachel, Nick?

NICK: I made my face go all serious, grave. I said:
    "My
    stepfather
    has her."

ADAM: What do you mean he
    "has her."

NICK: Long story.

ADAM: Is she gonna come back?

NICK: Hard to say.
    When my
    Stepfather
    Has her,
    There's no telling when she'll be back.

ADAM: Look. Maybe I should go . . .

NICK: No.
    I mean . . .
    If you want to
    Go ahead
    But like
    My mom'll ask all sorts of questions and . . .
    And who knows?
    You stick around, maybe Rachel will get back.
    And there was this
    weird silence
    And I didn't know what to do —

I got him here,
To my house,
To my room,
Which is what I wanted —
I guess —
But I just stood there like a fucking retard
If I had a gun in that moment?
I would've stuck it in my mouth and pulled the trigger
But Adam saved me.

ADAM: Your mom's pretty cool.

NICK: No she's not.

ADAM: I think she's cool.

NICK: That's cause she was hitting on you.

ADAM: She was not.

NICK: You don't know my mom.
You coming here is like
The first time she's been that close to a man in

ADAM: What about your stepdad?

NICK: My *stepdad's* got plenty of other places to dunk his you know what.

ADAM: And she was hitting on me?

NICK: Dude, what are you blind or something?

ADAM: Your mom is kinda hot.

NICK: Dude. That's my mom you're talking about.

ADAM: Sorry. I was just
Kidding.
Hey, where's Rachel's room?

NICK: Upstairs. Second floor.

ADAM: Can we like
You know

NICK: You wanna check out my sister's room?

ADAM: Well,
Yeah,
I mean

NICK: What are you a stalker?

ADAM: No,
I just thought

NICK: What do you think she'd do if she found out?

ADAM: Forget it, man

NICK: "Hey Sis, guess what, you know that guy you've been mooning about? The one you met on the Internet?"

ADAM: Forget it, Nick.

NICK: "Yeah, well he came over and you know what he wanted to do?"

ADAM: Nick.

NICK: "He wanted me to sneak him into your room."

ADAM: Shut up.

NICK: "So he could sniff around your panty drawer."

   Hey.

   Don't push.

ADAM: Just shut the fuck up, all right?

NICK: I was just kidding

ADAM: Look. This totally sucks. I'm gonna go.

NICK: NO

   I mean

   You can go if you want to

   But.

   I wanna show you something.

ADAM: What?

NICK: I took him over to a file cabinet in the basement storage area.

ADAM: This better be good.

NICK: I opened the bottom drawer

   reached towards the back

   pulled out a thin folder.

   I sat next to Adam on the floor,

   And looked him sharp in the eye.

   What's my name?

ADAM: Uhhh . . . Nick?

NICK: What's my *full* name?

ADAM: This is stupid.

NICK: Come on, what's my full name?

ADAM: Your full name is Nick Sutcliffe.

NICK: Right. Nick Sutcliffe.

   What does it say at the top here?

ADAM: "Birth Certificate."

NICK: And what does it say here?

ADAM: "Nick . . . "

   Wait a minute.

NICK: Creepy, isn't it.

ADAM: That's not your last name.

NICK: That *is* my name.

   Only no one —
   Except my mom and me —
   And now you —
   Knows it.

ADAM: How do you know it isn't somebody else's?

NICK: How old am I Adam?

ADAM: Fourteen?

NICK: And what does it say here.

ADAM: Date of birth // November 9, 1989

NICK: November 9, 1989.

   My birthday, Adam.

ADAM: Dude that's fucked up.

   Wait.

   Isn't that today?

NICK: Yep.

ADAM: Oh.

NICK: I'm fifteen today.

ADAM: Oh

NICK: I was fourteen yesterday.

   But I'm fifteen today.

ADAM: Oh

   Well

   Happy uhh

   birthday

   dude

NICK: Thanks.

ADAM: Wait:

   Did you ever ask your mom about this?

NICK: No fucking way.

ADAM: But don't you wanna know?

NICK: Sure I wanna know.

   I don't go a single night,
   Where I don't toss and turn in my bed
   Wondering
   Who's my real dad?
   See:

Until I found this

My mother?

That psycho upstairs?

Led me to believe that her "first" husband was my dad.

And when he shot himself

ADAM: He shot himself?

NICK: When I was eleven.

He disappeared one night.

Cops found him the next morning

In his car

In the parking lot of a Jewel Osco

Sucking on the wrong end of a rifle barrel.

ADAM: Holy shit.

Wait:

What's a Jewel Osco.

NICK: Supermarket chain.

Back in Chicago.

They don't have them here.

ADAM: Nick — that's

Whoa.

NICK: It wasn't until we were packing up the house there

That I found this.

Realized

My whole fucking life was a lie.

The dead guy in the parking lot —

The guy who I thought was my father —

He wasn't my father.

He was just

Some dead guy.

ADAM: Dude . . .

If that happened to me,

Man I'd go straight to my mom

Shove this right in her face and be like

"What the fuck?!?!"

NICK: Oh I've been tempted.

But

I'm holding onto this little secret

In case I ever need to go nuclear on her

ADAM: Whoa.

NICK: A beautiful silence hung in the room.

A silence filled with awe. With mystery.

Adam looked

Beautiful

ADAM: What about Rachel? Who's her dad?

NICK: There she was again.

RACHEL.

Who is *Rachel's* dad?

That asshole

Was so obsessed by that little bitch

He couldn't recognize me in that moment.

Rachel

Was more REAL to him

Than ME.

Me: they very person who

INVENTED

Rachel

For Christ's sake.

I wish I could describe the rage inside of me in that moment

I wanted to tear his heart out, shove it down his throat.

I wanted to laugh in his face and say

"You fucking FOOL.

You FUCKING TWIT.

THERE IS NO RACHEL,

YOU PIECE OF SHIT.

I

AM RACHEL

YOU'RE SITTING RIGHT NEXT TO "HER."

DO YOU WANT TO FALL IN LOVE WITH ME NOW?

ARE YOU DYING TO MEET ME NOW?

ARE YOU DYING TO STICK YOUR COCK IN ME NOW?

YOU JERK OFF FOR HER EVERY NIGHT,

WILL YOU JERK OFF FOR ME NOW?

HUH?

HUH?

I could so destroy you . . . .

But I take pride in my self-control.

ADAM: What about Rachel? Who's her dad?

NICK: Who's Rachel's dad?

Well,

Knowing my mom?

Your guess is as good as mine.

Hey: Here's an idea. Next time you talk to Rachel, why don't you ask her?

RACHEL: Why are you asking me about my stepdad?

ADAM: Just curious

RACHEL: I don't want to talk about him.

ADAM: Y Not?

RACHEL: Certain subjects are off limits. OK?

ADAM: OK. Well what do u want 2 talk about.

RACHEL: I don't want to talk anymore.

I want to watch.

ADAM: Let me turn the webcam on.

NICK: After resisting the temptation to tear Adam's throat out,

I poured drinks.

ADAM: What's this?

NICK: Absolut Mandarin.

Here.

ADAM: What if your mom finds out?

NICK: My mom buys like three cases of this stuff a week.

There's never any orange juice in the house

So she gets her Vitamin C intake with this.

She's always too fucked up to notice if one goes missing.

To Mom! Cheers!

ADAM: Holy shit.

NICK: What?

ADAM: You downed that.

NICK: The longer you nurse it,

The longer it takes to get where you want to go.

Your turn.

ADAM: I don't know

NICK: Come on! A-dam! A-dam! A-dam! // Yeah!

ADAM: Fuck!

NICK: Gross isn't it. I don't know how my mom drinks this stuff like water.

Here. Have another one.

ADAM: No, dude, I'm cool with one.

NICK: Don't be such a pussy

ADAM: Fine.

NICK: Drink it.

ADAM: OK.

Fuck!

So what do you wanna do?

NICK: You.

ADAM: Whatever. Seriously — what do you wanna do?

NICK: You. Come on. Let me do you. I'll do you like you wanna do Rachel.

ADAM: Shut up, man

That's gross.

NICK: You're right. It's totally gross. Disgusting. Filthy. Makes me wanna throw up. Here.

ADAM: I don't want anymore.

NICK: Fine. Means I'll have even more for myself.

ADAM: Alright. Pour me another one.

NICK: So what *is* new on the Rachel-the-cock-tease front?

Where are you going?

ADAM: I'm getting out of here, dude,

You're being a total dick.

NICK: Don't go . . .

Please. Please don't go.

ADAM: Don't call her a cock tease.

NICK: Look:

I'm sorry.

ADAM: You said you were gonna help me.

NICK: I know.

I'm sorry.

Another shot?

ADAM: Fine.

You think she really likes me?

NICK: Does Michael Jackson like doing it to little boys?

ADAM: Come on, I'm serious.

NICK: Yeah. She likes you.

The other day? She left her chemistry notebook on the kitchen table?

Front cover and back was covered.

With your name.

She drew little hearts.

"Rachel n Adam 4Ever"

You really like her?

ADAM: Dude, I've never . . .

Felt

This way.

NICK: You're totally whipped.

ADAM: I mean

She's so

Cool

Like

Her picture?

She's

But not like in that way that

You'd be like

"Dude, she's way out of my league."

You know what I mean?

NICK: She likes you.

ADAM: I feel

Totally weird

You know?

Like

I'm

Forget it.

NICK: Like what?

ADAM: It's gonna sound queer but . . .

I think I love her

Which is weird 'cause

NICK: 'Cause you haven't met her.

ADAM: Yeah.

NICK: You think you'll like her as much when you meet her?

ADAM: I think so.

I hope so.

You think she'll like me?

NICK: Dude,

She will not be disappointed.

ADAM: I've imagined it.

Meeting her

NICK: What do you imagine?

ADAM: It's stupid.

NICK: No.

ADAM: We're like

On the beach? Chilling?

And it's like six o'clock so the light's all

Orange?

And we're just walking

NICK: What's she wearing?

ADAM: She's wearing like a skirt. Tank top. Sandals so

You can see her toes

And her toenail polish

Is like

Chipped.

And we're just walking side by side

And she's laughing

And there's like

Water

And waves

And little kids playing on the beach

And we're like

In our own world

NICK: I'm gonna have another.

So you're walking on the beach

ADAM: Yeah,

Just talking

And the sun's coming down

So we like

We sit

Looking at the ocean

This shit's getting to my head, I need to lie down.

NICK: Me too.

Ocean.. sky . . . seagulls . . . ?

ADAM: Yeah, yeah.

And we're just sitting there

Quiet you know?

Like we're all wrapped up in some

Feeling

And then,

Without either of us knowing who made the first move

We're

Holding hands.

NICK: Like this?

ADAM: Yeah.

NICK: What does it feel like?

ADAM: It's like a surge of
      Good.
NICK: I'd like to feel that.
ADAM: Then she touches my face.
      And I touch hers.
      And her hair.
      And we're looking in each other's eyes
      Those green eyes . . .
NICK: Yeah?
ADAM: And like when we started holding hands
      Neither of us making the first move
      We kiss.
NICK: Like this?
ADAM: I'm totally wasted.
NICK: Me too.
      Don't stop.
      (They're all over each other.)
OLIVIA: Now when you do it,
      I need you to promise me that you'll tell him
      That you love him.

6

NICK: The question the choice the question the choice the question the choice
MOLLY: What are these?
NICK: What are these?
MOLLY: Nick, can you hear me? What are these?
NICK: Do I tell the truth?
MOLLY: Nick
NICK: Or do I make shit up.
MOLLY: Nii-iick
NICK: The low-grade migraine, sweat glands juicing up, a hardening between
      my legs
MOLLY: Earth to Nick. Do you copy?
NICK: Me speeding up
MOLLY: What are these
NICK: The air taking on the consistency of peanut butter
MOLLY: NICK!

NICK: The question the choice the question the choice
    I mentioned before
    That what separates the pros from the amateurs
    Is the capacity to improvise mid game.
    Now, I'd be totally lying to you
    If I told you that I planned what happened that night.
    I guess I wanted it to happen,
    But wanting something,
    And that thing actually happening . . . .
    That night ended up a little one-sided —
    Turned out I did most of the giving.
    I remember feeling on the one hand like
    Well
    How
    God
    must feel.
    At the same time
    Having Adam in my mouth
    Hearing him say,
ADAM: Rachel. Oh. Fuck. Rachel.
NICK: You can imagine how that felt.
    Wished it was the barrel of a gun instead of Adam that was in my mouth.
    When we were done,
    Adam puked.
    We passed out.
    When I woke up,
    he was already gone.
MOM: Nicky? Hon?
NICK: What.
MOM: Could you come in my room a sec?
NICK: What.
MOM: You slept late.
NICK: I got stuff to do, Mom.
MOM: You look —
NICK: Who's the lucky guy tonight?
MOM: Nick . . . .
NICK: That's an awful lot of eye shadow you're wearing
MOM: Nick . . .
NICK: You just might convince him you're still 25

MOM: Ha. Ha. Sit down.

NICK: Can this wait?

MOM: It'll only take a minute.

NICK: Fine.

MOM: I liked your friend. Aaron, was it?

NICK: Adam. You liked him but you can't even remember his name.

MOM: I'm sorry Nicky,

I'm just . . .

Where did you two meet?

NICK: Around.

MOM: Just "around"?

NICK: What about "around" don't you understand?

MOM: Well . . .

Could you be more specific?

NICK: What's with the interrogation?

MOM: I'm not interr//ogating I'm

NICK: I mean what's next,

Are you gonna put a hood over my head? Attach electrodes to my nip-
ples? Take some souvenir photographs?

MOM: Nicky.

NICK: I mean what do you want me to say? Huh? I met him around. Why is
that so difficult to believe? You meet all sorts of people. In all sorts of
places. How am I supposed to remember shit // like that.

MOM: Language, Nicky.

NICK: *Stuff*

Like that?

MOM: Well, it's not exactly as if you have parades of friends walking through
that door.

NICK: Whatever.

MOM: Adam is the first friend you've brought to the house since we moved
here

I don't think it's unreasonable to ask a simple question // about where

NICK: Yeah, and I answered your question. Around.

OK?

Now can I go?

MOM: What's happening to you?

NICK: Jesus

MOM: You didn't used to be this way. You used to talk to me.

Go ahead, Nick. Leave.

But before you leave let me make something clear:
Until you're willing to tell me where you met that boy

NICK: Oh, he's "that boy" now, // I see how it is

MOM: *Until* you're willing to tell me where you met that boy,
You are not allowed to bring him into this house // again.

NICK: But I thought you liked // him, Mom

MOM: You are not allowed to see him under *any* circumstances.
Have I made myself clear.

NICK: Clear

as

mud,

Mom.

MOM: Who are you?

NICK: And you don't have to worry about him coming over anymore.
Not after the way you acted.

MOM: Excuse me?

NICK: I know you're a lonely old hag
But did you have to hit on him?

MOM: WHAT.

DID.

YOU.

SAY?

NICK: I know you like them young,
But that was a little ridiculous.

MOM: Oh God. Oh my God.
Oh sweetie sweetie sweetie sweetie I didn't mean that

NICK: You hit me

MOM: Baby, I'm sorry I'm sorry

NICK: Why did you hit me?

MOM: Sweetie
Don't cry . . .
Please
Don't cry . . . .
You're OK. We're OK. Shhhh. It's OK.
You used to be like a little cat.
I'd go from one room to the next
And I wouldn't notice
That you had followed me.
You were so quiet.

Content to be just close by.
I used to call you Kitty.
But when you got bigger
You hated me calling you that.
Then you were Nicky.
Don't stop being Nicky . . .
Please honey,
You'll always be my Nicky.

7

NICK: The question the choice the question the choice the question the choice
MOLLY: What are these?
NICK: What are these?
MOLLY: Nick, can you hear me? What are these?
NICK: Do I tell the truth?
MOLLY: Nick
NICK: Or do I make shit up.
MOLLY: Nii-iick
NICK: The low-grade migraine, sweat glands juicing up, a hardening between
    my legs
MOLLY: Earth to Nick. Do you copy?
NICK: Me speeding up
MOLLY: What are these
NICK: The air taking on the consistency of peanut butter
MOLLY: NICK!
NICK: The question the choice the question the choice
    Adam cut me off. I'd come into the chat room, be like
    "Hey, what's up?"
ADAM: JustWant2ChillWithU has left the chat room.
NICK: I'd Instant Message him.
ADAM: JustWant2ChillWithU is now off-line.
NICK: I sent him e-mails.
ADAM: Message to
    JustWant2ChillWithU@aol.com has been returned to sender.
NICK: The silence felt like fifty kicks to the stomach.
    I would have walked onto the 101 in the direction of oncoming traffic —
    And I'm not kidding when I say I seriously considered this option —

Were it not for Rachel.

She was still alive for Adam —

Though barely.

He started getting harsh with her.

Mean.

He told her one day:

ADAM: I think u r a fucking cock tease.

NICK: Wasn't the same Adam

That wrote in his profile way back when

ADAM: I want to fall in love with a girl

NICK: "Love" was no longer part of his vocabulary

RACHEL: But I love you.

How can you say such a thing?

ADAM: *"LOVE"*

NICK: Adam had gone from saying the word and meaning it

To making it sound like the punch line of a mean joke.

ADAM: *"LOOOOVVVEEE"*

RACHEL: How can you be so cruel?

ADAM: Me? Cruel?

What about u?

"I *can't* meet you."

"It's *complicated.*"

I'm a fucking idiot.

I never want 2 talk 2 u again.

RACHEL: Please. Don't say that, Adam. I love you.

ADAM: Prove it.

RACHEL: I will.

ADAM: How.

RACHEL: Turn on your webcam?

ADAM: Fuck no.

RACHEL: I'll show you how much I love you.

ADAM: Turn on your webcam.

RACHEL: You know my stepfather won't let me have one.

ADAM: I believe that. Whatever.

RACHEL: Please, don't go.

I'll do anything.

ADAM: Anything.

RACHEL: Yes.

Anything.

ADAM: I want to meet u.

    r u there?

RACHEL: OK.

    Fine.

    I'll meet you.

ADAM: U will?

RACHEL: Yes.

    Friday.

    4:30.

    By the carousel on the pier.

ADAM: Friday.

    R u sure?

RACHEL: I've never been more sure of anything in my life.

ADAM: OK.

RACHEL: Will you do something for me?

    I want to watch.

ADAM: I'll

    I'll turn my webcam on.

NICK: Of course this was a date Rachel couldn't keep.

    Could you imagine? Me standing on the pier

    by the carousel,

    squeezed into a miniskirt and tank top

    "Hi Adam, It's me, Rachel."

    I've gotten the shit kicked out of me before

    It's no fun.

    I don't like pain —

    Though I will admit —

    And it's totally fucked, I know —

    But there was a certain amount of pleasure

    In imagining Adam inflict it.

    Better that than total silence from him,

    Right?

    I guess that's what you call being love sick.

    It was in this state of utter uselessness

    That it became clear:

    If I needed to keep Adam

    I had to do the unthinkable.

FEMALE NETIZEN: Capiche911 has entered the chat room.

TONY: <u>JustWant2ChillWithU</u>

You're Adam, right.

ADAM: Yeah.

TONY: Nice to meet you, Adam.

ADAM: Who r u?

TONY: Adam Moody, right?

ADAM: Who the fuck r u?

TONY: I'd watch your language if I were you, Adam.

We don't like it when people use the F word to me

ADAM: Oh yeah?

TONY: There was one kid —

God bless him —

Who said that word to me one too many times,

You know what happened to him?

ADAM: What?

TONY: Cops found him one night

Hanging from a tree.

You wanna know how he was hanging from that tree?

ADAM: Um . . . A rope?

TONY: Railroad spikes.

That's right. Some sick fuck crucified him with railroad spikes.

To a tree.

Sick, don't you think.

ADAM: Yeah.

TONY: Even sicker

He was missing parts.

ADAM: Like what parts.

TONY: Use your imagination.

Can you use your imagination,

Or do I need to help you out?

Adam. Moody. of 1211 Camino Del Sur.

ADAM: Who r u?

TONY: That's a good question, Adam.

But I think a better question is

WHO

The

FUCK

R

U

!

We got a little problem here, Adam.

It seems you've been wanting to stick your toothpick dick

In places

Where your toothpick dick don't belong.

ADAM: I don't know what u r talking about.

TONY: "I don't know what you're talking about."

That's funny, Adam Moody of 1211 Camino del Sur.

I'll put it to you even simpler:

Stay.

The Fuck.

Away.

From Rachel.

ADAM: You know Rachel?

TONY: Yeah.

I know Rachel.

And I know what you're trying to do to her.

ADAM: I'm not doing anything.

TONY: You filthy little piece of shit,

"I'm not doing anything" —

I'll come over there right now,

take that webcam of yours and shove it right up your ass, you little prick,

Don't think I don't know what you're up to

Don't think I don't know what you do in front of that camera every night

I've seen it and it's disgusting. You're fucking sick,

You know that? Doing that in front of a fifteen-year-old girl?

What's the matter with you?

ADAM: It wasn't my idea

TONY: You spineless piece of shit.

You know what I have a mind to do?

I have a mind to send someone over there right now

To slowly cut your balls off in front of that webcam of yours

I would love to watch that. I'll sit here drinkin my fuckin bottle of Yoohoo

watch you scream like a little bitch, "pleeeeeeaaaaaase don't cut my baaaaaaalls off."

Scared now?

Consider this little conversation a warning:

Stay.

The Fuck.

Away.

From my stepdaughter.

ADAM: She's

Your stepdaughter . . . ?

TONY: Really scared now, aren't you.

I'll say it again. And slowly this time, so you get the message, nice and clear:

Stay.

The Fuck.

Away.

From.

My.

Stepdaughter.

Cause man to man,

Adam Moody of 1211 Camino del Sur.

Only one of us can have her.

And that one of us

Is not you.

You dig?

FEMALE NETIZEN: Capiche911 has left the chat room.

RACHEL: He did what?

ADAM: He said he was gonna crucify me to a tree

Using railroad spikes

RACHEL: He's such a bastard

ADAM: He said something . . .

RACHEL: What did he say?

ADAM: He said

TONY: Only one of us can have her.

And that one of us

Is Not You.

RACHEL: I'm so ashamed.

This is awful.

ADAM: What did he mean?

RACHEL: I'll tell you everything when I see you Friday

ADAM: I don't know if Friday's such a good idea

RACHEL: Fuck him.

I'm meeting you.

I'm tired of being his slave.

He can go fuck himself.

ADAM: Rachel, be careful

RACHEL: I'm tired of being careful.

 I'll see you Friday.

 Where we said we'd meet.

OLIVIA: Now when you do it,

 I need you to promise me that you'll tell him

 That you love him.

8

NICK: The question the choice the question the choice the question the choice

MOLLY: What are these?

NICK: What are these?

MOLLY: Nick, can you hear me? What are these?

NICK: Do I tell the truth?

MOLLY: Nick

NICK: Or do I make shit up.

MOLLY: Nii-iick

NICK: The low-grade migraine, sweat glands juicing up, a hardening between my legs

MOLLY: Earth to Nick. Do you copy?

NICK: Me speeding up

MOLLY: What are these

NICK: The air taking on the consistency of peanut butter

MOLLY: NICK!

NICK: The question the choice the question the choice

NICK: I waited on the pier,

 Out of sight from the carousel,

 So Adam wouldn't see me.

 When he showed

 He was so . . .

 He'd dressed for the occasion.

 He had a bouquet of roses in his hand.

 I watched him for a bit

 Everything moved so fast

 Except for him

 Except for me.

 We moved like we lived in a world made of peanut butter.

ADAM: WHAT
    The FUCK
    Are YOU
    Doing here?
NICK: Adam,
    Please,
    Hear me out.
ADAM: You sick little faggot,
    I should kick your ass
NICK: Please, Adam.
    I swear
    I never would've come here
    If it wasn't
    Important.
ADAM: Two seconds.
NICK: Rachel's missing.
ADAM: Bullshit.
NICK: I swear to you on my life.
    Our stepdad
    He took her
ADAM: What do you mean he took her?
NICK: He found out that she had a date to meet you
    He went ballistic.
    Beat the shit out of my mom,
    Smashed up Rachel's room,
    her computer
    She ran into my room
    Scared,
    Crying,
    Adam,
    She was crying,
    She told me she was meeting you
    She begged me to come and tell you what happened
    Then my stepdad came into the room,
    Pulled her by the hair and dragged her out of the house
ADAM: I don't believe you.
    What the fuck are you doing?
NICK: Look.
    Does this look like I'm lying?

ADAM: Holy shit — what the fuck is that?

NICK: He put his cigar out on my shoulder.

ADAM: I'm
      I'm sorry.

NICK: Yeah, well fuck you!

ADAM: Don't cry man,
      I'm sorry —

NICK: I don't know where he took her
      I'm so fucking scared, Adam

ADAM: Come on,
      I'll take you back to your house.

NICK: NO!
      I can't go there.
      I'll sleep on the beach
      Anything.
      But not there.

ADAM: Come on.
      I'll take you over to my house.

NICK: As we left the pier
      Adam took the flowers he'd gotten for Rachel
      And dumped them in a trash can.
      Adam didn't have any Absolut Mandarin in his house.
      We didn't need it.
      I cried the whole time
      I was so raw.
      This time though
      When I had him in my mouth
      He didn't say

ADAM: Rachel, Fuck, Rachel

NICK: He said my name.
      I fell asleep on his bed.
      I don't know what time it was
      But the words

MALE NETIZEN: You've got mail.

NICK: Coming from his computer
      Woke me
      Eyes half opened I watched his back
      And the light from the computer monitor
      outlining the muscles of his arms.

His shoulders started to shake . . . .

His breathing . . .

Like he was hyperventilating.

TONY: You little fuck.

>I told you to stay away from her,

>Adam Moody of 1211 Camino del Sur.

>But since you didn't listen.

>Take a good long hard look at this picture.

>*You* did this.

NICK: The photo . . .

>Whoa.

>Body of a girl,

>About 5'6''

>at the side of the freeway.

>Thighs all bruised.

>Clothes torn.

>A few feet away from her body,

>Her head.

>She could've had dirty blonde hair,

>But you couldn't tell 'cause it was all matted in blood.

>She didn't have much of a face left.

>I got the picture off this Web site where you can download crime scene photos.

>Sick shit.

>Adam ran to the bathroom.

>Locked the door.

>I could hear him puking his guts out.

>I knocked.

ADAM: Go away.

NICK: Adam

>It's me

>Nick

ADAM: Go away.

>Please.

>Go away.

NICK: So I left.

OLIVIA: Now when you do it

>I need you to promise me that you'll tell him

>That you love him.

9

NICK: After leaving his house
   I stayed out all night.
   I'd reached my own gullibility threshold,
   And it broke my heart to realize
   That I was a 10.
   I believed everything,
   I wondered
   What Ms. Spiegel,
   My Theater Arts teacher,
   Would've thought about my Dark Play?
MS. SPIEGEL: The best theater takes the audience on a journey into the darkest,
   Most *dangerous,*
   Regions of the human soul.
NICK: Was my Dark Play dark enough?
   Dangerous enough?
MS. SPIEGEL: At the end of the journey
   The audience,
   Having faced that
   Darkness,
   That
   Danger,
   Can recognize the darkness and danger lurking in their own souls,
NICK: I sure as hell recognized the darkness and danger lurking in my soul
MS. SPIEGEL: And actively take steps to
   Change
   It.
NICK: I couldn't do shit to change it.
   There was only one thing left for me to do:
TONY: heinousbusterSVU has entered the chat room.
OLIVIA: Adam? Adam Moody?
ADAM: Who r u?
OLIVIA: My name is Olivia Stabler.
   I work with the Special Victims Unit of the New York City Police De-
   partment.
ADAM: Riiight.
OLIVIA: In the criminal justice system, sexually based offences are considered
   especially heinous. In New York City, the dedicated detectives who inves-

tigate these vicious felonies are members of an elite squad known as the Special Victims Unit.

ADAM: What

ever.

OLIVIA: I'm a member of this elite squad. I've been asked to come here to southern California to help investigate a string of especially heinous brutal sex murders that have taken place in the area too complex and heinous for local law enforcement. Given our expertise in solving heinous cases I'm here to nail the heinous bastards that have been committing these heinous crimes.

ADAM: What do u want with me?

OLIVIA: Adam, Sweetie. I need to ask you a favor.

I don't really care how you write when you're chatting with people your own age.

But when you chat with me,

chat like an adult.

ADAM: What are u trying 2 say?

OLIVIA: I detest teen talk.

U and *R* are letters. If you mean "you are" — spell it out

Y-O-U-A-R-E. Same with "2." That's a number, not a preposition.

ADAM: Oh.

OLIVIA: How old are you Adam?

ADAM: Sixteen. Going on seventeen.

OLIVIA: You're almost a man.

ADAM: I guess.

OLIVIA: You guess.

Adam. Either you are almost a man or you aren't. Which is it?

ADAM: I'm almost a man.

OLIVIA: Good. So write like one.

You knew Rachel Sutcliffe.

Adam?

I'm asking you a simple yes/no question: did you know Rachel Sutcliffe.

ADAM: No.

OLIVIA: I see. What about her brother? Nick? Nick Sutcliffe?

ADAM: I don't know anyone named Nick.

OLIVIA: OK.

I understand your need to deny that you know him.

To deny that you knew her.

To deny all the things you've done that . . .

Well,

things

that if I were in your shoes

I might deny too.

ADAM: Fuck off.

OLIVIA: Language, Adam.

How do you think that poor, decapitated girl would feel

If she knew you denied knowing her?

How will you live with yourself knowing you did that?

I ask you again:

Did you know Rachel Sutcliffe.

ADAM: Yes.

OLIVIA: How well did you know Rachel?

ADAM: I

Don't want you to think I'm like . . .

A freak or anything for saying it but —

OLIVIA: Adam:

What did I say to you before about teen language?

ADAM: That you don't like it.

OLIVIA: That's right. And what was wrong with that sentence.

ADAM: Which sentence?

OLIVIA: Scroll up. The one that reads: "Don't think I'm *like* . . . a freak for saying this"

Adam. You can't be "like" anything. You either are or you aren't a freak.

ADAM: Right.

OLIVIA: So what is it you want to tell me about Rachel

That makes you afraid I'll look at you as a freak?

ADAM: I

I loved her.

OLIVIA: That's what I thought.

And that's why I've sought you out.

We need your help.

NICK: At that point

To explain why she needed Adam's help,

Olivia rolled in a Titanic-sized wheelbarrow of caca

I can't remember exactly what I had Olivia tell Adam

Some bullshit

About our stepfather and some

criminal conspiracy

surrounding Rachel's murder.

That involved

illegal drug trafficking

"Coyotes" smuggling illegal aliens across the U.S.-Mexico border

child pornography

snuff movies

Internet identity theft . . . .

OLIVIA: Al Queda // sleeper cells

NICK: Right: al Queda sleeper cells

    The details aren't what's important,

    What's important is that

    Olivia tried to convince Adam

    If he "followed the money" —

    She actually *said* that —

OLIVIA: Follow the money

NICK: the trail would lead to Nick.

OLIVIA: Right now as we sit here chit-chatting, they're out there

    Perpetrating their rape of southern California.

    Adam.

    The Syndicate has used Nick

    To procure victims for them on the World Wide Web.

    Teenagers like you. Underage. Sometimes even younger.

    You drink milk, don't you?

ADAM: Um. Yeah?

OLIVIA: You've seen the faces of those kids staring at you from the cartons?

    What do you think happened to them?

    Nick had every intention of turning you

    From a normal, well-adjusted, middle-class young man

    Into one of those faces staring you down while you eat your Cap'n Crunch.

ADAM: I don't believe you.

OLIVIA: You are one lucky teenager. That could have been your head

    Lying in a ditch at the side of the freeway.

ADAM: I'm not gullible.

    I'm not stupid.

OLIVIA: That could have been you, had it not been for Rachel getting in the way.

ADAM: I am NOT gullible.

    I am NOT stupid.

OLIVIA: Of course you aren't, Adam.

    So it should be clear to you:

    Nick sold Rachel out.

    How do you think her stepfather knew she was planning to meet you?

    Adam?

    Don't get me wrong:

    Nick was a victim here too —

    But Nick stopped being a victim on the day he had his sister murdered.

    Depravity begets depravity.

    And now Nick is beyond depraved.

    He's become an inhuman monster.

    He must be put down.

    We need you to eliminate him.

ADAM: Wait

    Are you saying . . .

    You want me to kill him?

OLIVIA: "Kill" is such an ugly word, Adam.

    Criminals kill.

    Law enforcement solves crimes.

ADAM: OK . . . .

    Hypothetically . . . .

OLIVIA: That's a good word, Adam. I'm impressed.

ADAM: Hypothetically . . .

    If all this

    Were real

    And hypothetically . . .

    If I went along with what you're asking . . .

    What do I do?

OLIVIA: Make contact with him.

    Have him meet you in a public place.

    The mall.

    When he shows, tell him you have to run an errand for your mother.

    Take him to Williams Sonoma on the second level.

    Buy a knife

    (we'll reimburse you, don't worry).

ADAM: What kind of knife.

OLIVIA: A big knife.

ADAM: Like a butcher knife.

OLIVIA: Exactly.

Take him to where they keep the dumpsters behind the Sears.
Get him up against the wall.
Start stabbing him.
Hypothetically.

ADAM: God.

OLIVIA: I know it's a heavy burden.
But think of the burden Nick will be to all of us if he's allowed to live.
Think of the favor you'll be doing Southern California.

ADAM: What about me? What do I get out of it?

OLIVIA: The rewards for you, Adam, will be great.

ADAM: What kind of rewards?

OLIVIA: Use your // imagination

TONY: Use your // imagination

RACHEL: Use your // imagination

NICK: Use your imagination.

OLIVIA: And with all that he's put you through, Adam
Isn't there a part of you
That *wants* to kill him?
Will you do it?

ADAM: Yes.

OLIVIA: Good.
One more thing:
Now when you do it
I need you to promise me that you'll tell him
That you love him.

ADAM: What?

OLIVIA AND NICK: You do love him, don't you.

NICK: Don't you?

10

NICK: Adam looked
Different
When we met in the food court of the mall.
He looked
Older.
Like a
Well

Like a man.

It was hard to look him in the eye.

ADAM: Hey.

NICK: Hey.

ADAM: Everything OK?

NICK: Yeah.

You?

ADAM: I'm fine.

Listen. I have to run an errand for my mother.

I need to find the Williams Sonoma.

NICK: We walked in silence.

He did everything Olivia instructed him to do

With calm

With grace

With

Dignity.

ADAM: Let's get out of here. Go find some place more quiet to

To talk.

NICK: We left the mall.

Walked back to the area behind Sears where they keep the dumpsters.

I was calm.

ADAM: I have something for you.

NICK: I didn't feel the first thrust.

ADAM: I love you

NICK: I didn't feel the second or third

ADAM: I love you

I love you

NICK: The fourth felt like a pinprick to a fingertip.

ADAM: I love you

NICK: Five,

Six,

Seven

Times

ADAM: I love you

I love you

I love you

I

NICK: I remember lying on the pavement

Feeling a smile spread across my face

The silhouette of Adam against the blue southern California sky
hovering above me for a second before he ran . . .
That's when I felt it
A wave
A hurricane
An earthquake
Mt. St. Helen's blowing her top.
A cloudburst and
A shower of wine
A swirl of color
Disappearing outlines
The sky splitting open,
Swallowing me
The earth cracking open
Levitating me
A gazillion tiny lightbulbs
Twinkling through the pores of my skin
The Virgin Mary and Mary Magdalene
Caressing,
Kissing
licking
my flesh
a skyscraper collapsing
a mother giving birth
No ME
I love you
No ME
I love you
Fire
Water
Light
Air
White.
I love you.
If this is what death is like.
I want to die every day.
But I lived.

11

MOLLY: What are these?

    Nick, can you hear me? What are these?

    Nick

    Nii-iick

    Earth to Nick. Do you copy?

    What are these

    NICK!

NICK: Do I tell her the truth?

    Or do I make shit up.

    She was about to get out of bed and leave

    When I said,

    "OK OK OK. I'll tell you. I'll tell you everything."

    And I told her.

    Everything.

    She didn't say anything for awhile.

    She just smoked her cigarette in silence.

    It was starting to get light outside.

    Finally, she put out her cigarette and said:

MOLLY: Nick, you are totally full of shit. Why do you always have to make shit up?

NICK: And she went to sleep.

    I go to college now

    I work nights at the campus library.

    I still live in the dorms,

    But I'm hoping to save enough money this quarter

    And over the summer

    So I can get my own place this fall.

    I guess you can say I have a girlfriend.

    That's her lying naked on the bed.

    Things are pretty much normal now. I guess.

    I mean

    There's still a lot of stuff I need to figure out

    but

    I'm pretty much indistinguishable from any other college kid.

    I'm still undecided about my major.

END OF PLAY

INTELLECTUALS
A COMEDY IN TWO ACTS

Scott C. Sickles

Scott C. Sickles received his Master of Fine Arts degree in dramatic writing from Carnegie Mellon University School of Drama. He is proud to have studied, there and elsewhere, with Arthur Giron, Kathleen George, Anthony McKay, Frank Gagliano, Millee Taggart-Ratcliffe and, most closely, with William C. Kovacsik.

His play *Shepherd's Bush*, depicting the private life of E. M. Forster, earned him a 1996 Pennsylvania Council on the Arts Fellowship. His other biographical drama *Lightning From Heaven*, which chronicles the affair between Boris Pasternak and his muse Olga Ivinskaya, won the 1999 West Coast Theater Guild/ Julie Harris Playwriting Award. He was named Outstanding Playwright of the 1996 Pittsburgh New Works Festival for *The Harmonic Convergence*. Samuel French, Inc. published his tender coming-of-age piece *murmurs* in *Off-Off-Broadway Festival Plays, 21st Series*.

Scott's plays have been produced in New York City, and across the United States, as well as in Canada and Australia. His creative home is the WorkShop Theater Company where he serves as associate artistic director. In addition to *Intellectuals*, productions there include: *From the Top, The Philosopher's Joke, RidiculouSublime!* (co-produced with Mind the Gap Theatre and featuring *Sarcophagus* and *Perfecting the Kiss); The Following Morning; Beautiful Noises* (Critics' Choice, Samuel French Festival; also produced by Mind the Gap Theatre in New York City, by the City Theater Company in Coral Cables, Florida, and around the country); *The Antique Shoppe; The Harmonic Convergence* (also produced by CCAC-South for the Pittsburgh New Works Festival, Release the Hounds Productions — Critics' Choice, Samuel French Festival — and Ensemble Studio Theater); *Manly Men Doing Manly Things* (also produced by Vital Theater Company, NativeAliens Theatre Collective, StageQ in Madison, Wisconsin, and Pittsburgh Playwrights Theater Festival), *M is for the Million Things: Plays About Mothers and Motherhood*, which includes the new short plays *The Mother Lode; Yea, Though I Walk; The Man in 119* and a reprisal of *The Antique Shoppe*.

Scott has dedicated his entire adult life to new play development. He hails from Pittsburgh where his work — producing the long-running reading series Sunday Night Live and as artistic director of Pittsburgh New Voices, a company devoted to new plays by local authors — inspired *Pittsburgh Magazine* to name him one of the city's three most influential theater personalities. Since arriving in New York City, he has served as company manager of Playwrights Horizons and, with Lori Faiella, helmed the Off-Off-Broadway companies Running Start Productions and Antipodes Theatrical before finding an artistic home at the WorkShop Theater Company. He has taught playwriting at Carnegie Mellon Drama, Pittsburgh New Voices, the WorkShop Theater Company, and privately. He has also served as a guest lecturer at Hofstra University.

He wishes to thank D. L. Lepidus for granting him the honor of having his first published full-length play included in this volume.

ORIGINAL PRODUCTION

Intellectuals was originally produced Off-Off-Broadway by the WorkShop Theater Company (Timothy Scott Harris, artistic director; Riley Jones-Cohen, executive director) in September 2006. The lighting design was by Deborah Constantine; the scenic design by Craig M. Napoliello with Amy Vlastelica; costumes by Isabel Fields; and the sound design by Nick DiCeglie, Kevin Reifel, and David Gautschy. The production stage manager was Michael Palmer. David Gautschy directed with the following cast:

MARGOT WELLES	Ellen Dolan
PHILIP EMBERS	Bill Tatum
BRIGHTON GALLOWAY	Bill Blechingberg
FEMALE STUDENT/SOPHIE/CHELSEA/LUISA	Kari Swenson Riely
ANTONIA BURNS	Patricia O'Connell
NICK DALDRY	Jess Cassidy White
HOSTESS/HERA JANE SMITH	Kim Weston-Moran

Prior to the WorkShop Theater Company production, *Intellectuals* has been developed by the Stage Directors and Choreographers Foundation at CAP 21 (directed by Carol Bennett Gerber), as well as by Algonquin Productions, the Carnegie Collaborative at Manhattan Theatre Club, the 42nd Street WorkShop, and the Carnegie Mellon Festival of New Plays (all directed by Michael Montel).

A NOTE FROM THE PLAYWRIGHT

Writing is often considered a solitary art form.

If only . . .

Even when I'm by myself, my mind stays busy creating a cavalcade of colorful characters embroiled in magnificent melodramas bandying about bons mots. They won't leave me alone. Even when I have writer's block, they taunt me, daring me to make them do things. (Pricks!) Where do these imaginary people come from?

They come from fear. Or rather, from FEAR! Fear of who I've been, what I've done, what I might do, what could happen to me, what won't happen to me that I want to happen to me, carbohydrates, loneliness, companionship, failure, success, looking stupid, looking too pompous, being laughed at when I don't want to be and not being laughed at when I do. In short: My Issues.

Once I've spewed My Issues onto the page, I then begin the humiliating process of Sharing the Play. This means involving those most lifelike of imaginary beings: actors. I first shared an incomplete draft of this play in a cold room at Theater Row Studios with Ali Hayden, Bill Kovacsik, Greg Stuhr, Patricia O'Connell, David Miceli, Tamilla Woodard, and Tracie Black. That was January 1997.

Since then, the play has gone through many readings, public and private; a developmental staging many drafts ago; three directors; countless trees (and allegedly one laser printer); and the involvement of just over *one hundred* actors.

Talk about scary.

Whenever I go back to work on the script, the voices of the characters are joined by those of the actors (both in their roles and speaking their own minds), by my directors and dramaturgs (official and unofficial), and by my own voice as well. That's a lot of people to have in one's head. Evidently, there's a good deal of room in there.

So, truth be told, playwriting is about as solitary as being trapped in the evacuation of Shanghai. As a playwright, one is never truly alone. I extend my deepest gratitude to everyone who has kept me company during this process. Without you, my head, my heart, and my spirit would be woefully empty.

I hope you enjoy my play, my collaborators, our voices, and My Issues!

—*Scott C. Sickles*

ACKNOWLEDGMENTS

Very special thanks to Riley Jones-Cohen for being right as usual; to my agent Barbara Hogenson as well as her associates Nicole Verity and Sarah Feider for their faith and dedication; David Mead, Eric Krebs Theatrical Management, and the John Houseman Studio Theater; the University of Pittsburgh's departments of theatre arts and philosophy; to the legion of actors who assisted in this play's development over the years; and especially to Michael Montel, Jane Trichter, and Tim Harris without whom this play would be longer than *Nickelby* with, of course, no intermission.

CHARACTERS

BRIGHTON GALLOWAY: a film professor in his early forties; confident in the classroom, but not in himself; gay and perennially single, or so he thought!

PHILIP EMBERS: a philosophy professor in his early fifties; locked in a struggle between the schools of thought he teaches and how they apply to his suddenly discontented life; married to . . .

MARGO WELLES: a therapist in her early fifties; embraces dogma but doesn't realize she'd rather embrace her husband; has decided to give lesbianism a whirl.

NICK DALDRY: an attractive man in his early-to-mid twenties; attracted to Brighton, yet with secrets from his family and a hidden past!

ANTONIA BURNS: a student of Philip's in her sixties; a mature woman with a thirst for life and a fondness for much younger men . . . a fondness she doesn't want her family to know about!

HERA JANE SMITH: an African-American lesbian attorney (it's a cliché and it's intentional) in her thirties who is not a radical feminist but does believe that every woman has Sapphic potential. (Also plays Hostess.)

LUISA: lovely woman in her early-to-mid twenties; peripatetic waitress with a past connection to Nick! Yes, Nick! (Also plays Female Student, Sophie, and Chelsea.)

for Alison Luce, Greg Stuhr, Patricia O'Connell,
Riley Jones-Cohen and Michael Montel

SCENE
Various locations in a medium-size university town, like Pittsburgh.

TIME
The present. Mid-October. The week before the middle of the fall semester.

ON STAGING THE PLAY
This play is meant to move is a fluid, cinematic style. Sets should be simple, minimal and suggested, not realistic. Whenever possible, transitions between scenes should take no longer than the cross fade. Transitions between "days" can take a bit longer. (I cannot stress enough the value of a run crew.)

The characters tend to think on their feet, so unscripted pauses are not recommended. A period means the end of a sentence, not the end of the world. The production, as well as the performances within it, should be light, funny, and elegant.

INTELLECTUALS

ACT ONE

Setting: Philip and Margot's living room. Monday night. 11:00 PM. The week before Mid-Semester Break.

At Rise: Margot Welles, a woman in her early fifties, dressed professionally, enters with suitcases. She puts them down in an obvious but out-of-the-way location. She looks at her watch, paces for a moment, looks out the window. Nothing. She fills a snifter with brandy and sets it out, just so. She checks herself in a mirror but does not primp.

Sound of a car pulling into the driveway.

Margot primps briefly and poises herself in the middle of the room.

The car shuts off; doors open and shut. Jovial men's voices are heard.

Philip and Brighton enter. Philip Embers is a scholarly man in his early fifties, dressed professorially. Brighton Galloway is in his early forties, dressed in business casual. The two men are laughing.

MARGOT: So, how was it?

(The laughter stops.)

BRIGHTON: Philip?

PHILIP: No, no. You go right ahead. I know it's killing you.

(As the conversation ensues, Philip looks around the living room for something.)

BRIGHTON: Thank you. Oh, my god. It was so bad, Philip actually suggested we call you during intermission so you could bring over rotten vegetables for the second act.

MARGOT: That was Philip's suggestion?

PHILIP: I was inspired. We couldn't call during intermission, though, because . . .

BRIGHTON AND PHILIP: There WAS no intermission!

BRIGHTON: We thought we'd need Amnesty International to get us out of there.

PHILIP: The only thing keeping us going was the comforting promise of coffee and dessert that awaits us here.

BRIGHTON: Hear hear!

(Awkward pause as there is no coffee and dessert in sight and Margot doesn't offer or explain.)

PHILIP: Which I'm sure awaits us in the kitchen. Brighton, you regale Margot with tales of terrible theater and I —

MARGOT: Philip.

PHILIP: No, no. You've been busy, dear. I will get the refreshments myself. Brighton, continue.

(Philip exits. Margot moves the suitcases into the middle of the room as Brighton speaks.)

BRIGHTON: Anyway, I must say, I've never seen a *King Lear* with so many dance numbers.

MARGOT: How many were there?

BRIGHTON: Merely two. In *KING LEAR!* The first extravaganza featured an actress spinning down center wearing Malcolm McDowell's outfit from *A Clockwork Orange*, complete with bowler hat and eyelash, and then . . . she pretended to be a clock!

MARGOT: *(Occasionally looking to see if Philip re-emerges.)* Oh, my!

BRIGHTON: The second one was even better! It was of course the storm. Lear bouncing across the stage, and by bouncing, I mean *bouncing*.

MARGOT: Bouncing?

BRIGHTON: This Lear was downright sprightly. Meanwhile, there's a chorus line of people slowly waving at him, making woosh noises — I'm not kidding — and for some reason, someone keeps running backwards, in a straightjacket, past the opening of the thatched hut. Yes, I said both "straightjacket" and "thatched hut." I nicknamed it "The Who's Marat/Sade."

MARGOT: Well, I'm sorry I missed it.

BRIGHTON: No. You're not.

PHILIP: *(Re-emerges.)* Brighton, the coffee is going to take too long; how about a nightcap, instead?

BRIGHTON: No thanks; I'm driving.

MARGOT: Me too.

PHILIP: Margot?

MARGOT: Yes, Philip?

PHILIP: *(Discovers full brandy snifter.)* Ah. You've already poured one. Is this for me?

MARGOT: Uh, yes. Indeed it is.

PHILIP: *(Trying to cover suspicion:)* Wonderful! You used the large snifter. And it's quite full. Why, this is very thoughtful of you, Margot.

BRIGHTON: OK! Time for me to go. I have to run home and write my review.

MARGOT: I can't wait to read it.

BRIGHTON: You've already heard half of it. Don't get me wrong: There is such a thing as good concept Shakespeare. I've seen it happen. Less than five times, but I have seen it. It might happen more often. If only Ph.D. candidates weren't allowed to direct. Good night!

(Exits.)

PHILIP: Did you get everything done that you needed to do?

MARGOT: I think so.

PHILIP: I'm sorry, I've forgotten. How long is your trip?

MARGOT: My trip?

PHILIP: Two suitcases. I didn't think you'd be gone that long.

MARGOT: Really, how long did you think I'd be gone?

PHILIP: Just a day or two at the most.

MARGOT: And where do you think I'm going?

PHILIP: Uh . . . OK, you caught me. I saw the suitcases and figured you had packed for an important trip that we most likely discussed at some point and I didn't want you to realize I had forgotten about it. But, I did. I'm sorry.

MARGOT: You didn't forget. I didn't tell you.

PHILIP: I see. Margot. What's wrong?

MARGOT: Nothing.

PHILIP: I went in to the kitchen to find the coffee and dessert. What I found instead was printed instructions taped to the coffeemaker about how to use it. Color photos and everything, quite beautifully produced.

MARGOT: I wanted it to be aesthetically pleasing.

PHILIP: You succeeded. Um. When I opened the refrigerator, I discovered a Tupperware orgy of lunch meats, breads and things you adorably labeled as "fixin's."

MARGOT: I had a very colloquial moment there, didn't I?

PHILIP: So, in light of your leaving notes on all of the food and beverages in our home, I must ask: Have you been reading Lewis Carroll?

MARGOT: *(Pause, indignant.)* Maybe.

PHILIP: Margot . . . What are you trying to tell me?

MARGOT: I . . . I think we need some time apart.

PHILIP: Did I . . . ? Should I have —

MARGOT: No, no. It's not you.

(Pause; gathers her thoughts.)

Philip. I've come to realize there are aspects of my life that I've left unexplored; aspects that, by their nature, I cannot explore with you.

PHILIP: Such as?

MARGOT: I've been doing some reading and —

PHILIP: Uh oh.

MARGOT: Excuse me?

PHILIP: Go on.

MARGOT: No, what did you mean by "uh-oh"? I tell you I've been reading . . . and you say —

PHILIP: I was not railing against the right of women to read. I was merely reacting to how you are, at times, readily influenced by trends you read about. You don't have to, as the youth might say, "go all Margaret Atwood on me."

MARGOT: I am not easily influenced by trends.

PHILIP: We have a basement with a pottery wheel, a home wine-making system and a loom, each of which have been used once or twice and then never again. But, let's not discuss this right now. You were leaving me.

MARGOT: I was saying: I've been doing some reading and realized, not just from this reading, but also from counseling women with similar unexplored alcoves in their experience, that my feminine potential has largely remained untapped. I wish to tap that potential.

PHILIP: Meaning?

MARGOT: I'm becoming a lesbian.

PHILIP: You are?

MARGOT: I don't know for how long. Just until I can determine if it's who I am.

PHILIP: And how long do you think it will be before you know whether or not lesbianism is your cup of tea?

MARGOT: I'm not enjoying your tone.

PHILIP: Margot, how do I say this? Lesbianism is a sexual orientation, not a car. You can't test-drive it.

MARGOT: There are many case histories of women who don't realize they're lesbians until their first experience.

PHILIP: Yes, but they at least wonder.

MARGOT: I've wondered.

PHILIP: Since when?

MARGOT: The point is: This is something I have to find out about and in order to do that —

PHILIP: You have to leave me. I can't believe this. You're casting aside twenty-two years of marriage —

MARGOT: I'm not casting anything aside.

PHILIP: I see. You're not deserting me. This is just a . . . separation.

MARGOT: Don't think of it as a separation, then. Think of it as more of a . . . sabbatical.

PHILIP: We have plans! The Museum Ball on Saturday. I reserved a table for us at the University's Fall Carnival.

MARGOT: Philip, please don't!

(Doorbell.)

BRIGHTON: *(Offstage.)* It's me!

PHILIP: It's open.

(Brighton enters.)

BRIGHTON: Sorry to do this, but I left my playbill here. Let's see. Where . . . Ah. There it is. OK, so I'm pretending I didn't leave this here on purpose to give myself an excuse to come back and ask you why you're acting so *Who's Afraid of Virginia Woolf*-y. You find me painfully transparent and tell me what's up.

PHILIP: By all means. Margot?

MARGOT: You'd find out tomorrow anyway. You see, Brighton . . . I've . . . come to, uh . . . some . . . conclusions . . .

PHILIP: Don't hesitate. Let it out! Don't let his potentially very negative reaction daunt you.

MARGOT: I'm not daunted.

PHILIP: You seem nonplussed.

MARGOT: I am perfectly plussed. Brighton, I know that because you are my friend and because you have struggled with similar issues in your own difficult, yet triumphant, life —

BRIGHTON: Spit it out.

MARGOT: I'm becoming a lesbian.

BRIGHTON: *(Pause.)* Oh, thank God. I thought you two were serious. You really had me.

MARGOT: It's not a joke.

BRIGHTON: It has to be. "I'm becoming a lesbian." No one "becomes" a lesbian. It's not like Judaism. You can't convert.

MARGOT: I'm not "converting."

PHILIP: It's more like a test-drive.

MARGOT: Brighton, listen to me. I've come to realize there are certain aspects of my life that I've left unexplored; aspects that, by their nature, I cannot explore with Philip. I've been doing some reading and I've realized, not only from this reading but from counseling women with similar unexplored alcoves in their experience, that my feminine potential has largely remained untapped. I wish to tap that potential.

PHILIP: You've been rehearsing that!

MARGOT: I have not!

PHILIP: Those are the exact same words you used to explain this cockamamie sabbatical to me before! The only way you could use the exact same words is if you rehearsed it.

MARGOT: Though it obviously has not occurred to you, Philip, perhaps the reason I am able to explain myself clearly with similar and, perhaps, identical language is because I have given the matter a great deal of thought.

PHILIP: Clearly, you have. Apparently, you also gave a good deal of thought to how you were going to break the news to me?

MARGOT: Yes, Philip.

PHILIP: Kept saying it out loud until you got it just right?

MARGOT: Yes, Philip.

PHILIP: And you don't call that rehearsal?

MARGOT: I respect your . . . Socraticism. However —

BRIGHTON: May I ask you a personal question, Margot?

MARGOT: Certainly.

BRIGHTON: Are you attracted to women?

MARGOT: I adore women.

BRIGHTON: I mean sexually.

MARGOT: What does that have to do with anything?

PHILIP: For starters, it's a prerequisite for lesbianism.

MARGOT: Well . . . I didn't want to make this about anything as superficial as sexual attraction and gender, but . . . sure.

PHILIP: "Sure?"

MARGOT: Yes. "Sure." A word used to express certainty.

PHILIP: Ah, I see what you're doing. Oh, Margot, I am onto you so. Is that how the kids say it today, Brighton?

BRIGHTON: They say "so onto you" but "onto you so" is more you.

MARGOT: And how and to what extent, Philip, are you "onto me so"?

PHILIP: You knew I would be reluctant to go along with your little experiment.

MARGOT: "Little?" Exploring one's identity is hardly —

PHILIP: Margot, have you been dissatisfied, disappointed, or otherwise disenchanted with our marriage?

MARGOT: What complaints could I possibly have?

PHILIP: Is that rhetorical or a "no"?

BRIGHTON: I think it's actually a direct question designed to place the blame on you for being ignorant of your matrimonial shortcomings.

MARGOT: It's a "no."

PHILIP: A "no"?

MARGOT: Yes! A "no."

PHILIP: Excellent. Then the passion sparking your odyssey of self-discovery has nothing to do with anything I've said or not said, done or not done, or with who I am, was, have been or could be?

MARGOT: That's right.

PHILIP: Then, Margot, I congratulate you!

MARGOT: You do?

BRIGHTON: No you don't.

PHILIP: This is a great moment. You must pull anchor and set forth. I shall impede you no longer. You've packed your things.
(*Beat. softly:*)
You've packed your things.
(*Beat.*)
Far be it from me to render that act in vain. Wait here. I'll bring the car around for you.

MARGOT: You will?

PHILIP: Unless there's some reason I shouldn't.

MARGOT: No. Please do!

PHILIP: Happy to oblige.

MARGOT: It's quite gentlemanly of you.

PHILIP: If I'm anything, it's a gentleman.

MARGOT: (*Beat.*) Do you need the keys?

PHILIP: I have my keys. Do you have yours?

MARGOT: Of course I do. I'm all set.

PHILIP: Good for you. Then, there's no point in waiting any longer. I'll get the car.

MARGOT: Thank you.

PHILIP: Fine. Excuse me.
(*Exits.*)

MARGOT: I must admit, he's taking this much better than I thought he would.

BRIGHTON: Yes! I'm so relieved that neither of you is behaving in any way that resembles passive-aggression or denial.

MARGOT: It is a relief, isn't it?

BRIGHTON: Margot, if you were having these thoughts, why didn't you talk to me?

MARGOT: I needed to do this on my own.

BRIGHTON: You were afraid I could talk you out of it.

MARGOT: I was worried you might say something to Philip.

BRIGHTON: And you were afraid I could talk you out of it.

MARGOT: This isn't easy for me. I'll need your help.

BRIGHTON: Lunch. Your office. Tomorrow.

MARGOT: Thank you, Brighton.

(Philip enters.)

PHILIP: Your chariot awaits.

MARGOT: Thank you, Philip.

(Margot picks up her luggage. She leaves one piece for Philip and looks at him expectantly.)

PHILIP: You can make two trips.

MARGOT: That won't be necessary. I've got it.

(She doesn't.)

BRIGHTON: Philip, do you need me to stay?

MARGOT: I've got it.

(She doesn't.)

PHILIP: No, thanks. I'm sure I'll see you in the morning.

MARGOT: I've got it.

(She does!)

(Cross fade to:)

TUESDAY

Setting: Brighton's office. Tuesday morning. A desk with a phone, a stapler, and papers. At Rise: Brighton gathers notes for his lecture. Philip enters, holding something in his hand.

BRIGHTON: Well, if it isn't the Happy Bachelor.

PHILIP: If you love someone, you must set them free!

BRIGHTON: The last time I did that, I had to contend with a rather uppity bail bondsman. What the hell were you doing last night?

PHILIP: I was blindsided. I thought she was bluffing; I wanted to call her on it. I didn't think she'd actually leave.

BRIGHTON: Not even when you started her car and drove it to the front door? Why so cheerful?

PHILIP: Voila!

(Presents a gold charm bracelet.)

BRIGHTON: For me? You shouldn't have! It's just what I wanted.

PHILIP: I gave this to her on our first anniversary. It has a little gold number for every year we've been married, musical notes from our days as symphony addicts, a little gold menu with the name of the restaurant where I proposed to her engraved on it. Misspelled.

(Beat.)

I found this hanging out of the jewelry box. Which means: She's coming back.

BRIGHTON: Or she's so disenchanted with you that she's left behind any and all physical evidence of your marital union.

(Sees that Philip is stunned.)

But that's probably wrong.

PHILIP: Have you spoken to her today?

BRIGHTON: I'm meeting her for lunch.

PHILIP: Really? Where?

BRIGHTON: Philip.

PHILIP: I'm not going to crash your lunch.

BRIGHTON: Of course you would. That's why we're eating in her office.

PHILIP: How nice. She has a nice office.

BRIGHTON: You want progress reports on my conversations with her.

PHILIP: Will you give me progress reports?

BRIGHTON: I'm a naturally indiscreet person. I'll keep each of you informed about the other, so be careful what you tell me and especially careful about what you ask.

PHILIP: Fair enough. And while you're . . .

BRIGHTON: Teaching Remedial Lesbianism?

PHILIP: I was wondering if you might . . .

BRIGHTON: You want me to convince Margot that lesbians are evil.

PHILIP: Just convince her that she wouldn't make a very good one. I mean, it's not as though you don't already have issues with lesbians.

BRIGHTON: I do not have issues with lesbians.

PHILIP: You don't like lesbians.

BRIGHTON: That is a gross generalization. I don't like the lesbians I have met. I'm sure there are plenty of lesbians . . . of quality out there. Our circles simply have not overlapped.

PHILIP: Fair enough. Lesbians bother you. I don't have to understand why.

BRIGHTON: (Exasperated:) What's not to understand? Lesbians —

PHILIP: The one's you've met.

BRIGHTON: Yes-yes-of-course-who-else! "Those people" — and I mean that in the best possible way — tend to exhibit the same annoying traits as most of the lesser gay men I have known: stereotypical behavior, prejudices, obsession with labels, an almost complete absence of any sense of humor. Where gay men think everything is a joke, lesbians often don't see the humor in humor. Of course, the abject hatred of men is a turnoff; the absence of any sense of style: It's garish or it's Santa Fe; the maximum of five haircuts, all of them unflattering.

PHILIP: But the lesbians, at least the ones I've encountered recently, seem to be "letting their hair down." So to speak.

BRIGHTON: And the theater! Oh, my God, the theater! Show after show about intelligent sensitive women escaping the clutches of Neolithic men, who just don't understand the uniqueness that can only happen between two women blah blah blah. "But these are my feelings" blah blah blah; "Our relationship" blah blah blah, "I disagree with your position on Insert Women's Issue Here" blah blah blah; "When she first touched me" "drenching rain" "long drought in my soul" blah blah! And all the while I'm sitting in the bleachers praying that SOMETHING ANYTHING will happen. But *does* it? NO! We have to sit through some dyke's fucking "Internal Journey."

PHILIP: I hadn't realized you felt this —

BRIGHTON: On the up side, you can be a fat lesbian and get a date. I hate people. Thank God I'm a teacher. Don't worry, Philip. If Margot wants to immerse herself in the waters of Sapphic sisterhood, I know just the pool in which she should dip her toe!

(Cross fade to: Margot's office. There is a desk with a computer and a chair. Brighton stands as Margot sits behind her computer.)

BRIGHTON: Welcome to Internet Personals!

MARGOT: Are you sure?

BRIGHTON: Absolutely. This is the fastest, most efficient way of surveying the playing field. Let's browse, shall we?

MARGOT: OK . . . Women seeking women, obviously.

BRIGHTON: Between ages . . . ?

MARGOT: Twenty-five and fifty?

BRIGHTON: Cradle robber.

MARGOT: I'm interested in younger perspectives as well.

BRIGHTON: You'll end up with a nut job harboring an Electra Complex.

MARGOT: Kind of relationship? Casual?

BRIGHTON: Only looking for sex.

MARGOT: Long-Term Serious?

BRIGHTON: Picked out the china pattern; looking for someone to go with it.

MARGOT: Long-Term Casual?

BRIGHTON: Probably your safest bet. Click that.

MARGOT: "Only search ads with photos"? I don't want to be superficial.

BRIGHTON: Remember that when your date asks if you're distracted by her goiter.

MARGOT: Fine. Here's one: "Young Soul Pioneer — "

BRIGHTON: Fruitcake!

MARGOT: "ISO Elegant Femme to Explore Life's Frontiers."

BRIGHTON: That doesn't reek of autoerotic asphyxiation to you?

MARGOT: Stop it. What does ISO mean?

BRIGHTON: "In search of."

MARGOT: Like Leonard Nimoy?

BRIGHTON: Probably.

MARGOT: Am I femme?

BRIGHTON: You're not butch.

MARGOT: Is butch bad?

BRIGHTON: I like it.

MARGOT: Look: She enjoys pondering the universe and writing poetry and keeps nature close to her at all times. There's nothing about oxygen-deprived orgasms.

BRIGHTON: Maybe there should be.

MARGOT: I'm going to reply. Dear "AlphaOmegan."

BRIGHTON: You're kidding.

MARGOT: *(Typing:)* "My name is Margot Welles."

BRIGHTON: Don't give her your full name.

MARGOT: " . . . Margot and I believe I am the femme for whom you have been looking."

BRIGHTON: Good.

MARGOT: "I am relatively new at this." I don't want her expectations to be too high.

BRIGHTON: These are Internet personals. If she has high expectations . . . Here. Type this: "My experience has mostly been with men."

MARGOT: Good. OK.

BRIGHTON: "so, judging from your description, you won't be too much of a stretch."

MARGOT: *(Laughs.)* Brighton! Be serious, please.

BRIGHTON: "You seem like the sort of woman with whom I might feel comfortable."

MARGOT: That's nice. Brighton, I know it must be difficult being in the middle of this —

BRIGHTON: Philip did not put me up to this.

MARGOT: He didn't ask you to —

BRIGHTON: Of course he asked.

MARGOT: And you didn't agree to —

BRIGHTON: I most certainly did not. Though I probably gave him a tacit impression I did. Margot, look: I love you. I would never do anything to compromise the integrity of your efforts.

MARGOT: Oh, Brighton. That is so sweet of you. Now: The virtual world certainly has provided an interesting overview. Can you recommend any place in the actual world?

BRIGHTON: The Women's Center downtown has a support group for bi-curious women and newly out lesbians.

MARGOT: Sounds good. Any place I should avoid?

BRIGHTON: The Women's Issues section at Barnes & Noble.

MARGOT: Thanks. Let's write one for me, now.

(Cross fade to: Philip's classroom. Tuesday afternoon. Philip stands behind a lectern. Female Student and Antonia are planted in the audience. Philip holds a copy of Plato's Meno.)

PHILIP: That wraps up Plato's *The Meno*. Any questions?

(Questions come from offstage.)

FEMALE STUDENT: Yes, uh, Professor Embers. Uh, I don't get the bit about knowledge versus true opinion. What's the difference?

PHILIP: A child burns himself on a hot stove. He has true knowledge that touching the stove is dangerous. Another child, who has not touched the stove, can only have the opinion that touching the stove is dangerous. That opinion may be correct, but his inexperience precludes it from being true knowledge.

FEMALE STUDENT: But don't they amount to the same thing?

PHILIP: Practically speaking, yes. In this instance, the child who has learned from the other's experience has lucked out.

FEMALE STUDENT: So sometimes the correct opinion is better than true knowledge.

PHILIP: Sometimes, but certainly not always. Can anyone think of an example where true knowledge wins out? Anyone at all?

ANTONIA: Love.

PHILIP: *(Beat.)* Go on.

ANTONIA: It's better to have experienced love and to know what love is from the inside, than to be around friends who are in love and observe them.

FEMALE STUDENT: But what about heartbreak? Is it better to have true knowledge that heartbreak is devastating or is it better to have the correct opinion?

PHILIP: *(To Antonia:)* Would you care to respond, Miss . . . I'm sorry, I don't recall your name.

ANTONIA: Burns.

(Pronounced: ann-toe-NEE-uh.)

Antonia Burns. And the answer is . . . true knowledge.

PHILIP: Why?

ANTONIA: So when people tell you they know what you're going through, you can tell them to go to hell.

PHILIP: *(Smiling wide:)* Well. There it is.

PHILIP: *(Checks time.)* Looks like we're out of time. The reading for next time is from Aristotle's *Nicomachean Ethics.*

(Above pronounced: nee-koe-MAH-kee-uhn.)

Have a good weekend.

(Cross fade to Brighton in his lecture hall.)

BRIGHTON: Your script must be filled with images. I don't mean long strings of adjectives. Be evocative. Be picturesque. Be concise, but vivid. Take the sequence we watched today from *Out of Africa.* Sure, we have John Barry's lush score and David Watkin's breathtaking cinematography as we watch Robert Redford fly Meryl Streep around. What makes those beautiful aerial images matter? What's happening? Anyone?

(Pause.)

Come on, people. This isn't quantum physics. Look at them! It's obvious —

NICK: *(offstage.)* . . . falling in love . . .

BRIGHTON: I'm sorry. I didn't hear that.

NICK: I said, they're falling in love.

BRIGHTON: Bravo. Wasn't that simple? Now, tell me this. How can you tell?

NICK: The way she reaches back for his hand and he takes it. How they both change once he does.

BRIGHTON: Are they saying anything?

NICK: No. It's just . . . what they're doing.

BRIGHTON: And what we're seeing them do. See, class. Actions and images. Thank you, Mister . . . ?

NICK: Daldry.

BRIGHTON: Thank you, Mister Daldry. Actions and images . . .

(Cross fade to an empty area of the stage. Philip enters with his overcoat and briefcase.)

ANTONIA: *(Offstage.)* Excuse me. Doctor Embers!

(Philip stops. Antonia enters. She is about sixty, very colorfully dressed but not too tacky.)

PHILIP: Miss Burns, right?

ANTONIA: Antonia.

PHILIP: I enjoyed your participation in class today.

ANTONIA: You know what they say . . . Experience brings wisdom, a gift unappreciated by the young.

PHILIP: Who said that?

ANTONIA: Actually, I did. I'm always pretending I'm quoting people. It disguises the fact that I'm trying too hard.

PHILIP: Trying too hard to . . .

ANTONIA: To be quotable, of course.

PHILIP: I'm of the opinion you should speak up more often. So, how can I help you?

ANTONIA: I have a few questions about the reading assignment.

PHILIP: You seemed to understand it perfectly.

ANTONIA: Not the Plato. That's fine. I mean the Aristotle. I read the passages you assigned.

PHILIP: You read them? Already?

ANTONIA: Yes.

PHILIP: Really?

ANTONIA: Yes?

PHILIP: *(Wistful:)* No student of mine has ever read ahead. I usually consider myself lucky if they read it at all, but . . . you . . . you read ahead.

ANTONIA: Doctor Embers, please. Your enthusiasm is making me blush.

PHILIP: No, it isn't. I get the impression not much does.

(Awkward moment.)

So, we were talking about . . .

ANTONIA: Aristotle. It's chilly. Do you mind if we talk over coffee?

PHILIP: I . . . I'd love to, but I can't tonight.

ANTONIA: Another time, then.

(They begin to exit in opposite directions. Philip turns to Antonia.)

PHILIP: I'm free tomorrow evening.

(Antonia stops and faces Philip. She is smiling.)

(Cross fade to: Brighton gathering his notes at the lectern. Nick Daldry enters and crosses to him. Nick is a charismatic man in his twenties.)

NICK: Mister Galloway.

BRIGHTON: Mister Daldry. Thank you for your participation in class today. It was nice hearing a voice that wasn't my own.

NICK: My pleasure. Actually . . . I was sort of making up for lost time.

BRIGHTON: How so?

NICK: The first time I took this class, I don't think I said a word.

BRIGHTON: Did I fail you because of it?

NICK: You gave me an A minus.

BRIGHTON: You must have earned it. I give nothing. So, if you've already passed the course, why are you taking it again?

NICK: I'm not. I was just sitting in.

BRIGHTON: Why?

NICK: Uh, well. I started out as a Psych major in undergrad. Then I took this course and I changed my major to film.

BRIGHTON: And now you're here to exact some kind of revenge on me for ruining your life?

NICK: On the contrary. You . . . God, this sounds so cliché, but . . . You . . . changed my life.

BRIGHTON: Really? Thank you.

NICK: That's not the reason I'm here, though.

BRIGHTON: Oh?

NICK: All right, here goes. When I first took this course, I was nineteen and I didn't think it would be appropriate, but now I'm in my twenties and I'm a little more experienced, with life and such, and I'm a little more confident, although you can probably tell I'm a little nervous right now.

BRIGHTON: A predicate, I'm begging you.

NICK: Would you like to go out with me tomorrow night?

BRIGHTON: *(Pause.)* To what end?

NICK: Um. A date?

BRIGHTON: What do you mean?

(No response.)

I see. You're an actor then. Researching a role? *Sweet Bird of Youth?*

NICK: No, I'm not an actor. And I'm not your student anymore.

BRIGHTON: But you are still a student.

NICK: Not in this department. I'm in the graduate film program.

BRIGHTON: This is a film course.

NICK: Taught through the English department.

BRIGHTON: In conjunction with Film Studies.

NICK: Still, you teach undergrad. I'm a grad student. There's no conflict of interest.

BRIGHTON: I don't know if it would be kosher. This isn't the theater department, you know.

NICK: OK. If you don't want to go . . .

BRIGHTON: I never said that. I'm . . . It's just . . . I'm having a Woody Allen meets Derek Jarman moment and it's just a little . . .

NICK: Buñuel?

BRIGHTON: Buñuel? No, not Buñuel. Buñuel?

NICK: You know: surreal.

BRIGHTON: It is surreal. Not quite Fellini surreal, but more like . . . it feels Canadian.

NICK: Like Atom Egoyan.

BRIGHTON: Yes. Only chronological. What time tomorrow?

(Cross Fade to:)

WEDNESDAY

Setting: Margot's office. Early Wednesday evening. At Rise: Margot primps a little. Philip enters.

PHILIP: Aren't you a vision.

MARGOT: Just happened to be in the neighborhood?

PHILIP: I'm checking up on you. I brought your mail as a ruse.

MARGOT: Clever.

PHILIP: I have my moments. What's the occasion?

MARGOT: I have a date.

PHILIP: Already?

MARGOT: And one tomorrow.

PHILIP: Impressive.

MARGOT: Surprised?

PHILIP: That you were able to get two dates this quickly? Not at all.

MARGOT: Funny; I was. They're not really "dates," of course. Just drinks.

PHILIP: I see. And then what?

MARGOT: Philip, please. I'm not that kind of girl.

PHILIP: I remember exactly what kind of girl you were. Drinks could lead to a concert or a play. Afterwards, if all went well, there might be dancing. Beyond that —

MARGOT: What are you and Brighton doing this evening?

PHILIP: Nothing. He has a date.

MARGOT: Who does?

PHILIP: Brighton.

MARGOT: Our Brighton?

PHILIP: How many do you know?

MARGOT: A date?

PHILIP: Yes.

MARGOT: He said "date"? He used that exact word.

PHILIP: Yes.

MARGOT: What do you think he meant?

PHILIP: He must have told you.

MARGOT: He didn't say anything.

PHILIP: Must be something in the air. He's meeting someone tonight. You're meeting someone . . .

MARGOT: It's just drinks.

PHILIP: I'm meeting someone too.

MARGOT: Are you?

PHILIP: A student.

MARGOT: Preschool or grammar?

PHILIP: Lovely girl. She reads ahead.

MARGOT: You must be in heaven. Careful, Philip. You don't want to commit moral turpitude with an ethics student. The irony alone is too much.

PHILIP: She's auditing.

MARGOT: How convenient.

PHILIP: Besides, it's not a date. Just coffee.

MARGOT: You have a nice time.

MARGOT: You, too.

PHILIP: *(Gestures for her to leave first. She goes. As she passes him:)* She better not look anything like me.

(Margot laughs in spite of herself and exits. Philip follows.)

(Cross fade to: Brighton's office. Brighton frantically tries on different ties. His telephone rings. He answers it.)

BRIGHTON: Hello?

(Spot up on Philip at a pay phone.)

PHILIP: You didn't tell me Margot has a date.

BRIGHTON: Philip?

PHILIP: Yes. Who else?

BRIGHTON: I thought you might be Nick.

PHILIP: Aren't you about to see him?

BRIGHTON: Yes.

PHILIP: Then why would you think it was him?

BRIGHTON: I was afraid he was calling to cancel.

PHILIP: Why would he do that?

BRIGHTON: Gee, Philip, I don't know: He could have sobered up; regained his eyesight; his medication could have reached its therapeutic window. THERE ARE A MILLION REASONS!

PHILIP: This isn't why I called you.

BRIGHTON: Let's look at the facts. He asked me out because he's attracted to the lecturer. But he's not going out with the lecturer. He's going out with the date. I'm a bad, bad date.

PHILIP: No, you're not.

BRIGHTON: How would you know?

PHILIP: I was just trying to be supportive.

BRIGHTON: Stop it.

PHILIP: Brighton, why didn't you tell me Margot has a date?

(Call-waiting beep.)

BRIGHTON: Hang on. My other line is beeping.

(Brighton clicks his phone. Philip's light Cross Fades to Margot on a cell phone, seated as though in a cab.)

BRIGHTON: Hello?

MARGOT: Philip tells me you have a date.

BRIGHTON: I told you too.

MARGOT: No, you didn't.

BRIGHTON: Oh. I thought I had.

MARGOT: You can share anything with me.

BRIGHTON: I know. I do.

MARGOT: There's no reason to hide anything, ever.

BRIGHTON: I know. I don't.

MARGOT: I know you don't.

BRIGHTON: Good.

MARGOT: Oh, Brighton. Has Philip mentioned any of his students to you?

BRIGHTON: No. Why?

MARGOT: He seems to be going on a date with one.

BRIGHTON: He hasn't mentioned this to me.

MARGOT: I believe you, Brighton. But I want to let you know that you can tell me these things about Philip. It doesn't bother me.

BRIGHTON: That's a relief. My other line is beeping.

MARGOT: I didn't hear anything. There's usually a click on this end.

(Brighton clicks the stapler near the phone.)

BRIGHTON: There it is again. Hang on.

(Brighton clicks his phone. Margot's light Cross Fades to Philip on the pay phone.)

BRIGHTON: Hello?

PHILIP: It's her, isn't it?

BRIGHTON: No.

PHILIP: I've been wasting nickel after nickel in this damn machine.

BRIGHTON: Where is your cell phone?

PHILIP: I dropped it in the toilet. Don't ask.

BRIGHTON: Don't worry, I won't. Philip, I've got to go.

PHILIP: What is she saying about me?

BRIGHTON: That you're dating your students.

PHILIP: Did she seem upset?

BRIGHTON: Philip, I have a date coming in a matter of minutes. My hair has declared independence. I stupidly ate onions at lunchtime. I don't even want to think about my skin.

PHILIP: Let me take your mind off of it. What did Margot —

(Call-waiting beep.)

BRIGHTON: That's my other line again.

PHILIP: You're not clicking the stapler into the phone, are you?

BRIGHTON: Hold on.

(Brighton clicks his phone. Philip's light Cross Fades to Margot's.)

MARGOT: Brighton, please don't put me on hold. I forgot to charge my phone and I'm on my last little bar.

BRIGHTON: Why have you both suddenly forgotten how to take care of your cell phones?

MARGOT: So it is him!

BRIGHTON: For Christ's sake.

MARGOT: Brighton, don't you think it's rather soon for Philip to start dating?

BRIGHTON: You're dating.

MARGOT: I'm exploring untapped feminine potential.

BRIGHTON: Margot, you're dating.

MARGOT: OK, fine. You're right. I'm just a little nervous. I haven't been on a date in twenty-five years. What does one do on a date these days?

BRIGHTON: You're asking me?

MARGOT: You've dated more recently than I have.

BRIGHTON: Yes, but

(Clicks the stapler.)

Hang on. I won't be but a minute.

MARGOT: The battery!

(Brighton clicks the phone. Margot's light Cross Fades to Philip's.)

BRIGHTON: Hello?

PHILIP: This fucking phone is bleeding me dry!

BRIGHTON: Philip.

PHILIP: Every two minutes, it asks me for a nickel. So, I've been giving it a nickel every two minutes. Then I run out of nickels. I give it a quarter. Two minutes later, it asks me for another fucking nickel! I just gave it a fucking quarter!

BRIGHTON: That must really suck for you. I need your advice, Philip. I'm going on a date. What should I do?

PHILIP: Be yourself?

BRIGHTON: OK, let's pretend for a moment that you're helpful. If you were helpful, what would you say?

PHILIP: Uh . . . Try to relax. Pay attention. Avoid politics. Ask questions.

BRIGHTON: See. That was helpful.

(Clicks stapler.)

Whoops! That's my stapler. Hold on.

(Brighton clicks the phone. Philip lights Cross Fade to Margot's. There is loud static. Margot's light flickers wildly.)

BRIGHTON: Hello?

MARGOT: *(Shouting:)* My battery's dying!

BRIGHTON: I've thought about your question!

MARGOT: What!

BRIGHTON: Try to relax! Pay attention! Ask questions!

MARGOT: What are you saying?! You're breaking up!

BRIGHTON: Relax!

MARGOT: I can't hear you!

BRIGHTON: RELAX! RELAX!

(Margot's light flickers out. The static ends abruptly.)

BRIGHTON: Hello? Margot?

(Brighton clicks the phone. Spot comes up on a very angry Philip.)

BRIGHTON: Philip?

OPERATOR'S VOICE: Please deposit five cents . . . for the next two minutes.

PHILIP: I JUST GAVE YOU A QUARTER!

BRIGHTON: Philip!

PHILIP: Brighton?!? I'm out of change!

OPERATOR'S VOICE: *(On "change.")* Please deposit five cents . . . for the next two minutes . . . or your call will be terminated . . . This is a recording.

PHILIP: What was that? I couldn't hear you!

BRIGHTON: I said, thanks for the advice.

PHILIP: You're welcome. Brighton, why didn't you tell me Margot had a —

(Philip's light blacks out.)

BRIGHTON: Philip? Hello? Thank God.

(Brighton hangs up the phone. Nick enters knocking on the door.)

BRIGHTON: Come in?

NICK: Hi. So, are you ready?

(Cross fade to: Coffee shop. Antonia sits with coffee, book, notes, and Philip.)

ANTONIA: I'm concerned about Aristotle. He writes that human beings act on their basic needs by fulfilling them as pleasurably as possible. So, ethically, we should live our lives as happily as possible, without depriving others or causing them displeasure.

PHILIP: But, what if . . . What if providing for your own needs necessarily means doing so at the expense of someone else's happiness?

ANTONIA: It probably depends on your perspective. If you're getting what you want, it seems fair. If you're not, you feel screwed.

PHILIP: I suppose that's so.

ANTONIA: I think Aristotle would recommend meeting your remaining needs as happily as possible.

PHILIP: That's a contemporary way of looking at it, but yes.

ANTONIA: Good! I like Aristotle. I'm all for happiness. How about you?

PHILIP: I'm certainly not opposed to it.

ANTONIA: So, what would make you happy right now?

PHILIP: Who says I'm not?

ANTONIA: You mean you are?

PHILIP: Sure.

ANTONIA: Could you be happier?

PHILIP: I suppose.

ANTONIA: And how would you meet those needs?

PHILIP: Are you thinking of something specific?

ANTONIA: What do you think of older women?

(Pause. Cross fade to: Theater Lobby. Nick and Brighton stand uncomfortably.)

BRIGHTON: It's ten of. I wonder if they're ever going to open the damn house.

(Brighton looks at Nick, who smiles back. Pause.)

NICK: Dinner was good.

BRIGHTON: Yes, it was.

NICK: You enjoyed the brisket?

BRIGHTON: I did. It wasn't too dry.

NICK: Good.

BRIGHTON: Sometimes that's a problem. Dry brisket.

NICK: Yeah, I've heard that. I wonder why that is.

BRIGHTON: I don't know. It must dry easily.

NICK: There's probably some . . . you know . . .

BRIGHTON: Window of opportunity.

NICK: Exactly. To keep the brisket from . . .

BRIGHTON: So . . .

NICK: So . . .

> *(Pause.)*
>
> I haven't been to this theater in years. In fact —
>
> *(Points out poster.)*
>
> — that's the last show I saw here.

BRIGHTON: No wonder you stayed away.

NICK: You didn't like it?

BRIGHTON: Oh, please! All those sidelong, "I really want to fuck you if only I could say so" glances between the two leads. It was like watching *Remains of the Day* with the sound off.

NICK: I thought it was a refreshingly honest interpretation of those characters.

BRIGHTON: It was *The Sound of Music!* Oh, and the Maria —

NICK: — is a very dear friend of mine —

BRIGHTON: — was lovely. Oh, look. They've opened the house.

> *(Brighton and Nick exit.)*
>
> *(Cross Fade to: Margot sitting alone, waiting, looking at her watch, checking herself in the mirror, occasionally craning her neck inquisitively to see if an offstage passerby is the one. No. She dials her phone and checks her messages. As she does, Sophie enters. She is goth-chick top to bottom: white face, black eye makeup, spider-web patterns on her hands, army boots, carrying a journal and a backpack with something moving inside it.)*

SOPHIE: *(Painfully droning voice.)* Hey . . . You're not, Margotte . . . are you . . . ?

> *(Margot closes her phone and smiles bravely.)*
>
> *(Cross fade to:)*

Setting: Brighton's office. Thursday morning. At Rise: Brighton gathers his lecture items. Philip enters.

PHILIP: How'd it go?

BRIGHTON: It was the *Heaven's Gate* of dates.

It was my fault. I was a pompous blowhard. I don't want to talk about it.

PHILIP: OK then, tell me about Margot's date.

BRIGHTON: You don't care about me at all.

PHILIP: You said you didn't want to talk about it!

BRIGHTON: It's only fair. She's your wife. It's only natural you'd be more interested in her romantic life than mine. Now, I don't have all the details, but she did say "I haven't had this much fun since counseling death row inmates."

PHILIP: Excellent. Brighton, question: If a student made a romantic overture toward you, what would you do?

BRIGHTON: Verbally pummel them with my opinions until they ran away screaming, but that's me.

PHILIP: Are you sure you don't want to talk about this?

BRIGHTON: What is there to say? It was a disaster. I am the romantic equivalent of Chernobyl. I've said it out loud. Eleven steps to go!

(Nick enters.)

NICK: Is this a bad time?

BRIGHTON: Uh . . . no. Nick Daldry, this is Philip Embers. He's with the philosophy department.

NICK: Pleasure to meet you.

PHILIP: Same here. Anyway, Brighton —

BRIGHTON: I'll spread good cheer. Pity you must go.

PHILIP: Indeed. Pleasure to meet you, Nick. Brighton, call me.

BRIGHTON: Oh, I will.

(Philip exits.)

BRIGHTON: This is a surprise. Did you leave something in the car?

NICK: I have to be honest with you.

BRIGHTON: No, you don't.

NICK: It was my fault.

BRIGHTON: Though I like where this is heading.

NICK: I was so nervous. I mean, you'd be nervous too if you suddenly found yourself out on a date with your crush from undergrad.

BRIGHTON: Oh.

NICK: Yeah. And, um. I think I was trying too hard and expecting . . . I don't even know what I was expecting. All I know is . . .

BRIGHTON: Nick.

NICK: I know. You're dying for a predicate. Do you want to go out again?

BRIGHTON: You wouldn't be happier getting root canal or . . .

NICK: Look at it this way. After last night, it's got to get better.

BRIGHTON: When you put it that way . . .

NICK: Tonight then?

BRIGHTON: Tonight?

NICK: Yes.

BRIGHTON: You're so young, too young to realize it's often considered insulting to ask someone out the day of. It means that you assume the person you're asking out has such a barren existence, that they couldn't possibly have plans of their own.

NICK: So, you're busy.

BRIGHTON: No, I'm free as a bird. See you at six.

(Cross fade to: A restaurant bar. There is a bar and a table for two sits in front of a Hostess. Nick and Brighton enter. They're having a good time.)

NICK: I'm shooting a documentary about Duncan James. He's this legendary seventy-two-year-old jazz vocalist. You hear the word *legend* and you think "been around forever and is very, very good." But his voice . . . there are a million experiences he brings to every note! I'd just sit there and listen to him tell story after story, never repeating a one, while I let the camera roll. It was truly a privilege.

BRIGHTON: I'd love to see some of the footage.

NICK: I think that can be arranged. I'm going to hit the head before we leave.

BRIGHTON: Are you sure there's time?

NICK: The movie doesn't start for another forty minutes.

BRIGHTON: Why won't you tell me which movie we're seeing?

NICK: It gives me a perverse sense of power.

BRIGHTON: Good Lord. Go pee. I'll meet you outside.

(Brighton and Nick exit in opposite directions. Beat. Antonia enters with Philip.)

PHILIP: I'll see if our table is ready.

ANTONIA: I'll be right here.

(Philip crosses to a hostess' lectern. Nick enters, passing Philip, and he and Antonia see each other. They are surprised.)

ANTONIA: Nicky.

NICK: Grandma? What are you doing here?

ANTONIA: Oh. Just grabbing something to eat.

NICK: Are you with someone?

ANTONIA: Me? No. I come here by myself all the time. How about you?

NICK: I'm all by myself too.

> (Hostess — *played by the actress who will be playing Hera Jane* — *enters and talks to Philip.*)

PHILIP: Yes, a reservation under Embers.

> (*Nick turns around and spots Philip who doesn't see him.*)

NICK: Oh.

ANTONIA: Do you know that gentleman?

NICK: Him? No. Do you?

ANTONIA: Oh, no. I'm here by myself.

NICK: Yes. Me, too.

PHILIP: That's fine. Thank you.

NICK: *(Overlapping:)* I'll be seeing you.

ANTONIA: *(Overlapping:)* Bye-bye.

> (*Nick and Antonia share the briefest of pecks and he bolts out. Philip makes his way over.*)

PHILIP: Who was that?

ANTONIA: My grandson. I tried to get him to stay a moment, but he had to run.

PHILIP: He looks familiar.

ANTONIA: He probably has one of those faces.

HOSTESS: Embers party of two, right this way.

PHILIP: After you.

> (*Hostess leads Antonia and Philip out. Margot and Chelsea, a pretty, breezy woman, enter. The Hostess calls out to them.*)

HOSTESS: *(Offstage:)* I'll be right back. You can have a seat at the bar, if you like.

MARGOT: Thank you. That's fine.

> (*Margot and Chelsea cross to the bar. Philip bolts back in and sees Margot. He bolts back out.*)

MARGOT: Chelsea is a very nice name.

CHELSEA: Thank you! That's so nice. Margot is a very nice name too.

MARGOT: Thank you.

CHELSEA: So, what made you respond to my ad?

MARGOT: Well —

CHELSEA: Not that anything *made* you. I mean, you did exercise free will when you responded, right?

MARGOT: Absolutely.

CHELSEA: You're not just saying that to be nice?

MARGOT: I don't say things to be nice. I'm a therapist.

CHELSEA: Oh. You're not the kind who tells women to leave their lovers, are you?

MARGOT: Well, it depends —

CHELSEA: Because I'm an optimist and I think things can be worked out.

MARGOT: That's generally a healthy outlook to have —

CHELSEA: At least they could have been, but my girlfriend's therapist — oops! Did it again. OK, rewind. What I meant was: my EX-girlfriend's therapist told her . . . Her therapist is Wanda O'Shell. Do you know her?

MARGOT: Not well, but I've met her.

(During the following, Philip enters and eavesdrops.)

CHELSEA: Loudmouth bitch; you don't want to know her well. She'll just tell you to leave the people you love and do her bidding. You would never do that, would you? Tell someone to leave someone who loves them?

MARGOT: Let's not talk about me.

CHELSEA: Just say you wouldn't! Even if it's a lie! Can't you just . . . JUST SAY IT?

(Philip smiles to himself and sneaks off.)

MARGOT: I would never do that, Chelsea, and I mean that.

CHELSEA: Thank you. Thank you!

(Chelsea dries her eyes. Margot looks at her watch.)

(Cross fade to: Nick and Brighton sitting next to each other as a projector light flickers above them. The Soundtrack is of an intense, horror science-fiction film. Brighton holds the popcorn. Nick holds the beverage.)

(Nick watches casually. Brighton watches with a confused but intense expression on his face. The Music swells for an intense moment and Climaxes. Brighton laughs, but never takes his eyes off the screen. Nick looks over at him and smiles. He's rather taken with Brighton. Nick puts the beverage down as Brighton eats some popcorn. Nick goes to put his arm around Brighton who starts coughing and gestures for the beverage. Nick leans back over and gets the drink for Brighton. He hands it over and Brighton gulps it down, stops takes a deep breath.)

NICK: *(Whispering.)* . . . you OK?

(Brighton nods and hands the drink back to Nick, who just holds it. They watch intently for a moment. Music swells suddenly and both Nick and Brighton jump. Sound effects are screechy and squishy. Brighton and Nick wince.)

BRIGHTON: *(Involuntarily.)* oooooo . . .

(*Nick puts his arm around Brighton, who becomes aware of it. Brighton nervously adjusts himself in his seat. Nick starts to play with Brighton's hair. Brighton brushes the hand away. Nick persists and Brighton brushes.*)

BRIGHTON: I'm watching this.

(*Nick stops playing, but keeps his arm around Brighton. They watch for a moment, very intensely. Brighton looks over at Nick. He examines Nick's face. Nick catches him looking and smiles back at him. Brighton looks away, but looks back. Nick squeezes Brighton's shoulder, bringing Brighton closer to him. Brighton relaxes and rests against Nick. They watch contentedly. Music Flares and Nick and Brighton jolt again.*)

(*Cross Fade to: Philip and Antonia at her front door.*)

ANTONIA: Thank you for a wonderful evening.

PHILIP: The pleasure was all mine.

ANTONIA: It was a lovely concert. It's fascinating, isn't it? New Composers of Classical Music. It's so rare to be able to applaud for a composer who's alive to hear you clapping. Meanwhile, I'm sure all those poor souls can think about is whether or not we'll still be applauding them hundreds of years from now.

(*Pause. Philip's mind is elsewhere.*)

Philip?

PHILIP: I'm sorry.

ANTONIA: What is it?

PHILIP: There's something . . .

ANTONIA: Are you married?

PHILIP: *(Laughs.)* More or less. My wife and I separated.

ANTONIA: I see. Recently?

PHILIP: *(Looks at his watch:)* Almost seventy-two hours ago.

ANTONIA: Oh.

PHILIP: My wife was at the restaurant tonight.

ANTONIA: I thought you seemed preoccupied.

PHILIP: I hope I wasn't too terrible a companion.

ANTONIA: You were fine.

PHILIP: Under the circumstances?

ANTONIA: Regardless.

PHILIP: That's very sweet. She wasn't there long. Besides, she was . . . on a date.

ANTONIA: Why are you smiling?

PHILIP: Am I?

ANTONIA: Did her date not go well?

PHILIP: Not from what I could see. I should probably feel ashamed of myself: spying on her.

ANTONIA: It's only natural that you feel this way. I'd be jealous as hell if I were you.

PHILIP: But, when you truly love someone . . . don't you want them to find their own happiness?

ANTONIA: Not within the first seventy-two hours after they leave you.

PHILIP: *(Laughs. Pauses. Takes her hand:)* Thank you.

ANTONIA: It was my pleasure. I hope you get her back.

PHILIP: Me, too..

(Pause.)

Would you . . . I shouldn't ask you this, but would you like to . . . help me get her back?

ANTONIA: How?

PHILIP: She and I were supposed to attend a museum fund-raiser this weekend. It's a lovely affair. Would you like to join me in her stead?

ANTONIA: I don't want to come between you and your wife.

PHILIP: If anything, you'd help bring us back together.

ANTONIA: You think she'll hear about us being there together and get so jealous she'll realize she was wrong to leave you?

PHILIP: It's passive-aggressive, I know.

ANTONIA: True. But that doesn't mean it wouldn't work. You don't think a younger woman would be more effective in incurring her jealousy?

PHILIP: Oh, no. It might annoy her, but she would just dismiss a co-ed as passing fancy. A mature, elegant, sophisticated —

ANTONIA: Older.

PHILIP: — vivacious, enchanting and, sure, older woman . . . You. She couldn't dismiss you. It would not be possible.

ANTONIA: You flatter me.

PHILIP: Not at all. You'd be saving my life.

ANTONIA: *(Beat.)* I don't know, Philip. If my family caught wind . . . My daughter is very active in the church. In fact, she married the minister.

PHILIP: That is active.

ANTONIA: He's one of those people who leads protests against family-planning clinics and runs a program to reform gays. After twelve years, she still expects me to be mourning my husband: wearing black, lighting candles, sleeping on his gravestone! I just want to tell her, "I don't think your father would have wanted me to become an asshole."

(Pause.)

So, what does a mature, vivacious, and enchanting woman wear to a museum?

(Cross fade to empty stage space. Brighton walks Nick home.)

BRIGHTON: *(In medias res:)* Because the film . . . dare I call it a film? The *movie* went right for the audience's basic fear response. It's manipulative. And I'm sorry, but if you bury a pick ax in someone's head, even once, they don't get back up. If you don't believe me, ask Trotsky.

NICK: Look, I'm not asking you if you thought it was good. Obviously, it's not particularly artful filmmaking.

BRIGHTON: I am so relieved you said that.

NICK: What I'm asking you is: Did you enjoy it?

BRIGHTON: On what level do you mean —

NICK: It's a B horror movie! Right off the bat, you know it's going to be bad. You don't have to analyze it. You can just watch it and enjoy being with . . . whoever you're with.

BRIGHTON: So, did *you* have a good time?

NICK: I had a blast.

(Long pause.)

NICK: Here we are.

BRIGHTON: OK. Well, then . . . Thanks for the evening.

NICK: My pleasure.

BRIGHTON: Yeah. Me too.

NICK: At some point, preferably in the near future, I would really like to kiss you good night.

BRIGHTON: Oh?

NICK: Would that be all right with you?

BRIGHTON: Uh . . . yeah.

NICK: Would now be an acceptable time?

BRIGHTON: Well, let me, uh, think . . . Now works.

(Nick crosses to Brighton and kisses him. It's a good kiss.)

NICK: Would you like to come up?

BRIGHTON: Sure.

(Cross Fade to:)

FRIDAY

Setting: Friday morning; The Women's Center. At Rise: Margot holds her coat and purse. Hera Jane — an African-American woman, beautiful and intelligent — enters. A Brahms selection plays over the first part of this scene.

HERA JANE: Hello. Are you Margot Welles?

MARGOT: Yes.

HERA JANE: Welcome. I'm Hera Jane Smith, the volunteer coordinator for the Women's Center. Sorry to keep you waiting.

MARGOT: Quite all right. Brahms was keeping me company.

HERA JANE: Good. I like to keep it on the classical station.

MARGOT: I love classical music. I used to go to the symphony all the time.

HERA JANE: Why'd you stop?

MARGOT: *(Beat.)* I don't know.

HERA JANE: Believe it or not, choosing classical music for the lobby was a controversial decision.

MARGOT: *(Gasps!)* Adult contemporary!

HERA JANE: Isn't it sad? Still, I suppose people should just enjoy whatever it is they enjoy, so long as they feel good about it.

MARGOT: But that's not how you really feel?

HERA JANE: That's right. You're a psychologist.

MARGOT: Whoops. Was I prying? Occupational hazard.

HERA JANE: No problem. I pry too. I'm an attorney.

MARGOT: Really? So this isn't what you do?

HERA JANE: It's one of several things. So, why do you want to volunteer? I'm sure you meet a vast array of people in your line of work.

MARGOT: I do. And it's fascinating. But, I'm hoping to help people more . . . like me.

HERA JANE: Women?

MARGOT: Lesbians in particular.

HERA JANE: You're a lesbian?

MARGOT: Sur — yes! "Yes, I am," as Melissa once said. I must confess, I'm really very new at, um . . . the gay thing.

HERA JANE: Welcome aboard.

MARGOT: Anchors away!

HERA JANE: How's it going? Are you meeting people?

MARGOT: Well . . .

HERA JANE: I see. Don't worry. I've been there.

MARGOT: Oh, have you?

HERA JANE: I could tell you stories.

MARGOT: I'd love to hear them.

HERA JANE: Oh? All right then. Uh. How about this? I have an extra ticket to the R&B Society tonight. Would you like to go with me?

MARGOT: Me?

HERA JANE: Oh, God. I can't believe I just . . . That sounded so forward.

MARGOT: No, no.

HERA JANE: What an impression I must be giving you of the Center . . . and of me.

MARGOT: No. Believe me, I know how difficult it can be to find people who enjoy Renaissance and Baroque.

HERA JANE: It's hard to find anyone who knows I'm not talking about Rhythm and Blues. You know a lot about music, don't you?

MARGOT: I support public broadcasting.

HERA JANE: At the risk of appearing forward again, would you like to join me? We could get some dinner. And I'd love to field any questions you have about . . . coming out and all that.

MARGOT: I would really appreciate that. I've been doing a great deal of research regarding the lesbian motif, but what I'm lacking is good field experience.

HERA JANE: (Beat.) You really do need to get out.

MARGOT: Oh, I am out.

HERA JANE: Of the books, I mean. I can show you around the Center now. Then later tonight, I can just show you around. Deal?

MARGOT: Sure!

(Cross fade to Margot and Hera Jane walking together. They are having a good time.)

MARGOT: They had such lovely voices.

HERA JANE: They did.

MARGOT: Their technique was so precise. Very evocative.

HERA JANE: It made me want to dance.

MARGOT: Really?

HERA JANE: That kind of music makes me close my eyes and transports me to . . . amazing places. It's almost otherworldly. Don't you think so?

MARGOT: (Beat.) Yes.

HERA JANE: You think I'm a lunatic. But it's very kind of you to indulge me.

MARGOT: I have made no such diagnosis. In fact, I must admit I'm a little jealous.

HERA JANE: Of what?

MARGOT: We went to the same concert, heard the same voices and melodies. And you. You shot across the universe, but . . . I never left the concert hall. I feel like I've cheated myself.

HERA JANE: We'll just have to go back and try it again.

MARGOT: I'd like that.

(Cross Fade to:)

SATURDAY

Setting: Margot's office. At Rise: Margot prepares to leave. The doorbell rings. Margot answers the door. Brighton blusters in.)

MARGOT: Good! Come in! I need to talk to you.

BRIGHTON: Yesterday, I woke up in the arms of a significantly younger man!

MARGOT: That's wonderful! I myself had a very eye-opening evening —

BRIGHTON: As I was leaving, he swore he'd call me. And he did!

MARGOT: What a positive step forward for you. That's so much better than the answering machine, a Post-it, or an e-mail. One of these days, you'll meet someone who will be healthy enough to break up with you in person.

BRIGHTON: He didn't break up with me.

MARGOT: Then why did he call?

BRIGHTON: To talk! Jesus! He enjoys my company, even when I'm not there.

MARGOT: So, you're saying he's gay, available, and genuinely interested in you?

BRIGHTON: Apparently.

MARGOT: You're going to dump him, aren't you?

BRIGHTON: What else can I do? Nobody's really this perfect! Therefore, he must be hiding his flaws, which is tantamount to deception in my book. I feel so betrayed.

MARGOT: No, you don't. You just want to feel betrayed, so you can avoid having this relationship, and not risk getting hurt.

BRIGHTON: And that's not a healthy response?

MARGOT: That's right; it's not. Now, what would be a healthy response?

BRIGHTON: Facing my fears with an open mind and positive attitude . . .

(Quickly adding:) by having he and I meet you for drinks this evening so you can advise me!

MARGOT: I can't; I have plans.

BRIGHTON: With your new gal pal? Philip will be so pleased.

MARGOT: I'm sure Philip is having too good a time with his "student" to care. Has he mentioned how old she is? Not that I am concerned about this. I mean really. It's none of my business.

BRIGHTON: You're right. It's not. Meet my needs instead! You can size up Nick. I can size up your friend, which you were going to ask me to do anyway.

MARGOT: Not tonight!

BRIGHTON: Drinks! Just meet us for drinks. You can convince me everything's all right, then Nick and I will get our own table, completely out of your eyeshot.

MARGOT: I don't know . . .

BRIGHTON: It's just drinks. It may also be needy, neurotic, selfish, and solipsistic. But it is just drinks.

MARGOT: You'll go to a completely different restaurant for dinner.

BRIGHTON: Deal. Where and when?

MARGOT: Seven o'clock at Adagio.

BRIGHTON: You're kidding, right?

MARGOT: Her choice; she goes there all the time; who am I to say no.

BRIGHTON: Fine.

MARGOT: Don't tell Philip.

BRIGHTON: Do I look like I have a death wish?

(Lights Cross Fade to Philip in pursuit of Brighton.)

PHILIP: Brighton? Brighton!

BRIGHTON: I'm not telling you.

PHILIP: I don't care where it is, so long as it's romantic.

BRIGHTON: Why do you want it to be romantic?

PHILIP: Because if the atmosphere is romantic and the company is as well, once they're finally alone, Margot and her date might become intimate and —

BRIGHTON: Philip, please! I have to eat with these people!

PHILIP: . . . And Margot will have to figure out that she's . . . whoever she is. Then all of this will be over and we can move on from there. You're sure the restaurant is romantic?

BRIGHTON: Yes! The critics agree: "Adagio is romantic!"

PHILIP: You're going to Adagio?

BRIGHTON: (Beat.) No?

PHILIP: Excuse me, Brighton. I have to make a phone call.

BRIGHTON: Philip. Promise me you will not do anything I will regret.

PHILIP: Sure.

(Cross Fade to: Brighton and Nick in Brighton's car. Classical music plays. They smile at each other. Nick gets bored with the radio.)

NICK: Can I change the station?

BRIGHTON: You may.

(Nick changes the radio from the classical station to news to static. He finds an adult contemporary station playing a Celene Dion ballad, e.g. "Only One Road." Brighton reacts.)

BRIGHTON: What in God's name are we listening to?

NICK: Celene Dion.

BRIGHTON: Make it stop.

NICK: You don't like listening to music written or sung by anyone who hasn't died.

BRIGHTON: You're right. Kill her and her so-called songwriters and I'll listen with glee.

NICK: I missed you.

BRIGHTON: You really get off on my pseudo-intellectual cultural elitism, don't you?

NICK: Way back when, when I listened to your lecture about *American Graffiti* and Truffaut's *Small Change* . . . what did you title the lecture — don't tell me . . . "Plot-Free Masterpieces: Don't Try This at Home."

BRIGHTON: That was it.

NICK: I think I fell for you right then and there.

(Silence. A new, similar song plays.)

BRIGHTON: Is that fucking song still playing?

NICK: It's a completely different song.

BRIGHTON: How can you tell?

NICK: (Changes the radio station to jazz.) Is this better?

(Cross Fade to: A high table in a bar, no stools. Margot and Hera Jane wait.)

MARGOT: I'm sure they'll be here any minute.

HERA JANE: No problem. The longer they take, the more time we have together.

MARGOT: You're sure this is OK? Inviting them to join us?

HERA JANE: Yes. It's perfectly fine. Perfectly fine.

MARGOT: Why'd you say it twice?

HERA JANE: What?

MARGOT: "Perfectly fine." You said it twice. I should have consulted you first.

HERA JANE: It doesn't matter now. We can make the best of it. It's just drinks.

MARGOT: What's wrong?

HERA JANE: I don't mean to be so . . . I'm not always comfortable around gay men.

MARGOT: Really? I'm sure you and Brighton will get along fine. He's very bright and witty.

HERA JANE: Aren't they all?

MARGOT: *(Beat.)* Um. I'm sure you'll have a great deal to talk about. You both enjoy culture and the arts. In fact, he's a theater critic.

HERA JANE: Not Brighton Galloway?

MARGOT: Yes.

HERA JANE: The gay misogynist theater critic?

MARGOT: Excuse me?

HERA JANE: Don't worry. I'm sure since he's your friend he's perfectly nice. Is this them?

(Brighton and Nick enter and cross to Margot and Hera Jane.)

MARGOT: Hello!

BRIGHTON: Thanks for inviting us. I hope we're not imposing.

MARGOT: No. Of course not. No.

BRIGHTON: You said that twice.

MARGOT: You must be Nick. I'm Margot Welles.

NICK: Pleasure to meet you.

MARGOT: Likewise. Nick, Brighton, I'd like you to meet my friend Hera Jane.

NICK: Cool name.

HERA JANE: Thank you.

BRIGHTON: Wonderful to finally meet you.

HERA JANE: Mm-hm.

BRIGHTON: OK . . .

NICK: I'll be right back. If the waitress comes, could you order a Sam Adams for me?

BRIGHTON: Sure.

NICK: Thanks. Pardon me, ladies.

(Nick exits. The others sit.)

MARGOT: He seems very nice.

BRIGHTON: Yeah.

HERA JANE: He's rather young, isn't he?

BRIGHTON: Yes. He is young. So, you're a lawyer?

HERA JANE: Yes.

BRIGHTON: Civil rights?

HERA JANE: No. Real estate.

BRIGHTON: That's fabulous.

HERA JANE: What made you think I was a civil rights attorney?

BRIGHTON: Just a guess.

HERA JANE: I thought it might be because I'm black.

BRIGHTON: Actually, it had occurred to me that being black, female, and gay might have incurred enough prejudice and injustice to spark a more globally reaching proactive political consciousness.

HERA JANE: I am very active. Politically.

BRIGHTON: Good for you.

HERA JANE: Are you?

BRIGHTON: I vote.

(Luisa the waitress — twenties, extroverted, and charming — comes to the table.)

LUISA: Good evening, everybody. Oh, hello.

HERA JANE: Hi.

LUISA: Always a pleasure to see you And new friends! Wonderful. Hi, there. My name is Luisa. What can I get you? Now, I know you want a Bloody Mary.

HERA JANE: That's right.

LUISA: *(Points to Nick's space.)* Brandy Alexander?

HERA JANE: Uh, no.

LUISA: Oh.

(Beat as she figures it out.)

Oh! OK. And you, Ma'am?

MARGOT: Gin and tonic.

LUISA: Sir?

BRIGHTON: Kamikaze, double, on the rocks.

LUISA: Great. I'll get those for you right away.

BRIGHTON: And . . .

(Points to Nick's space.)

He'll have a Sam Adams.

LUISA: Oh, so you do have one more?

BRIGHTON: *(Beat; appalled she'd assume he's alone.)* Yes!

LUISA: Well, that's great. I'll just . . . Uh-huh.

(Exits.)

BRIGHTON: Great restaurant. It's very romantic.

HERA JANE: Yes. It is.

BRIGHTON: Come here often?

HERA JANE: Somewhat.

BRIGHTON: I haven't been here in ages. Margot, when was the last time you were here?

(Nick enters.)

MARGOT: So, Nick. You used to be a student of Brighton's?

NICK: He's the reason I became a filmmaker.

HERA JANE: Brighton, you write films don't you?

BRIGHTON: I write screenplays.

HERA JANE: What's the difference?

BRIGHTON: Films have been shot.

HERA JANE: Well . . . Someday.

NICK: What fun things have the two of you planned for the weekend?

HERA JANE: I was thinking we might take in that program of women's monologues the Magnolia Project is doing. What is it called again?

BRIGHTON: *(Shudders; hissing:)* "The Velvet Embrace . . . " Subtitled "Prayers From the Goddess of the Only True Love."

HERA JANE: I take it you didn't enjoy it.

BRIGHTON: My wrists opened by themselves.

HERA JANE: What was so wrong with it?

BRIGHTON: I don't know. What could be wrong with an endless and agonizing series of two-dimensional feminine stereotypes yammering on in the past tense using adjective-noun groups that no one would ever really use. What was that line? "But mother, you've never experienced love with another woman. The gossamer fluidity."

(Pause.)

Gossamer fluidity. Did she fuck a goose?

HERA JANE: And gay men's theater is any better?

MARGOT AND NICK: Don't get him started —

BRIGHTON: I am so with you. With lesbians portraying themselves as codependent, introspective windbags and gay men as swishy activists running around naked talking about how funny they think they are, it's no wonder everyone hates us.

HERA JANE: Stereotypes do, unfortunately, have clear origins. Feminists often have no sense of humor. Gay men often swish and lisp. Critics are often frustrated artists who can't break into the worlds they judge.

BRIGHTON: That's completely true. We're *all* like that. Just the way many lawyers are soul-less purveyors of deception.

MARGOT: All right. That's —

HERA JANE: *(Overlapping Margot:)* You know, it's people like you —

MARGOT: Enough! This stops now!

HERA JANE: I'm sorry, Margot. But your friend here is attacking —

BRIGHTON: Typical. Blame the man.

MARGOT: You are both being ridiculous. Now, as much as I'd like you to work out whatever differences you have, I'd like to have a pleasant evening. If that means Nick and I do all the talking, so be it. Understood?

BRIGHTON: *(Simultaneous with Hera Jane:)* Repression isn't healthy —

HERA JANE: *(Simultaneous with Brighton:)* I will not be a victim —

MARGOT: Or the evening ends now. What'll it be?

(Philip and Antonia, dressed for an elegant evening out, enter and cross to the others. Antonia sees Margot and stops short of the table. She doesn't see Nick, but Nick sees her.)

BRIGHTON: Oh, my God.

NICK: Oh, shit.

(Hides behind menu.)

PHILIP: Hello, Margot. What a surprise.

MARGOT: Yes. It is.

PHILIP: *(To Hera Jane:)* You must be . . .

MARGOT: This is Hera Jane.

PHILIP: Ah. The wives of Zeus and Tarzan.

HERA JANE: Excuse me?

MARGOT: I think it's a lovely name.

PHILIP: So do I. I never meant to imply otherwise. Everyone, I'd like you to meet —

MARGOT: Antonia?

ANTONIA: Hello, Doctor Welles.

PHILIP: You know each other?

ANTONIA: Doctor Welles is my therapist.

MARGOT: Have you been cruising my lobby, Philip?

PHILIP: I most certainly have not! Antonia is auditing one of my lectures.

MARGOT: She's the "student" you took to the symphony?

PHILIP: And to the Museum Ball tonight.

MARGOT: You're going?

PHILIP: We are.

MARGOT: I thought we agreed to send a check.

PHILIP: I did. They sent me tickets. And here we are.

BRIGHTON: *(Trying to prevent World War Three.)* Lovely to meet you, Ma'am. I'm Brighton Galloway. And this is —

ANTONIA: Nicky?

NICK: Hi, Grandma.

ANTONIA: Um. Do you know Phil —

PHILIP: Yes, Nick. Brighton introduced us the other morning. Good seeing you again.

NICK: Likewise. So, Grandma, are you and Professor Embers —

ANTONIA: So how do you and Mister . . . Galloway, was it? How do you know each other?

HERA JANE: They're on a date.

ANTONIA: Really?

BRIGHTON: As are we all, apparently! Why don't you join us?

(Sees Margot and Hera Jane glaring.)

At a completely different place and time.

(Luisa enters.)

LUISA: Your drinks will be ready in a moment.

NICK: Luisa?

LUISA: Nicky! Oh, my God!

(Nick and Luisa hug.)

BRIGHTON: You know everyone, don't you?

NICK: Luisa, this is Brighton.

LUISA: Nicky's film professor from undergrad?

BRIGHTON: The very one.

LUISA: Well, that's —

ANTONIA: Hello, Luisa.

LUISA: Mrs. Burns? Mrs. Burns! Oh, hello. You're here with Nicky . . . and his . . . his professor . . .

BRIGHTON: So, Luisa. How do you know Nicky?

LUISA: I'm his . . . um . . . wife.

(Blackout.)

END OF ACT ONE

ACT TWO

SATURDAY

Setting: Outside Adagio; immediately following. At Rise: Brighton enters with Nick in pursuit.

NICK: Brighton!

BRIGHTON: This is why I hate valet parking!

NICK: If you just let me explain!

(Grabs hold of Brighton; does not let go.)

BRIGHTON: It's impossible to effectively storm out! Unhand me, sir!

(Luisa rushes in.)

LUISA: Nick!

BRIGHTON: Your wife wants you.

LUISA: What are we going to do?

BRIGHTON: I have an idea! How about you let go of me and then I get my car, drive away and forget I ever met you.

NICK: No.

BRIGHTON: No? I'm not taking a survey. I'm announcing my exit strategy.

(Brighton just glares. Margot enters bickering with Philip. As they walk through, Brighton tries to get Philip's attention.)

MARGOT: In what universe is it appropriate to crash someone else's date?

PHILIP: I apologize.

BRIGHTON: Philip.

PHILIP: I misread your mixed signal.

MARGOT: I sent you no signal; mixed or otherwise.

BRIGHTON: Philip, I need to —

PHILIP: You told Brighton where you and your date were meeting.

MARGOT: Because I was meeting him here, too!

PHILIP: And that's the only reason?

(Margot groans in frustration and exits.)

BRIGHTON: Philip, I really need you to —

PHILIP: Margot!

(Philip exits after Margot. As Brighton exits with Nick in tow, leaving Luisa behind, as Antonia and Hera Jane calmly stroll in.)

BRIGHTON: Philip!

NICK: Brighton!

LUISA: Nick . . .

ANTONIA: Luisa, there you are. So, tell me are you and Nicky still —

LUISA: We're fine. Absolutely fine.

ANTONIA: You said that twice.

LUISA: I'll be right back.

(To Hera Jane:)

Hi.

HERA JANE: Hello?

(Luisa lets out an awkward laugh and exits into the restaurant. Antonia and Hera Jane share an awkward pause.)

HERA JANE: So, how long have you known, um . . .

ANTONIA: *(Completing the question.)* Philip? I introduced myself on Tuesday. The day after Dr. Welles left him.

HERA JANE: She left him Monday night?

ANTONIA: Late Monday. Technically, one could consider it Tuesday morning.

HERA JANE: Uh huh.

(Luisa enters, looking to see if Nick is back.)

ANTONIA: It's no wonder they're behaving this way. With the separation so recent.

LUISA: We're not separated! We're fine!

(Luisa exits as Philip and Margot enter.)

MARGOT: Will you please just drop it!

HERA JANE: If you'll excuse me.

(Hera Jane leaves Antonia and approaches Philip and Margot.)

PHILIP: And you just happened to pick this restaurant?

MARGOT: For the last time, Philip, she picked it.

PHILIP: You didn't object. Then, you told Brighton. And now, you expect me to believe that, even on a subconscious level, you didn't want me to be here?

(Hera Jane approaches Margot as, at the same time, Brighton re-enters with Nick, still not letting go, and approaches Philip. Antonia approaches Luisa.)

HERA JANE: Margot.

BRIGHTON: Philip.

BRIGHTON AND HERA JANE: May have a word with —

(They stop and regard each other with contempt. Hera Jane takes Margot aside as Brighton takes Philip aside.)

BRIGHTON: Philip, I need you to —

(Notices Nick sticking by him.)

Do you mind?

NICK: Mind what?

BRIGHTON: Let go of my arm or I will rip it off your body, beat you about the head and shoulders with it and shove it up your ass!

NICK: *(Stifles a laugh.)* You are so cute!

(Brighton stares daggers at Nick for a second then turns to Philip.)

BRIGHTON: So, Philip, I was saying . . .

(Brighton, Philip, and Nick exit, leaving Antonia to eavesdrop on Hera Jane and Margot.)

MARGOT: You were saying?

HERA JANE: When did you and your husband separate?

MARGOT: Oh, ages ago.

HERA JANE: *(Shoots Antonia a look.)* Really?

MARGOT: Oh, yes. Monday night, in fact.

(Antonia relishes the moment with great smugness.)

MARGOT: Though it was close to midnight, so technically, it could have been Tuesday morning. Why?

HERA JANE: Margot, that's not "ages ago." That's —

(Philip, Brighton, and Nick re-enter.)

PHILIP: I will do nothing of the kind!

BRIGHTON: Why not? You're already taking his grandmother home!

(To Antonia.)

Hello, good seeing you again.

(To Philip.)

I can't drive him home. I'm traumatized.

(Luisa enters.)

HERA JANE: — if I could get a word in —

NICK: If you would just listen to me —

ANTONIA: If you need someone to listen, Nicky, I —

LUISA: *(To All.)* Would any of you like dessert to go? We have tiramisu, a three-berry zabaglione, and a dark chocolate cherry tartufo that's out of this world!

HERA JANE: It's been less than a week! A few hours short of five days! That is not a lot of time!

MARGOT: I'm sorry, I was distracted by the dessert options.

Time is relative. For most people, five days might not be a long time after ending a marriage —

PHILIP: *(Breaking away from Brighton.)* Ending?!?

BRIGHTON: Philip!

MARGOT: Or at least "pausing" a matrimonial union before exploring other romantic options.

HERA JANE: Exploring romantic options?

PHILIP: Oh! Hasn't she told you? About her little experiment?

ANTONIA: Speaking of experimenting —

NICK: I say we pray.

LUISA: Good idea.

(Nick, Luisa, and Antonia lower their heads in prayer. Nick maintains his hold on Brighton, who stands there uncomfortably.)

HERA JANE: Experiment?

PHILIP: You see, Hera Jane . . . May I call you that?

HERA JANE: No.

BRIGHTON: *(To Nick.)* OK, Nick! You win! I will listen to what you have to say!

NICK: Wow, that prayer really worked fast.

BRIGHTON: Not here. Let's go someplace private so we can talk all of this out. OK? I'll get the car.

NICK: I'll go with —

BRIGHTON: No no no. You need to stay here with your grandmother and your um . . .

(Shoots Luisa a look.)

And pray. For us. For me, especially. I'll be right back; I promise. I promise. *(Luisa and Antonia lower their heads in prayer. Brighton exits. Nick relaxes and thanks God in his prayer.)*

MARGOT: Brighton has exactly the right idea. Just as he will drive Nick home and procure an explanation, you and I will go someplace private so that I may proffer one to you, if you'd be so gracious as to listen.

HERA JANE: Sure.

MARGOT: *(Beat.)* And, Philip: You can spend the remainder of your evening explaining to Antonia how you could have led her on so mercilessly, toying with her affections, all to implement an insipid plot to make me jealous.

PHILIP: I didn't deceive her! She was in on it!

ANTONIA: And the Lord be Our Shepherd, Amen. Time to go!

MARGOT: Antonia, is this true?

ANTONIA: I swear, I didn't know his wife was going to be you!

MARGOT: It would have been all right if his wife were a stranger?

ANTONIA: I don't know about "all right." It certainly would have been better.

PHILIP: Margot, can't you see —

MARGOT: I'm sorry, Philip, but I don't have time to deal with any of this right now. Except for dessert:

(*To: Luisa.*)

Miss, two zabagliones to go, please.

HERA JANE: Actually, I'd prefer tiramisu.

MARGOT: And a tiramisu.

(*Luisa exits. SFX: car driving by. Margot waves to the "passing car."*)

MARGOT: Nick, can she give you a ride home or will you need Philip?

NICK: But I'm getting a ride with . . . oh, shit . . .

PHILIP: If you'd like a ride, Nick —

NICK: (*Nervous look to Antonia.*) I'm sure Luisa won't mind. It'll give us a chance to catch up.

(*Luisa enters with a doggy bag, which she hands to Margot.*)

LUISA: (*Hands Margot bag.*) Two zabagliones and a tiramisu.

MARGOT: Thank you.

LUISA: (*To Hera Jane.*) Sorry I brought up . . . you know . . . the Brandy Alexander.

HERA JANE: Don't worry about it. It wasn't meant to be.

LUISA: I hope you fare better with the dessert course.

MARGOT: Hera Jane, shall we? And Philip!

PHILIP: I won't follow you!

MARGOT: Thank you!

(*Margot and Hera Jane leave.*)

LUISA: (*To Philip.*) Thanks for coming to Adagio. I hope you'll all come back soon.

(*To Antonia:*)

See you in church.

ANTONIA: Tomorrow?

LUISA: Soon. Bye!

ANTONIA: Good night, Nicholas.

NICK: Grandma.

(*Antonia and Philip exit.*)

LUISA: Stranded?

NICK: I need to go after him.

LUISA: Do you want to borrow my car?

NICK: I actually need you to go with me. And I know you're at work, but I need you to come now.

LUISA: (*"Of course."*) Sure.

(*Cross Fade to: Antonia's backyard, later that evening. Philip and Antonia continue.*)

ANTONIA: Let's sit out here for a while and breathe in the night air. I'll put on some strong tea. There's nothing like a hot cup of tea on a cool night to help clear the mind.

PHILIP: So we can see how perfectly and completely I've botched things.

ANTONIA: So we can figure out what to do next.

PHILIP: What's left to do? After tonight, I don't think things can right themselves.

ANTONIA: From earth scorched by molten rock do the loveliest flowers grow.

PHILIP: Let me guess . . .

ANTONIA: I'm quoting me again. I'm still working on that one, but I thought it apropos.

PHILIP: Do you have anything in your repertoire about futility, stupidity, and psychosis?

ANTONIA: Philip, I need to ask: How often do you and your wife argue?

PHILIP: Almost never.

ANTONIA: That's why things seem so bad; you don't have anything to compare it to.

PHILIP: (*Laughs.*) Now it's my turn to ask you: Why do you even see a therapist? You're fine.

ANTONIA: At first it was grief. Then it was guilt over what my family expected of me. Now, it's just to . . . keep things in perspective.

PHILIP: So, you've been her patient for . . .

ANTONIA: Twelve years.

PHILIP: Wow.

ANTONIA: Yes. Wow.

PHILIP: I'm sorry.

ANTONIA: I imagine we'll work something out.

PHILIP: I'm not sure. It would appear that we've reached an impasse.

ANTONIA: My husband and I reached many an impasse. Somehow we always managed to find a way to overcome them. We either compromised or we didn't. We both knew how we felt about things, acted on those feelings, stuck to our guns and life went on. Do you love her, Philip?
(*Pause.*)
It won't hurt my feelings if you say yes. It'll only upset me if you lie to me.

PHILIP: It sounds as though you already know the answer.

ANTONIA: So then: What are you going to do about it?
(*Cross Fade to: Brighton alone in his apartment. There is offstage knocking.*)

NICK: (*Offstage.*) Brighton! Brighton, it's me.

BRIGHTON: Please go away.

NICK: *(Offstage.)* Brighton, let me in.

(No response.)

If you don't let me in, I will serenade you. Loudly. With songs written by living composers.

(Brighton rushes and lets Nick in.)

BRIGHTON: You wouldn't dare.

NICK: I'm desperate.

BRIGHTON: It's attractive.

NICK: Really?

BRIGHTON: No.

(Luisa enters.)

BRIGHTON: Oh, this is all I need.

NICK: If you'd let me explain . . .

BRIGHTON: Explain what? Why you have a wife or why you never bothered to mention her?

NICK: I would have told you, but . . . I, uh . . . forgot.

(Silence.)

NICK: Brighton?

BRIGHTON: *(Needing a moment:)* I'm digesting it.

(Pause.)

You . . . forgot?

NICK: Yeah.

BRIGHTON: Mm-hm. Uh, question: WHAT THE FUCK DO YOU MEAN YOU FORGOT?!?

NICK: I don't have time for this! I need to see my grandmother!

BRIGHTON: Oh, yes, the grandmother! It's too bad she didn't get a picture of us together and you didn't get a picture of her with Philip. You could blackmail each other. It'll certainly make Thanksgiving interesting. All those Pinter pauses.

(Acts it out:)

"Grandma, I have something to say. Pause."

(Pauses.)

"Pass the potatoes."

And she could say, "Potatoes? Silence."

(Pause.)

"Sure. Beat."

(Beat.)

"I'll pass the potatoes."

NICK: You don't know what this is like for me, OK! You don't have fundamentalist Christian parents!

BRIGHTON: Oh, don't I?

NICK: Do you?

BRIGHTON: No, but you didn't know that! You took it for granted. Much like I assumed you were . . .

NICK: Not married?

BRIGHTON: Bingo! How can you forget you're married?

NICK: It's not like we ever see each other. Luisa's an actress. She's been on tour.

BRIGHTON: Why isn't she on tour anymore?

LUISA: It was LES MIZ. Tomorrow finally came.

NICK: I really have to go. Luisa will explain. Really, she tells it better than I do.

BRIGHTON: So, this marriage of yours is, what? Folklore?

LUISA: There really is a perfectly logical —

BRIGHTON: I don't have to stay here and listen to this. I'm going out.

(Gets his keys out.)

Lock up when you leave.

(Nick lunges at Brighton and they wrestle over his keys. Nick plants a ridiculously long kiss on Brighton. Brighton relents. Nick grabs the keys and exits. Pause. Brighton notices Luisa is still here. She settles in.)

LUISA: Once upon a time . . .

(Cross Fade to: Hera Jane's house. Margot looks around as Hera Jane prepares two glasses of wine.)

MARGOT: What a lovely home. Did you decorate yourself?

HERA JANE: Yes.

MARGOT: It's very . . . Southwestern.

HERA JANE: I like the Southwest.

MARGOT: *(Pause.)* Look.

HERA JANE: It's OK. I'm sure you didn't mean for your ex-husband to come by.

MARGOT: No.

HERA JANE: And if your friend the critic says he didn't mean for it to happen, either . . . who am I to doubt him.

MARGOT: We weren't really going to see *The Velvet Embrace* were we?

HERA JANE: Oh, God no. I read his review and . . . I agreed with it. He was so smug. I couldn't stop myself. Some wine?

MARGOT: I'd love some. Oh, you've already poured it.

(Margot and Hera Jane sit.)

HERA JANE: Why waste time?

MARGOT: Why indeed.

HERA JANE: A toast. To wasting no more time.

MARGOT: I'll drink to that.

> *(Hera Jane sips her glass. Margot drinks all of hers.)*

HERA JANE: Do you like the music?

MARGOT: It's very nice.

HERA JANE: I was in the music store this morning and I saw this CD: *Classical Music for Lovers*. I thought, "How cheesy." Then I read the back of the case and there are some impressive recordings. And the best part: no Ravel.

MARGOT: Oh? Well, good. The absolute last thing we need right now is . . . Ravel.

HERA JANE: How's the wine?

MARGOT: Wonderful.

HERA JANE: You seem tense.

MARGOT: Tense? Me? No.

HERA JANE: Here.

> *(Sets the wine glasses aside.)*

I'm very good at this.

MARGOT: At what?

HERA JANE: Turn around.

> *(Hera Jane rubs Margot's shoulders. Margot is more perplexed than anything.)*

HERA JANE: I was right. You are tense.

MARGOT: I carry all my stress in my shoulders.

HERA JANE: You need to lighten the load a little. How's that.

MARGOT: Feels great.

HERA JANE: I told you I was good at this.

MARGOT: I just . . . want to take another sip of that delicious wine.

HERA JANE: Sure.

> *(Hera Jane gets Margot's glass and holds it up for her to drink. Margot takes the glass and drinks. Hera Jane takes the glass from Margot's hand, making sure to make contact. Hera Jane kisses Margot. It's a romantic kiss. Margot stiffens. Hera Jane attempts to be more passionate, but Margot pulls away. Hera Jane gives up, frustrated. It's a very awkward moment.)*

MARGOT: I'm really sorry.

HERA JANE: *(Wants to mean it, but doesn't:)* It's all right.

MARGOT: Things are moving a little fast, that's all.

HERA JANE: That's not it.

MARGOT: Really, it is. You're a very attractive woman —

HERA JANE: Do you find me attractive?

MARGOT: I just said so.

HERA JANE: No. You just said that I am attractive. In a general sense. What I'm asking is . . . are you attracted to me?

MARGOT: Well . . . Sure.

HERA JANE: *(Beat.)* OK, Margot, look. I used to believe that every woman, no matter who she was, had a lesbian inside waiting to surface. It was the bond of sisterhood and the innate aesthetic beauty of the female body and the sensitive poetic souls of women that led me to believe this. You know when I changed my mind?

MARGOT: When?

HERA JANE: Thirty seconds ago.

There are plenty of women who have revelations late in life. From there, they make tremendous changes. But these women want to be with other women. And, Margot . . . You're not one of them.

MARGOT: You're probably right.

HERA JANE: Oh, I'm right. If there are two things in this life about which I am certain it's that *The Velvet Embrace* sucked and you're straight.

This whole "experiment" of yours, Margot . . . It's one thing to experiment with your mind. The mind plays tricks on itself, so it's natural for it to want to play tricks on others. But the heart is sacred. It doesn't know good from bad, right from wrong; it doesn't know anything. It only feels. It only wants, and it wants what it wants because it doesn't know better. It's not always right, but at least it's honest. But when your experiment involves another person's heart, that's when you have to check and see if it's really worth it. Ask your heart what it wants. You'll find out if it's right.

MARGOT: Wow. You are one smart lady.

HERA JANE: I'm a Wellesley girl; it comes with the territory. Good luck, Margot.

MARGOT: Thank you. And let me just say, if I were a lesbian, I hope that you'd be the woman to whom I would be attracted.

HERA JANE: You might want to work on your complimentary skills if you want this marriage of yours to succeed. But, I appreciate the thought.

(Cross Fade to: Brighton's apartment. Luisa tells her story to an unenthused Brighton.)

LUISA: *(In medias res.)* And after that summer, we became inseparable. Then, in the *third* grade —

BRIGHTON: Did you get married in the third grade?!?

LUISA: No?

(Pause as he glares at her.)

Oh . . . Sorry. OK then: Fast-forward to the summer between junior and senior year of high school.

BRIGHTON: Thank you.

LUISA: Nicky's father, the local pastor and pillar of the community, realizes his only son has never had a girlfriend. He goes through hell, high water, and countless Daughters of the American Revolution to find him one. We endure no less than six ice cream socials at which only chocolate and vanilla are served because, and I quote "strawberry is for whores." Ultimately, none of the lovely corn-fed young ladies hold the boy's interest, so he invites Nick to come to one of the meetings he holds at church. In these meeting, men go in "doubting their manhood" and emerge as "good Christians." The Pastor says it's "just to observe" — kind of like Take Your Gay Son to Work Day. Naturally, Nicky starts to panic, so I offer to be his girlfriend.

So, one Friday night we stay out really late: until about . . . nine thirty. Can you remember when nine thirty was late? We sneak up onto the porch swing and pretend to shush each other and giggle. We're actually whispering things like "OK, OK, giggle on three. One. Two. Now. Uh-ha-ha-ha-ha! Shhhh!" Finally, we hear someone coming to the door so we, just as we rehearsed, started rubbing noses. Suddenly, Pastor Daldry bursts through the door! We stop rubbing noses and stand up. He looks us over and asks, "What's going on here, Children?" We tell him the truth. "Nuuuthing." The Pastor gets this huge grin on his face, pats his son on the shoulder and from that moment on, Nicky and I are a "couple."

Our parents were so happy! They set the date. They bought the rings. Next thing we knew it was: "I do — I do" — "You may now kiss the bride" — "Everybody do the electric slide" and we were hitched. And that's the story of how I married your boyfriend.

BRIGHTON: I see.

LUISA: Can you guess where they sent us on our honeymoon?

BRIGHTON: I can't imagine.

LUISA: Colonial Williamsburg. Don't ask me why. Anyway, that night, I was sitting in bed watching gymnastics on cable. Nick comes in, after spending about a year in the bathroom, and starts trying to be romantic with me. I start laughing. He's like, "What's so funny?" and I'm like,

"What do you think you're doing?" He says, "Well, it is our wedding night." And I'm like, "Yeah and I'm watching this." And he goes, "Don't you think we should . . . " So I finally come out and say it. "Nick. We're gay." He almost passes out. And I say, "Honestly, Nick. Do you think I'd have married you if we weren't?" And he's like, "You knew?" And I was like, "Hello!"

BRIGHTON: I'm sorry; did you say "Nick . . . we're gay."

LUISA: Nick asked the same question. I thought it was obvious.

BRIGHTON: It's not.

(Beat.)

So, tell me, Mrs. Daldry the First, have you managed to find someone special yourself?

LUISA: There's someone I have my eye on. Unfortunately, every time I get a chance to do something about it, she's seeing someone else.

BRIGHTON: I know the feeling. It sucks.

LUISA: Though, come to think of it, maybe you could help me.

BRIGHTON: Me? Sure.

(Cross Fade to: Antonia's backyard. Nick is heard offstage.)

NICK: Grandma!

ANTONIA: (Enters in a hurry.) I'm out back. In the garden.

(Nick enters.)

NICK: Hi.

ANTONIA: That was quite an evening, wasn't it?

NICK: Quite. Have you . . .

ANTONIA: Discussed it with anybody? Your parents, in particular?

NICK: Have you?

ANTONIA: Come and sit down. Give me a kiss.

(Nick kisses Antonia. They sit together.)

ANTONIA: Do you know how I met Philip?

(Nick shakes his head.)

I'm enrolled in his ethics class. That's right: Your grandmother is a college freshman!

NICK: And you haven't told my parents?

ANTONIA: Are you kidding? They think "matriculating" makes you go blind.

NICK: I know; they warned me. Why is my mother like this?

ANTONIA: I suspect it's her idea of rebellion. You should have seen how angry she got when she dated a musician and we liked him.

NICK: So she traded in a musician for a fascist?

ANTONIA: You shouldn't call your father a fascist.

NICK: He is a fascist.

ANTONIA: I know, dear, but please don't call him that. It reminds me of how badly I raised your mother.

NICK: So, I take it you're not going to squeal.

ANTONIA: Nicky, I was pretending to be on a date with my professor. Can you imagine how they'd react to that?

NICK: They wouldn't know which of us to stone first. Of course, I could probably draw fire away from you with the whole sodomy thing. I'm sorry, was that too much information?

ANTONIA: *(Laughs.)* It's all right. I subscribe to premium cable channels. Don't tell your mother.

NICK: *(Simultaneous; starting on "Don't tell".)* I won't tell Mom.

(Pause.)

Well. It's a pleasure meeting you, Ma'am.

ANTONIA: The pleasure is all mine.

(Takes Nick's hand.)

Tell me. Are you in love?

NICK: Oh, yeah.

ANTONIA: That's wonderful.

NICK: How about you?

ANTONIA: I'm . . . in like.

NICK: Now, now.

ANTONIA: It's more complicated.

NICK: I know the situation. I was asking about you.

ANTONIA: Can you keep a secret? What am I saying; of course you can.

NICK: Are you in love?

ANTONIA: Maybe. A little.

NICK: I'm sorry.

ANTONIA: Yes, well . . . Would you like to come in. I've got ice cream. Strawberry!

NICK: The frozen dairy treat of whores? I wish I could, but I should head back. I left my boyfriend alone with my wife.

ANTONIA: Are you suicidal?

NICK: Quite the opposite.

(Cross Fade to: Nick's place. Brighton waits on the couch. Luisa rushes over.)

LUISA: OK, he's coming, he's coming, he's coming.

(Brighton and Luisa sit together. They hear keys in the door and start rubbing noses. Nick enters and sees them as they stand up quickly.)

LUISA: Oh, my God! It's my husband!

NICK: Very funny.

LUISA: Is everything OK with your grandmother? I mean, she's not going to say anything —

NICK: All is well.

LUISA: *(Beat.)* Thank God. Then my work here is done.

(Kisses Nick good-bye. Throws her arms around Brighton.)

Bye, Brighton. Thank you, thank you, thank you so much!

(Kisses him and exits.)

NICK: What was that all about?

BRIGHTON: She just needed some advice from her new Fairy Godfather. So, your wife tells me she's a lesbian.

NICK: Indeed, she is.

BRIGHTON: And you didn't mention this because . . .

NICK: For starters, I didn't think you'd believe me.

(Holds Brighton.)

But mostly because the thought of your love life being saved by a long monologue from a lesbian was too priceless to pass up.

BRIGHTON: *(Stunned silence.)* You are the worst person in the world.

NICK: It must suck that you're stuck with me.

BRIGHTON: Nick. How do I say this . . .

NICK: What's there to say? We're good, aren't we?

BRIGHTON: Ever since we started seeing each other, I've been questioning you. I have defied you to make me trust you. At any time, I should have been able to say, "Nick. I accept your explanation. I know that from now on, you'll keep me informed about any and all spouses you might have. I trust you."

NICK: Now you know you can.

BRIGHTON: I know I should be able to. But . . . I don't know why I'm like this. Maybe it's because I'm afraid the moment I allow myself to trust you will be the moment I shouldn't. That's the way it always seems to work for me, so . . .

NICK: So . . . you're dumping me?

BRIGHTON: It's for the best.

NICK: But, I love you.

BRIGHTON: How can you say that? We've only known each other for —

NICK: I've known you for almost five years. Ever since I took your class —

BRIGHTON: That's not me. That's . . . a guy who only shines when he stands alone in front of a captive audience. What you're feeling isn't love. It's . . . Stockholm Syndrome.

NICK: Fine. I admit I fell in love with an ideal.

BRIGHTON: An ideal to which I could not possibly measure up.

NICK: No one could measure up to that —

BRIGHTON: I'm sorry: "Up to which I could not possibly measure."

NICK: You have no idea what a relief it was to discover how absolutely, totally, insanely flawed you are.

BRIGHTON: *(Pause.)* Thank you?

NICK: I know we're just getting to know each other.

BRIGHTON: I know you well enough.

> *(Pause.)*
>
> You are a young, kind, passionate, talented, lovely young man with a very bright future. In short, you are the opposite of me.

NICK: Aren't opposites supposed to attract?

BRIGHTON: Only in the movies. Besides: You deserve better.

NICK: Maybe I don't want better. Maybe I want you.

BRIGHTON: In some way, that is the nicest thing anyone has ever said to me.

NICK: How about you? How do you . . . feel about me?

BRIGHTON: How do you think I feel about you, Nick?

NICK: I want to hear it.

BRIGHTON: I . . . Oh, God.

> *(Brighton exits, leaving Nick alone.)*
>
> *(Cross Fade to: Antonia greeting Margot in the garden.)*

MARGOT: I appreciate your calling me.

ANTONIA: I thought it important that we clear some things up right away. Like I said before, I had no idea you and Philip —

MARGOT: I believe that. What I can't bring myself to understand is why you went along with it.

ANTONIA: Because sometimes imitation isn't the highest form of flattery. Sometimes, it's envy . . . covetousness. To have someone want what you have. I wanted his wife, whoever she was, to wish she was me, in my shoes, with the man I was with. Perhaps it's petty and wrong, but it was for a good cause.

MARGOT: What good could have possibly come of this?

ANTONIA: Saving your marriage, obviously.

MARGOT: I'm going to refer you to a new therapist, now that we have this . . . conflict of interest.

ANTONIA: So, you do still have feelings for Philip.

MARGOT: I beg your pardon.

ANTONIA: If you didn't feel something for him, you wouldn't need to refer me, would you?

MARGOT: It has nothing to do with emotions.

ANTONIA: Shouldn't it?

MARGOT: I'm sorry things turned out this way. I hope you enjoyed the symphony.

ANTONIA: We did.

MARGOT: I'm glad.

ANTONIA: It was very romantic.

MARGOT: Good for you.

ANTONIA: In fact, Philip was very romantic himself.

MARGOT: Good for him.

ANTONIA: In fact, it had been so long since I had been romanced, I'd forgotten that "romance" could be a verb. As much as I enjoyed it, I'm sad to admit that all the effort, the romance, the spectacle; none of it was for me.

MARGOT: I see.

ANTONIA: Good for you. Now, how does it make you feel?

MARGOT: Thank you, Antonia. You've given me a lot to consider.

(Margot exits. As Antonia watches her go, Philip enters behind her.)

ANTONIA: Did you get what you needed?

PHILIP: I think so.

ANTONIA: I'm glad.

PHILIP: You didn't have to do this for me.

ANTONIA: Are you kidding? I enjoyed our little caper. And look at all I got out of it. I've witnessed the births of new concertos and symphonies. I suddenly have a great friend and ally in a grandson I realize I barely knew. It really has been a great week.

PHILIP: (Beat.) Your husband was a very lucky man.

ANTONIA: I always thought so.

(Philip gives Antonia an appreciative kiss. Margot enters talking.)

MARGOT: When you're spying on someone, you should really wait several more minutes after they leave the scene before standing under a porch light!

PHILIP: This isn't what it looks like!

MARGOT: I know exactly what it is!

PHILIP: I don't think you do!

MARGOT: You got Antonia to lure me here so you could spy on our conversation!

PHILIP: I was wrong. You hit the nail right on the head.

MARGOT: How could you do this?

ANTONIA: I'll just go inside and leave you two to talk this out. If you need anything, I'll be right inside that window.

(Antonia exits. Margot and Philip face off. If possible, Antonia peers out a "window" to observe them.)

MARGOT: You're supposed to know me, Philip!

PHILIP: How do you expect me to know what you need from me, when you not only refuse to tell me, but when your behavior is unrecognizable as your own.

MARGOT: What behavior? All I'm doing is searching for someone or something that can provide me with a little happiness.

PHILIP: Now that I don't?

MARGOT: I never said that.

PHILIP: Adagio! Why did you have to take her to Adagio?

MARGOT: I didn't. She invited me!

PHILIP: You couldn't have refused? It didn't occur to you to say, "I'd rather not go there. You see, that's where my husband proposed to me. In fact, every five years, we'd celebrate our anniversaries there."

MARGOT: Of course it occurred to me.

PHILIP: Then why didn't —

MARGOT: Because, I wanted to go! Because it's romantic and gorgeous and I love it and I accepted a rare invitation to go there when it wasn't routine.

PHILIP: Our anniversaries are not routine.

MARGOT: Yes, Philip, they are.

PHILIP: Why, because they happen every year at the same time? That's what makes them anniversaries, Margot!

MARGOT: And where do you get off bitching about my going on a date to Adagio after what you did?

PHILIP: What in God's name did I do?

MARGOT: How could you not know?

PHILIP: I can't read your mind, Margot. If something's offending you, you actually do have to tell me what it is. But, no! Instead of giving me a straight answer, I'm left looking for clues, hoping that some sort of sign might fall out of the heavens and make things clear and that's just not going to happen!

(Brighton bursts in.)

BRIGHTON: Margot! Philip! It is you! I saw you from the street! What is this place? It's like some homespun magical oasis of calm. I hate that.

Oh, God, it's a miracle I found you! This is the worst . . . The most horrible . . . I mean, it's . . . It's over! He said he . . . And I-I-I . . . I . . .
walked out! Just like — I mean, I swore I would never . . . to anyone the
way they did — and — and now . . . me . . . It's like I've become every
man I swore I'd never forgive. And why?! Oh, you'll love this; it's a real
ass-kicker! Because . . . because . . . it didn't make sense! It didn't make
sense. Someone I could . . . and trust comes into my life and . . . tells
me . . . he-he-he . . . and I . . . cast it aside. Because it didn't make
sense . . . Look at who I'm talking to . . . about casting aside the people
we . . . Honestly, what the hell is wrong with you two? I-I . . . I've got
to . . . I'll see you.

(Brighton exits. Pause.)

PHILIP: I'd call that a sign.

MARGOT: It was more than that. It was a wake-up call.

PHILIP: You think so?

(Takes her uncomfortably in his arms.)

Oh, thank God.

MARGOT: What are you doing?

PHILIP: You're finally coming to your senses about what you've done.

MARGOT: What I've done? You're saying it's my fault Brighton is a mess?

PHILIP: Brighton? Who was talking about Brighton?

MARGOT: Brighton was, for one.

PHILIP: Sure, at the beginning.

MARGOT: I was talking about him, for another.

PHILIP: But in the end, he was talking about you.

MARGOT: During which part of that did the subject become "me"?

PHILIP: The part heavy with disdain, of course.

MARGOT: That part wasn't about me. That was about "us."

PHILIP: Us?

MARGOT: Yes. Us! Both of us. You and me.

PHILIP: *(Questioning the grammar.)* Not "you and I"?

MARGOT: I'm pretty sure "you and me" is right.

PHILIP: So, you're saying his disdain was evidence of some mutual culpability
on both our parts?

MARGOT: Exactly!

PHILIP: Hm. I liked this better when it was just about Brighton.

MARGOT: You are impossible!

PHILIP: What did I say this time?

(Margot storms off. Philip watches her go. Antonia enters.)

PHILIP: After all that, she still hasn't come to her senses!

ANTONIA: Philip, I think we should sit down and talk about this.

PHILIP: But I have to go after her!

ANTONIA: No, you don't.

PHILIP: But if I don't —

ANTONIA: Give her a chance to realize you're not there. Besides, we have to prepare for tomorrow.

PHILIP: That's right. I almost forgot. Lead the way.

(Antonia leads Philip off.)

(Cross Fade to: Brighton in his car. He is driving, clearly upset. He turns on the radio. The same Celine Dion ballad blares loudly!)

BRIGHTON: Aw, fuck!

(Brighton reaches to change the station, but he doesn't have the energy for it and waves his hand at the radio dismissively and continues to drive. He starts listening to the words of the song and rolls his eyes. Then a verse reflecting his current situation plays. He listens more intently. As the song plays, his eyes begin to tear up, the lip begins to quiver, and he gets choked up. He pulls over and starts to bawl.)

(Cross Fade to: the Adagio Bar. Hera Jane sits quietly with a cocktail. Luisa enters in mufti; sees Hera Jane, takes a moment to gather confidence and approaches.)

LUISA: How was the dessert course?

HERA JANE: Hm? Ah, yes. In the freezer. Untouched.

LUISA: Literally or metaphorically.

HERA JANE: Yes.

LUISA: I'm so sorry.

HERA JANE: Me, too.

LUISA: I could have told you.

HERA JANE: Really? How?

LUISA: You are a Bloody-Mary person: strong, spicy and natural. That doesn't go with the sweet and creamy Brandy Alexander.

HERA JANE: How about with a Gin and Tonic?

LUISA: There was hope until the two zabagliones. Bubbles and pine on one side and custard with sweet wine on the other? Strangely duplicitous.

HERA JANE: And what does the tiramisu say about me?

LUISA: Oh please! Cheese, espresso, cocoa and cookies? The things that make life worth living!

HERA JANE: And your husband?

LUISA: I just got done straightening things out between him and his boyfriend.

HERA JANE: He's an attractive young fellow. What does he see in . . . that man?

LUISA: Believe it or not, there's a lot of good to find there. In fact, if it weren't for Brighton, I might not have the nerve to do this.

(Writes her number down on a matchbook.)

This is my phone number.

HERA JANE: I'll use it.

LUISA: I look forward to that.

HERA JANE: What are you doing now?

LUISA: Why do you ask?

HERA JANE: I don't like to waste time.

LUISA: Then, I'd better warn you: I don't like to move too fast.

HERA JANE: Oh, I prefer taking it slow.

LUISA: All right, then. Slow it is.

HERA JANE: Starting now?

LUISA: Sure.

(Cross Fade to: Nick's. Pounding on the door. Nick comes to answer it.)

NICK: Who is it?

BRIGHTON: (Offstage.) I'm an idiot. Open the door.

(Nick lets Brighton in.)

NICK: OK, so you know the password.

BRIGHTON: First of all, we need to set some ground rules.

NICK: Oh, do we?

BRIGHTON: In the future, when you borrow my car, do not leave the radio set to some easy-listening station with the volume turned all the way up. That song was playing again and I hate that song and I hate that singer and now, because of her, I really hate Quebec. There's enough hate in the world without you leaving my radio on.

NICK: I seem to be missing something. Didn't we just break up?

BRIGHTON: Can't you see I'm in denial about that?

NICK: Well, I'm not.

BRIGHTON: Why not? Have you met someone in the past half hour?

NICK: Maybe. Maybe I had a quickie with the cable guy or — or the mailman or the plumber.

BRIGHTON: Don't be ridiculous. Where are you going to find any of those people at this hour? Oh. By the way, the answer to your question: yes.

NICK: I don't recall asking any yes/no questions.

BRIGHTON: Oh, for God's sake! Yes, I love you, you fucking idiot.

NICK: That's what I wanted to hear.

BRIGHTON: Yeah, well, I hope you're happy now.

NICK: You're right about one thing. We have to establish ground rules.

BRIGHTON: Such as?

NICK: I would strongly prefer it, irrational trust issues or not, that you not leave me again.

BRIGHTON: I think that's doable.

NICK: Good.

BRIGHTON: After all, I could end up being trapped in the car with that song again. I think I'd rather face life with you.

NICK: You know, now that it's played such an important role in our relationship —

BRIGHTON: Absolutely not! That is not nor will it ever be "our song."

NICK: We don't have another one.

BRIGHTON: We'll find another one. Honestly, you are not a well man. And this is coming from me!

NICK: Shut up.

(Nick embraces Brighton. They don't let go.)

BRIGHTON: So, does this mean we're back together?

(Nick smacks Brighton upside the head. The embrace still holds.)

I'll take that as a yes.

(Cross Fade to:)

FALL CARNIVAL

*Setting: A picnic grove with grill, table, and cooler. No real fire is necessary.
At Rise: Philip puts charms on the bracelet as Margot enters.*

MARGOT: I was hoping you'd be here.

(Philip acknowledges her but does not speak.)

MARGOT: I won't take too much of your time. I just didn't want things to end the way they did last night. You see, after I drove off, I thought I saw your headlights following me. So, I pulled over, ready to confront you. And the car passed me and, I discovered: It wasn't you. And then . . . I got really angry because you didn't follow me. What sense —

(Philip holds up the bracelet.)

MARGOT: Is that my bracelet? I've been looking all over for that.

(Margot reaches for it, but Philip holds onto it and motions for her to sit.)

MARGOT: OK . . .

(Sits next to Philip who hands her the bracelet. She looks through it and discovers . . .)

I see you've been busy. Let's see . . . Interlocking symbols of femininity: Lesbianism, right? And . . . what the hell is this? Big-eyed rodents: infestation? You gave me an infestation charm? Why does this even exist?

(He hands her a magnifying glass.)

You always carry one of these?

(She takes it and looks at the charm through it. She laughs.)

Ah. Three blind mice. Me, you, and Brighton?

(He nods assent.)

And what's this? Sheet music?

(Philip hands Margot an envelope. She opens it.)

The symphony. You renewed our subscription?

(He nods assent.)

It would be perfect if you got our old seats, too.

(He points.)

Oh, my God, you did? After all this time they were still available?

(He gives her a look.)

You're right. They are terrible seats. Most people would think so anyway. My, but you've been busy.

(Philip shrugs.)

This is very nice of you, really it is. But we can't, Philip. Not after this past week. Certainly not after last night.

PHILIP: Yes, we can.

MARGOT: What was up with the silent treatment?

PHILIP: Talking has been getting me into too much trouble lately and, besides, I wanted to show you I could listen.

MARGOT: Fair enough. It's still a little chilly out. Do you have any —

(Philip hands her a cup of coffee.)

I see you already poured it.

PHILIP: Remember before when I was quiet? It's your turn now.

MARGOT: *(Beat.)* OK.

PHILIP: Margot. I've come to realize that there are aspects of my life, I've left unexplored; aspects that, by their nature, I cannot explore . . . without you.

MARGOT: Without me?

PHILIP: I still have the floor. As I was saying, I've been doing some thinking —

MARGOT: Uh-oh.

PHILIP: Excuse me?

MARGOT: My apologies. Go on.

PHILIP: No, what did you mean by "uh-oh"? I tell you I've been thinking . . . and you say —

MARGOT: I was not railing against anyone's right to think. I was merely reacting to how you are, at times, carried away by your thoughts, which lead to leaps of logic that are — for lack of a truly appropriate existing word — Evel Knievel . . . lian. You don't have to, as the youth might say, "go all Ayn Rand on me."

PHILIP: I do not get carried away —

MARGOT: Calling imaginary bluffs, crashing dates, matrimonial espionage. But, let's not discuss this right now. You have the floor.

PHILIP: Yes, I was saying. I've been doing some thinking and realized, not just from this thinking, but also from interacting with people who possess similar unexplored alcoves in their experience, that our marital potential has largely remained untapped. I wish to tap that potential.

MARGOT: Meaning?

PHILIP: I want you to come home. I want our marriage back.

MARGOT: Do you really think we can?

PHILIP: Absolutely not.

MARGOT: OK, now you're sending a genuinely mixed message.

PHILIP: I don't want our marriage back the way it was. It wasn't working that way. Only, I didn't know that. And you couldn't wait for me to figure it out. So, you left.

MARGOT: That's not why I left. Well, yes it was, but I didn't know that at the time. I really thought I was embarking on a journey to explore my untapped feminine potential. Fortunately, I found someone on that journey to help me realize how . . .

PHILIP: Delusional?

MARGOT: I was about to say "misguided."

PHILIP: Tomato-tomahto.

MARGOT: I learned that what I wanted was you. Of course, by that point you had become a raving jackass. Now, I realize, it's apparently the raving jackass that I've missed the most.

PHILIP: Here I am.

MARGOT: Indeed. Here you are.

PHILIP: I took you for granted and I am sorry. I will never do that again and do you know why?

MARGOT: Because you've learned to be sensitive and understand my feelings without my having to indulge you with an overt explanation?

PHILIP: No. Because you are going to indulge me with overt explanations instead of assuming I can take a hint or read your mind.

MARGOT: And in exchange, I get what?

PHILIP: I will then be appropriately attentive. Even if it involves spontaneity.

MARGOT: Are you sure you can handle being spontaneous?

PHILIP: I didn't do too badly with the charms.

MARGOT: No, you didn't.

PHILIP: Well, Margot . . .

MARGOT: What do you think we should do?

PHILIP: I'm tired of thinking. Thinking . . . doesn't really work for us.

MARGOT: I wish I could disagree.

PHILIP: A wisc person once said, "From earth scorched by molten rock, the loveliest flowers can grow."

MARGOT: That's nice. I'll bet that same wise person said, "It had been so long since I had been romanced, I'd forgotten that 'romance' could be a verb."

PHILIP: You guessed it.

MARGOT: When I was talking to her on the porch, she was quite forceful with me; almost bitchy. As your wife, it was pissing me off, but as her therapist, I must admit I was very proud.

PHILIP: Answer me this and I know it's corny. What does your heart want?

MARGOT: My heart wants . . . This is corny. My heart wants . . . music.

PHILIP: Check. Bad seats and all.

MARGOT: It wants . . . romance. The verb.

PHILIP: Check. What else?

MARGOT: It wants . . . It just wants us to be happy.

PHILIP: That's what Aristotle would say.

MARGOT: For once, he and I agree. What does yours want?

PHILIP: Guess.

MARGOT: Let's see. If thoughts and words keep getting us into trouble, what's left?

PHILIP: How about this.

(Kisses her, soft and long.)

Does that work for you?

MARGOT: *(Pause.)* Sure.

(Philip and Margot kiss passionately, laying down on top of the picnic table. As they make out, Brighton and Nick enter with a cooler. They see the necking couple and shush each other and an entering Antonia, Luisa, and Hera Jane. They start to unpack the cooler around Philip and Margot who continue kissing, oblivious.)

END OF PLAY

LIVING ROOM IN AFRICA

Bathsheba Doran

PLAYWRIGHT'S BIOGRAPHY

Bathsheba Doran's plays include *Nest* (Signature Theater, D.C.), *Living Room in Africa* (Off-Broadway, Edge Theater, Susan Smith Blackburn Award Finalist), *2 Soldiers* (various, published), *The Parents' Evening* (Cherry Lane), *Until Morning* (BBC Radio 4), and adaptations of *Great Expectations* (Off-Broadway with Kathleen Chalfant at the Lucille Lortel), Maeterlinck's *The Blind* (Classic Stage Company), and *Peer Gynt* (dir. Andre Serban).

Doran was born in the UK, but she moved permanently to the States on a Fulbright scholarship in 2000. She is the recipient of three Lecomte du Nouy Lincoln Center playwriting awards, and her work has been developed by MTC, NYTW, the O'Neill Playwrights Center, the McCarter Theatre, Lincoln Center, and Sundance among others. She is a former playwriting fellow of Juilliard, and she received her M.F.A. from Columbia University. She has worked as a comedy writer for VH1 (*Best Week Ever*) and BBC TV (including *Smack the Pony*).

She is currently under commission from Atlantic Theater in New York, and South Coast Repertory in California.

ORIGINAL PRODUCTION

Living Room in Africa was produced by Gloucester Stage Company at Gloucester Stage in 2005. Production information is as follows:

MARIE	Polly Lee
NSUGO	Jackie Davis
MARK	Richard Arum
EDWARD	Nathaniel McIntyre
ANTHONY	Billy Eugene Jones
MICHAEL LEE	Sean McGuirk

Set Design	Jenna McFarland
Costume Design	Kristen Glans
Lighting Design	Scott Pinkney
Sound Design	Matt Griffin
Production Stage Manager	Adele Nadine Traub
Directed by	Danny Goldstein

Living Room in Africa was produced Off-Broadway by Edge Theater at The Beckett Theater at Theater Row in 2006. Production information is as follows:

MARIE	Ana Reeder

```
NSUGO  . . . . . . . . . . . . . . . . . . . . . . . . . . Marsha Stephanie Blake
MARK  . . . . . . . . . . . . . . . . . . . . . . . . . . . . . . Michael Chernus
EDWARD  . . . . . . . . . . . . . . . . . . . . . . . . . . . . . Rob Campbell
ANTHONY  . . . . . . . . . . . . . . . . . . . . . . . . . . . Maduka Steady
MICHAEL LEE  . . . . . . . . . . . . . . . . . . . . . . . . . . . . Guy Boyd

Set Design  . . . . . . . . . . . . . . . . . . . . . . . . . . . . David Korins
Costume Design  . . . . . . . . . . . . . . . . . . . . . . . . .Jenny Mannis
Lighting Design  . . . . . . . . . . . . . . . . . . . . . . . . Matt Richards
Sound  . . . . . . . . . . . . . . . . . . . . . . . . . . . . . . . . . . . Eric Shim
Original Music  . . . . . . . . . . . . . . . . . . . . . . . Michael Friedman
Production Stage Manager  . . . . . . . . . . . . . . . . . . . . Jeff Meyers
Directed by  . . . . . . . . . . . . . . . . . . . . . . . . . . . Carolyn Cantor
```

AUTHOR'S NOTE

The script produced Off-Broadway was a slightly edited version of what follows, and it is available upon request. *Living Room in Africa* was developed with the Juilliard School and the O'Neill Playwrights Conference.

For Lucy

When tremendous changes are involved no one can be blamed for looking to his own intent. We consider that we are worthy of our power.

Thucydides, *A History of the Peloponnesian War*

The key-note is to be: the prolific growth of our intellectual life, in literature, art, etc. — and in contrast to this: The whole of mankind has gone astray.

Ibsen, *Notes and Fragments*

CHARACTERS

MARIE: late twenties
EDWARD: late twenties
MARK: mid-twenties
ANTHONY: mid-twenties
NSUGO: late twenties
MICHAEL LEE: early sixties

PLACE

A living room in Africa

TIME

The present

LIVING ROOM IN AFRICA

ACT ONE, SCENE 1

A living room in Africa. Boxes waiting to be unpacked. We're in a large some-what dilapidated house. On one wall, a faint outline where a zebra skin used to hang. Various pieces of contemporary Western art lean against the walls in-congruous in their surroundings. A winding staircase leads to the second floor. The room is still for a moment. Mark and Marie enter.

MARIE: Do you like the house?

MARK: Yes it's very . . . lots of wicker.

MARIE: I like it. The city, where the gallery is going to be, that's about an hour's drive away. We'll go there for dinner, I thought. Maybe tomorrow. And Edward will want to show you the site and everything.

MARK: The city's an hour's drive?

MARIE: Yes but there's a local village. That's only about a twenty-minute walk.

MARK: What do you do there?

MARIE: It's a sort of . . . a permanent market. You can get a cup of coffee. And now there's a swimming pool.

MARK: They have a pool?

MARIE: As of today. Edward had it built. Or dug, I suppose. For the local chil-dren.

MARK: What's wrong with the river?

MARIE: Mark!

MARK: What? I thought everybody swam in the river.

MARIE: They do. It's polluted. Hence the swimming pool.

MARK: Polluted with what?

MARIE: A disease.

MARK: Polluted is from something unnatural. Like traffic.

MARIE: It's something to do with rats.

MARK: Weil's disease. It's a parasite.

MARIE: I don't know. It's very dangerous. We have been informed by everyone not to swim in the river. But the children still swim in it. Or some of them. Because they won't listen.

Edward thought a pool would distract them. Although of course it can't fit as many of them in.

MARK: They have the same problem in England. Remember the summer Mum and Dad wouldn't let us swim in the river in Oxford?

MARIE: Oh yes. Well it's that then. Here.

MARK: So where's Edward?

MARIE: At the swimming pool. Today is the opening ceremony. He's giving a speech. They're naming it after him. "The Edward Lawrence Swimming Pool."

MARK: He didn't want to put your name on it?

MARIE: We're not married.

(A beat.)

MARK: Could I have a drink?

MARIE: Oh. Oh I'm sorry. What would you like?

MARK: Do you have any beer?

MARIE: We have gin. Edward thought it would be appropriate to drink gin in Africa. Like the colonialists of old.

(She makes him a gin and tonic. Everything she needs is on a subtle and convenient drinks trolley, including ice.)

MARIE: I can't believe you're here.

MARK: I can't believe you're here.

MARIE: I know. It's so far away.

(She hands him his drink, and he takes a long sip.)

MARK: That's good.

MARIE: Is it? Good. Edward's got in the habit of having one every evening when he gets home from work.

MARK: It's really hot.

MARIE: So, how are you? Is everything well?

MARK: Yes. Yes, everything's . . . well.

How are you?

MARIE: I'm happy.

MARK: Good. You look well.

MARIE: I am. I really . . . Mark, I really think I've found my rhythm. And it's much slower than I thought it was.

MARK: Well it couldn't have been faster.

MARIE: You should try one of these.

(She hands him a red reed, from a neat wooden box.)

MARIE: The natives chew them. Local culture.

(She laughs slightly.)

I'll go and stir the soup. It's cold soup you'll be relieved to know. Of mango.

(She exits.)

MARK: You're cooking?

(Mark laughs slightly, then stands up and walks around the room a little. He picks up a few pieces of African bric-a-brac.)

(Outside, there is a scream. Then some voices speaking, indistinguishable. Then nothing.)

MARK: Marie?

(A young black woman enters from upstairs of the house.)

MARK: Hello. Hi.

(She walks straight past Mark and into another room. A moment later Marie comes back in.)

MARK: Who was that woman?

MARIE: That? That was Nsugo.

MARK: And she is . . . ?

MARIE: She helps.

MARK: She's the help?

MARIE: Yes, she's the help.

MARK: You've enslaved the natives?

MARIE: (Sharply.) She's not a slave, Mark, is she? She's being paid. A lot.

MARK: How much?

MARIE: I'm not telling you.

MARK: (Winding her up.) Just tell me how much.

MARIE: She came with the house.

It's just because she's black. Everyone's black here. What am I supposed to do? And Edward wanted it. Alright? I hate it.

She's teaching me to cook, actually.

MARK: Since when have you been interested in cooking?

MARIE: Since now. I told you. I'm changing.

So how is everyone?

MARK: Fine. I bumped into your friend Pete. He said to tell you "hello."

MARIE: Is that it?

MARK: Yes.

MARIE: Well say "hello" back, I suppose. Or not. I don't know. If Marie says "hello'" in Africa, does anybody hear?

MARK: He read one of your poems in the paper.

MARIE: Which poem?

MARK: In *The Times*.

MARIE: Oh that. That was a while ago.

MARK: What are you working on now?

MARIE: I don't really want to talk about work.

MARK: Alright.

MARIE: I'll take you on a tour tomorrow. It's unbelievable.

MARK: What is?

MARIE: The poverty.

MARK: Not much point in showing it to me then, is there? If it's unbelievable.

MARIE: No. I suppose not.

There's lots of other things to do.

MARK: Like what?

MARIE: You can hand-feed giraffes, about half an hour from here. I thought we'd do that. And there's a place to watch . . . hippos bathe. I thought we could do that. And there's a lake a couple of hours away. I can't remember what it's called, but it's supposed to be beautiful. There are . . . flamingoes.

MARK: That sounds good. The flamingoes.

You should call Pete.

MARIE: Why?

MARK: Because he used to be a friend of yours. I don't think you should cut yourself off so much.

MARIE: The phone's expensive.

MARK: Can't Edward pay?

MARIE: I like to keep things separate.

MARK: You really chew that stuff. Often?

MARIE: Yes, why?

MARK: Your teeth have gone slightly red.

MARIE: Really? Have they? I'll have to clean them.

Are you tired? You must be tired.

MARK: No. I feel slightly dirty. I think I should wash.

MARIE: There's a shower, upstairs. They put it in specially.

MARK: Congratulations.

MARIE: Thanks, I feel good about it. Edward wants to try and install air-conditioning although I don't think the wiring here can take it.

Actually I don't know anything about it but nobody else thinks the wiring here can take it. There'd be a fire.

MARK: Are you planning to do a lot of home improvements?

MARIE: Obviously, I'm not. Edward is. He's going to be investigating air-conditioning. I'm supposed to be sourcing rugs.

MARK: How long do you think you'll be staying? About?

MARIE: I don't know. A year, two years. About. I do like it here.

I'll still be coming back to visit. Just like I did from New York. And Germany.

MARK: This is a lot more inconvenient that flying to New York. Also . . .

MARIE: Also what?

MARK: I'm getting married.

> *(A beat.)*

MARIE: To who?

MARK: To a girl.

MARIE: Oh.

MARK: You haven't met her.

MARIE: What's her name?

MARK: It's Lilly.

MARIE: That's wonderful. When did you meet her?

MARK: I've been with her for about eight months.

MARIE: Quick.

MARK: I . . . really . . . It turns out, you just know. When you've met the right person. I've wasted rather a lot of time.

MARIE: You've never mentioned her.

MARK: I have actually.

I really want you to meet her.

MARIE: I will meet her.

MARK: When?

MARIE: At Christmas.

MARK: Oh come on, I'm getting married. I'm getting married!

MARIE: I've only been here a month . . . I can't just fly back because you want me to meet your girlfriend. Your fiancée.

MARK: Why not?

MARIE: You want me to fly back for dinner?

MARK: I just flew here.

MARIE: Do you know, I think we've got some champagne? Edward actually brought it over from New York. He's so strange. He brought some champagne, and all the tea we had. Isn't that strange? *(A beat.)*

> Mark. . . Don't be angry. We'll both fly over for the wedding. Of course. I can't wait to meet her. What's she like?

> This is wonderful. *(A beat.)*

> What color hair does she have?

MARK: Blonde. It's blonde.

MARIE: What does she do?

MARK: She's a doctor.

> *(A beat.)*

> Mum and Dad love her.

MARIE: Why didn't you introduce me to her last time I was in London?

MARK: She was away that weekend.

MARIE: It wasn't a weekend.

MARK: I'm going to have children.

MARIE: Really? How many?

MARK: Four. I've decided. You're not going to know them.

MARIE: I will know them. I can visit. And they can visit. Imagine what a wonderful time they'd have here. Imagine the photographs. They could ride elephants.

MARK: No one is going to visit you here.

MARIE: What do you mean no one is going to visit me here?

MARK: This country is dying, isn't it? I'm sure anyone who can is trying to move away.

MARIE: Not everyone's dead.

MARK: You're not really staying here . . .

MARIE: I'm writing.

MARK: You could write in England.

MARIE: I don't want to live in London again.

MARK: Mum and Dad said you turned down a teaching fellowship there.

MARIE: Edward got this opportunity.

MARK: What about your career?

MARIE: Poets don't have careers.

MARK: The best career a poet can hope for is to *teach.*
    (A beat.)

MARIE: I do have a life, Mark. I'm sorry if you don't like it, but I'm not planning to change it. For you.

MARK: Because of Edward?

MARIE: Partly.

MARK: It's ridiculous.

MARIE: What is?

MARK: You just showed me the house, you sleep in separate bedrooms!

MARIE: Not everyone wants what you want, Mark.

MARK: I assumed . . . We all assumed that you two must be . . . by now . . .

MARIE: Well we're not.

MARK: Why?

MARIE: It may not be the way everyone else is, but I'm not the way everyone else is.

    You may not like it here but I do.

MARK: Really? In this godforsaken village.

MARIE: It's not forsaken.

MARK: There's nothing here!

MARIE: They think the gallery is going to make a big difference.

MARK: Only to people looking for an interesting article in the Sunday papers.

MARIE: To the whole area. A lot of people are getting work through it.

MARK: Edward! And I'd love to know how much he's being paid. Not that he even needs paying. How much did he make from selling that last piece?

MARIE: He's in charge of about twenty men, actually. He's overseeing the construction. They are all being paid. Anyway, what have you suddenly got against Edward?

MARK: I don't think he . . . I don't think he takes care of you.

(A beat.)

MARIE: He does, Mark. Oh, he does. We both take care of each other.

MARK: Don't you want to be with someone who . . .

MARIE: I can bear Edward. I can't bear most people.

(A beat.)

MARK: Alright.

I'll take that shower.

MARIE: You're not angry are you?

MARK: No.

MARIE: Good. Because you just got here.

(Mark exits. Marie makes herself a drink. Nsugo enters with plates.)

MARIE: We already had a fight.

Will you taste the soup?

NSUGO: Yes.

(Nsugo exits with the plates into the dining room.)

MARIE: I think it's good. Tomorrow I'll try and make it without you helping. Then you can taste it and give me a mark out of ten.

(Nsugo re-enters, and straightens up the room.)

NSUGO: Alright.

MARIE: We're still going to have our cooking lessons while Mark's here. He can amuse himself for an hour. And I'm still going to write. I don't have to stop everything just because he's arrived, do I? Or do I?

NSUGO: He is coming a long way to see you.

MARIE: Yes. But I can't spend every second with him because I'll kill him by the middle of the week. That's how it is with brothers, isn't it? You love them so much in theory.

Do you have a brother?

NSUGO: One brother.

MARIE: Does he live around here?

NSUGO: He is living in Ghana. It is expensive to go there.

MARIE: Yes. Do you get along well?

NSUGO: I do not know my brother so much now. He is married in Ghana. I do not know the wife.

MARIE: My brother is getting married too.

(Nsugo is about to exit.)

MARIE: Nsugo? How do you manage it all? Michael Lee told us you have four children. Would you like to bring them here, sometimes? So you can be near them?

How old are they?

NSUGO: One is eight and one is nine.

MARIE: What about the others?

NSUGO: The others are dead now.

MARIE: What? What did they die of?

NSUGO: There is sickness.

MARIE: Yes.

Are you well?

NSUGO: I am well.

MARIE: Good.

(Edward enters.)

EDWARD: Hello!

NSUGO: I can finish with the table.

(She exits.)

EDWARD: How was your day?

MARIE: I wrote. There's a place in the village. I got a lot of stares.

EDWARD: What place?

MARIE: With the wooden tables. It looks rather like a shack.

EDWARD: Oh there. It is a shack.

MARIE: It's a cafe. And they're very nice. I had papaya juice and coffee. And a chapatti.

(Edward makes himself a gin.)

EDWARD: What's the coffee like?

MARIE: Strong.

EDWARD: When are you going to show me what you're working on?

MARIE: Not yet.

EDWARD: Do you want to talk it through?

MARIE: No.

EDWARD: So where's Mark?

MARIE: Upstairs. Showering.

EDWARD: How is it seeing him?

MARIE: He wants me to go home.

EDWARD: He always says that. He misses you. This tonic is rather flat.

MARIE: And he thinks it's odd that we have a black cook.

EDWARD: I know, but what are we supposed to do? Everyone here's black.

MARIE: I know.

EDWARD: She needs the money. It's a good thing. We don't need her. I miss cooking.

MARIE: I know.

EDWARD: I mean it. We come here, we've got all of this money as far as they're concerned, she asks us for a job, she used to work here . . . I mean for god's sake, what were we supposed to do? She's got four children.

MARIE: Two.

EDWARD: No, four.

MARIE: No, when Michael Lee was here she had four children. Now she has two. She just told me.

EDWARD: What did they die of?

MARIE: She wasn't specific.

EDWARD: We should find out.

MARIE: Why?

EDWARD: Well because . . . We ought to know.

MARIE: She's fine. I asked.

EDWARD: I'm worried now.

Do you think we should ask her to get a doctor's certificate?

MARIE: No I don't.

EDWARD: What should we do?

MARIE: She said she's fine.

EDWARD: Because she needs this job.

MARIE: Yes she does.

What would happen if we gave her whatever you'd pay a maid in New York? She'd be able to up and go to Spain after a couple of weeks. Get a nice suntan.

Sorry. I don't know why I said that.

(A beat.)

EDWARD: Tomorrow I thought we could eat at that place that's started up by the gallery. You see. It's already happening. Regeneration. Before we've even opened.

MARIE: Alright. And I thought we might hand-feed giraffes.

EDWARD: How many times have we hand-fed giraffes since we moved here?

MARIE: Three.

EDWARD: Right.

MARIE: And their tongues are grey.

EDWARD: Very powerful hearts giraffes. Got to keep the blood pumping all the way up that great long neck.

MARIE: They are such an extraordinary shape. I think of them as the animal equivalent to bananas.

     Can we have a dinner party while Mark's here?

EDWARD: Who would we invite?

MARIE: There's the people from the gallery.

EDWARD: Who? The builders? I don't think that would be . . .

MARIE: When does everyone else arrive?

EDWARD: In a couple of months when we're ready to open.

MARIE: What about that guy you told me about? Anthony.

EDWARD: Oh him. The contractor. We could have him, I suppose.

    That would be nice.

    Who's going to cook?

MARIE: You cook. You never cook any more.

EDWARD: It'll look odd. I don't think any of the men Anthony knows cook.

MARIE: What do they do, beat their wives?

    You can enlighten him.

EDWARD: What would I cook?

MARIE: Chicken and potatoes, please.

EDWARD: Would I cook it African style or Western?

MARIE: Can you cook it African style?

EDWARD: Sort of.

MARIE: Can you cook it African style as good as Anthony's wife? Wives.

EDWARD: Probably not.

MARIE: Then Western.

EDWARD: When?

MARIE: At the end of the week. It can be Mark's good-bye.

EDWARD: I can't believe he flew all the way to see us already. Well to see you.

MARIE: I know. The idea of getting in a plane fills me with dread.

EDWARD: It's a shorter flight from London than we had from New York.

MARIE: Really? Maybe that's where I'll go next.

EDWARD: I thought you were spending Christmas in New York.

MARIE: Mark's getting married.

EDWARD: Really? To what?

MARIE: To Lilly, whoever she is. Lilly the fucking doctor.

EDWARD: We should open some champagne for him. Make a special event out of it. We'll still have another bottle.

   (Mark enters.)

MARK: Good shower.

MARIE: Thanks.

EDWARD: Hello!

MARK: Hi.

   (Mark and Edward hug.)

EDWARD: So you got here OK. Obviously.

MARIE: He took the bus.

MARK: Two busses.

EDWARD: Really? That's very enterprising of you. Everyone normally takes a cab.

MARIE: Except the people on the bus.

EDWARD: Except the people on the bus. Indeed.

EDWARD: I hear you're getting married.

MARK: Yes.

EDWARD: So who is she?

MARK: To Lilly. She's a doctor.

MARIE: She has blonde hair.

EDWARD: I think we've got a bottle of champagne somewhere.

   (He exits.)

MARIE: Mark. I am very, very happy for you.

   (Hugging him.)

   I can't wait to meet Lilly.

MARK: She's nervous to meet you.

MARIE: Good.

   (Edward comes back in with the champagne, and champagne glasses. He hands the others their glasses and then pops opens the bottle. He pours them their drinks.)

EDWARD: I told you we should bring the champagne.

MARIE: Yes, it's wonderful isn't it, with champagne? You have a bottle, and you never know what the occasion will be to use it, but one always comes along and here it is.

EDWARD: When's the wedding?

MARK: Next spring.

EDWARD: Well we'll be there!

   So what's she like?

MARK: Her name's Lilly. She's a doctor.

EDWARD: Lilly's a beautiful name. I always wanted to name a daughter Lilly.

MARK: *(Sarcastically.)* You two thinking about having kids?

MARIE: Did you see the soup? I helped to make it.

EDWARD: Oh that was you. Very impressive. I just added some salt.

MARIE: Why would you add salt to a mango? That makes no sense.

EDWARD: So that it isn't too sweet? So that it has taste?

MARIE: The taste of salt.

MARK: I hear you built the villagers a swimming pool.

> *(Nsugo enters.)*

NSUGO: The table is ready.

> *(She exits.)*

EDWARD: I'm going to have to talk to her about this. I don't feel comfortable.

MARIE: What exactly are you going to say?

MARK: What's the problem?

MARIE: Edward thinks the cook may have AIDS.

EDWARD: I'm worried. She's doing the cooking. What if she cuts her finger or something?

MARIE: You don't have to eat the food she has prepared if you don't want to. I will.

EDWARD: Mark . . .

MARIE: The cook here may or may not have AIDS. She says she doesn't. Anyway, you don't get it from eating food.

EDWARD: You're being deliberately perverse.

MARK: You don't get it from food.

MARIE: She's not going to give us food with her blood in it. Is she? Shall we go through?

> *(Outside, a scream.)*

MARK: What is that?

EDWARD: We don't know. It's rather worrying.

MARK: Yes it is.

Do you ever go and see who it is?

MARIE: People scream everywhere. They screamed in New York. They screamed in Germany. Don't you ever hear people screaming in London?

MARK: I suppose so.

MARIE: And I doubt you go outside to deal with it.

EDWARD: You can't go out and investigate at night. The animals.

MARK: Really?

EDWARD: You can actually be eaten by a lion here. We were warned.

MARK: Do you have a gun?

EDWARD: Yes we do, we have a gun. Although I have no idea how to shoot it. Or any intention of learning.

MARIE: We're thinking, if a lion sees the gun, that will be enough.

MARK: I don't think that's how it works with lions.

MARIE: No. Me neither. Shall we go through?

(Exit.)

SCENE 2

It is seven o'clock in the evening, a week later. The house is more unpacked. Mark and Anthony are seated, with drinks nearby. Anthony is showing Mark some photographs.

ANTHONY: That is the supermarket I built in the city. It took nearly a year. Everybody there uses it now. That was my biggest job. That is what got me the job to build the gallery.

This is the swimming pool.

MARK: Edward's swimming pool?

ANTHONY: Yes. Yes. But they drained it. We have to refill it. And this is the gallery. How it is at the moment. It will not be finished for another two or three months, but you can see here . . . this is the front. This will all be glass.

That is my friend, Nick. He is working on the roof, you see?

And that's me, see? I am telling everyone where the door will go. My friend took that picture. Not Nick. My other friend. He is also working on the building. He is a plumber.

(Marie enters hurriedly.)

MARIE: Edward!

(To the others.)

I'll be with you in a minute.

(She stops and smiles at them.)

Are you alright for drinks?

MARK: Yes.

MARIE: Edward! The rice . . .

(She turns back to the other's laughing slightly.)

I've burned the rice.

ANTHONY: Where is Nsugo?

MARIE: She . . . We had to . . .

You see her children are sick. Her other children. She's taking care of them.

ANTHONY: Oh.

MARIE: We . . .

MARK: Weren't you looking for Edward?

MARIE: Yes. Thank you.

(Marie exits upstairs. Mark tries to hand the photographs back to Anthony.)

MARK: Good work.

ANTHONY: Keep them.

MARK: No, that's alright.

ANTHONY: No, you show them to people. Maybe they'll want me to build something. In England.

MARK: I'm afraid I don't know anyone that —

ANTHONY: Just in case. I have many copies. And then you will have a picture of me. One day you will look at it and say "that was Anthony."

(Mark takes the photographs and puts them down.)

ANTHONY: You have been here for a week. What do you think of my country?

MARK: I like it. It's very beautiful.

ANTHONY: Yes, it's beautiful. The women are beautiful, right?

MARK: Yes.

ANTHONY: You like them, huh?

I could find you a woman if you want. There are many women you could see.

MARK: Many thanks but I'm leaving tomorrow.

ANTHONY: Yes. You are leaving. I want to leave. Maybe go to America. Edward knows a lot of people in America. He could get me a visa. I could build things there. Maybe swimming pools. Everyone has a swimming pool in California, right?

MARK: I don't know. I think a lot of people do.

ANTHONY: Edward knows a lot of rich people, right?

MARK: Some.

ANTHONY: He has a lot of money. The other man who came, Michael Lee, he was going to get me a job. But so far nothing.

You've been to America?

MARK: Yes.

ANTHONY: Do you like it there?

MARK: Not really. I prefer England.

ANTHONY: Where do you live in England?

MARK: London.

ANTHONY: Oh, London. What do you do there?

MARK: I research. Energy. Different types of energy. What the best way for us to make power is.

ANTHONY: Here we use coal.

MARK: I know.

ANTHONY: Is that one of the best ones?

MARK: There are advantages and disadvantages.

ANTHONY: Same with everything. If I leave here I won't see the mountains but I will make a lot of money, maybe.

(Marie enters hurriedly.)

MARIE: Edward's in the shower. Mark, can you look at the rice? It's not . . .

MARK: What's wrong with it?

MARIE: I don't know, can you just fix it?

(Mark exits.)

MARIE: Thank you.

(To Anthony.)

Can I get you another gin? Oh you're still drinking. Alright. I'll have one.

(Marie gets herself a drink.)

MARIE: Edward says you're doing wonderful work at the gallery.

ANTHONY: He likes me, yes?

MARIE: Oh yes.

ANTHONY: I am not lazy. I make sure everything gets done.

MARIE: That's good.

ANTHONY: The workers, they want to take a long time. I crack the whip.

MARIE: Why do they want to take such a long time?

ANTHONY: There is no other work after this job. Not for them.

MARIE: You know some very rich men have put their money in this project. So if the men want to take a little bit longer I think that's OK.

They hope the gallery will create jobs.

ANTHONY: Only three or four. And not for these men.

(Mark comes back in.)

MARK: I've put more rice on.

MARIE: *(To Anthony.)* Do you like rice?

ANTHONY: Sure, rice. Rice is very popular.

(Edward comes in.)

EDWARD: Hello. Hello, Anthony.

ANTHONY: Hey Edward!

(They slap each other's palms.)

MARIE: Darling, there was a problem with the rice which I have solved.

EDWARD: What problem?

MARIE: I burnt it. Mark's put more on. Thank you, Mark.

  (To Edward.)

  But I think you should turn down the chicken.

EDWARD: How does she burn rice?

MARK: She didn't put enough water in.

  (Edward and Anthony laugh. Mark leaves the group to browse the bookshelves.)

ANTHONY: *(To Marie.)* You can't cook. Wow!

MARIE: Edward does the cooking.

  (To Edward.) Are you going to turn down the chicken?

EDWARD: *(Sharp.)* In a minute.

MARIE: Can you cook, Anthony?

ANTHONY: No.

MARIE: That's something we have in common then.

EDWARD: Who wants some more?

  (Anthony holds out his glass.)

EDWARD: Are there any local wines here we should try?

  (Mark holds out his glass as well, and Edward crosses to serve him.)

ANTHONY: I don't know.

MARIE: What do people drink?

ANTHONY: Beer. Or there is a spirit called Khadi. That's good. Made from berries.

EDWARD: We should get some. Where do you get it?

ANTHONY: At the store.

  (A beat.)

MARIE: Do you want some Khat?

  (She shows Anthony the red reeds.)

ANTHONY: No. I don't chew it.

MARIE: Oh.

  Why don't you?

ANTHONY: It's not good for you. Some people, friends of mine, they chew Khat all day, every day, they don't do anything anymore. I have chewed it sometimes. It can make you see things.

MARK: Is it hallucinogenic?

EDWARD: Slightly. I'll turn down the chicken.

  (Edward exits.)

MARIE: Have you always lived here?

ANTHONY: Yes.

MARIE: Are you married?

ANTHONY: Yes. I am.

MARIE: Do you have children?

ANTHONY: One.

MARIE: Boy or a girl?

ANTHONY: A girl. She is one.

MARIE: I wish you had brought your wife.

ANTHONY: She is with the baby.

MARIE: I like babies. You could have brought them. Next time.

ANTHONY: Edward and I must talk about work.

MARIE: I could have talked to your wife.

ANTHONY: She does not have much English.

(Edward comes back in.)

MARIE: I was telling Anthony, next time he should bring his wife.

(A beat.)

EDWARD: Anthony, I didn't know you were married.

ANTHONY: I am married. One year.

MARIE: He has a baby.

EDWARD: Why didn't you tell me?

(Anthony shrugs.)

EDWARD: You should have brought them with you. We'd love to meet them.

ANTHONY: You two. You will have children soon?

MARIE: I don't know about soon.

Mark's getting married next year.

ANTHONY: So Edward. We have a problem with the swimming pool.

EDWARD: What problem?

ANTHONY: It has been drained.

EDWARD: Oh why on earth have they done that?

ANTHONY: There was some blood in the water. A child hurt his head.

EDWARD: So they drained it? That seems a bit excessive.

ANTHONY: In the river, the water runs. In the pool the blood floats.
There were other children in the pool so —. There was a lot of blood.
People swallowed the water.

MARK: The child who hurt his head. He's alright, is he?

ANTHONY: Yes. But some people do not want to put more water in the pool.
You have to talk to them.

EDWARD: Oh dear. Do you think I should send the family some flowers?

MARIE: It's not your fault.

EDWARD: I know, but it's my swimming pool.
Why don't they want to refill it?

ANTHONY: Some say the child was sick. He should not have been in the swimming pool. He was supposed to be separate. You should not send his mother anything.

MARIE: Sick with what?

ANTHONY: I don't know.

(To Edward.)

You must get me the job to fill it. It will be a day's work. I need two men.

EDWARD: You shouldn't only stand and watch, Anthony. I did hire you to work as well.

ANTHONY: OK. One man. I'll take Nick.

EDWARD: I'll talk to them tomorrow.

MARK: What's the child sick with?

Is it AIDS?

ANTHONY: I don't know. Maybe. Some say.

MARK: How many others were in the pool?

ANTHONY: It was full.

EDWARD: There couldn't have been that much blood.

ANTHONY: There was a lot of blood.

MARK: Is someone checking the other children?

ANTHONY: No one is checking the other children. It is fine.

MARK: It's not fine. The other children should be seen by a doctor. This child should be seen by a doctor.

ANTHONY: This child was seen by a doctor!

MARK: Edward, I think you should arrange for a medical check.

EDWARD: Mark, there are medical facilities. I do not control the use people make of them.

(Pause.)

ANTHONY: This disease is very dangerous. You all have to be careful. It is very contagious. You can catch it from cups and plates and sometimes clothes. You have to stay separate. Remember Edward? How I make sure you have a special cup in the gallery? That is why.

MARK: That's not how you catch it.

ANTHONY: What do you know?

MARK: I know you don't catch it from cups. You catch it from blood.

ANTHONY: It is in the air.

EDWARD: I know it feels that way Anthony. But it's not. There has been a lot of research about it. In the West.

ANTHONY: How you get it?

EDWARD: Through sex. Mainly.

ANTHONY: No.

MARK: Yes!

ANTHONY: Then why do the children have it?

EDWARD: If the mother has it . . .

ANTHONY: Oh the mother . . .
Yes.

MARIE: That's why you have to use a condom. Anthony. You must tell every-
one to use a condom.
(To Mark.)
That's one of the problems here.

EDWARD: *(To Mark.)* Condoms aren't actually that easy to get over here. We
brought a few hundred with us from New York, but we're not quite sure
what to do with them.

MARK: I'm sure.

ANTHONY: Many people think that condoms can give you AIDS.

MARK: What?

ANTHONY: But you say it is to protect you from the mother.

EDWARD: No —

MARK: Hey! Condoms do not give you AIDS. Spread the word.

ANTHONY: Alright. Relax man. Relax Max . . .

MARK: *(To Anthony.)* Why are you laughing? It's not funny. This is serious!

ANTHONY: *(Sharply.)* Not for you.
(A beat.)

MARIE: Why do people think it's happening?

ANTHONY: I don't know. Some people say from god. Maybe the men get it
from the women. Like Edward said.

EDWARD: I did not say that. Please don't tell people that, Anthony.

MARK: Hey! Anthony! Where do you think the women get it from?

ANTHONY: Maybe a punishment. I don't know. Only god knows. It has happened before.

MARIE: When has it happened before?

ANTHONY: Fever. Sickness. No food, sometimes. Everywhere. It is part of living in Africa. That's why I want to move to America.

MARK: It's in America too. Did you know that? It's everywhere!

MARIE: There's medicine in America.

ANTHONY: I did not know that. Why don't they bring it here?
(Pause.)

EDWARD: It's too expensive.

MARIE: At the moment.

ANTHONY: The people who are sick in America. Why do they have it? Is it a punishment?

EDWARD: No. It's a disease. It's no one's fault.

ANTHONY: When the white man first came to this country, he got sick and died from fever. Because the land was not his to take.

Now, here in Africa we get sick and die. Because we have done nothing with the land since the white man left. Why not? Why is this country not like America? There are rivers, there are trees, there are men to build. But there is no energy.

There is a punishment for this I think.

EDWARD: I think the food's ready.

MARK: It's no one's fault.

ANTHONY: And yes, a woman gets it if she has been whoring. Everyone knows. The mother of this child today, she sees many men.

MARK: My god . . .

MARIE: Mark —

MARK: I'm going for a walk.

MARIE: Mark, stay.

MARK: *(To Anthony.)* Whores don't get it! People get it! And it's not their fault! *(Exiting.)*

I don't want any dinner. Sorry.

MARIE: Mark. Please. We're not supposed to go out at night.

MARK: *(To Anthony, from the door.)* You get it from sex. Use a condom.

MARIE: Mark, he's married.

ANTHONY: Hey, Mark! I am a Christian. That is why I don't use a condom.

MARK: Oh because you're a Christian?

ANTHONY: Just like you.

(A beat. Mark exits.)

ANTHONY: Hey! What's his problem?

EDWARD: I'm so sorry.

MARIE: Edward —

EDWARD: What do you want me to do?

MARIE: He's upset. He's leaving tomorrow. He can't leave like this.

EDWARD: He'll be back in five minutes. He doesn't know where to go. There is nowhere to go.

MARIE: I'll get him. He's probably just waiting outside.

ANTHONY: I will leave.

MARIE: No. Let's sort this out. Mark didn't mean —

He's concerned. He's concerned for your people.

ANTHONY: My people are not his concern.

MARIE: I'll go and get him.

Please.

Let's not. Let's not be this way. We are four people. In a room.

(She exits.)

EDWARD: Two people.

ANTHONY: I won't stay.

EDWARD: Are you sure?

I am so sorry about Mark.

They're both very highly strung.

ANTHONY: You have to look after everyone, yes. It is tiring. I get tired. That is why, you and me at work. In the sun. Shirts off. Only time a man can think, yes?

EDWARD: Why didn't you tell me you were married, Anthony?

Anthony?

ANTHONY: I cannot take my wife to America.

EDWARD: Why not?

ANTHONY: It's too much trouble. It's OK. I have a brother in Tanzania who sends his wife money. I will send my wife money.

EDWARD: Wouldn't you miss her? What about the baby?

ANTHONY: When are you going away?

EDWARD: After the gallery is established.

ANTHONY: I could go with you. I could be your assistant. I think you like having me around. I think I make you laugh.

EDWARD: I don't think you should leave your wife and child Anthony. I don't want to play any part in that.

ANTHONY: I am a good builder, Edward. You are not a good builder. If I had not pushed you that wall would have come down on your head. Remember.

EDWARD: Yes.

ANTHONY: I saved your life. Do you remember? I said now we are brothers.

(Edward starts for the door.)

EDWARD: Let's go. I should find Mark and Marie. They shouldn't be out there.

(Anthony does not move.)

ANTHONY: Do not leave me like Michael Lee left me, Edward. He promised me many things. I have been to this house many times before and the last time I left it he said "see you in America." And since then I have received one T-Shirt in the mail with one postcard with a picture of some boats.

We are good friends, you and I. We have become friends. We work together, like men, every day under the sun, sweating and building. You make promises. You must not betray me. It is easy to get on a plane and fly away.

(He starts to exit and then turns back.)

My wife is sick, Edward. She is a whore.

(Anthony exits. A moment and then Marie enters.)

EDWARD: Where's Mark?

MARIE: Apologizing to Anthony.

That didn't go very well.

EDWARD: No.

MARIE: Maybe because it was the first time.

It's terrible about the swimming pool.

EDWARD: Yes it is. The swimming pool was meant to be a good thing.

MARIE: It is a good thing. And we'll get it refilled and we'll start again.

(Mark enters.)

MARK: I'm sorry, I don't like him.

EDWARD: You didn't see his best side,

MARK: What is his best side?

EDWARD: He's very bright. And he's ambitious.

MARK: He hates women. That's not very bright.

EDWARD: It's a different culture here.

MARK: Some cultural difference aren't acceptable. Not when they're based on ignorance and prejudice.

EDWARD: That's universal.

MARK: That doesn't make it alright!

My god, they're all killing each other! "I don't use condoms . . ."

MARIE: That's the church.

MARK: They should have taken our church and told us to shove it!

EDWARD: I agree. But they didn't.

MARIE: I'd really be very interested to meet his wife. Do you think we could have them both round, Edward?

MARK: You two just love to socialize don't you. What the hell do you think you and his wife are going to talk about, Marie?

MARIE: I don't know. That's precisely why I'd like to meet her.

EDWARD: Apparently his wife has AIDS.

He just told me.

MARIE: She just had a baby.

MARK: Why doesn't he . . . You know he sees prostitutes? He probably gave it to her.

EDWARD: He doesn't see prostitutes.

MARK: How do you know? He offered to take me to one. He had a look on his face . . .

I want to go home.

EDWARD: Are we going to eat?

MARIE: *(To Mark.)* Well you're going tomorrow.

EDWARD: *(To Marie.)* We'll be back to see him soon.

MARIE: Does anybody mind if I work for a while?

EDWARD: Don't you want to taste the chicken?

MARIE: No!

MARK: I'm not hungry either.

MARIE: I'll be down later.

(Marie exits.)

MARK: It's my last night. You'd think she might want to spend some time together.

EDWARD: She said she'd be down later.

She was writing every night before you got here. I've never seen her work like this. It's good. She was blocked for a long time in New York.

MARK: She sent me some things from New York. I thought they were good.

EDWARD: They were good. But she was struggling.

MARK: You help her a lot.

EDWARD: Other people have always helped poets.

MARK: I don't think she should chew those sticks.

EDWARD: She's always liked drugs. Mild drugs. It's very common here. It's like alcohol. She drank in Germany, she smoked pot in New York, and now she's chewing Khat in Africa. That's Marie.

MARK: I don't want to visit here again, Edward. Have you any idea how long you're going to be staying?

EDWARD: I'll be out here at least another year.

Marie is free to do whatever she wants. I don't hold her here, Mark. I get the distinct impression that you feel I do, but I don't I assure you.

MARK: Well good, I'll report that to the family.

EDWARD: I didn't realize you'd be giving a report.

MARK: We worry about her.

EDWARD: Mark. She's fine. She's happy.

MARK: Of course she's happy here. She's a depressive. They feed off misery.

EDWARD: One depression. In her twenties. It's normal.

MARK: She's not a stable person.

EDWARD: She doesn't seem unstable to me at all.

MARK: You don't know her like I do.

EDWARD: I've known her as long as you have.

MARK: I'm her brother. Who are you?

EDWARD: In a way. I'm her brother too.

MARK: She —

EDWARD: Mark. You've got a new family now. Leave me to mine.

Listen, I was thinking of trying to get the people round here interested in bio-gas.

MARK: Oh.

EDWARD: I've always thought that bio-gas is underestimated. We did a class about it at school once. It always sounded very practical to me. Do you know that it could create a third of the energy we get from coal?

MARK: It leaves a lot of waste.

EDWARD: So does nuclear power.

MARK: I know. The thing is, there is no solution.

EDWARD: Come on, Mark. There is a best option. Do you think we could get bio-gas off the ground here? Is that something you might be interested in helping us with?

MARK: I live in London.

EDWARD: We have e-mail.

MARK: I could send you some literature if you'd like.

EDWARD: That would be wonderful. I just want to get people talking, you know? About what can be done. To show that there are still possibilities. It's like the swimming pool. I know it's nothing. But it gives people hope, you see. And that's important.

MARK: Hope in what?

EDWARD: Hope that there are alternatives. Hope that happiness is accessible. That this is a country, or a village, where there can be a swimming pool. And people can . . .

MARK: Frolic?

EDWARD: Sure. Why not? Why shouldn't they? Let them frolic, for how ever long.

MARK: Not long now.

EDWARD: There'll be other people, Mark. They'll always be more people. And some might get out. Like Anthony. He's got great spirit.

(A beat.)

EDWARD: I'm sorry that what you've seen has shocked you, Mark. But isn't it better to have seen it? You'll wake up in London with your new wife one morning and you'll know what's happening on the other side of the world.

MARK: I already knew.

EDWARD: But you didn't feel this way in London. So sad. You've learned something more. Isn't that useful.

MARK: I don't know if it's useful.

Before it was abstract. I blamed the church, I blamed the colonialists, I blamed the governments. Now I blame you.

You're enjoying it, Edward.

(Mark exits.)

SCENE 3

It is late afternoon, a few weeks later. The boxes are gone and now there's a rug. It is raining outside, and it has been for several weeks. Edward is sitting with a drink, writing on a notepad. Marie enters. She circles the room vaguely. Edward looks up, then returns to his work.

EDWARD: How's it going up there? What are you working on?

MARIE: I don't know . . . It's getting very long. I'm worried. It's not . . . People don't like long poems anymore.

(A beat.)

EDWARD: An article.

MARIE: Another article?

EDWARD: It's for *The New York Times.* Bringing art to the people. That kind of thing. It might attract the gallery more funding.

MARIE: You've got enough funding.

EDWARD: You can't have too much. What do you think of this? "It is a commonplace about art that it is supposed to uplift. Here, such inspiration is sorely needed for a people currently blighted by such socio-economic hardship. The gallery, not yet complete, is already causing tremendous excitement among locals, generating a sense of hope, not simply in the future, but in the interest the West is taking in their plight by devoting money, time and energy to this ambitious project."

MARIE: That's good.

It's not true, though, is it?

EDWARD: People are excited.

MARIE: Really?

EDWARD: Some people. And wait till it opens. Imagine, imagine what it's going to mean to these people to be able to go in, for free, and look at a

Rothko. And we've got some Van Goghs. One definitely, we might get another one, I'm working on it. And there's going to be local art. I've already seen two transparencies of paintings that are coming in from Zimbabwe.

MARIE: That's hardly local.

EDWARD: I met an artist from the city a few weeks ago. The plumber brought him in, and showed me his work. I'm definitely going to try and use it. It's wonderful.

MARIE: What is it?

EDWARD: He makes bowls. Wooden bowls. They're quite beautiful. I was going to ask you if we should get one.

MARIE: A bowl?

EDWARD: Yes, I thought we could use it for fruit. They're not expensive.

MARIE: You can't leave fruit out in a bowl here. You have to eat it immediately. Otherwise the flies come.

EDWARD: We could just have one on display.

MARIE: Form but no function.

EDWARD: Its function would be to be beautiful.

MARIE: An empty bowl. Yes, I suppose it would be rather poignant. We can get one if you'd like.

EDWARD: The flies have gone anyway now. With the rain.

MARIE: I wish the rain would stop.

EDWARD: Apparently it doesn't stop. Not for months. I don't know how much of the gallery we're supposed to get done with the weather like this. And four men were off last month anyway.

MARIE: I feel . . . very heavy.

EDWARD: I hope you're not getting ill.

Although Michael Lee did say there was a very good doctor in the city. We could ask him about it next week.

MARIE: It's so strange he's staying with us. We don't know him.

EDWARD: He's not staying long. He just wants to pick up a few things. It is his house. I didn't know what else to say.

MARIE: Why did he leave?

EDWARD: The bank closed down their branch last year. He and his wife went back to Boston.

He sounds nice.

MARIE: Everyone's getting out.

EDWARD: Not everyone.

We're getting in a lot of contemporary art from New York. And a few pieces from Germany.

MARIE: Oh great. What did you get? Sculptures made of toothpaste? Five can-
vasses all painted red? Don't tell me, the artists' urine in different shaped
bottles, labeled with what he'd drunk that day.

EDWARD: The toothpaste sculpture is quite an important piece. Actually.

MARIE: Sorry.

EDWARD: I did get it for the gallery. It's a coup, I thought.

MARIE: How much did you pay for it?

EDWARD: We're getting everything cheap. It looks good on the artists' résumés
to have pieces hung abroad.

MARIE: How much?

EDWARD: Why do you want to know?

MARIE: Because I think a sculpture made of toothpaste is a stupid idea.

EDWARD: It's original.

MARIE: I think there's a reason it hasn't been done before.

All good stories have been told at least a thousand times before.

EDWARD: Yes what you do is so much more important than what I do.

(Pause.)

MARIE: Edward. I don't feel well.

EDWARD: Should I call that doctor?

MARIE: No, I . . .

I feel like I'm changing. And I don't feel in control of it particularly.

EDWARD: But it's not like before.

MARIE: I'm getting up, aren't I? I get up, I shower, I walk about the house, I
write. I just feel . . . heavy.

It's probably just the rain.

(A beat.)

EDWARD: It's hard for you staying home all day.

MARIE: Yes.

EDWARD: And now Nsugo gone. There's no one to talk to.

MARIE: Can we ask her to come back? Just to clean?

EDWARD: She needs to be with her children.

MARIE: Says who?

EDWARD: We both did. I gave her some money.

I give Anthony money, I give Nsugo money, at least the rug was cheap.
I don't feel very well, either.

I think it is the weather. It must be.

(Pause.)

MARIE: If there's going to be so much press I think we should tell them what's
going on here.

EDWARD: Everybody knows, Marie. There's just not anything anyone can do. We just have to wait. This will pass. And there will be new life here Marie. That's what this article is. That's what I'm saying. New people will come.

MARIE: Yes. Yes of course how silly of me.

EDWARD: What's silly of you?

MARIE: To forget. That life is cheap.

(Pause.)

EDWARD: After here, I was thinking Paris. I've been offered some consultancy. It's an open offer. We could go whenever we want. Next year. The year after. Paris is good for writers.

We wouldn't have to stay in the city if we didn't want to. There are some beautiful parts of France. Parts that have barely changed since the twelfth century.

MARIE: Paris is for lovers.

(Pause.)

MARIE: (*Without emotion.*) I have to say . . .

I do want to make love Edward . . .

I need to.

(Edward looks down at his article.)

EDWARD: Maybe you'll meet someone when we have the opening. Can you hang on for a couple of months?

(A long, uncomfortable pause. Marie starts laughing. It's not a particularly happy sound.)

MARIE: What's wrong with us? Here we are in the middle of Africa in this big house, with these walls of paintings, and our books Edward, the books we've put together on the shelves . . .

Oh god what are we doing?

EDWARD: We're happy aren't we?

MARIE: Are we?

EDWARD: I am. I thought you were too. Do you really want to risk everything we have? For sex?

MARIE: You're going to leave me eventually.

EDWARD: Don't be ridiculous. You're the one who might run off and leave me!

MARIE: Well neither of us can go anywhere here.

(A beat.)

It really is funny to think there are places in France where you sit all day long at a little table outside a little café, waiting to be served the good red wine and thinking how beautiful it all is. How peaceful.

(Loud knocking.)

EDWARD: Who's that?

MARIE: Shall I answer?

EDWARD: Who would visit?

(A moment, then Marie exits and returns with Anthony, soaking from the rain.)

ANTHONY: I need to talk to you, Edward!

EDWARD: You're soaking.

ANTHONY: There is much rain.

EDWARD: Do you want a drink?

ANTHONY: I need to talk to you.

EDWARD: Alright . . .

ANTHONY: In private. Please.

(A brief pause. Marie exits.)

EDWARD: What is it?

ANTHONY: I have seen a doctor. I am well.

EDWARD: Good.

(Remembering.)

Good!

ANTHONY: A good doctor. In the city. I do not have the disease. I checked. I was scared after that night, Edward. I went to this doctor. Here is the report.

(He hands a sodden document to Edward.)

ANTHONY: The doctor says I am lucky. He tells me many people will die. It is like you said. You get it from the blood.

(Edward hands the paper back to Anthony.)

ANTHONY: My wife, she will die. And the child. He is sure.

EDWARD: I'm so sorry, Anthony.

ANTHONY: My wife, she says I must come to you.

EDWARD: Anthony, I can't . . .

What?

ANTHONY: My wife says it's OK for me to leave. She will stay here alone. It is best. She says. She says it, Edward.

EDWARD: Anthony, I said I would investigate.

ANTHONY: Then investigate!

EDWARD: We still have the gallery. I'm not leaving.

ANTHONY: But when you do, you will take me with you?

EDWARD: You're just going to leave your wife to die here? Alone?

ANTHONY: You, you live in this big house. You don't understand how it is for me. How it is for everyone. Where I live . . . you do not know, Edward, what I come from every day when I come to the gallery. Everyone where

I live is dying! There is silence everywhere while people wait for their death to come for them. No one speaks about it, we just walk through it, we are stepping over bodies to walk to the road. No one is clearing the bodies, Edward. There are people lying outside their house, you don't know if they sleep or if they are dead now.

EDWARD: In our village?

ANTHONY: There is a smell and there is nowhere in the village you can go that does not have that smell. Some people think you can catch it just from the smell. I think that too, sometimes, at night. But I do not understand why I think that because the smell is sweet.

EDWARD: This village?

ANTHONY: Step off the road and walk down the hill and you would see Africa. There are hundreds of families. With no running water, no proper doors, or windows, or beds, Edward, or chairs like these! It is nothing! Nothing! You would refuse to live this way.

I refuse it too, Edward.

EDWARD: Anthony. There are people who are working on a cure.

ANTHONY: The doctor said it is too late.

EDWARD: Not for everybody.

ANTHONY: Yes, for everybody here. This is Africa.

We must build a gallery somewhere else, where people are alive and they can come to see your pictures.

Why don't you go back to America?

EDWARD: I'm here. I'm building a gallery.

ANTHONY: You know the other friends of mine who are working with us? Nick? Steve? They have a foam in their mouths. When they are talking you can see the white. They will not come back to work, after the rains.

EDWARD: You'll have to find people to replace them. This week. I'll meet them there.

ANTHONY: Everyone is sick! Everyone I know is sick! There is no one to work! But I can still work. We should work somewhere else.

EDWARD: Anthony it's not as simple —

I can't just telephone someone —

ANTHONY: You can! You said you can! You said you know many people.

Did you send a photograph to anyone, Edward?

It was expensive. To make the photographs. It was expensive to see this doctor.

EDWARD: I will send the photographs. I promise. I'll do it tomorrow.

ANTHONY: You promise me, you promise me, you promise me these things.

I cannot make you keep your promises.

EDWARD: Look, I have to work now, Anthony.

Would you like to borrow something? For the rain?

ANTHONY: No.

(He starts to exit.)

EDWARD: Is there anything we can do? For your wife?

ANTHONY: I have asked you to help me.

(Anthony exits. A pause.)

EDWARD: Marie!

Marie!

(Marie enters from the upstairs.)

EDWARD: Marie!

MARIE: What? I'm working now.

EDWARD: Anthony says —

It's a lot of people who are ill.

I'm worried.

MARIE: You're worried about what? The people?

EDWARD: That this might have been a mistake.

I need to call London.

MARIE: And say what?

EDWARD: The sponsors have a right to know exactly what the situation is.

MARIE: Everyone does know. It's in the papers.

EDWARD: No, not the way he described it.

He said the dead just lie outside their houses. That no one will clear them. That there's a village near here —

MARIE: We know the village —

EDWARD: Not that village! Another village! Off the road!

MARIE: Where off the road?

EDWARD: I don't know! Off the road! Walk down the hill! That's where everyone is! Dying! It's a twenty-minute walk!

Everyone said we were crazy to come in the first place.

MARIE: That's not true. Some people were ever so excited for us, going all the way to Africa.

EDWARD: You know, if this is a doomed project it's better to accept that now than spend more money.

MARIE: So you'd just leave? Just leave them here? What about their jobs?

EDWARD: The men are too sick to build the gallery!

MARIE: You said there were always more people!

EDWARD: There's that job in Paris. What about Paris?

MARIE: That's not what we talked about.

EDWARD: If you'd heard him.

MARIE: I didn't need to hear him. I knew! This isn't new information!

EDWARD: It is to me!

It was the way that he put it.

MARIE: Oh.

You didn't understand before.

I don't want to leave. We said we'd be here at least a year. We agreed. I'm writing. I can't just move.

EDWARD: We might have to. I'm calling the sponsors.

MARIE: Don't call them.

EDWARD: They have a right to know.

MARIE: A sense of hope remember. You said you were doing it to give a sense of hope.

EDWARD: Look at what happened with the swimming pool. In less than a week they had to drain it.

MARIE: The interest the West is taking, you said. Devoting time, money, and energy. So we're just going to leave? It's too difficult?

EDWARD: What do you want me to do! I can't solve this!

MARIE: I want you to stay!

EDWARD: What, and watch? I don't want to!

MARIE: But I do!

EDWARD: You want us to stay and watch? Soon we'll be the only ones here.

MARIE: We should watch, Edward. And care! And not just turn away because it frightens you!

EDWARD: We're not staying here.

MARIE: Aren't we?

EDWARD: No.

MARIE: You mean you're not staying here.

EDWARD: You are?

MARIE: Yes.

EDWARD: Who's going to pay for the house?

(A beat.)

MARIE: Don't you dare think I can't manage without you, Edward. I can.

(Marie gets her coat.)

EDWARD: What are you doing?

(A beat.)

For god's sake, Marie. It's getting late. It's pouring with rain. You can't —

MARIE: I'm sick of this house. I'm sick of staying in this house, all day, every day, doing nothing!

EDWARD: So let's leave!

MARIE: I'm not just going to leave, Edward!

EDWARD: What, you'll stay here without me?

MARIE: Yes, yes why not? We're not lovers. We don't have to be together. It's a convenience, isn't it?

EDWARD: You've been chewing that stuff. I can see. Your eyes look funny. Just sit down. Please. Just sit down for a moment.

MARIE: You never chose me. For your very own. So I don't sit when you tell me to sit. I don't sit when someone we know is dying in the middle of Africa!

EDWARD: Who the hell do we know?

MARIE: We know Nsugo!

I liked her.

My god, Edward, I'm not going to sit!

(Marie exits.)

ACT TWO, SCENE 1

It is late afternoon, a week later. It is still raining. Michael Lee has just arrived. He is surveying the room.

MICHAEL: I like what you've done with the place.

EDWARD: Good.

MICHAEL: All the pictures. Very nice. I don't go in for the modern stuff myself so much. I like the pre-Raphaelites.

My wife was on me to get an original. You can still get them, you know. But they're expensive.

Good investment though, right?

EDWARD: Can be. Absolutely.

MICHAEL: How much are these worth? Out of curiosity?

EDWARD: Which?

MICHAEL: That one. What did you pay for that?

EDWARD: That's worth about eight thousand dollars.

MICHAEL: You're kidding me.

(He takes a closer look.)

MICHAEL: It's just newspaper print, right?

EDWARD: You're paying for the artist, really. This guy's doing very well at the moment.

MICHAEL: I guess he is if he can cut up a newspaper and people are paying eight thousand dollars for it.

EDWARD: It's increased in value since I bought it.

MICHAEL: No kidding.

EDWARD: I've been following him since he was young.

MICHAEL: *(Examining the picture.)* What's it say here? I can't see without my glasses.

EDWARD: It's not really about the words.

MICHAEL: Oh boy. Some old lady in New Jersey poisoned her grandchild. There's no date.

So people pay a lot of money for this kind of thing, huh?

I like a painting. No one does a nice painting any more. Why is that?

EDWARD: Some do.

If you're interested I could show you some contemporary painting.

When I get back to New York.

MICHAEL: Sure. Sure.

You know why I like the pre-Raphaelites? All that hair. Women never have hair like that any more.

Why is that?

EDWARD: I'm not sure.

MICHAEL: Do you smell something?

EDWARD: No.

MICHAEL: There's a funny smell.

You know what I used to have hanging in this room. A zebra skin. Jean hated it. That really stank. I'd spray it but I couldn't get rid of the stink.

EDWARD: Can I get you anything? Some tea?

MICHAEL: I'll have a scotch.

EDWARD: I'm afraid we don't have any.

MICHAEL: I bought you a bottle on the plane.

EDWARD: Thank you.

(Michael nods to a plastic bag and Edward takes a bottle from it and pours himself and Michael Lee a drink.)

MICHAEL: So you're moving back to New York, huh?

EDWARD: Next week.

MICHAEL: The gallery didn't work out?

EDWARD: No. There's a lot of sickness in the village. It's a bad time.

MICHAEL: I heard.

EDWARD: Although we haven't made an official announcement so I'd be grateful if you didn't say anything at the moment.

I'm sorry we're leaving the house sooner than we said.

MICHAEL: No problem. Found a buyer.

EDWARD: Really?

MICHAEL: Company from Washington. Didn't tell me much. They make paper.

EDWARD: When do they come?

MICHAEL: In a few weeks. They want to use it as a base, is all they said. So I'm selling and I'm out of here. It's worked out fine.

EDWARD: I'm glad.

MICHAEL: Jean always said I was crazy to buy this place anyway, but I fell in love with it. Everyone else from the bank lived in city. But I didn't mind the drive. I liked the idea of being somewhere remote.

You been hunting yet?

EDWARD: No, no I haven't.

MICHAEL: You should do that before you leave. You can pay a guide. It's a lot of fun. I got a lion, once.

EDWARD: Really?

MICHAEL: You're not supposed to hit the lions. But I saw it and I shot it. Didn't even think about it. Instinct. And a lion would eat you soon as look at you so I didn't lose any sleep over it.

EDWARD: Who lived in this house before you did?

MICHAEL: Bought it from an old British lady. Broke her heart to sell it to me. I guess her family had been here for generations. But most of the other British moved from here years ago anyway, and her daughter persuaded her to move back to England.

(Trying to remember.)

Or Scotland. I forget.

Have you been happy here?

EDWARD: Yes I have.

MICHAEL: Best years of my life, in some ways.

But Jean hated it here. Got bored. Nothing for her to do. She works back in the States so she was glad to leave. And the country will drive you crazy after a few years anyway. It was time to go.

EDWARD: How does it drive you crazy?

MICHAEL: I was on a train once, my wife wanted to take a train, don't ask me why, and it stops in the middle of nowhere, so I ask a guy why, and he told me it's because the driver had gone to take a leak. And I said, "is he planning on coming back any time soon," because we hadn't moved for about twenty minutes, and he said "relax man. This is Africa."

Half the time that train moved so slowly you could walk next to it. But the country's beautiful. I'll give them that. Beautiful scenery. And the wildlife. Oh boy.

You know you can hand-feed giraffes somewhere around here?

EDWARD: Yes, we've been.

MICHAEL: You can bet when the British were here the trains ran on time.

EDWARD: Well we built the railway.

MICHAEL: Exactly.

Everyone's always attacking the West. We shouldn't be here, we shouldn't be there. But in reality, everyone uses the goddamn railroad. Everyone's always getting at the Americans. But my god, when the British had power, they used it too.

EDWARD: Yes they did.

MICHAEL: What are you gonna do? Progress corrupts.

The British did some pretty terrible things in Africa, didn't they?

EDWARD: Yes.

MICHAEL: Why did you cut off all those people's hands in the Congo?

EDWARD: That was the Belgians.

MICHAEL: It's a good time to leave. This country's in the toilet. Even driving here from the airport. I was shocked. Everything's closed.

There used to be a restaurant in town where you could eat zebra. Is that gone?

EDWARD: I haven't seen it.

MICHAEL: Pity. You could eat anything. Zebra, impala, the impala was good . . . Warthog. Over two years I tried everything on the menu. Except turtle. Couldn't bring myself to eat turtle. You know what I mean? I kept thinking about their little heads.

EDWARD: I do find it rather difficult not to feel guilty about leaving. Just leaving so abruptly. Leaving everyone behind. Did you find that?

MICHAEL: What are you supposed to do? Take them with you?

EDWARD: No, no of course not.

Do you remember Anthony?

MICHAEL: Oh yes.

EDWARD: He wants me to help him.

MICHAEL: He was the same with me. I said to him once, "Why do you want to move to America? Look to Africa. Stay and rebuild it." I tried to inspire him, you know.

EDWARD: There's not a tremendous amount of work for him here. Especially now I'm leaving.

MICHAEL: There's no work in the States. It's a terrible time.

EDWARD: I know. I tried to explain to him.

MICHAEL: Edward. Guess what? You're not the bank.

EDWARD: No.

MICHAEL: You've had some success. Good for you. It does not mean you owe the world.

EDWARD: I know.

MICHAEL: Do the right thing. Give to charity. Sit on some boards. But don't let everyone that comes along bleed you dry. Take it from me. Or after every conversation you have, you realize you've been robbed.

EDWARD: I made some calls for Anthony. Nobody's very interested.

MICHAEL: I know. I did the same. I made a few calls but it didn't work out. Immigration's tight.

EDWARD: Sure.

MICHAEL: Everyone's got problems of their own.

EDWARD: I freelance. I don't have a company to put him in or anything.

MICHAEL: You came here, you employed him, now it's over.
(He finishes his drink.)

MICHAEL: Are you putting me in the back bedroom?

EDWARD: No. No, I thought the one next door. You see, Nsugo is staying with us at the moment.

MICHAEL: You had her move in?

EDWARD: She and her children are staying here for a while.

MICHAEL: The kids are staying here? All four.

EDWARD: No, just two. I hope that's alright.

MICHAEL: You're renting the place. If that's what you want to do.

EDWARD: Marie took them in —
Oh, there she is.
(The two men rise as Marie enters from upstairs.)

MARIE: The children are asleep.

EDWARD: Marie, this is Michael Lee. Michael, this is Marie.

MICHAEL: How do you do?

EDWARD: Well. I am well.

MICHAEL: Is Nsugo coming down? I brought her something.

MARIE: She's singing to the children. I can't make her stop.

MICHAEL: I'll go up and say hello.

MARIE: She says they'll be dead by morning. I don't think they will. They seem a little better, to me. I don't know. I'm not a doctor. But there's no point in them seeing a doctor now, she says. I agree with her. They're not going to get well.

MICHAEL: What's wrong with them?

MARIE: There's a boy and a girl. She's eight and he's nine.

EDWARD: Unfortunately the children, Nsugo's children, have AIDS. Marie found them in the village. And their living circumstances were less than . . . so she brought them here.

MARIE: Does any one want any soup? I'm going to cook some soup, I think. Nsugo and I chopped up some vegetables this morning.

(To Michael.)

I've been learning to cook. I couldn't cook at all before I came here.

EDWARD: We've been eating a lot of soup.

MARIE: Yes, that's all I can do at the moment. But with soup you get so much. So many different vitamins. And it's easy to swallow. Especially for the children. They have a foam in their mouth. It's . . . what's the word?

EDWARD: Michael said he ate on the plane.

MARIE: Candida.

I'll make a big pot.

(Marie exits.)

EDWARD: I am sorry about this. When she found them, the children were so sick you see, and Marie and Nsugo had become close, she couldn't bring herself to leave them there.

MICHAEL: Yes, I see. It's admirable.

So they're next door to me?

EDWARD: Yes. I hope they won't disturb you. They . . . there is an element of crying.

MICHAEL: Are you going crazy?

EDWARD: Well it's not easy.

Marie brought them in, what could I say?

MICHAEL: I always told Jean, you don't let it go too far. Nothing against the Africans. But we're talking about different worlds. You don't want to confuse the two. Let them see how we live and they'll resent it. And who can blame them? But that's the way it is, so best to keep it all separate.

EDWARD: Yes.

I'm not really sure what to do.

MICHAEL: You're leaving soon. When?

EDWARD: At the end of next week.

MICHAEL: So. There you go.

EDWARD: The thing is . . .

Marie says she doesn't want to come with.

MICHAEL: She wants to stay here by herself?

EDWARD: She feels very attached to Nsugo and the children.

MICHAEL: What about you?

EDWARD: It's a complicated situation.

MICHAEL: Where would she stay? Does she know I'm selling the house?

EDWARD: I'll tell her.

MICHAEL: It will pass. She's emotional. It's understandable. But she isn't going to stay here if she doesn't have anywhere to live.

EDWARD: I have to say, she's not been herself recently. At all.

Obviously I can't just leave her here. I'm responsible.

MICHAEL: Of course.

What does she do again?

EDWARD: She's a poet. She's quite widely published.

MICHAEL: So she's a little flaky.

EDWARD: Yes. A little.

It's very stressful here, that's all. It's getting to her. To both of us.

I am worried about her.

There was one time, a long time ago, in London. She suffered a very serious depression. She wasn't in her right mind, exactly. For a brief period. Six months or so. It's extremely common with artists.

MICHAEL: Oh sure.

EDWARD: I worry . . .

MICHAEL: Do you think it's happening again?

EDWARD: Possibly.

MICHAEL: Have you taken her to see a doctor?

EDWARD: I was actually hoping that you could recommend one.

Although I've mentioned the idea a few times to her and she doesn't want to see anyone.

MICHAEL: What about her family?

EDWARD: I don't want to worry them. I just need to get her on the plane.

(Marie enters.)

MARIE: I've put it on a low light.

(She sits.)

MARIE: Have you noticed the lizards?

EDWARD: I saw a few this morning.

MARIE: There's more than a few. Nsugo says the lizards mean death.

EDWARD: Really?

MARIE: Oh yes. It's an old legend. God asked man if he wanted to be reincarnated after he died. Man decided yes.

They sent a lizard with the answer to god.

But the lizard was a vain lizard. He walked slowly so everyone would notice that his skin glittered in sunlight.

So of course. The lizard was overtaken by an evil hare. The hare ran up to god and said: I was sent by man, they do not want be reincarnated.

God made it so. And when the lizard did finally get there, it was all too late.

And ever since then the lizard has been bad luck. The San people say anyway.

There are lizards everywhere I'm noticing.

MICHAEL: Edward was telling me you're a writer. You must like these old stories.

MARIE: I particularly like this one.

MICHAEL: Are you working on anything at the moment?

MARIE: Yes.

EDWARD: Every time I try to talk to her, she's writing.

MICHAEL: Poems?

MARIE: One poem.

MICHAEL: What kind of poetry do you write?

MARIE: What kind?

MICHAEL: Does it rhyme?

(Marie looks at Edward.)

EDWARD: Sometimes. Sometimes it rhymes, doesn't it?

Are you ready to go and get this one published?

MARIE: Edward, it's a long poem — no one's going to publish it. It's pages and pages.

EDWARD: Maybe this one will be the book.

MARIE: Yes, maybe.

I think maybe it's the best thing I've written.

EDWARD: I'd like to see.

MARIE: It pours out of me. All day.

MICHAEL: Sounds like maybe you should take a break kid.

MARIE: I do sleep. But there are the children. We have to keep washing the sheets. We keep running out of them because the children can't control their bowels any more. So I wash them. And then their little bodies.

They hardly notice the shower though. I thought they'd be so excited.

MICHAEL: If they're that sick we should take them to a hospital.

MARIE: Should we? There are hundreds more. I don't think there's room for all of them. And these two are peaceful here.

MICHAEL: Edward tells me you plan to stay after he leaves.

MARIE: Yes. I think that's best. There's so much to do.

MICHAEL: You realize of course that I have to give the house to somebody else.

MARIE: Who?

MICHAEL: Some men.

MARIE: Some white men?

MICHAEL: Yes. White men.

MARIE: Yes, they will come I suppose. There's going to be so much space, they wouldn't let it go to waste, would they?

EDWARD: So we can't keep the house, you see.

MARIE: I can go back to the village. With Nsugo.

But I wish you'd let us stay here, Mr. Lee.

MICHAEL: You can call me Michael.

MARIE: I wish you would. There's running water here, that's a help. And we can cook easily. I thought we could turn the place into a sort of hospice. That would be more useful than a swimming pool. Nsugo was telling me that the people think the swimming pool cursed the village.

EDWARD: Why do they think that? This was all going on before the swimming pool.

MARIE: Because it's so drained and hopeless.

MICHAEL: What's this?

EDWARD: I built them a swimming pool.

MARIE: You mustn't let it upset you. You misunderstood what can be done. But now it's clear.

EDWARD: Oh really? Thank god. What are we supposed to do? I've been wondering.

MARIE: We must bear witness.

We can't give very much. Acknowledgment. Regret.

Admit our fault.

EDWARD: How is this our fault?

MARIE: I do not know your fault.

(To Michael.)

Or yours.

I will tell you mine. When I was eighteen I was driving in a car with Mark.

(To Michael.)

Mark is my brother.

And a black man, our age, was in the road, in the way of the car, so we had to slow down. And Mark said "naff off, nigger." And we both burst out laughing. And I don't know why.

(A beat.)

MICHAEL: I have a friend here, not near here, but a few hours drive away, who I thought we might have dinner with while I'm visiting. He's an American, a doctor. Lived here for twenty years.

EDWARD: That sounds like fun. What do you think?

MARIE: Would you like me to see a doctor, Edward?

EDWARD: I'm worried about you. You're scaring me.

MARIE: There's nothing to be frightened of, Edward. Nothing at all.

It's time for us to separate. That's all. Do you understand?

I can't go where you're going. It's become imaginary to me, do you see? I couldn't live there. And I don't think I could live with you.

EDWARD: You can't stay here by yourself.

MICHAEL: Marie, I really do think you should see a doctor. Edward tells me you've not been feeling well.

MARIE: Who are you?

MICHAEL: My name is Michael Lee.

MARIE: That isn't what I asked.

EDWARD: He wants to help us.

MARIE: You want to help?

Then I beg you.

Don't sell this house.

Please.

(She kneels in front of Michael.)

MICHAEL: Edward?

EDWARD: Marie. Stand up.

MARIE: Edward, do you remember when we got here there was screaming?

(To Michael.)

We heard it at night for the first few weeks. Nsugo told me later it was the women mourning. But they've stopped that now. No reincarnation. Soon it will be quiet. Let us stay until then.

MICHAEL: *(To Edward.)* I'm taking my bags upstairs.

MARIE: You can't look at me can you?

MICHAEL: You know what I see when I look?

A girl that's been here too long.

MARIE: Try and stay downstairs as much as you can. The children wake very easily. I'll take the bags.

(Marie gets up, and crosses to Michael Lee's bags. She picks them up and exits upstairs. A brief pause.)

MICHAEL: Very emotional.

EDWARD: What do you think I should do?

MICHAEL: Take a look at what she's writing.

EDWARD: Why?

MICHAEL: You'll be able to tell, won't you? From that. I think she needs medical attention. For a start she needs something to calm her down. I'll call the doctor in the morning, see what he thinks.

EDWARD: I can't look at her work without her permission.

MICHAEL: She doesn't have to know. Edward, this is serious. You've got a week before leaving her here. I think we'd better find out.

EDWARD: Find out what?

MICHAEL: How far gone she is. Now don't worry. We'll get her out of here. Get her to the doctors in New York. She'll be right as rain in a few weeks.

EDWARD: Alright.

MICHAEL: Good.

EDWARD: Thank you, Michael.

MICHAEL: My pleasure.

(Nsugo enters.)

MICHAEL: Nsugo.

Michael Lee. Remember? Jean sends her best. She bought you something. Marie took it upstairs.

It's a sweater.

NSUGO: Hello Mr. Lee.

EDWARD: Do you need something?

NSUGO: Your woman needs soup, Edward. She is not eating enough.

EDWARD: Shall I get it?

NSUGO: I can get it.

I thank you both. For letting us stay here. Also my children.

(She exits into the other room.)

MICHAEL: Does she know you're leaving?

EDWARD: I haven't said anything. I don't know if Marie has.

(Nsugo reappears with the bowl of soup and exits slowly up the stairs.)

SCENE 2

It is six in the evening, a few days later. The room is in boxes. Nsugo and Marie are sitting together, shelling peas.

MARIE: I don't understand why they're not back by now.

NSUGO: They have gone to the city.

MARIE: It's getting dark.

NSUGO: Yes.

MARIE: How long can it take?

NSUGO: They have gone to the bank.

MARIE: Yes, with my work. Now why would they do that.

I'll go and check on the children.

NSUGO: The children are sleeping.

(A beat.)

MARIE: I'll put out the champagne glasses.

(She gets up and starts looking for them in open boxes.)

MARIE: It doesn't matter if Anthony comes before they do. Then we can all be here toasting them as they come in. They'll get the shock of their lives.

(She finds the glasses, and begins unwrapping them, putting them out on the now empty drinks trolley.)

MARIE: There was a party once, in Berlin, that Edward and I went to, and the bar was made of ice. And the barman would pour your drink down an ice funnel, and it would come out cold in your glass. It really was something. It really was.

We used to go out a lot. We'd go to lots of places. We'd go and listen to music, or out to the theatre, or to eat, or parties. There were a lot of parties. And we'd go and we'd watch and laugh. At all the strange people.

NSUGO: You will miss Edward?

(A beat.)

MARIE: I'll miss the idea of Edward. An earlier idea I had of him.

Never mind. We can do without Edward.

NSUGO: Michael Lee told me this morning that I cannot stay here.

MARIE: No, we can stay here for two, maybe three weeks after they leave. After that I thought I could rent somewhere in the city. I have some money. I don't think anything costs very much. We can stay there with the children. And I can try and get a job. We both can.

NSUGO: There is no work.

MARIE: I'll find work.

NSUGO: I can go back to the village.

MARIE: There's really no need.

I think we ought to keep the children somewhere clean if we can.

They've been a lot better since they've been here. Remember? You thought they'd be dead by now. Some people are lucky. There are women, prostitutes, who should be dead. But they're not. They don't even have it. No one knows why. People are experimenting on them.

You will come with me, won't you? I have some money.

Nsugo, I want you to be my friend. Do you think we can be friends?

NSUGO: Sure.

MARIE: No but real friends? Do you want to try to do that?

Nsugo and Marie. They met in the big house in a village in Africa. Then they moved to town.

What do you think?

NSUGO: I think one day you will go back.

MARIE: I'm not going back. Edward flies to New York tomorrow. I am not flying with him.

NSUGO: Why is this?

MARIE: In America, when I lived in America, it was very hard not to feel like the world was coming to an end, and the end would be caused by human error.

NSUGO: A country sees many things and lives through many times. This is one blink in god's eye.

MARIE: I can hear them.

(A moment, then Edward and Michael Lee enter from the outside.)

EDWARD: At least it's stopped raining.

MICHAEL: Why won't they pave the damn roads road here!

(They stop on seeing the two women.)

EDWARD: Hello.

(Marie stands.)

MARIE: Give me my work.

(A beat. Edward hands her a sheaf of papers.)

MARIE: You crept into my room, while I was asleep, and stole from me?

EDWARD: Yes.

(She exits. A moment. He exits after her.)

MICHAEL: These two . . . What are you gonna do?

You making another soup?

NSUGO: Yes. Pea soup.

MICHAEL: What was that dish you made I liked so much?

NSUGO: Goat curry.

MICHAEL: That's right. Hardly any one eats goat in America. Did you know that? I don't know why.

NSUGO: Are there many goats?

MICHAEL: As many as anywhere else, I guess. Or we could get some. But no one wants to eat them.

NSUGO: The meat is tough. Cow is better.

MICHAEL: Yeah, we eat a lot of steak.

How's Marie doing?

NSUGO: She is well.

MICHAEL: No, no she isn't.

We took a look at Marie's poems. That she writes. Upstairs. You know her poems?

NSUGO: Yes.

MICHAEL: She expresses the desire in her writing, to hurt herself, to hurt other people. Does Edward get a beating! Oh boy. Edward the lizard. Edward's a lizard, and I'm a machine, apparently.

(Edward comes back in and makes himself a drink.)

EDWARD: She's furious.

MICHAEL: She'll get over it.

I gotta tell you, Edward, I can't believe she's published.

EDWARD: Well she is.

EDWARD: They're a downer. Who wants to read a downer?

EDWARD: That's the thing. She was always funny, Marie. Before. She was always very witty. Especially her writing. They never publish the other stuff. She's got piles of it in storage.

NSUGO: Some is funny.

(A beat.)

EDWARD: She read it to you?

MICHAEL: We've just got to sit her down, tell her what the doctor said.

EDWARD: He didn't even meet her.

MICHAEL: He was pretty clear.

EDWARD: Because you kept pushing him. Because we paid him!

MICHAEL: She's your wife, Edward. If you want to give up on her and leave her here that's up to you. I wouldn't leave a member of my family here, not in a million years.

EDWARD: She's not actually my wife.

(A beat.)

EDWARD: Oh. I assumed . . .

EDWARD: No. We're not family. We're not blood.

NSUGO: Family doesn't start with blood. That is time.

MICHAEL: But you two have been together for years, right?

EDWARD: Yes. Years.

MICHAEL: OK.

(To Nsugo.)

Has she said anything to you?

NSUGO: She says she will not go. She has said that we will live together.

MICHAEL: Is that what you want? You want to live with a crazy white lady? She needs treatment.

NSUGO: What would the doctor do to her?

EDWARD: He'd talk to her. Make her feel better.

MICHAEL: Put her on pills.

NSUGO: She doesn't say to me that she feels bad.

EDWARD: You didn't know her before we came here. She was very different. She was always laughing, always making other people laugh. She was . . . Extraordinary.

MICHAEL: We have to make her understand that she can't just stay in the middle of Africa.

NSUGO: Why can't she stay here? I am staying here.

(A beat.)

MICHAEL: Marie needs to be with her family, Nsugo.

EDWARD: She's taking you to live in the city?

She doesn't have much money, Nsugo.

This is for you.

(He holds out a significant number of bills to Nsugo and wait until she takes the money from him.)

EDWARD: Thank you for everything you've done for us.

NSUGO: This is a lot of money.

EDWARD: It's really not that much for me.

Please take it You've worked for us, and I'm paying you. It's a bonus. This is the end of our time together. It's traditional.

NSUGO: With this money I can take the children.

EDWARD: Yes. Away from here. Where would you go?

NSUGO: To my family in Ghana.

EDWARD: Yes. Yes, Michael told me you had family there. Why are the champagne glasses out?

NSUGO: Anthony is coming to say good-bye.

(Marie enters from the upstairs.)

EDWARD: Anthony is?

MARIE: I invited him to come and have a drink with us. He came over earlier. The poor thing went to the gallery site, now that the rain's stopped, I suppose he wanted to be there bright and early. And of course he arrived, and saw it all abandoned, and understandably he was quite confused because nobody told him, so he came over here. I explained the situation. I think he'd like to discuss it with you.

MICHAEL: Oh boy, that's going to be fun.

MARIE: I didn't mention that you were here, Michael. I thought it would be a nice surprise.

MICHAEL: Makes no difference to me. I'm going to finish packing. You still not coming with us?

MARIE: No, Nsugo and I are taking a house.

MICHAEL: Oh yeah? Good for you.

Nsugo, I've got a closet I need to empty in the kids' room.

MARIE: They're asleep.

MICHAEL: I need my things.

Oh, I know. I sicken you.

MARIE: Yes you do. You both do, actually.

MICHAEL: You should be thanking us. We're trying to help you.

MARIE: I don't need help.

MICHAEL: Oh yes you do sweetheart. I read your work.

EDWARD: Michael —

MICHAEL: And you're one sick little puppy.

(A beat.)

EDWARD: It's very dark. You know it is.

MARIE: What did you expect it to be? Why do you think I didn't want to show you?

MICHAEL: We also showed it to a doctor.

MARIE: And what did he say?

MICHAEL: He said you're a danger to yourselves, a danger to others, and we have to get you home.

MARIE: How am I a danger to others?

MICHAEL: Stab me with a knife? Is that what you want to do?

MARIE: Oh yes, I wrote that, didn't I?

Only last night. I was just making some notes.

MICHAEL: They're potentially libelous, the things you wrote. Just so you know.

MARIE: You really took everything, didn't you. Right out of my desk. While I was sleeping. The subterfuge is amazing. Did the two of you wear night goggles?

MICHAEL: Nsugo, I need to get into that room.

(He exits. Nsugo follows.)

MARIE: We're all dangers to ourselves. Aren't we? And to others. Especially to others. Aren't we?

EDWARD: Marie?

I loved it. This poem.

(Pause.)

MARIE: No one will publish it, will they?

EDWARD: Come home. Make the rounds. Convince them.

MARIE: I'm too tired.

EDWARD: I gave Nsugo some money. She won't be staying here. She's got family in Ghana.

(Pause.)

MARIE: I'm still staying Edward.

EDWARD: What about me?

MARIE: What about you?

EDWARD: Aren't you going to miss me?

I'm going to miss you.

I don't want you to leave me.

MARIE: You're the one leaving, Edward.

EDWARD: We can't stay here! You'd have to be crazy to stay here.

MARIE: You know there is nothing more insulting than having your sanity questioned. Really nothing. So stop it. Because it frightens me.

EDWARD: You're behaving strangely!

MARIE: These are strange times. These are strange times, Edward! How do you expect me to behave?

Don't you see? We're not equal, Edward, you and I. You're always the sane one and I the mad. You're rich, I'm poor. And you giving to me, giving to me, giving me a meal at a fancy, fancy restaurant . . .

And both of us knowing how lucky I am to have you. To have your patronage.

I don't want it any more.

Stop patronizing me. I can't bear it.

EDWARD: You know what I can't bear? That once I had to sit by your bed and listen to you tell me that you didn't want to be alive any more. That I had to convince you that you should be. Mark couldn't do anything, your parents couldn't do anything, your friends couldn't do anything. I had to deal with it! And every day I know that I might wake up one morning, and you'll have forgotten what I told you and we'll have to start all over again. Are we starting all over again, Marie? Is that what this is? Because I don't know what to do!

MARIE: I'm sick of everyone thinking I need to be rescued! From myself!

What do you think? That you swooped in out of the sky from Germany and suddenly everything was alright again? It was exhausting to pull myself out of that. You didn't do it, I did!

EDWARD: Oh and I had nothing to do with it? I took you back with me, gave you somewhere to live, cooked for you, looked after you —

MARIE: You were miserable there without me. Weren't you? And you've never once acknowledged it.

EDWARD: What if we got married. Would that help?

MARIE: Oh Edward. Not out of pity. Not out of fear. Just go home.

(A knock on the door.)

That's Anthony.

EDWARD: I don't know what to say to him.

Why did you do this?

MARIE: Because you weren't even going to say good-bye!

(She exits and enters again with Anthony.)

EDWARD: Anthony.

ANTHONY: *(To Edward.)* Marie told me you were leaving.

EDWARD: Yes.

ANTHONY: I hear the gallery is closing Edward.

No work. You did not tell me. I went there this morning, now that the rains have stopped, I thought we would continue as normal. But nobody was there.

EDWARD: I'm sorry. The funders changed their minds. The economy is very difficult everywhere at the moment. Not just here.

ANTHONY: You didn't want to say good-bye?

EDWARD: I was going to say good-bye. It's been very busy. The decision was only made last week.

Good-bye, Anthony.

ANTHONY: Can I have a drink? It is my birthday today, did Marie tell you?

EDWARD: No.

(Marie exits to get the champagne. The two men stand in silence until she comes back and pours them a drink.)

EDWARD: Happy birthday.

ANTHONY: So.

My wife died this week.

EDWARD: I'm sorry.

ANTHONY: Another woman is taking care of the child now.

I am absolutely free to go with you.

EDWARD: I'm going alone, Anthony. I keep telling you.

ANTHONY: That is not what you told me before.

EDWARD: Yes it is, Anthony! I didn't promise anything!

ANTHONY: I thought we were friends. You would leave a friend here? I should have listened to the old people. You cannot be friends with the white man. They laughed at me. They have been laughing at me for a long time. Since Michael Lee.

EDWARD: This has nothing to do with being white.

ANTHONY: This has many things to do with being white. False promises, no care, here is some money, now I am taking the money away.

EDWARD: Look, you want to move to America, Anthony? Then find a way. Instead of sucking everybody else dry.

I'm sorry. I can't help you any more.

ANTHONY: I don't believe you!

EDWARD: I've done a lot for you, Anthony. I gave you money.

ANTHONY: I worked for you.

EDWARD: More money than that! What did you do with it?

ANTHONY: I took my wife to a hotel in the city. This is where she died. I paid. She is still there. I left her in the room.

EDWARD: Alright, you want more money? Fine. I'll pay for your flight. How's that? You can fly to America.

(Edward is searching for his wallet.)

EDWARD: There's no work in America. You know that. You'll be as poor there as you are here. Worse maybe. And there's immigration . . . Just don't come to me. Please.

I don't have any more cash. I'll write you a check. A thousand dollars. That will get you there.

I'm writing you a check. Right now. That's all I'm doing. Then you're on your own.

ANTHONY: Why are you like this now, Edward? You were not like this before.

EDWARD: Because I'm sick of it! I'm sick of everyone thinking I know the answers!

(He holds out the check.)

EDWARD: Take the money.

ANTHONY: What can I do with a check of American dollars?

EDWARD: Take it.

ANTHONY: I have no way to make money from this piece of paper.

EDWARD: I don't have any cash!

ANTHONY: You would have to come with me to the bank in the city.

EDWARD: There's no time. We're leaving first thing in the morning.

MARIE: Edward!

EDWARD: What?

MARIE: Why are you being so ugly?

ANTHONY: I saved your life, Edward.

(Michael Lee enters with his luggage and stares at Edward waving the check in front of Anthony.)

MICHAEL: *(To Edward.)* What are you doing?

EDWARD: Giving him money.

MICHAEL: *(To Anthony.)* I see you haven't changed.

ANTHONY: You came back . . .

MICHAEL: I leave in the morning.

(A beat. Anthony finishes his drink.)

ANTHONY: Good-bye.

EDWARD: Good-bye Anthony.

MARIE: Anthony.

ANTHONY: Yes?

MARIE: I am so sorry.

ANTHONY: My wife. She was not a whore. It was me. I gave it to her. It is my fault.

(He exits.)

MICHAEL: I'm taking these to the car.

(We hear a shot.)

(A moment. Michael Lee exits. No one moves. Michael returns.)

MICHAEL: He's dead.

EDWARD: He can't be.

MICHAEL: He is. He used the shot gun. There's blood everywhere.

(Nsugo runs in.)

NSUGO: What has happened?

EDWARD: Anthony shot himself. He shot himself.

MICHAEL: Can you get some towels?

(Nsugo and Marie exit.)

MICHAEL: You OK?

EDWARD: Am I OK?

MICHAEL: Coward's way out. That's all it is Edward. Not your fault. You were holding out a check for christ sakes.

(Nsugo passes through with towels. Michael Lee follows. Edward is alone, holding his check.)

(Michael comes back in. He is treading blood onto the floor.)

MICHAEL: We can't leave him in the kitchen.

Who the hell do you call about something like this?

MICHAEL: Does he have any family?

We're going to have to bury him. Edward? We're going to have to bury him. I'll get a shovel.

EDWARD: The blood. The blood will attract the animals.

MICHAEL: We've got the gun.

(He exits. Marie enters. More blood on the floor.)

MARIE: Edward?

Edward.

(Edward stands there.)

MARIE: *(Very gently.)* Edward. Go inside.

(Edward exits. Michael Lee walks passes through with a shovel. Nsugo enters.)

MARIE: Is Edward crying?

NSUGO: Yes.

Marie, I am going to Ghana.

MARIE: I know.

NSUGO: You will be here by yourself.

I think you are my friend. A friend can remember, and say out there, across the sea is Nsugo. She was my friend in Africa.

A friend does not have to stay in Africa too.

A friend can tell what she has seen in her poems. People will remember this story.

MARIE: Yes.

NSUGO: I will remember also. Nsugo and Marie. They met in the big house in Africa.

She tried to save her children. I am grateful.

(Edward enters.)

EDWARD: Michael wants to bury him.

What should I do?

MARIE: We're not burying him like an animal.

NSUGO: Many here are buried this way now.

MARIE: Edward?

(Edward exits.)

MARIE: We'll buy him a coffin.

That's something we can do, isn't it?

Much cheaper than taking him to America.

(Edward enters.)

EDWARD: Michael's gone. He's spending the night at the airport.

MARIE: He's left everything behind.

But you'll stay? For his funeral.

EDWARD: Of course.

MARIE: Anthony was a Christian.

EDWARD: We'll find a priest.

MARIE: They say suicides are damned.

EDWARD: I know.

MARIE: We won't tell them.

And do we sit with the body, wash the body? That's what you do is it? I don't know . . .

EDWARD: I don't know . . .

MARIE: I think that's what you do. Sit with it all night. I think we should do that.

NSUGO: So I will make the soup

(She exits with the peas.)

EDWARD: Is this my fault?

Is it?

Shall we stay here? I will.

MARIE: I don't know.

(She looks at him. He kisses her, clumsily. She lets him.)

EDWARD: We can go wherever you want. If you don't want to go back to America then what about Paris?

MARIE: Yes. Yes that's a place I suppose.

Paris.

We could try Paris.

(The lights start to fade. They sit holding on to each other. Two lost and frightened children.)

EDWARD: It's near London. Mark's getting married in the spring.

END OF PLAY

NO CHILD . . .

Nilaja Sun

To the teachers of America . . .
You are our country's great!

PLAYWRIGHT'S BIOGRAPHY

Nilaja Sun is the solo writer and performer of the Off-Broadway smash *No Child . . .*, which concluded its run at the Barrow Street Theatre in June 2007. For her creation and performance of *No Child . . .*, Nilaja garnered a Lucille Lortel Award, an Outer Critics Circle Award, a Theatre World Award, an Obie Award, the John Gassner Playwrighting Award, and she was named the Best One-Person Show at the U.S. Comedy Arts Festival. In her long-term relationship with Epic Theatre Center, Nilaja has appeared in *No Child . . .*, *Einstein's Gift*, *Pieces of the Throne*, *Time and the Conways;* she was also named the first Artistic Associate of Epic Theatre. Other New York credits include *Huck and Holden* (Cherry Lane Theatre), *The Cook* (Intar), *The Adventures of Barrio Grrrl!* (Summer Play Festival), *Law and Order: SVU*. As a solo performer, Nilaja's projects include critically acclaimed *Blues for a Gray Sun* (INTAR), *La Nubia Latina*, *Black and Blue*, *Insufficient Fare*, *Due to the Tragic Events of . . .*, and *Mixtures*. A native of the Lower East Side, she is a Princess Grace Award winner and has worked as a teaching artist in New York City for eight years.

ORIGINAL PRODUCTION

Originally produced Off-Broadway in New York at the Barrow Street Theatre by Scott Morfee and Tom Wirtshafter, *No Child . . .* received its World Premiere by Epic Theatre Center, New York City in May 2006. It was commissioned by the New York State Council of the Arts. Permission for use of *Our Country's Good* by Timberlake Wertenbaker was granted by the Estate of Thomas Keneally and Timberlake Wertenbaker. First presented at the Royal Court Theatre, London on 10 September 1988.

NOTES

This play may be performed with one actor or with as many as sixteen actors. The play takes place in several locations but is best staged in a fluid style with lights and sounds suggesting scene changes.

CHARACTERS

(In order of appearance:)

JANITOR BARON: eighties, Narrator

MS. SUN: thirties, teaching artist

MS. TAM: twenties, teacher

COCA: sixteen, student

JEROME: eighteen, student

BRIAN: sixteen, student

SHONDRIKA: sixteen, student

XIOMARA: sixteen, student

JOSE: seventeen, student

CHRIS: fifteen, student

MRS KENNEDY: school principal

SECURITY GUARD: Jamaican

PHILLIP: sixteen, student

MRS. PROJENSKY: Russian substitute teacher

MR. JOHNSON: Teacher

DOÑA GUZMAN: seventies, grandmother to Jose Guzman

TIME

Now

PLACE

New York

NO CHILD . . .

SCENE 1

School. Morning. Janitor enters, mopping floor as he sings.

JANITOR: *Trouble in mind.*
I'm Blue.
But I won't be blue always.
Cuz the sun's gonna shine
in my back door someday.
(To audience.)
Hear that? Silence. Beautiful silence, pure silence. The kind of silence that only comes from spending years in the back woods. We ain't in the back woods (though I'm thinking 'bout retirin' there). It's 8:04 AM — five minutes before the start of the day. And, we on the second floor of Malcolm X High School in the Bronx, U.S.A. Right over there is my Janitor's closet, just right of the girls' bathroom where the smell of makeup, hair pomade, and gossip fills the air in the morning light. There's Mrs. Kennedy's room — she the principal. For seventeen years, been leading this group of delinquents — Oh I'm sorry, academically and emotionally challenged youth. She got a lot to work with! Seventeen feet below my very own, lay one hundred-thousand-dollar worth of a security system. This include two metal-detecting machines, seven metal-detecting wands, five school guards, and three N.Y.C. police officers. All armed. Guess all we missing is a bomb-sniffing dog. Right over there's Ms. Tam's class, she one of them new teachers. Worked as an associate in the biggest investment firm in New York then coming home from a long dreary day at work, read an ad on the subway — ya'll know the ones that offer you a lifetime of glorious purpose and meaning if you just become a New York City teacher. Uh-huh — the devil's lair on the IRT. I adore Ms. Tam, she kind, docile, but I don't think she know what she got herself into. See, I been working here since 1958 and I done seen some teachers come and go, I said I seen teachers come and go. Ah! One more time for good luck, I seen teachers come and go and I do believe it is one of the hardest jobs in the whole wide world. Shoot, I don't gotta tell you that, y'all look like smart folk! The most underpaid, underappreciated, under-paid job in this crazy universe. But for some miracle, every year God

creates people that grow up knowing that's what they gonna do for the rest of they life. God, ain't He sometin'! Now, you might say to me, "Jackson Baron Copeford the Third. Boy, what you doin' up dere on dat stage? You ain't no actor." That I know and neither are these kids you about to meet. *(He clears his throat.)* What you about to see is a story about a play within a play within a play. And a teacher (or as she likes to call herself — a teaching artist — just so as people know she do somethin' else on her free time). The kids call her Ms. Sun and in two minutes from now she gonna walk up them stairs towards the janitor's room and stop right at Ms. Tam's class. She gonna be something they done never seen before. Now I know what you're thinking: "Oh, Baron. I know about the public schools. I watch Eyewitness News." What I got to say to that? HUSH! You don't know unless you been in the schools on a day-to-day basis. HUSH! You don't know unless you been a teacher, administrator, student, or custodial staff. HUSH! Cuz you could learn a little sometin'. Here's lesson number one: Taking the 6 train, in eighteen minutes, you can go from Fifty-ninth Street, one of the richest congressional districts in the nation, all the way up to Brook Ave. in the Bronx, where Malcolm X High is, the poorest congressional district in the nation. In only eighteen minutes. HUSH!

SCENE 2

Before class.

MS. SUN *(On the phone in the hallway.)* Mr. Pulaski! Mr. Pulaski! Hi, it's Nilaja Sun from Bergen Street. 280 Bergen. Apartment four? Hey! Mr. Pulaski, thanks for being so patient, I know how late my rent is . . . By the way, how's your wife Margaret? Cool. And your son Josh? Long Island University. That's serious. Oh he's gonna love it and he'll be close to home. But yes, I apologize for not getting you last month's rent on time, but see the IRS put a levy on my bank account and I just can't retrieve any money from it right now. Well, it should be cleared by Tuesday but the real reason why I called was to say I'm startin' a new teaching program up here in the Bronx and it's a six-week-long workshop and they're paying me exactly what I owe you so . . . what's that? Theater. I'm teaching theater. A play actually. It's called *Our Country's Good* . . . Have you heard of it? Well it's about a group of convicts that put on a play . . . So the kids are actually gonna be doing a play within a play within . . . What's that?

Ah, yes, kids today need more discipline and less self-expression. Less "lulalula" and more daily structure like Catholic school during Pope Pious the Twelfth. On the flip side of the matter, having gone to Catholic school for thirteen years, I didn't even know I was black until college. *(She roars her laughter.)* Sir? Sir, are you still there? *(Bell rings.)* I gotta go teach, sir. Are we cool with getting you that money by the twenty-fifth? How about the thirtieth? Thirty-first? I know, don't push it. You rock. Yes, I'm still an actor. No, not in anything right now. But soon. Yes, sir, happy Lent to you too, sir.

SCENE 3

Classroom.

MS. TAM: Ms. Sun? Come on in. I'm Cindy Tam and I'm so excited to have your program here in our English class. Sorry we weren't able to meet the last four times you set up a planning meeting but so much has been going on in my life. Is it true you've been a teaching artist for seven years? In New York City? Wow. That's amazing. I'm a new teacher. They don't know that. It's a challenge. The kids are really spirited. Kaswan, where are you going? Well, we're going to be starting in a few minutes and I would strongly suggest you not leave. *(Listens.)* OK, but be back in five minutes, um, Veronica, stop hitting Chris and calling him a motherfucker. I'm sorry, please stop hitting Chris and calling him a motherfucker. Thanks, Veronica. Sorry, like I said, very excited you're here. Where is everyone? The kids usually come in twenty to thirty minutes late because it's so early. I know it's only a forty-one-minute class but I've been installing harsher penalties for anyone who comes in after fifteen. After five? OK, we'll try that. Well, what we can do today is start the program in ten minutes and wait for the bulk of them to come in, eat their breakfast, and . . . You wanna start now? But there are only seven kids here. The rest of them will ask what's going on and what am I gonna say to each late student? *(Scared out of her wits.)* OK. Then, we'll start. Now. Class! Please welcome Ms. Sun. She's going to be teaching you a play, and teaching you about acting, and how to act and we're gonna do a play and it's gonna be fun.

COCA: Fun? This is stupid already. I don't wanna act. I wanna do vocabulary.

JEROME: Vocab? Hello, Ms. Sun. Thank you for starting the class on time. Since we usually be the only ones on time.

BRIAN: Niggah, you ain't never on time.

JEROME: Shut up, bitch motherfucker.

MS. TAM: Jerome, Brian? What did I tell you about the offensive language?

JEROME: Yo, yo. We know. Pork-fried rice wonton coming up.

MS. TAM: I heard that, Jerome.

JEROME: Sorry, Ms. Tam.

BRIAN: *(Accent.)* Solly, Ms. Tam.

MS. TAM: Go on, Ms. Sun! *(Beat.)*

MS. SUN: Ah, well, I'm Ms. Sun and I will be with you all for the next six weeks and by the end of those glorious weeks, you would have read a play, analyzed the play, been cast in it, rehearsed it, and lastly performed it. It's gonna be a whirlwind spectacle that I want you to start inviting your parents and friends and loved ones to come see . . . What's that? No, it's not *Raisin in the Sun . . .* No, not *West Side Story.* It's a play called *Our Country's Good.*

COCA: Ew. This is some patrionism?

MS. SUN: Patriotism? No. It's a play based in Australia in 1788 and it's written by a woman named Timberlake Wertenbaker.

BRIAN: Yo, Justin Timberlake done wrote himself a play. "Gonna rock yo' body. Today. Dance with me."

MS. TAM: Brian, focus?

BRIAN: "People say she a gold digga, but she don't mess with no broke niggas."

MS. TAM: Brian!!! Put down the Red Bull.

BRIAN: Beef-fried rice.

MS. TAM: Brian.

BRIAN: Vegetable-fried rice.

JEROME: Ay yo! This some white shit. Ain't this illegal to teach this white shit no mo'?

MS. SUN: Are you done?

JEROME: Huh?

MS. SUN: Are you done?

JEROME: What?

MS. SUN: With your spiel? With your little spiel?

JEROME: Yeah.

MS. SUN: Because I'm trying to tell you what the play is about and I can't when you keep on interrupting.

JEROME: Oh my bad. Damn. She got attitude. I like that.

SHONDRIKA: I don't. What's this play about anyway?

MS. SUN: Well, what's your name?

SHONDRIKA: Shondrika.

MS. SUN: Well, Shondrika . . .

SHONDRIKA: Shondrika!

MS. SUN: Shondrika?

SHONDRIKA: Shondrika!!!

MS. SUN: Shondrika!!!

SHONDRIKA: Close enough.

MS. SUN: Ah-hah . . . *Our Country's Good* is about a group of convicts.

XIOMARA: What are convicts?

JEROME: Jailbirds, you dumb in a can. Get it? *(Laugh/clap.)* Dominican! Dominican!

MS. SUN: . . . And they put on a play called *The Recruiting Officer.* You'll be reading . . .

COCA: We gotta read?

JEROME: Aw hell no.

MS. TAM: Yes, you'll be reading, but you're also gonna be creating a community.

JEROME: Ay yo! Last time I created a community the cops came. *(Latecomers enter.)*

MS. TAM: Kaswan, Jose, Jennifer, Malika, Talifa, Poughkeepsie, come on in, you're late. What's your excuse this time, Jose?

JOSE: Sorry, Miss. But that faggot Mr. Smith was yelling at us to stop running to class. Fucking faggot.

MS. SUN: ENOUGH!

JOSE: Who? Who this?

MS. SUN: Hi. I'm Ms. Sun. Take your seats now. And as of today and for the next six weeks, when I'm in this classroom, you will not be using the word *faggot* or *bitch* or *nigga* or *motherfucker* or *motherfuckerniggabitchfaggot.* Anymore. Dominicans shall not be called and will not call each other dumb in a cans or platanos.

COCA: *Ah, y pero quien e heta? Esa prieta?*

MS. SUN: *La prieta soy yo, senorita. (Coca is speechless.)*

BRIAN: Shwimp fwy why! Shwimp fwy why!

MS. SUN: We will respect our teacher's ethnicity.

BRIAN: Shwimp fwy why??? *(No one else laughs.)*

MS. SUN: Ladies will not call each other heifers or hos.

SHONDRIKA: Shoot! That's what I'm talkin' about.

MS. SUN: We will start class on time. We will eat our breakfast beforehand. And from now on we are nothing but thespians.

XIOMARA: Lesbians? I ain't no Rosie O'Donnell.

MS. SUN: No, no! Thespian! It means actor, citizen, lover of all things great.

XIOMARA: I love that hard cash that bling-bling.

MS. SUN: Say it with me, class, thespian.

XIOMARA: *(Bored.)* Thespian.

MS. SUN: Thespian!

JEROME: *(Bored.)* Thespian.

MS. SUN: Thespian!

COCA: Thespian, already, damn!

MS. SUN: Now, let's get up and form a circle.

SHONDRIKA: Get up? Aw hell no!

JOSE: Miss, we not supposed to do exercises this early.

MS. TAM: Come on guys, stand up. Stand up.

COCA: Miss, this is mad boring.

MS. SUN: Boredom, my love, usually comes from boring people.

BRIAN: OOOOOOOOOOOOH!

COCA: *(Dissed.)* What's that supposed to mean?

BRIAN: That's O.D., yo! Oh she played you, yo!

JEROME: Ay yo, shut yo trap! Miss, I could be the lovable and charming leading man that gets all the honies' numbers?

MS. SUN: We'll see.

JEROME: Miss, can I get your number? *(Beat.)* Nah, I'm just playing. Let's do this, yo. Get up. *(They get up.)*

MS. SUN: OK, thank you . . .

JEROME: Jerome!

MS. SUN: Jerome. Great circle! Let's take a deep breath in and out. In . . .

BRIAN: Ohm! Nah! I'm just playing. Keep going. Keep going. Keep going. Keep going.

MS. SUN: . . . and out . . . In . . .

COCA: I'm hungry. What time it is?

MS. SUN: . . . and out . . . stretch with me, will you? Now, who here has ever seen a play? *(No one raises their hand . . . but Chris.)* Really? Which show?

CHRIS: Star Wars. It was a live reenactment.

MS. SUN: Was it in a theater?

CHRIS: Yeah. We all wore outfits and costumes and acted alongside the movie.

JEROME: Damn, Chris, you like SupaDupaJamaicanNerdNegro.

CHRIS: And for that, I zap you. *(To Ms. Sun.)* You really gonna make us act onstage?

MS. SUN: Yup.

CHRIS: I'm scared.

MS. SUN: Yeah, well guess what? Before I walked in here, even with all my acting and teaching experience, I was scared and nervous too, but you get over it once you get a feel for the audience and you see all of your parents and your friends and your teachers smiling at you. Did you guys know that public speaking is the number one fear for all humans — even greater than death?

JEROME: What? They ain't never lived in the hood.

JOSE: But, Miss, you should be scared of this class, cuz we supposed to be the worst class in the school.

MS. TAM: It's true. They are.

MS. SUN: Really, well, in the past thirty-five minutes, I've met some pretty amazing young adults, thinkers, debaters, thespians . . .

BRIAN: Lesbians.

MS. SUN: Keep breathing! *(Bell rings.)* Oh no, listen, read scenes 1 through 5 for the next time. Thanks guys, you are great.

MS. TAM: Wow. That was amazing. You're really great with the kids. *(Beat.)* Just to let you know. They're probably not going to read the play and they are probably going to lose the handout and probably start to cut your class and their parents probably won't come to the show. Probably. OK, bye.

MS. SUN: Bye. *(She watches her leave.)* For all our sake, Ms. Tam, I hope you're probably wrong.

SCENE 4

School hallway.

MRS. KENNEDY: Ms. Sun, hi, Mrs. Kennedy — the principal, so glad to meet you. Sorry about the attendance, Ms. Tam is a new teacher and we need all these kids to pass five Regents exams in the next two months. The pressure's on. Let me know when you'll be needing the auditorium. There are four schools in this building and it's like fighting diseased lions to book a night in it. But, you're priority. We've given you one of the most challenging classes. But I believe in them. I believe in you. Tyesha, can I have a word? *(She walks off. Security guard stops Ms. Sun.)*

SECURITY GUARD: Y'ave pass ta leave. I said do you have a pass to leave? Oh, you a teaching artist? Oh. Cuz you look like one a them. Well, excuse me for livin'! *(To other guards.)* Just trying to do mi job. I don't know the difference 'tween the teachers, teaching artists, parents, Board of Ed. people, and these animals comin' in here. I don' know da difference. Just tryin' to do mi job. *(To student.)* Girl, girl! Whatcha t'ink dis is? You can't go in wifoot goin' tru da detector. I don care if you just walked out and now you come back in. Rules are rules. Put ya bag in and yo wallet and your selfish phone.

(Beep.) Go back. Ya belt.

(Beep.) Go back. Ya earrings.

(Beep.) Go back. Ya shoes. Don't sass me!

(Beep.) Go back. Ya hair . . . t'ings.

(Beep.) Go back. Ya jewelry. Oh, oh I don' have time for your attitude. Open your arms, spread your legs. Oh, oh I don' care about your science class. Should know betta' than to just waltz in 'ere ten minutes 'fore class. Got ta give it one whole hour. Lemme see yo I.D. Don' have? Can't come in. Excuse?!!! What ya name is? Shondrika Jones! I don' care about ya Regents. Go, Go, Go back home. Next time don' bring all dat bling and don' bring all dat belt and don' bring all dat sass. Who ya t'ink ya is? The mayor of New York City? Slut! *(To another student.)* Boy, boy, don't you pass me! *(Light shift.)*

JANITOR: *(To audience.)* Your tax dollars at work! As Ms. Sun makes her way back home on the train, she thinks to herself.

SCENE 5

Subway car.

MS. SUN: What will these six weeks bring? How will I persuade them to act onstage? *(Beat.)* Why did I choose a play about convicts? These kids aren't convicts. The kids in Rikers are convicts. These kids are just in tenth grade. They've got the world telling them they are going to end up in jail. Why would I choose a play about convicts? Why couldn't I choose a play about kings and queens in Africa or the triumphs of the Taino Indian? This totally wouldn't jive if I were white and trying to do this. How dare I! Why would I choose to do a play about convicts?

SCENE 6

Classroom.

JEROME: Because we treated like convicts every day.

MS. TAM: Jerome, raise your hand.

JEROME: *(Raises hand.)* We treated like convicts every day.

MS. SUN: How do you mean?

SHONDRIKA: First, we wake up to bars on our windows.

COCA: Then, our moms and dads.

SHONDRIKA: You got a dad?

COCA: Yeah . . . so? Then our mom tells us where to go, what to do, and blah, blah, blah.

JEROME: Then, we walk in a uniformed line towards the subways, cramming into a ten-by-forty-foot cell *(Laughs.)* checking out the fly honies.

BRIAN: But there ain't no honies in jail, know what I'm saying?

JEROME: Unless, you there long enough, what, what!

MS. SUN: Then, class, you'll walk into another line at the *bodega* at the corner store, to get what?

XIOMARA: Breakfast.

MS. SUN: And what's for breakfast?

XIOMARA: Welch's Orange and a Debbie snack cake.

MS. SUN: Exactly, then what?

SHONDRIKA: Then, we go to school.

CHRIS: . . . Where a cool electronic object points out our every metal flaw.

JEROME: Damn, Chris, you read way too much sci-fi!

SHONDRIKA: Then we go to a class they tell us we gotta go to, with a teacher we gotta learn from and a play we gotta do.

MS. SUN: And now that you feel like prisoners . . . open to page twenty-seven. Phillip says, "Watkin: Man is born free, and everywhere he is in chains." What don't people expect from prisoners?

JOSE: For them to succeed in life . . .

MS. SUN: But, in the play . . .

COCA: They succeed by doing the exact opposite of what people expect.

MS. SUN: And so . . . how does that relate to your lives?

SHONDRIKA: Shoot, don't nobody expect us to do nothing but drop out, get pregnant, go to jail . . .

BRIAN: . . . or work for the MTA.

XIOMARA: My mom works for the MTA, nigga. Sorry, Miss . . . NEGRO.

SHONDRIKA: So, dese characters is kinda going through what we kinda going through right now.

MS. SUN: Kinda, yeah. And so . . . Brian . . .

BRIAN: By us doing the show, see what I'm saying, we could prove something to ourselves and our moms and her dad and Mrs. Kennedy and Ms. Tam that we is the shi . . . shining stars of the school, see what I'm saying?

MS. SUN: Great, turn to Act One, Scene 6. Can I have a volunteer to read? *(Ms. Sun looks around.)*

SHONDRIKA: Shoot, I'll read, give me this: "We are talking about criminals, often hardened criminals. They have a habit of vice and crime. Habits . . ."

JOSE: Damn, Ma, put some feeling into that!

SHONDRIKA: I don't see you up here reading, Jose.

JOSE: Cuz you the actress of the class.

SHONDRIKA: *(Realizing she is the "actress" of the class.)* "Habits are difficult to BREAK! And it can be more than habit, an I-nate — "

MS. TAM: *(Correcting.)* Innate . . .

SHONDRIKA: See, Ms. Tam why you had to mess up my flow? Now I gotta start from the beginning since you done messed up my flow. *(Class sighs.)*

BRIAN: Aw. Come on!!!

MS. TAM: Sorry, Shondrika.

SHONDRIKA: Right. "Habits are difficult to break. And it can be more than habit, an innate tendency. Many criminals seem to have been born that way. It is in their nature." Thank you. *(Applause.)*

MS. SUN: Beautiful, Shondrika. And is it in your nature to live like you're a convict?

SHONDRIKA: No!

MS. SUN: Well, what is in your nature? Coca?

COCA: Love.

MS. SUN: What else? Chris?

CHRIS: Success. And real estate.

MS. SUN: Jose, how about you?

JOSE: Family. Yo. My brother and my *buela.*

MS. SUN: Brian?

BRIAN: And above all, money, see what I'm sayin', know what I mean, see what I'm saying?

MS. SUN: Yes, Brian, we see what you're saying . . . and now that you know that you actually can succeed, let's get up and stretch!

COCA: Get up? Aw — hell no!

JOSE: This is mad boring.

XIOMARA: I just ate. I hate this part.

JEROME: Can I go to the bathroom? *(Bell rings. Lights shift.)*

JANITOR: Not so bad for a second class. Although, due to discipline issues, attention problems, lateness, and resistance to the project on the whole, Ms. Sun is already behind in her teaching lesson. And, the show is only four weeks away. Let's watch as Ms. Sun enters her third week of classes. The show must go on! (I'm good at this. I am!)

SCENE 7

Classroom.

COCA: Miss. Did you hear? Most of our class is gone for the day . . . They went on an important school trip. To the UniverSoul Circus. There's only five of us here.

MS. SUN: That's OK, Coca. We'll make due with the five of us, including Ms. Tam.

MS. TAM: *(Tired.)* Ewww . . .

MS. SUN: So, we will start the rehearsal section for *Our Country's Good.* We have the lovely Xiomara as Mary Brenham.

XIOMARA: *(Deep voice.)* I don't want to be Mary Brenham, I want to be Liz . . . the pretty one.

MS. SUN: I think I can make that happen. Chris as the Aborigine.

CHRIS: It's good.

MS. SUN: And Phillip as . . . Phillip as . . . Ralph! Phillip, do me a favor, go to page thirty-one and read your big monologue about the presence of women on the stage.

PHILLIP: *(Inaudibly.)* "In my own small way in just a few hours I have seen something change. I asked some of the convict women to read me some lines, these women who behave often no better than animals." (Pause.)

MS. SUN: Good, Phillip, good. Do me a favor and read the first line again but pretend that you are speaking to a group of a hundred people.

PHILLIP: *(Inaudibly.)* "In my own small way in just a few hours I have seen something change."

MS. SUN: Thank you, Phillip. You can sit down now. *(She goes to work on another student.)* No, Phillip, get back up. Someone is stealing your brand-new . . . what kind of car do you like, Phillip?

PHILLIP: *(Inaudibly.)* Mercedes LX 100, Limited edition.

MS. SUN: That! And, you have to, with that line there, stop him from taking your prized possession. Read it again.

PHILLIP: *(Inaudibly.)* "In my own small way I have seen something change."

MS. SUN: Now open your mouth . . .

PHILLIP: *(Inaudibly but with mouth wide.)* "In my own small way . . . "

MS. SUN: Your tongue, your tongue is a living breathing animal thrashing about in your mouth — it's not just lying there on the bottom near your jaw — it's got a life of its own, man. Give it life.

PHILLIP: *(Full on.)* "In my own small way I have seen something change!" *(The bell rings.)*

MS. SUN: That's it. That's it. Right there . . . *(She is alone now.)* God, I need a Vicodin.

SCENE 8

School. Night.

JANITOR: It may not look it, but this school has gone through many transformations. When I first arrived at its pristine steps, I marveled at the architecture . . . like a castle. Believe it or not, there were nothin' but Italian kids here and it was called Robert Moses High back then. Humph! See, I was the first Negro janitor here and ooh that made them other custodians upset. But I did my job, kept my courtesies intact. Them janitors all gone now . . . and I'm still here. Then came the 60s, civil rights, the assassination of President Kennedy right there on the TV, Vietnam. Those were some hot times. Italians started moving out and Blacks and Puerto Ricans moved right on in. Back then, landlords was burning up they own buildings just so as to collect they insurance. And, the Black Panthers had a breakfast program — would say "Brotha Baron! How you gonna fight the MAN today?" I say "With my broom and my grade D ammonia, ya dig?" They'd laugh. They all gone, I'm still here. Then came the 70s when they renamed the school Malcolm X after our great revolutionary. I say, "Alright, here we go. True change has got to begin now." Lesson number two: Revolution has its upside and its downside. Try not to stick around for the downside. Eighties brought Reagan, that goddamn crack ('scuse my cussin') and hip-hop. Ain't nothing like my Joe King Oliver's Creole Jazz Band but what you gonna do. And here we come to today. Building fallin' apart, paint chipping, water damage, kids running around here talking loud like crazy folk, half of them is raising themselves. Let me tell ya, I don't know nothing about no No Child, Yes Child, Who Child What Child. I do know there's a hole in the fourth-floor ceiling ain't been fixed since '87, all the bathrooms on the third floor, they all broke. Now, who's accountable for dat? Heck, they even asked me to give up my closet, make it into some science lab class cuz ain't got no room. I say, "This my sanctuary. You can't take away my zen. Shoot, I read *O* magazine." They complied for now. Phew! Everything's falling apart . . . But these floors, these windows, these chalkboards — they clean . . . why? Cuz I'm still here!

SCENE 9

Classroom.

COCA: Miss, did you hear? Someone stole Ms. Tam's bag and she quit for good. We got some Russian teacher now.

MRS. PROJENSKY: Quiet Quiet Quiet Quiet Quiet Quiet Quiet. Quiet!

MS. SUN: Miss, Miss, Miss. I'm the teaching artist for . . .

MRS. PROJENSKY: Sit down, you.

SHONDRIKA: Aw, snap, she told her.

MRS. PROJENSKY: Sit down, quiet. Quiet, sit down.

MS. SUN: No, I'm the teaching artist for this period. Maybe Miss Tam or Mrs. Kennedy told you something about me?

JEROME: *(Shadowboxes.)* Ah, hah, you being replaced, Russian lady.

MS. SUN: Jerome, you're not helping right now.

JEROME: What?! You don't gotta tell me jack. We ain't got a teacher no more or haven't you heard? *(He flings a chair.)* We are the worst class in school.

MRS. PROJENSKY: Sit down! Sit down!

MS. SUN: Guys, quiet down and focus. We have a show to do in a few weeks.

COCA: Ooee, I don't wanna do this no more. It's stupid.

CHRIS: I still want to do it.

JEROME: Shut the fuck up, Chris.

JOSE: Yo man, she's right. This shit is mad fucking boring yo.

COCA: Yeah!

XIOMARA: Yeah!

BRIAN: Yeah!

SHONDRIKA: Yeah!

COCA: Mad boring.

JEROME: Fuckin' stupid.

MRS. PROJENSKY: Quiet! Quiet! Quiet!

MS. SUN: What has gotten into all you? The first two classes were amazing, you guys were analyzing the play, making parallels to your lives. So, we missed a week when you went to go see, uh . . .

SHONDRIKA: UniverSoul Circus.

MS. SUN: Right! But, just because we missed a week doesn't mean we have to start from square one. Does it? Jerome, Jerome! where are you going?

MRS. PROJENSKY: Sit down, sit down, you! Sit down!

JEROME: I don't gotta listen to none of y'all. *(He flings another chair.)* I'm eighteen years old.

BRIAN: Yeah, and still in the tenth grade, nigga. *(Brian flings a chair.)*

MS. SUN: Brian!

JEROME: I most definitely ain't gonna do no stupid-ass motha fuckin' Australian play from the goddamn seventeen-hundreds!

MS. SUN: Fine, Jerome. You don't wanna be a part of something really special? There are others here who do.

JEROME: Who? Who in here want to do this show, memorize your lines, look like stupid fucking dicks on the stage for the whole school to laugh at us like they always do anyhow when can't none of us speak no goddamn English.

MS. SUN: Jerome, that's not fair, no one is saying you don't speak English. You all invited your parents . . .

COCA: Ooee, my moms can't come to this. She gotta work. Plus the Metrocard ends at seven.

XIOMARA: My mom ain't never even been to this school.

JEROME: That's what I'm sayin'! Who the fuck wanna do this? Who the fuck wanna do this?

MS. SUN: I'll take the vote, Jerome, if you sit down. Everyone sit down.

MRS. PROJENSKY: Sit down!

MS. SUN: Thank you, ma'am. OK, so, who, after all the hard work we've done so far building a team, analyzing the play in your own words (that is not easy, I know), developing self-esteem *y coraje* as great thespians . . .

BRIAN: Lesbians.

MS. SUN: Who wants to quit . . . after all this? *(She looks around as they all raise their hands . . . except for Chris.)* I see.

CHRIS: Miss. No. I still wanna do the show.

JEROME: That's cuz you gay, Chris. Yo, I'm out! One. Niggas. *(Pause. Ms. Sun is hurt.)*

MS. SUN: OK . . . Well . . . Ms?

MRS. PROJENSKY: Projensky.

MS. SUN: Ms. Projensky.

MRS. PROJENSKY: Projensky!

MS. SUN: Projensky.

MRS. PROJENSKY: Projensky!!!

MS. SUN: Projensky!!!

MRS. PROJENSKY: Is close.

MS. SUN: Do they have any sample Regents to take?

MRS. PROJENSKY: Yes, they do.

MS. SUN: Great. I'll alert Mrs. Kennedy of your vote.

PHILLIP: *(Audibly.)* Ms. Sun?

MS. SUN: Yes, Phillip, what is it?

PHILLIP: Can I still do the show? *(Beat.)*

SCENE 10

Principal's office.

MRS. KENNEDY: So they voted you out? Well, Malcolm X Vocational High School did not get an eight-thousand-dollar grant from the Department of Education of the City of New York for these students to choose democracy now. They will do the show. Because I will tell them so tomorrow. If they do not do the show, each student in 10F will be suspended and not be able to join their friends in their beloved Great Adventures trip in May. The horror. Look, I understand that they consider themselves the worst class in school. News flash — They're not even close. I know that they've had five different teachers in the course of seven months. I also can wrap my brain around the fact that 79 percent of those kids in there have been physically, emotionally, and sexually abused in their tender little sixteen-year-old lives. But that does not give them the right to disrespect someone who is stretching them to give them something beautiful. Something challenging. Something Jay-Z and P Diddly only wish they could offer them. Now, I will call all their parents this weekend and notify them of their intolerable behavior as well as invite them to *Our Country's Good.* Done. See you next Wednesday, Ms. Sun?

MS. SUN: Yes, yes. Thanks! Yes! . . . Uh, no, Mrs. Kennedy. You won't be seeing me next Wednesday. I quit. I came to teaching to touch lives and ed-
ucate and be this enchanting artist in the classroom and I have done
nothing but lose ten pounds in a month and develop a disgusting smoking habit. Those kids in there? They need something much greater than
anything I can give them — they need a miracle . . . and they need a miracle like every day. Sometimes, I dream of going to Connecticut and
teaching the rich white kids there. All I'd have to battle against is soccer
moms, bulimia, and everyone asking me how I wash my hair. But, I
chose to teach in my city, this city that raised me . . . and I'm tired, and
I'm not even considered a "real" teacher. I don't know how I would survive as a real teacher. But they do . . . on what, God knows. And, the
worst thing, the worst thing is that all those kids in there are me. Brown
skin, brown eyes, stuck. I can't even help my own people. Really revolutionary, huh?

It seems to me that this whole school system, not just here but the
whole system is falling apart from under us and then there are these test-
ing and accountability laws that have nothing to do with any real solu-
tions and if we expect to stay some sort of grand nation for the next fifty
years, we got another thing coming. Because we're not teaching these
kids how to be leaders. We're getting them ready for jail! Take off your
belt, take off your shoes, go back, go back, go back. We're totally abandoning these kids and we have been for thirty years and then we get annoyed when they're running around in the subway calling themselves
bitches and niggas, we get annoyed when their math scores don't pair up
to a five-year-old's in China, we get annoyed when they don't graduate in
time. It's because we've abandoned them. And, I'm no different, I'm
abandoning them too. *(Beat.)* I just need a break to be an actor, get
health insurance, go on auditions, pay the fucking IRS. Sorry. Look, I'm
sorry about the big grant from the Department of Ed. but perhaps we
could make it up somehow next year. I can't continue this program any
longer, even if it is for our country's good. Bye! *(Light shift.)*
JANITOR: (Sings.)
I'm gonna lay. Lay my head
On some lonesome railroad line.
Let that 2:19 train —

SCENE 11

Outside of school.

MS. SUN: *(Sings.)*
> *Ease my troubled mind —*

JEROME: Ms. Sun?

MS. SUN: Hi. Jerome.

JEROME: You singing? *(Beat.)* We were talking about you in the cafeteria. Had a power lunch. *(He laughs.)* Most of us were being assholes . . . sorry . . . bad thespians when we did that to you.

MS. SUN: You were the leader, do you know that, Jerome? Do you know that we teachers, we have feelings. And we try our best not to break in front of you all?

JEROME: Yeah, I know, my mom tells me that all the time.

MS. SUN: Listen to her, sweetheart, she's right. *(Beat.)* Look, the show is off. I'll be here next year, and we'll start again on another more tangible play, maybe even *Raisin in the Sun.* Now, if you'll excuse me, I have an audition to prepare for. *(She turns to leave.)*

JEROME: Ms. Sun, "The theater is an expression of civilization . . . "

MS. SUN: What?

JEROME: I said, "The theater is an expression of civilization. We belong to a great country which has spawned great playwrights: Shakespeare, Marlowe, Jonson, and even in our own time, Sheridan. The convicts will be speaking a refined, literate language and expressing sentiments of a delicacy they are not used to. It will remind them that there is more to life than crime, punishment. And we, this colony of a few hundred, will be watching this together. For a few hours we will no longer be despised prisoners and hated gaolers. We will laugh, we may be moved. We may even think a little. Can you suggest something else that would provide such an evening, Watkin?" *(Beat.)* Thank you.

MS. SUN: Jerome, I didn't know . . .

JEROME: . . . that I had the part of Second Lieutenant Ralph Clark memorized. I do my thang. Guess I won't be doing it this year though. Shoot, every teacher we have runs away. *(Beat.)*

MS. SUN: Listen, Jerome, you tell all your cafeteria buddies in there, OK, to have all their lines memorized from Acts One and Two and be completely focused when I walk into that room next week — that means no talking, no hidden conversations and blurting out random nonsense, no gum, and for crying out loud, no one should be drinking Red Bull.

JEROME: Aight. So you back?

MS. SUN: . . . Yeah, and I'm bad. *(She does some Michael Jackson moves.)*

JEROME: Miss, you really do need an acting job soon. *(Light shift.)*

JANITOR: Things are looking up for our little teaching artist. She got a new lease on life. Got on a payment plan with the IRS. Stopped smoking, ate a good breakfast, even took the early train to school this mornin'.

SCENE 12

Classroom.

COCA: Miss, did you hear? We got a new teacher permanently. He's kinda . . . good!

MR. JOHNSON: What do we say when Ms. Sun walks in?

SHONDRIKA: Good morning, Ms. Sun.

MR. JOHNSON: Hat off, Jerome.

JEROME: Damn, he got attitude! *(Beat.)* I like that!

MS. SUN: Wow, wow. You guys are lookin' really, really good.

MR. JOHNSON: Alright, let's get in the formation that we created. First, the tableau.

MS. SUN: *(Intimate.)* Tableau, you got them to do a tableau.

MR. JOHNSON: *(Intimate.)* I figured you'd want to see them in a frozen non-speaking state for a while. Oh, Kaswan, Xiomara, and Brian are in the auditorium building the set.

MS. SUN: *(Intimate.)* Wow. This is amazing. Thank you.

MR. JOHNSON: Don't thank me. Thank Mrs. Kennedy, thank yourself, thank these kids. *(To class.)* And we're starting from the top, top, top. Only one more week left. Shondrika, let's see those fliers you're working on.

SHONDRIKA: I been done. "Come see *Our Country's Good* cuz it's for your own good."

MS. SUN: Beautiful, Shondrika. Let's start from the top. *(Sound of noise.)* What's all that noise out in the hallway?

BRIAN: Ay, yo. Janitor Baron had a heart attack in his closet last night. He died there.

COCA: What? He was our favorite . . .

JEROME: How old was he, like a hundred or something?

SHONDRIKA: I just saw him yesterday. He told me he would come to the show. He died all alone, ya'll. *(Long pause.)*

MS. SUN: Thespians, I can give you some time . . .

JEROME: Nah, nah we done wasted enough time. Let's rehearse. Do the show. Dedicate it to Janitor Baron, our pops, may you rest in peace.

MS. SUN: Alright, then, we're taking it from the top. Chris, that's you, sweetheart.

CHRIS: "A giant canoe drifts onto the sea, clouds billowing from upright oars. This is a dream that has lost its way. Best to leave it alone." *(Light shift.)*

JANITOR: My, My, My . . . them kids banded together over me. Memorized, rehearsed, added costumes, a small set, even added a rap or two at the end — don't tell the playwright! And, I didn't even think they knew my name. Ain't that something? I think I know what you saying to yourselves: I see dead people. Shoot, this is a good story, I wanna finish telling it! Plus, my new friend up here, Arthur Miller, tells me ain't no rules say a dead man can't make a fine narrator. Say he wish he thought of it himself. Meanwhile, like most teachers, even after-hours, Ms. Sun's life just ain't her own.

SCENE 13

Sun's apartment. Night.

MS. SUN: *(On phone.)* Hi. This is Ms. Sun from Malcolm X High. I'm looking for Jose Guzman. He's a lead actor in *Our Country's Good* but I haven't seen him in class or after-school rehearsals since last week. My number is . . . *(Light shift. On phone:)* Hi. This is Ms. Sun again from Malcolm X High. I know it's probably dinner time but I'm still trying to reach Jose or his grandmother, Doña Guzman . . . *(Light shift. On phone:)* Hi. Ms. Sun here. Sorry, I know it's early and Mrs. Kennedy called last night, but the show is in less than two days . . . *(Light shift. On phone:)* Hi. It's midnight. You can probably imagine who this is. Does anyone answer this phone? Why have a machine, I mean really . . . Hello, hello, yes. This is Ms. Sun from Malcolm X High, oh . . . *Puedo hablar con* Doña Guzman. Ah Hah! Finally. Doña Guzman, ah ha, *bueno, Ingles,* OK. I've been working with your grandson now for six weeks on a play that you might have heard of. *(Beat.)* *Un espectaculo* . . . ah ha, *pero Ingles,* OK. I haven't seen him in a week and the show is in twenty-four hours mañana actually . . . Como? His brother was killed. Ave Maria, *Lo siento, señora* . . . How? Gangs . . . no, no, *olvidate,* forget about it. I'll send out prayers to you *y tu familia. Buenas.* (*She hangs up. Light shift.*)

JANITOR: Chin up now!

SCENE 14

School auditorium.

JANITOR: Cuz, it's opening night in the auditorium . . . I'm not even gonna talk about the logistics behind booking a high school auditorium for a night. Poor Mrs. Kennedy became a dictator.

MRS. KENNEDY: I booked this auditorium for the night and no one shall take it from me!!!

JANITOR: The stage is ablaze with fear, apprehension, doubt, nervousness, and, well, drama.

MR. JOHNSON: Anyone seen Jerome?

MS. SUN: Anyone seen Jerome?

COCA: His mom called him at four. Told him he had to babysit for the night.

MS. SUN: But, he's got a show tonight. Couldn't they find someone else? Couldn't he just bring the brats? Sorry.

MR. JOHNSON: What are we going to do now? His part is enormous.

PHILLIP: Ms. Sun?

MS. SUN: What, Phillip?

PHILLIP: . . . I could do his part.

MS. SUN: (*With apprehension.*) OK, Phillip. You're on. Just remember . . .

PHILLIP: I know . . . someone is stealing my Mercedes LX one hundred Limited Edition.

MS. SUN: And . . . ?

PHILLIP: . . . Let my tongue be alive!

DOÑA GUZMAN: Doña Guzman, *buenas. Buenas. D*oña Guzman. The *abuela de* Jose.

MS. SUN: Jose, you made it. I'm so sorry about your brother.

JOSE: Yeah, I know. Where's my costume at? *Buela, no ta allí.*

DOÑA GUZMAN: *Mira pa ya, muchacho.* We had very long week *pero* he love this class. He beg me *"mami, mami, mami, Our Country Goo, Our Country Goo, Our Country Goo."* What can I do? I say yes. What I can do, you know.

MS. SUN: Oh *señora.* It's parents like you . . . thank you. *Muchissima gracias por todo.* Sit, sit in the audience *por favor.*

MRS. KENNEDY: Ms. Sun, everyone is in place, there are about seventy-five people in that audience, including some parents I desperately need to speak to. We're glad you're back. Good luck!

SHONDRIKA: Miss, you want me to get the kids together before we start?

MS. SUN: Yeah, Shondrika, would you?

SHONDRIKA: Uh huh.

JANITOR: Now, here's a teacher's moment of truth. The last speech before the kids go on!

MS. SUN: Alright. This is it. We're here. We have done the work. We have lived this play inside and out. I officially have a hernia.

COCA: *(Laughing.)* She so stupid. I like her.

MS. SUN: We are a success . . . no matter what happens on this stage tonight. No matters which actors are missing or if your parents couldn't make it. I see before me twenty-seven amazingly talented young men and women. And I never thought I'd say this but I'm gonna miss you all.

SHONDRIKA: Ooh, she gonna make me cry!

MS. SUN: Tonight is your night.

COCA: Ooee, I'm nervous.

PHILLIP: Me too.

MS. SUN: I am too. That just means you care. Now let's take a deep breath in and out. In . . .

BRIAN: OHM! Nah, I'm just kiddin'. Keep going. Focus Focus.

MS. SUN: . . . and out. In and out.

SHONDRIKA: Miss, let's do this for Jose's brother and Janitor Baron.

MS. SUN: Oh, Shondrika, that's beautiful. OK, gentlemen, be with us tonight! PLACES. *(Light shift.)*

CHRIS: A giant canoe drifts out onto the sea, best to leave it alone.

COCA: This hateful hary-scary, topsy-turvy outpost. This is not a civilization.

XIOMARA: It's two hours, possibly of amusement, possibly of boredom. It's a waste, an unnecessary waste.

PHILLIP: The convicts will feel nothing has changed and will go back to their old ways.

JOSE: You have to be careful OH DAMN. *(Nervously, he regains his thought.)* You have to be careful with words that begin with *IN.* It can turn everything upside down. INjustice, most of that word is taken up with justice, but the *IN* turns it inside out making it the ugliest word in the English language.

SHONDRIKA: Citizens must be taught to obey the law of their own will. I want to rule over responsible human beings.

PHILLIP: Unexpected situations are often matched by unexpected virtues in people. Are they not?

BRIAN: A play should make you understand something new.

SHONDRIKA: Human beings —

XIOMARA: — have an intelligence —

BRIAN: — that has nothing to do —

JOSE: — with the circumstances —

COCA: — into which they were born.

CHRIS: THE END. *(Raucous applause. Light shift.)*

JANITOR: And the show did go on. A show that sparked a mini-revolution in the hearts of everyone in that auditorium. Sure, some crucial lines were fumbled, and some entrances missed and three cell phones went off in the audience. But, my God, if those kids weren't a success.

SCENE 15

Backstage.

COCA: Miss, I did good, right? I did good? I did good. I did my lines right. I did my motivations right. I did good, right. I did good? I did good? I did good? *(Assured.)* I did good. I did good. I did good. Oh, Miss. I been wantin' to tell you. You know I'm pregnant right? . . . Oh don't cry . . . Damn. Why do everyone cry when I say that? No, I wanted to tell you because my baby will not live like a prisoner, like a convict. I mean we still gotta put the baby-proof bars on the windows but that's state law. But that's it. We gonna travel, explore, see somethin' new for a change. I mean I love the Bronx but there's more to life right? You taught me that. "Man is born free" right . . . I mean, even though it's gonna be a girl. *(Beat.)* I know we was mad hard so thank you.

JOSE: Ms.? I don't know but, that class was still mad boring to me.

PHILLIP: *(Audibly.)* Ms. Sun?! I wanna be an actor now!

SECURITY GUARD: Oh, Oh! We gotta clear out the auditorium. You can't be lolly-gagging in here. Clear it out. Clear it out. Clear it out! By the way, I never done seen dem kids shine like they did tonight. They did good. You did good. Now, you got ta clear it out!

MS. SUN: *(To herself.)* Jerome . . . Jerome. *(Beat.)* "And we, this colony of a few hundred, will be watching this together, and we will no longer be despised prisoners and hated gaolers. We will laugh, we may be moved. We may . . ."

JEROME: *(Gasping.)* ". . . even think a little!"

MS. SUN: Jerome? What are you doing here?

JEROME: *(Panting.)* Mom came home early. Told me to run over here fast as I could . . . *(He realizes.)* I missed it. I missed it all. And I worked hard to learn my lines.

MS. SUN: Yes, you did Jerome. You worked very hard. *(Long beat.)*

JEROME: You gonna be teaching here again next year?

MS. SUN: That's the plan. But, only tenth graders again. Sorry.

JEROME: Oh no worries. I'm definitely gonna get left back for you. Psyche . . . Lemme go shout out to all them other thespians. You gonna be around?

MS. SUN: No, actually I have a commercial shoot early tomorrow morning.

JEROME: Really, for what?

MS. SUN: *(Slurring.)* It's nothing . . .

JEROME: Aw, come on you could tell me.

MS. SUN: Really, it's nothing.

JEROME: Lemme know. Lemme know. Come on lemme know.

MS. SUN: It's for Red Bull, damn it. Red Bull.

JEROME: Aight! Ms. Sun's finally getting paid. *(Light shift.)*

SCENE 16

JANITOR: And on to our third and final lesson of the evening: Something interesting happens when you die. You still care about the ones you left behind and wanna see how life ended up for them. Ms. Tam went back to the firm and wound up investing 2.3 million dollars towards arts in education with a strong emphasis on cultural diversity. Phillip proudly works as a conductor for the MTA. Shondrika Jones graduated summa cum laude from Harvard University and became the first black woman mayor of New York City. Alright now. Jose Guzman lost his life a week after the show when he decided to take vengeance on the Blood that killed his brother. Jerome. I might be omnipresent but I sure as heck ain't omniscient. Some of the brightest just slip through the cracks sometime. Do me a favor — you ever see him around town, tell him we thinkin' about him. And Ms. Sun. Well, she went on to win an NAACP Award, a Hispanic Heritage Award, a Tony Award, and an Academy Award. She was also in charge of restructuring of the nation's No Child Left Behind law and lives happily with her husband, Denzel Washington. His first wife never had a chance, poor thang. She still comes back every year to teach at Malcolm X High; oh, oh, oh, recently renamed Saint Tupac Shakur Preparatory. Times — they are a-changin'! *(He grabs his broom and sings. Lights shift as he walks toward a bright light offstage.)*

Trouble in mind

It's true

I had almost lost my way

(Offstage light brightens as if the heavens await. He knows to walk "into" it.)

But, the sun's gonna shine

In my back door someday

That's alright, Lord. That's alright!

END OF PLAY

THE PAIN AND THE ITCH

Bruce Norris

PLAYWRIGHT'S BIOGRAPHY

Bruce Norris is an actor and writer whose plays include, *The Infidel* (2000), *Purple Heart* (2002), *We All Went Down to Amsterdam* (2003), *The Pain and the Itch* (2004), and *The Unmentionables* (2006) all of which had their premiere at Steppenwolf Theatre, Chicago. His plays have also been produced at Lookingglass Theatre, Chicago (an adaptation of Joe Orton's *Up Against It,* 1994 and *The Vanishing Twin,* 1996), Philadelphia Theatre Company, Woolly Mammoth Theatre (Washington, D.C.), Playwrights Horizons (New York), The Royal Court Theatre (London) and the Galway Festival (Galway, Ireland). He is the recipient of the Whiting Foundation Prize for Drama (2006) as well as two Joseph Jefferson Awards (Chicago) for Best New Work, and the Kesselring Prize, Honorable Mention, for 2006. As an actor he can be seen in the films *A Civil Action* and *The Sixth Sense.* He lives in Brooklyn, New York.

ORIGINAL PRODUCTION

The Pain and the Itch received its World Premiere at Steppenwolf Theatre (Martha Lavey, Artistic Director; David Hawkanson, Executive Director) in Chicago, Illinois, on June 30, 2005. It was directed by Anna D. Shapiro; the costume design was by Janice Pytel; the lighting design was by James Ingalls; the sound design was by Michael Bodeen; and the production stage manager was Rob Satterlee. The cast was a follows:

MR. HADID	James Vincent Meredith
CLAY	Zak Orth
KELLY	Mariann Mayberry
CASH	Tracy Letts
KALINA	Kate Arrington
CAROL	Jayne Houdyshell
KAYLA	Lillian Almaguer/Hailey Gould

The Pain and the Itch was produced by Playwrights Horizons (Tim Sanford, Artistic Director; William Russo, General Manager) in New York City, on September 1, 2006. It ws directed by Anna D. Shapiro; the set design was by Daniel Ostling; the costume design was by Jennifer von Mayrhauser; the lighting design was by Donald Holder; the sound design was by Michael Bodeen; and the production stage manager was Susie Cordon. The cast was as follows:

MR. HADID	Peter Jay Fernandez
CLAY	Christopher Evans Welch

KELLY . . . . Mia Rogers
CASH . . . . Reg Rogers
KALINA . . . . Aya Cash
CAROL . . . . Jayne Houdyshell
KAYLA . . . . Ada-Marie L. Gutierrez/Vivien Kells

CHARACTERS

MR. HADID
KELLY
CLAY: married to kelly
KAYLA: their daughter, four years old
CASH: Clay's brother, one year older
KALINA: twenty-three, looks younger
CAROL: mother of Cash and Clay

NOTE: Cash is a well-dressed, successful doctor, not a deadbeat or oddball. Kalina is of Eastern European extraction and speaks with a pronounced accent. Mr. Hadid is likewise from abroad.

His accent is North African or perhaps Somali. He is bearded and wears a skullcap or tight-fitting hat of some kind. There is also a Baby. Clay or Kelly carry it around in a high-tech papoose, so it is never directly seen, though it is frequently heard.

TIME

The time is Thanksgiving evening and a later morning in January (the present). Lights should change to indicate a shift in time, but this should be done simply, and nothing (such as extra music or sound) should be added to further "enhance" these shifts. The scenes directly involving Mr. Hadid occur in the immediate present, which is to say, January. When the scenes move to the past (Thanksgiving), it maybe be possible — though not necessary — for Mr. Hadid to drift offstage, so that the past "takes over."

SETTING

The set is a very nice urban home. Expensive modern decor. Not homey. Tasteful neutral tones predominate. There is a visible front door and a staircase to a second floor. There is a sitting area as well as a prominent dining table. In a recessed alcove, there is a colossally large TV, the screen of which faces the audience.

THE PAIN AND THE ITCH

ACT ONE

Afternoon. Snow falls outside. Kelly and Clay sit side by side on the sofa. Clay holds the Baby. They both stare at Mr. Hadid, who holds his face in his hands and sobs quietly. This goes on for some time. Finally:

MR. HADID: I am sorry.
CLAY: *(Rapidly.)* No.
KELLY: *(The same.)* Don't.
CLAY: It's OK.
KELLY: It is *so* OK.
CLAY: More than OK. You should feel absolutely —
KELLY: However you need to . . . however the feelings have to. . . I mean, it's *loss,* for god's sake.
CLAY: And that *loss,* the *grief* that arises from *loss* . . . it would be unnatural to try to *suppress* —
KELLY: You can't.
CLAY: You can't do that.
KELLY: It's *harmful* to do that
CLAY: It is. No. What you're doing. It's the *right* thing, and an *emotion,* I mean, this is something we've been working on. The importance of *honoring* emotions in the moment that — *(To Kelly.)* What?
(Kelly is trying to stop him.)
CLAY: What? I'm *agreeing* with you.
(She mouths some words to Clay.)
CLAY: *(Quietly, to Mr. Hadid.)* I thought we were in agreement.
(Mr. Hadid wipes his eyes.)
MR. HADID: I am better now.
CLAY: But, what we wanted to say was —
(Then the Baby starts crying. Loud.)
CLAY: Uh-oh. Hey now. Hey mister.
KELLY: I'll do it.
CLAY: Hey mister angry face.
KELLY: Clay.
CLAY: I got him.
KELLY: Let me do it.
CLAY: Whatsamatter Groucho? Hey Groucho Marx.

KELLY: Clay.

CLAY: *(Laughing.)* Ohhh he's *mad*, isn't he? Look at that face! Grrrrrr!

KELLY: Would you let me do it?

CLAY: Heyyyyyy. Shhhhhhh.

KELLY: Please just give him to me.

CLAY: *(Handing Baby over to Kelly.)* He's stopping. He's stopping.

KELLY: Well, don't *bounce* him.

MR. HADID: Now I make *him* cry.

KELLY: No no no. Not you.

CLAY: I was only shushing *him*.

KELLY: We didn't mean *you*.

CLAY: No, he just gets a little hyper if he doesn't sleep through the night, but *you* should go ahead and . . . *(To the Baby.)* Huh? Feeling better now, huh? Yeah. *(To Kelly.)* I wasn't *bouncing*.

KELLY: Jiggling, anyway.

(As they were talking, Kayla has come downstairs, unnoticed. She picks up the TV remote and presses a button. The TV screen is filled with cartoons of clowns and loud children's music fills the room. The Baby cries louder.)

CLAY: *(Loud, to Kayla.)* Sweetie?

KELLY: Honey?

CLAY: Kayla?

KELLY: Not now, sweetie.

CLAY: Later, OK?

KELLY: We can watch that later, is that OK?

CLAY: After the grown-ups are done.

(Kayla switches off the set and calmly leaves the room.)

KELLY: *(To Kayla, as she leaves.)* Thank you, sweetie.

CLAY: *(Same.)* That's very nice of you. Very polite.

KELLY: *(Same.)* You're very thoughtful.

CLAY: Very considerate.

(She is gone. The Baby has stopped.)

MR. HADID: You were going to say.

KELLY: Yes.

CLAY: Yes. So. OK. So the situation was: The day before. We're having breakfast.

KELLY: I had just started going back to the office again.

CLAY: It's the Tuesday before the holiday, *(Re: the Baby.)* and he had just been born and she's on her way in to the office in the morning and I'm making breakfast, I'm making eggs for Kayla.

KELLY: And Kayla goes Mommy *look.*

CLAY: *Shrieks* and says it.

KELLY: And I look and there in her hand, right out of the *bowl* on the table —

CLAY: Kitchen table.

KELLY: This bowl has *avocados* in it and one of these avocados has been, what? Has been —

CLAY: Let's just say *gnawed.*

KELLY: *Gnawed* on.

CLAY: Extensively gnawed *upon.*

KELLY: Right down to the *pit,* has been *consumed.* Something, some sort of —

CLAY: Non-human.

KELLY: Unless you know some *human* that bites into an avocado like it was an *apple,* all right? So, yes, some *non-human creature* has entered our *house* and is now *feasting* on our avocados.

CLAY: And of course the mind devises these *scenarios.*

KELLY: But the bottom line is *one:* What sort of *toothed creature* are we dealing with, *two:* What is the point of *entry,* and *three,* where exactly is it *now?*

MR. HADID: Do you have a pet?

(*Pause.*)

KELLY: (*An uncomfortable subject.*) Uhhhh . . . no.

CLAY: No.

KELLY: No.

CLAY: No, we —

KELLY: No, although Kayla loves hamsters, about which I have said absolutely not.

CLAY: What with the allergies.

KELLY: No, Clay used to have a cat. But there's toxoplasmosis.

CLAY: From the litter box.

KELLY: First trimester, harms the fetus.

CLAY: *Potentially.*

KELLY: *Can* harm.

CLAY: It's not a certainty, but —

KELLY: It's a risk.

CLAY: A *low* risk.

KELLY: Not a risk I *personally* would want to take.

CLAY: Not that I'm questioning the decision because ultimately it is a *life* we're talking about and you have to ask yourself do I give priority to a *cat's* life? Or to . . . to . . . to?

KELLY: To a human life.

CLAY: Right. Right. Right. So. Right. So, we made the decision. *I* made the decision.

KELLY: You can say we.

CLAY: To have him killed.

KELLY: *(To Mr. Hadid.)* Some people might say put to sleep.

CLAY: *(Laughs.)* Well, I mean, he's not exactly *sleeping,* is he? He's *dead,* right? Chester is *dead* now and and and —

KELLY: Clay.

CLAY: And *we did it.* Or rather, the *vet,* at our request.

KELLY: *(To Mr. Hadid.)* He was euthanized.

CLAY: So, no. We don't have pets.

KELLY: But if you see this on your kitchen table. Your *child* sees it. *Touches* it. And admittedly, I am someone who tends to, on occasion —

CLAY: Overreact.

 (Kelly silently stares straight ahead.)

CLAY: Well, honey, I mean, *(Laughs.)* . . . I mean, at least *fixate.*

KELLY: *(To Mr. Hadid.)* We're being so rude. Can I get you something?

MR. HADID: I am fine.

KELLY: We have seltzer. Or iced tea.

CLAY: *(To Kelly.)* Or those green tea things in the bottles.

KELLY: Or caffeine-free Diet Coke. Or with.

CLAY: *(To Kelly.)* Or bottled water. Or tap water.

MR. HADID: I am fine.

 (Uncomfortable pause.)

CLAY: It just means a lot to us that you would —

MR. HADID: *(Interrupting.)* Unless you have some apple juice?

KELLY: Oh! Uhhhh . . . ?

CLAY: Do we?

KELLY: No. Just. Well.

CLAY: Not the good kind.

KELLY: We have, what is it, like *Mott's?*

MR. HADID: It is apple juice?

KELLY: Yeah.

MR. HADID: I will have that, thank you.

 (Kelly and Clay both stand. Kelly exits, taking the Baby. Clay sits.)

CLAY: *(For lack of anything better to say.)* I used to have a beard. Years ago. Seriously. My dad had a moustache. But on *me,* with the shape of my face, I always thought the full beard. Kelly, though, she . . . didn't so much . . . care for it . . . but I could grow another. One of these days.

(Pause.)

CLAY: It's just, we want you to get an accurate picture of who we *are*. Which is so hard because you're tempted to fall back on *clichés*. Which is frustrating if you want someone to *understand* the things that motivate you. Or all of us. As a people. *(He laughs.)* Well. There you go. Sounds *clichéd*. No, what I mean is . . . That this society, *our* society, as a whole. . . . *(Flailing.)* OK. Once again. What does that *mean?* "Society as a Whole." I don't even know what that *means*. I can only talk about *us*. The things that motivate *us,* because —

MR. HADID: *(Raises his hand.)* Excuse me? I cannot stay terribly long.

CLAY: But . . . the others are going to be here.

MR. HADID: I have a little time.

CLAY: Especially Mom.

MR. HADID: I have some time.

CLAY: And . . . didn't you want the *juice?*

MR. HADID: Perhaps you could finish the story of the avocados.

CLAY: Exactly. Yes. So: That was Tuesday. Wednesday, I call the exterminator. And then, of course, it was Thursday, which was the holiday.
(Lights change. Snow stops. Evening. It is now Thanksgiving. Tasteful home entertainment music begins to play. Kayla now wearing a party dress, runs through the room, shrieking. She is being chased by Kalina. Cash enters from the kitchen.)

CASH: Why do you rule out a *squirrel?*

CLAY: No. They came. They looked everywhere. They said it's not.

CASH: The squirrel is a foraging animal.

CLAY: They said this is something that has an appetite for *fruit*. Which to them did not suggest a squirrel.

CASH: A *fruit?*

CLAY: Yes.

CASH: Avocado's a vegetable.

CLAY: The fruit of the avocado tree.

CASH: Tree?

CLAY: Yes.

CASH: Think it's a *bush*.

CLAY: And even if it *was* a squirrel.

CASH: Could've been nuts in the vicinity.

CLAY: Even if it was.

CASH: Squirrel comes around, he's *foraging* for nuts, gets *distracted* by the avocado . . . *(Continued.)*

CLAY: *(Overlapping.)* It's *not,* but —

CASH: *(Continuous.)* . . . gets to that avocado pit, squirrel's thinking, hey, I just discovered the motherfucking Hope Diamond of nuts.

(Carol enters from the kitchen carrying a pretty tablecloth.)

CAROL: Clay, who is the actor, the one, you know, the one who does the narration for the nature shows?

CLAY: Uhhh. . . . I don't know.

CAROL: The one with the baritone voice?

CLAY: I don't know.

CAROL: Because there was a nature show on the other night and it was all *about* squirrels.

CLAY: It's not a squirrel, alright? It's not.

CASH: Rodent of some kind.

CLAY: But even *if.* Still. That's a vector of disease. There's the droppings. There's fleas.

CASH: Avocado's a vegetable.

CLAY: There's lice. And I'd rather not have that around my children, OK?

CAROL: *(Exiting to the kitchen.)* Anyway, that man, the one I meant, with the baritone voice? Well, he *narrated* that show.

(Again, Kayla runs through the room with Kalina chasing her. Kayla is screaming with laughter.)

KALINA: *(To Kayla.)* I am going to get you!!! You not fast enough!! Ha! I will capture and torture you!!

(They almost crash into Kelly, who enters as they tear through the room. Kelly carries place settings.)

CLAY: *(Calling after them.)* Not too loud, Sweetie. Your brother's still sleeping, OK?

KELLY: *(To Clay, not Cash, whom she ignores.)* I just wish you had called the other place. That's all I said.

CLAY: You asked me to call and I called. You didn't say —

KELLY: Of *course* they're cheaper if they use *neurotoxins.*

CLAY: You didn't specify. You just said call. You said handle it. *(Continued.)*

KELLY: *(Overlapping.)* Might as well spray Agent Orange on our children.

CLAY: *(Continuous.)* Which I *did,* so don't act like I'm incompetent.

KELLY: *(Searching in a closet.)* Your mother needs that big salad bowl. And I did say specifically no glue traps.

CLAY: I took them out. I took them out.

KELLY: *(From inside.)* I just don't think that allowing your daughter watch an animal writhe to a slow sadistic death in a puddle of glue is the best way to solve the problem.

CLAY: You know, if I happen to handle things my own way —

(Kelly, while digging through the closet, has pulled out a set of golf clubs.)

KELLY: Clay, you hired her. Can you explain to that woman the notion of a kitchen?

CLAY: Maybe she doesn't understand what you're saying.

KELLY: Well, then tomorrow we can hire a *translator* for the cleaning person. *(Calling.) Carol? I found it.*

(Kelly exits.)

CASH: Hey Clay.

CLAY: *(Calling after her.)* But see, do I come to your office and criticize the way *you* do things?

CASH: Got yourself some *golf clubs* I see.

CLAY: *(The same.)* If I'm the person here every second except three hours a week? Is that unreasonable?

(Kelly re-enters holding the chewed-upon avocado.)

KELLY: *(Lowered voice.)* You do *see* this, right? You see *teeth marks,* all right? This isn't *academic.* It's about your *children.* So, at the *moment?* Whether or not you're reasonable? That actually isn't the *topic* right now.

(Mr. Hadid interrupts from across the room. Music stops. Lights change.)

MR. HADID: May I ask a question?

CLAY: Oh. Sorry.

KELLY: Of course.

CLAY: Absolutely.

KELLY: Yes, please . . . Anything that's not clear.

MR. HADID: I have seen these shoes.

CLAY: These what?

MR. HADID: The shoes you are wearing.

CLAY: I . . . you mean *me?*

MR. HADID: Yes.

KELLY: Sorry. We're confused.

MR. HADID: The shoes on your feet.

CLAY: *(Laughs.)* Yeah?

MR. HADID: Do you know how much you pay for them?

KELLY: *His* shoes.

MR. HADID: I very much admire this style of shoe.

KELLY: Ohhhh.

CLAY: *(Relieved.)* Oh. Uhhhhh . . . uhhhh . . . Wow. God, let me think. *(To Kelly.)* Do you . . . ?

KELLY: They're from that place.

MR. HADID: They were expensive?

CLAY: Oh . . . uhhhh . . . well, except we usually wait for everything to go on sale.

KELLY: I'm one of those people with like a bargain *obsession*.

CLAY: So probably less than you think.

MR. HADID: But do you know how much? In dollars?

CLAY: Uhhhh . . . gosh *(To Kelly.)* . . . do you . . . ?

KELLY: Uhh . . . no, I don't . . . I . . . hmm. No.

CLAY: Really can't . . . uh, they're definitely comfortable.

MR. HADID: *(Politely.)* I am sorry.

CLAY: No, no.

KELLY: We could possibly find out.

MR. HADID: At a more convenient time.

KELLY: We don't really keep those kind of receipts.

MR. HADID: No no. Please go on.

(Back to the previous moment: lights, music, etc.)

KELLY: *(Brandishing the avocado.)* So, at the *moment?* Whether or not you're reasonable? That actually isn't the *topic* right now.

CASH: Hey Clay.

(Kelly exits to kitchen.)

CASH: Lemme take a look at your kid.

CLAY: *(To Cash.) Shhhh* . . . could you? A little? Do you mind?

CASH: *(Re: Kelly.)* She's not paying attention.

CLAY: I know. Just. Try to.

(Clay turns down the music.)

CASH: What's the big deal?

CLAY: It's not a big deal.

CASH: Not a big deal to *me*.

CLAY: Me either.

CASH: Happy to.

CLAY: Thanks.

CASH: Just tell me when.

CLAY: Not yet, but —

CASH: Awaiting your signal.

CLAY: Maybe when they come upstairs.

CASH: Standing by, chief.

(Pause.)

CLAY: I mean, I just don't want it to *seem* like a big deal.

CASH: What, you mean to your *wife?*

CLAY: No.

CASH: I'm not gonna say anything.

CLAY: I know.

CASH: To Mom?

CLAY: No, I just.

CASH: I'm discreet.

CLAY: I mean to Kayla.

CASH: She scared of me?

CLAY: No.

CASH: You told her who I am.

CLAY: Yeah.

CASH: You said this is Uncle Cash.

CLAY: Yeah.

CASH: So how am I making it a big deal?

CLAY: You know how.

CASH: I do?

CLAY: Yes you do.

CASH: I'm not sure I do.

CLAY: The way you are.

CASH: The way I am.

CLAY: The way you can be.

CASH: What way is that?

CLAY: You know.

CASH: Tell me what way.

CLAY: I think you know.

CASH: Say what you mean.

CLAY: The attitude.

CASH: *My* attitude.

CLAY: You know the attitude.

CASH: My *professional* attitude?

CLAY: General attitude.

CASH: So my *personality.*

CLAY: And I'd prefer it if you wouldn't.

CASH: Have the attitude.

CLAY: Today, anyway.

CASH: Because of the *children.*

CLAY: Kids don't understand when you . . . I'd just prefer it.

CASH: That's your preference.

CLAY: Yes it is.

CASH: About my attitude.

CLAY: Right.

CASH: Gracious. Well then, on behalf of the *children*.

    (*Kalina tiptoes through the room, hiding from Kayla, a finger to her lips, and exits again.*)

CASH: Soooo . . . Big *golfer* now, huh?

CLAY: For example.

CASH: Now there's a sport.

CLAY: Case in point.

CASH: The ladies *love* the golfers.

CLAY: Hmm-mm.

CASH: Strolling the links in a pair of crisp white shorts.

CLAY: Hate to break this to you

CASH: The ladies *cream* for the golfers.

CLAY: . . . but I'm not looking for your approval.

CASH: Not a dry panty in the clubhouse.

CLAY: Hey, you know what? Forget it.

CASH: Why?

CLAY: If this is how it's gonna be.

CASH: How what is?

CLAY: Big surprise.

CASH: What did I do?

CLAY: So it's going to be like this?

CASH: Like what?

CLAY: That's your choice? Years can go by, but *still*.

CASH: What's it like?

CLAY: Like this. Like unpleasant.

CASH: I don't find you unpleasant.

CLAY: Yeah yeah yeah.

CASH: Ohhhh, you mean *me*.

CLAY: Never changes.

CASH: But I'm making *pleasantries*.

CLAY: Yeah. Right. Uhhh . . . here's a thought: *Kiss my ass?*

CASH: Well, *that* was unpleasant.

CLAY: I'll take her to the pediatrician, you know? Thought you wouldn't mind.

CASH: I don't mind.

CLAY: If I ask every once in very rare while for a favor.

CASH: So not only do you want me to do your kid this medical favor but I also have to maintain a certain *attitude* —

CASH: A favor for which, by the way, most people would make an *appointment.*

CLAY: So don't say you don't mind when clearly you —

CASH: For which most people would *pay.*

CLAY: You might have warned me you were planning to be like this.

CASH: You might have warned me that you were still a little fascist.

CLAY: *(Seeing Carol and Kelly.)* Shhhh.

(Carol and Kelly enter carrying place settings.)

KELLY: . . . and I'm stranded there on the runway in *Orange County.* At *John Wayne Airport,* which I think says it all, and I'm talking to this young white man next to me who is headed to West Africa to do his *missionary work* like *trick or treat* for the Republican party —

(Kayla has entered, searching for Kalina. She has one hand inside her pull-up. She exits again.)

KELLY: Clay, did you put her in a pull-up?

CLAY: Yes I did.

KELLY: Why is she scratching like that?

CAROL: *(Re: table settings.)* Which way does this go, now?

KELLY: I'll do it. And this Man opens his bag, and remember, I'm actually *conversing* with this person, opens his carry-on and it is filled, top to bottom, with *Bibles, American Flags,* and laminated pictures of our *president.*

CAROL: Oh. Thank God, only two more years of that little *smirking* face.

KELLY: And I'm thinking *how dare you,* you TGI Fridays customer. You TJ Maxx shopper with your iceberg lettuce and your ranch dressing and the right *to vote. How dare you.* I mean the *audacity.*

(Kayla and Kalina run through screaming again, this time in the other direction.)

KALINA: *(As they pass through.)* I cannot catch her!!! She is too fast for me!! Is crazy fast girl!!

CLAY: *(Upon seeing them.)* Sweetie? C'mere a second.

KELLY: And I'm sorry, Carol, I'm all for inclusion. But that part of the country? Those are not my people.

(Kelly and Carol have exited to the kitchen again. Pause.)

CASH: Shouldn't leave food lying around.

CLAY: What food?

CASH: Why ya got that rodent problem.

CLAY: We don't leave food lying around.

CASH: Mom said you got a maid.

CLAY: Cleaning person. Yes.

CASH: Maybe pay her a little more.

CLAY: We pay her very well.

CASH: To make sure there's no food lying around.

CLAY: There isn't.

CASH: *(Shrugs.) Avocados* you said.

CLAY: Where do you suggest they ripen?

CASH: She's foreign, right?

CLAY: Who?

CASH: Maid. Foreigner?

CLAY: You have a problem with that?

CASH: Probably wants more money.

CLAY: We pay her very well.

CASH: It's why she came here, right? Make money?

CLAY: We give her lunch. We give her a room to put her stuff in.

CASH: Mom says she steals.

CLAY: *What!!?*

    (Kalina appears on the stairs.)

KALINA: Cash, come look with me at the baby sleeping!!!

CLAY: Mom's out of her fucking mind.

KALINA: *(Rapturously.)* Oh god!! He is so cute when lying like this in the sleep- ing position!!

CASH: *(To Clay, ignoring Kalina.)* What happened to your cat?

KALINA: *(Joining them.)* This is what I want is the babies!!! To be married and have my stomach filled with the big babies and feeling the kicks!!

CASH: What happened to Chester?

KALINA: Cash!!! Come to look!!!

CASH: Had a cat you wouldn't have a rodent problem.

KALINA: *(To Cash.)* Aaaarghggh!! *(To Clay.)* He is so boring, your brother! He always like to do nothing. And so I never do anything also. Yesterday I say to him hey. I say why we not sometime go dancing? He says *(Imitat- ing him.)* I'm not a *faggot*. I say, *Cash.* Don't be stupid. Is sexy to dance, you know? Does not make you the faggot to be liking to dance! And on top of the things, is way to have fun and meet the people. He say why do I want to meet the people? I say, uhhh, because *you are human being?* I say I wish that I can go and meet the faggots because I believe the fag- gots are having more of the fun than *you! (To Cash.)* Oh, hee hee ha ha. Go and be with the laughing. You are fucked over, you know?

CASH: Up.

KALINA: *(To Clay.)* Is totally fucked over to be thinking like this, yes?

CASH: The preposition you are looking for is *up*.

KALINA: *(To Cash.)* Hey. Excuse me. I know fucked over. OK? Is expression.

CASH: *(Laughs, quietly.)* Whatever. Fuckin' nitwit.

KALINA: What do you call me?

CASH: *(Laughing.) Fucked over.*

KALINA: Excuse me, what do you call me now?

CASH: *(To himself.)* I take it back. I *am* fucked over.

KALINA: I know this word, Cash. The word *nitwit*. Do not be calling me the names in front of your family, alright? Do you hear? Is not right, you know?

(Mr. Hadid, standing by the dining table, interrupts again. Lights change.)

MR. HADID: Excuse me once again.

CLAY: Hmmm?

MR. HADID: I am wondering about the table.

CLAY: Yeah?

MR. HADID: This one.

CLAY: Yeah?

MR. HADID: Very nice.

CLAY: Oh thanks.

MR. HADID: Very good table.

CLAY: Parsons table, yeah.

MR. HADID: And you could fix it.

CLAY: Fix what?

MR. HADID: The table. It is easy to fix. If you were to use the sandpaper? To rub it with the sandpaper. And you fill in these little holes. Here. And here. And then you use the beeswax. In this way, you bring out the pattern of the grain.

CLAY: Well. But. You know. It's *distressed.*

MR. HADID: But you could fix it.

CLAY: No, I mean, it's *supposed* to look like that.

MR. HADID: Ahhhhh.

CLAY: It's *made* that way.

MR. HADID: *(Smiles.)* Ahhhh. And do you know how much you pay for it?

CLAY: *(Reluctant.)* Oh. Uhhhhh . . . gosh.

MR. HADID: It was expensive?

CLAY: Interestingly, not as much as the chairs.

MR. HADID: But can you say how much? In dollars.

CLAY: The thing is . . . The thing is maybe we should talk about that *later.*

MR. HADID: Forgive me.

CLAY: No no no. It's fine. It's just we're trying to talk about *one* thing and then —

MR. HADID: None of my *beeswax*.

CLAY: No no no no.

MR. HADID: And I have interrupted.

CLAY: You're our *guest*. Please.

MR. HADID: I will be more careful.

CLAY: Can I get you anything else? Something to eat?

MR. HADID: Please. Continue.

(*The previous scene resumes.*)

KALINA: I know this word, Cash. The word *nitwit*. Do not be calling me the names in front of your family, alright? Do you hear? Is not right, you know?

(*Kayla has re-entered, looking for Kalina. Cash is chuckling.*)

KALINA: Oh, big funny joke. How we are laughing now.

CLAY: (*Quietly, to Kayla.*) Sweetie, don't scratch, OK? You just make it worse.

CASH: (*To Kayla.*) Hey. C'mere a second.

(*He checks with Clay, who silently indicates for Cash to proceed.*)

KALINA: (*To Clay.*) Ohhhhh, you know, last month we are going to New York? Cash and I are going to New York and we go to the Ground Zero and it is so *sad*, you know? To think how all the people die? And is still just big empty hole sitting there with nothing? *So sad*. Do you ever go to New York to see the Ground Zero?

CLAY: No.

(*As Kalina talks, Cash leads Kayla by the hand out of the room.*)

KALINA: Is good to go there so maybe you will.

CLAY: Maybe.

KALINA: For the nation.

CLAY: Maybe we will.

KALINA: And I buy these *boots* there, too!

CLAY: Those are great.

KALINA: I spend so much *money!* But still is good because is hard to find good shoes sometime.

CLAY: Uh, how long have you been in the U.S.?

KALINA: Four and half years. Oh, hey!! You know what it is I am thinking? In place where I am little girl, in village? We have the *weasels*, you know? And always they are getting into the places where there is the food? And I am also thinking maybe the weasels are in this place.

CLAY: It's possible.

KALINA: Is so weird! I say to Cash you have *brother* here and you not ever see him? Is *wrong*, you know? Because your *family*, this is the people who would *kill* for you. And you for them.

CLAY: Right.

KALINA: But you are so lucky to have Kelly, who make so much money so that you can do *nothing* all day but to be the perfect father for the children? So lucky for you!!

(Cash re-enters with Kayla as Carol and Kelly enter with place settings. Cash continues to kitchen.)

KELLY: . . . *in* which, of course, corporate media is totally complicit, since if you decide you're going to *hurt* people, as our president seems *determined* to do, then of course it helps to *vilify* them in advance so that we don't have to *feel so bad* when we start dropping bombs on them. Oh, uhhh —

(Kalina is lighting a cigarette.)

KELLY: *(To Kalina.)* Wait. Wait. Excuse me? Hello?

CLAY: Oh, yeah. We don't . . . in the house, generally —

KALINA: Ohhhh yes! I forget, Kelly! It is so true!

CAROL: *(Re: place settings.)* Oh, look. I'm doing everything backwards, aren't I?

KELLY: I'll do it. You sit.

KALINA: *Hey Kayla!!!? You go with me while I do the smoking!! (To Clay.)* Is OK, yes?

(Clay looks to Kelly.)

CLAY: Umm . . . actually . . ?

KALINA: *(Understanding.)* Ohhhh, I see it now. I am to show bad example. Is OK. *Hey Kayla! See how I am doing the smoking? This is soooo bad so don't do it when you are bigger. Even if it make you look sexy and things? Don't do it.*

KELLY: Clay, are you going to open that bottle of wine?

KALINA: *(As she exits.) Don't ever to be like me.*

CLAY: Mom? Glass of wine?

(Clay exits to kitchen. Kayla tugs at Kelly's leg as she sets the table.)

CAROL: I get so confused lately. I start to worry that I could have some of the *warning signs.*

KELLY: *(To Kayla.)* Not now, sweetie.

CAROL: Do you know that joke about the woman whose doctor says to her I have some terrible news for you, Mrs. Jones, he says I'm afraid you have *Alzheimer's* disease? And *she* says . . . *(Confused.)* oh, no, wait. Oh, *poop.*

KELLY: *(Calling to the kitchen.)* Clay*, can you also bring the candles?*

CAROL: No, see . . . now I have it all wrong.

CLAY: *(From offstage.) They're on the table.*

KELLY: *No they're not.* (*To Carol.*) I'm listening. The doctor says you have Alzheimer's.

CAROL: Oh! Oh! Now I remember. This is it. He says you have *cancer.*

KELLY: Ah. Very different.

CAROL: The doctor in the *joke.* He says, "You have incurable *cancer.*" You have to say that part first.

KELLY: (*To Kayla.*) Sweetie pie, *please?* (*To Carol.*) Right. So the doctor says "you have *cancer.*"

CAROL: He says you have incurable cancer and the woman says oh how terrible and *then* the doctor says but, you see, it's even *worse* than that —

KELLY: (*Smiles, knowing the punch line.*) Ohhhhh. Right, right. OK, I get it now.

CAROL: Oh, you've *heard* it.

KELLY: Uhhh . . . he says it's worse than that you also have Alzheimer's and she says oh thank god I thought you were going to tell me I had cancer.

CAROL: Now see, that just makes me laugh.

KELLY: (*To Kayla, finally.*) What, sweetie? Use your words.
(*Kelly bends down and Kayla whispers in her ear as Clay enters from the kitchen, with the bottle of wine.*)

CAROL: Isn't it odd, Clay? Both Charlton Heston *and* Ronald Reagan. With the Alzheimer's? Isn't that a coincidence? Both actors. And both Republicans.

CLAY: Oh, right. Well. Fuck 'em.

CAROL: Well, *precisely.*

KELLY: (*Taking Kayla toward the stairs.*) OK, sweetie. Mommy's gonna change your Huggie then you can help me set the table.

CLAY: No no no no no! What do you mean? What are you . . . ? I just put one on her.

KELLY: She says she's itchy.

CLAY: (*To Kayla.*) Sweetie, Daddy just gave you a brand new Huggie, remember? We don't need another Huggie.

CAROL: (*With concern.*) Ohhh, is Kayla wearing her little Huggie?

CLAY: Mom, can we not make her self-conscious, OK?

KELLY: Clay she's not comfortable.

CLAY: Well, that's not the point, is it? (*To Kayla.*) See, Sweetie, the Huggies aren't just *free,* you know, the Huggies cost *money.*

KELLY: For Christ's *sake,* Clay.

CAROL: (*To Kayla.*) I know some big girls who wear *grown-up* pants because *their* mommies and daddies —

CLAY: Mom? Why don't you just relax?

KELLY: Maybe we could *all* relax.

CLAY: *(To Kelly.)* Well, who deals with this every single day, huh? Is it you? Or is it me?

KELLY: Fine. Let her scratch.

CLAY: *(To Kayla.)* Daddy's the Huggie changer, right pumpkin? We don't need to bother Mommy.

(Kalina returns from outside.)

KALINA: *(To Kayla.)* I know what it is that is wrong with Kayla. Yes I do. She need *to be teekled!!! And I am coming to get her and teekle her!!!*

(Kayla shrieks and races away, Kalina following.)

KALINA: *(Exiting.) Stop!!! I command you to stop for my teekling!!*

(Carol sits by Mr. Hadid. Clay turns to him. Lights change.)

CLAY: See, I feel sorry for people out there. These people without kids. And I hate to use the cliché, it sounds like such a cliché, but it's a *gift*, right? To be able to, with your kids, to recapture some of . . our . . . *innocence.* Get some of that back. Reconnect with the innocence. Because if you *don't,* then, you know? Then it . . . it . . . it's *lost.* It *collapses,* like, like, like . . .

MR. HADID: Like a soufflé.

CAROL: *(To Mr. Hadid.)* Ohhh, do you know the word *soufflé?*

MR. HADID: Of course, yes.

CLAY: *(Re: his glass.)* Did you want more of that, or — ?

MR. HADID: Yes, please. Thank you.

(Clay takes his glass and exits.)

CAROL: Loss is so difficult.

MR. HADID: Yes.

CAROL: How old was she?

MR. HADID: She was forty-two.

CAROL: And you have a son?

MR. HADID: One son, yes ma'am.

CAROL: Let me ask you something. I was watching a documentary the other night on PBS. I don't know if you watch PBS. I'm a subscriber. And sometimes I volunteer for the pledge drives. But mostly I think what else is there to watch? I mean, really, well, there's the Discovery Channel. But 99 percent of what's on television I just look at it and I . . . I don't *disapprove,* I mean, more power to all that. Diversity and everything. Diversity is so important. But it's like with *junk food,* isn't it? I say to my first graders, if *all* you eat is junk food, then you can hardly expect to feel good about yourself. And you know, I was showing them a wonderful program all about families around the world, from each continent, and when they got to some tribesmen in New Guinea, who wear very little clothing, just some leaves and . . . *gourds,* but it's the *tropics,* after all, well, some of the children started to *laugh.* And you know, that just upset me so much. So I said to them, well now, let's all just *think* for a minute. Let's think how *you* would like to be laughed at. If you went to New Guinea right now, dressed in your *American* clothes? That wouldn't be very nice, would it? How do we ever expect to reach out to new cultures and embrace new ideas if all we can do is *laugh? (Back to her main point.)* And plus, Bill Moyers is so wonderful. So I was watching the documentary, which was all about *Genghis Khan.* Did you see that?

MR. HADID: I don't think so.

(Kayla has approached Carol. She holds one hand behind her back.)

CAROL: Well, look who's here now. Do you want to say hello? Do you want to do that? Hmm?

(Kayla shakes her head.)

CAROL: Oh, oh now, wait. Is that a surprise? Maybe let's not. OK? Because remember how some surprises aren't so nice? Remember? So only if it's a nice sur —

(Kayla produces a screwdriver. Carol flinches.)

CAROL: *Ohhh.* Alright. Well, that's a nice thing. I like screwdrivers. Screwdrivers are useful. Thank you. This will be *very useful.*

(Kayla exits.)

CAROL: I'm sorry. *How* old was she, did you say?

MR. HADID: Forty-two.

CAROL: She had diabetes?

MR. HADID: Yes ma'am.

CAROL: What a terrible way to . . .

MR. HADID: Yes ma'am.

CAROL: You see, because we don't *listen* to each other. We don't. My husband, for example. He was not a good listener. But the lovely thing about *Eastern* Wisdom, *I* think, what we learn from . . . from the . . . wait, where are the monks from? Oh, you know, the monks. The country with the meditation. The Asian country.

MR. HADID: China?

CAROL: No no no, smaller.

MR. HADID: Korea?

CAROL: No, but landlocked.

MR. HADID: Nepal?

CAROL: Oh, what is wrong with me? No, from our meditation class. More to the West.

MR. HADID: Bhutan?

CAROL: And It's mountainous. With the yaks, you know. The yaks and the political problems?

MR. HADID: Mongol — ?

CAROL: *Tibet!* Thank you. Tibet. With the Dalai Lama. The Tibetan monks. And what we learn from them is, it seems to me, it's the value of *listening.*

(Pause. Mr. Hadid nods.)

CAROL: Tell me again, *how* old was she?

(Kayla and Kalina dash in, using Nerf bats as guns to shoot at each other. Kayla is shrieking. Music returns.)

KALINA: *(Makes shooting sounds.)* Ahhhh! No! The bullets they are hitting her but still she lives!! She is *Supergirl! Nooo!* She shoots me! *Arrrgghhhghh!!!!*

(Clay enters from the kitchen. He is wearing an apron and oven mitts.)

CLAY: *(Interrupting.)* Hey. Sorry. Sweetie? No shooting, OK? Let's not shoot.

KALINA: Is OK. Is no real bullets.

CLAY: It's just we don't do shooting games.

KALINA: Oh, yes.

CLAY: Not to be all preachy about it.

KALINA: Noooo, is true. With the guns being so bad in the nation.

CLAY: *(To Kayla.)* But you're having some fun, aren't you, huh? Aren't you, Special K?

CAROL: Clay, did you know this? That Charlton Heston wears a *toupee?*

KALINA: *(To Kayla.)* Hey!! I know!! *Now I am to sword fight with you!! (en garde)* Ha-haaa!

(They begin fencing.)

CLAY: Wait. Sorry. Kalina? Uhhhh . . . martial arts? Guns. It's all the emphasis on *conflict?*

KALINA: *(Stopping.)* Ohhhhh, yes.

CAROL: And *John Wayne,* too. A toupee. And one doesn't normally think of him as *vain.* Now, someone told me that *he* did a movie about Genghis Khan. Now that's just silly. That's *miscasting.*

(Kelly has entered with a centerpiece.)

KALINA: *(To Kelly, who ignores her.)* Oh Kelly!!! So pretty!! Look at table!! Is she so perfect or what!?

CAROL: Now, tell me the one who played Gandhi.

KELLY: Ben Kingsley.

CAROL: No, that's not it.

KELLY: It was Ben Kingsley.

CAROL: No, I don't think so. I think he was Indian.

KELLY: Ben Kingsley is English.

CAROL: No, this actor is olive-skinned.

CLAY: Ben. Kingsley.

> *(Kelly continues upstairs as Cash returns with a martini.)*

CAROL: Well, I don't think you're right but anyway, the English actors are just *better*. Don't you think? Especially in historical films. You can't have American actors playing those parts, it never *sounds* right. Wait, now who is the one from that movie about the Conquistadors?

CLAY: *(On his way back to kitchen.)* Uhhh . . . I don't know.

CAROL: And I think he also was in *Dr. Zhivago*.

CLAY: I don't know.

CAROL: Oh, yes you do. Of course you do. You know.

CLAY: *(Calling from the kitchen.)* I don't know.

CAROL: *(To Kalina.)* Well, I don't really go to the *commercial* sort of movies anyway. I suppose it's all the talking in the audience. Although I know that people in certain communities enjoy that, all the talking, and I don't want to discourage that if it's their *custom*. Now, where I live we have a University Cinema. They show the smaller movies and those I like.

CASH: *(To himself, opening a magazine.)* The ones black people don't go to?

> *(Clay returns with bottle and glasses as Kelly returns from upstairs with the Baby.)*

CLAY: Anybody? Glass of wine before we eat?

KALINA: Ohhh, yes please for me, thank you.

CASH: Oughta go to porn films, Mom. People don't talk during those.

CAROL: I have no objection to pornography.

CASH: Although they do *moan* from time to time.

CAROL: We do have a thing called the First Amendment.

KELLY: Right, but Carol —

CAROL: In fact, we knew a couple that had quite an extensive collection of pornography.

CLAY: Who?

CAROL: The Teverbaughs.

CLAY: Doctor Teverbaugh.

CAROL: That's right.

CLAY: Pornography?

CAROL: It was their interest.

CLAY: My orthodontist.

CASH: I *thought* his fingers tasted funny.

CAROL: It can be a marital aid. If the couple has the shared interest, it can help the marriage.

CASH: But then it's not *porn.* How can that be *porn?*

CLAY: *(Looking at the ceiling.)* Shh, shh. Hey, you guys?

CASH: You can't look at porn with your *wife.* That's the moment it ceases to function as *porn.*

CLAY: Hey. Shhh. Shhh.

KALINA: Is not *sexy,* though. This is the problem. The porn, you know, is just not *sexy.*

CLAY: *Shhhhhhh!!!!!* Shut up. Shut up.

CAROL: Oh, don't say *shut up.*

(All stop. Clay turns off the music and stares at the ceiling.)

KELLY: What?

CAROL: What?

CLAY: Did you hear that?

CASH: What?

CAROL: What?

CLAY: Shhh. Listen.

(They do.)

CLAY: You didn't hear that?

KELLY: No.

KALINA: Where are we hearing?

CLAY: Up on the roof.

CAROL: *(To Kayla.)* Maybe Santa came *early!*

CLAY: Shhhh!!

(They listen. Nothing.)

CLAY: No one heard that?

(All mumble no.)

CLAY: Never mind.

KALINA: Because you know I have in the past the boyfriend who was in the porns? And he says you know is all just faking!!! Is not their real *feelings,* you know? And also the bright lights and the fat peoples. Is not sexy.

CAROL: Still, people should be free to choose.

KALINA: OK sure, is fine if you like to look at the fat peoples. I like much more the romantic love scenes. These to me are the more sexy.

CASH: I always watch *The Bridges of Madison County* when I want to ejaculate.

KELLY: OK, but Carol. While I can agree with you that, there may be this theoretical household where pornography is *shared* as a quote unquote *marital tool,* isn't the porn collection far more likely to be the private hobby of *one particular* partner? And how exactly does *that* aid the marital situation?

CAROL: You may be right.

CASH: *(Reading, not looking up.)* I could beat off to the *Reader's Digest.*

KELLY: Not to belabor the topic.

CAROL: I don't mind the topic.

KELLY: But it's different when children are involved.

CAROL: *(Amused.)* Though it may not be the ideal topic for a holiday established by Puritans.

KALINA: Is weird holiday, you know? Where we all eat of the same bird which then makes us feel sleepy.

CAROL: *(Happy to change the subject.)* Well, someday let's all celebrate a holiday in your country!!

KALINA: Ecch. Why? Oh, no, Carol. Is stupid place. Is nothing to do. Is just old men who piss in street all of the time. And the cars too expensive for the people. America is much better for living. Here *everyone* have the cars. Even the poor black people have the car. Why do the black people get the cars? They have no *money.* Get cars with the credit cards. Credit cards good deal for the black people. And they just *send* to them in the *mail!* Send them the card and say here, black people, go buy the car with this!!

CAROL: *(Re-interpreting positively.)* Corporations *do* prey on the disadvantaged. That is so true.

KALINA: Mmm, this wine is so delicious the taste of it!

CAROL: *(To Kalina.)* But see, it's just, that's the thing about PBS, I always think, how it gives you a broader perspective on the different cultures. You know, Clay has the cleaning lady that always wears the scarf on her head? And I said to her your scarf is so *pretty,* did you bring that from your country?

CLAY: Yeah. Hey, Mom?

CAROL: Although I'm not sure she understood me — *(To Clay.)* Hmmm?

CLAY: Did you accuse her of *stealing?*

CAROL: *What!!?* I *never* — No!!

CLAY: That's what Cash says.

CAROL: *Absolutely not!!* I would *never* in a million . . . *(Continuous.)*

CASH: *(Overlapping.)* What you said to me.

CAROL: *(Continued.)* . . . *years!* Oh, *stop it.* I didn't say that *at all.* I would *never.*

CASH: What you said was in her bag.

CAROL: Oh, that is *offensive*. All I said was the *bread*. She had the *bread*.

CLAY: When?

CAROL: But I would never *accuse* a person to their fa — I didn't say anything to *her*.

KELLY: What bread*?*

CAROL: You know, that bread that you get with the nuts in it. I just saw her *bag*, but it was only *half* of the loaf, and I certainly never *accused* anyone —

CLAY: Well, *Mom*. Whatever you saw —

CAROL: I was looking for the fabric softener sheets and I went in that back room where she keeps her things —

CLAY: But *so what!!?* Even if she *did*. It's *bread*.

CAROL: I'm *agreeing* with you. My goodness.

CLAY: Let her take anything she wants.

CAROL: That's what I'm *saying!!* Of course it's *nothing!* When you stop and think of everything we *have*.

KELLY: Are you talking about the *fig* bread?

CAROL: With the figs and the nuts.

KELLY: There's a whole loaf of that in the bread box.

CAROL: When you think of the *abundance*. It's almost shameful that anyone in the world would ever go *hungry*.

CASH: I'm hungry right now.

CAROL: That is exactly why I always support the worker's party candidates.

KELLY: Well, Carol. I mean, forgive me, but *really*.

CAROL: I'm making a statement.

CLAY: Yeah, the statement is I flush my vote down the toilet.

CAROL: The Socialist Worker's Party is hardly down the *toilet*.

KALINA: *Socialist!!??!!*

CAROL: I like to *believe* in what I vote for, not calculate between the lesser of —

KALINA: *(To Kayla, laughing hard.) She says she is Socialist!*

CAROL: *(Calmly.)* Well, my husband wasn't a *dedicated* socialist . . .

KALINA: *Here!!??!!*

CAROL: But I think that history will show, in the long run —

KELLY: Well, sure, if you're talking *economically*, if you mean following the Scandinavian model.

KALINA: *(Realizing they are serious.) Excuse me now.? But are you crazy!!??!!* *(The Baby starts to cry.)*

KELLY: *(To Baby.)* Shhhhh. OK. OK.

KALINA: *Are you completely insane people!!?? Because I have to tell you this is how you are sounding!!*

CASH: Can we go back to talking about porn?

KALINA: *I'm sorry but this is craziest thing that you say!*
(Kelly opens the front of her shirt to allow the Baby to nurse.)

KELLY: *(To Baby.)* Shhhh, shhhh.

CAROL: The point is, If *we* have so much, shouldn't there be a *system* so that everyone can have bread *all* of the time? Then *no one* has to steal.

CLAY: *Mom! No one stole any bread!*

CAROL: Don't be argumentative! I'm *saying* I want to *give* them bread.

KALINA: Why *give* them? The people can get the jobs!

CASH: Fuckin' A.

KALINA: *I* have job! I *pay* for the bread!! Is no one going to give *me* bread!

CAROL: Then at least the skills so that they can make their *own* bread.

KALINA: To be lazy and do nothing like the blacks and the Mexicans does not mean *I* have to give them the bread! The lazy people do not for nothing get my bread!!

CLAY: *(Peacemaker.)* OK. OK. OK.

CAROL: But we *like* to give! It's *blessed* to give.

KELLY: *(Condescendingly, to Kalina, as the baby nurses.)* Well, excuse me. Listen, I — the obvious point *is* . . . Sorry what's your *name?*

KALINA: It is Kalina.

CASH: *(To Kalina.)* She knows your name.

KELLY: Right. I think the point is, I *hope?* That the accumulated wisdom of your nineteen years might not be all that comprehensive, OK? *(Continuous.)*

CASH: *(Overlapping.)* She's twenty-three.

KELLY: *(Continued.)* And that there might be some value in not *shouting* at people who actually read the paper and keep up with world affairs.

KALINA: OK, and what I am saying to you now, Kelly? Because you are so much smarter and things? What I am saying is I don't understand all the words that you say.

CASH: *(To Kalina.)* She's trying to insult you.

KALINA: *(Ignoring Cash.)* What is the word *coomolated?*

CASH: No no no no no. Look. *(To Kalina.)* First of all. See, in this country, some of the rich people, you see, they feel *verrrry guilty.*

CLAY: *Rich?* You call this *rich?*

CAROL: Oh, let's let it drop.

CASH: They feel so *frivolous.* They feel *ashamed.*

CLAY: This isn't rich. Trust me, I can show you *rich.*

CASH: They think *oh no people are starving* and they can't *enjoy* how rich they are because they feel so *tacky.*

CLAY: This is why you finally come to our house? To pass *judgment* on us?

CASH: They say *If we were really good people we'd give eeeeverything away.*

CLAY: So don't come next time.

CASH: But the truth is, they don't *really* want to give away their stuff. Their golf clubs and their fifty-two-inch TV. Not to some starving illiterate natives in some desert somewhere. Not *really.*

CLAY: Whose car gets eight miles to the gallon, Cash? Huh? Not *ours!*

CAROL: Why don't we play a game? What's the name of that game we played?

CASH: See, they *feel* bad because what they practice doesn't square with what they preach. Which makes them every bit as bad as the materialistic barbarians they despise!

(Clay laughs derisively.)

CAROL: What's that game where you draw the little pictures?

CASH: And you want to say to these people: Hey, you don't have to change what you *practice.* That's way too *hard.* Just change what you fucking *preach.*

CLAY: Oh, fuck *you.* Up on your mountaintop.

CAROL: *(Clapping hands like a schoolteacher.)* Alright! We're all going to change the subject right now!

KELLY: How lovely to see your brother again, Clay. I've missed him so much.

CLAY: You don't speak for us, OK? Don't presume to speak for us.

(Then Kelly's nipple is bitten.)

KELLY: *Owww!!!* Jesus. *Fucking teeth.*

(She stands and exits upstairs, with the now crying Baby.)

CAROL: *(To Kalina.)* You know what movie I *did* enjoy. The one . . . oh, you know the one. It's Italian. And there's a very funny man in it. And it's during the holocaust. Not that I have to have a happy ending. But I do like to feel that I'm a better person for having watched it.

CASH: And you don't get that from porn?

(Kayla turns on a loud bright cartoon.)

CLAY: Sweetie? Pumpkin?

CAROL: *(To Kayla.)* Oh! What is *that?* Hmm? Doesn't that look *fun!* I want to watch that with *Kayla!*

KALINA: *(To Cash.)* You don't want the wine? It is so delicious!

(Cash waves her away.)

CLAY: *(To Kayla.)* OK, but not too loud. OK Sweetie?

(Kalina joins Kayla and Carol. Clay, gingerly, sits next to Cash.)

CLAY: So . . . you got to . . . you got a look at it?

CASH: Your kid, you mean?

CLAY: Yeah, her . . . her . . . you know, her —? *(He points to his genitals.)*

CASH: Yeah. I can give her something for that.

CLAY: That'd be great. Thanks.

(Cash pulls out a prescription pad.)

CASH: What's today, the twenty-sixth?

CLAY: Twenty-seventh. So, what? So, like a pill?

CASH: Ointment.

CLAY: It's just so red and inflamed. Down there. You know?

CASH: Yeah.

CLAY: Been that way a couple of days.

CASH: Looks painful, yeah.

CLAY: Ever seen anything like that before?

CASH: Uhhh . . . dunno.

CLAY: All . . . *scaly.* And there's this . . . this . . . sticky —

CASH: Discharge. Yeah. This'll stop her scratching it.

(Cash begins writing.)

CLAY: We're really happy you came.

CASH: Mmm.

CLAY: Good for kids to see their family.

CASH: They don't see their family?

CLAY: Extended family.

CASH: *(As he writes.)* So use this twice a day. Like before she goes to sleep and then again in the morning. Just the ulcerated area around the outer part of the vulva. And around the anus, too, you know, if she starts scratching back there.

CLAY: OK. Not just me. Kelly too. I'm sure she is.

CASH: Mm-hmm.

CLAY: Always seemed like you guys had a lot in common.

(Cash nods.)

CLAY: And you know, whatever you might think, you really don't know her. You don't. She's a complicated person who's been through a lot, and I know you don't care or possibly even *recall?* But a few years ago? Before we had Kayla? She was going through some difficult stuff but we got through it, you know, we got past it, and one of the things I came away with is an understanding of what an amazing person she is.

CASH: *(Tears off and hands Clay the prescription.)* So just take that to any pharmacy.

CLAY: Right. And that'll clear it up.

CASH: The sores . . . little blisters. Should, yeah.

CLAY: And you think it has to do with fleas. Or lice. From something getting in the house.

CASH: Could be.

CLAY: Don't you think?

CASH: Could be that.

CLAY: Since they carry all those diseases.

CASH: Could be any number of things.

    (Clay stares.)

CLAY: Well, is this the right medicine or not?

CASH: It's *medicinal.*

CLAY: Meaning *what?* Meaning it'll *cure* it?

CASH: Depends on what you mean by cure.

CLAY: Well *what does she have,* Cash? *(Drops his voice.)* Huh? Don't fuck around with me.

CASH: What do you want me to say? I'm a *plastic surgeon,* all right? I dunno everything.

CLAY: But what's with the *attitude?* Huh? You think this is *funny?* Or *ironic,* or something?

CASH: Although the word *anus* is funny.

CLAY: Go ahead and smirk at *me.* I don't care.

CASH: *(Snickering.)* Anus.

CLAY: But to amuse yourself at the expense of a *child?*

CASH: Hey. Take your nerve tonic, *Aunt Polly.*

CLAY: Just because some of us are trying to do something a little less *cowardly.*

CASH: Look. Do me a favor.

CLAY: A little less *selfish.*

CASH: Go talk to your *wife,* all right? Because, honestly?

CLAY: Wait wait wait wait wait shhhhhhh! *(To the others, re: TV.) Turn that off.*

CAROL: What's the matter? Why are you shout — ?

CLAY: *Off, please!! Can we please turn that off!!?*

    (Clay grabs remote, turns off the TV.)

KALINA: *(To Clay.)* What is problem?

CLAY: *I'm saying everybody please be quiet.*

    (Kelly has entered from kitchen.)

KELLY: What happened?

CLAY: *(Staring at the ceiling.) Shhhh!! Shut up shut up!!!*

KELLY: What are you doing?

CLAY: Could we all be quiet and *listen?* Could we do that, please?

(Pause. All is silent.)

CLAY: You're telling me you didn't hear that?

(All reply: What? No. Hear what?, etc.)

CLAY: *No one* heard that. You are seriously *kidding* me.

KALINA: I still don't know for what is we are listening.

CLAY: There was movement. No one else heard some sort of overhead movement? Am I the only one who cares?

CAROL: All *right.*

CLAY: Apparently so.

CAROL: We're all listening.

CLAY: Apparently I am.

KELLY: Have a *spasm,* that helps.

CAROL: Shhhhh. Everyone. Quiet now.

(All look up at the ceiling. They wait. In the middle of the silence:)

CASH: *AHHHHH!!!! LOOK OUT!!!!*

(Everyone jumps. Cash cracks up.) (Overlapping:)

CAROL: Oh, Cash, really. For heaven's sake, don't *do* that. That is just not funny.

CLAY: Very funny — Hysterically funny. Try growing up for a change, you cretin.

KELLY: Wow. Really sophisticated. It's such a pleasure to see you again, Cash, it truly is.

KALINA: See? This is what he is like. Is so stupid. Some of the times. Cannot believe it.

(Then, Kayla screams.)

CLAY: No, no, pumpkin. Uncle Cash was just playing a yelling game.

CASH: *(To Kayla.)* Let's play the yelling game.

(Kayla screams again.)

CLAY: Sweetie. Let's not do that, OK? Serious now. *(To Cash.)* Thanks a lot.

(Kayla does it again. Cash laughs.)

CLAY: *I want you to stop that. Daddy's not kidding, now!*

CAROL: *(To Kayla.)* Come here sweetie. Let me see your dress. Look at that pretty dress you have. That's your special dress, isn't it?

KALINA: *(Reaching in her bag.)* Hey Kayla! How about I show you the makeup?! I give you sexy makeover like the supermodel!!

KELLY: Uhhh . . . I don't think . . . uh, Clay?

KALINA: Oh no, Kelly, is OK. Is my job, you know, and all the makeup is the hypoallergenics so in truth is actually being good for the skin. *(To Kayla.)* So now you will be the hot sexy girl, yes?

KELLY: Uhh . . . yeah. Let's maybe not indoctrinate her into masculine objectification *just yet.*

(Kalina turns to Cash for clarification.)

KALINA: Ob-jee-dee-fi-kay?

CASH: She doesn't want her to look hot.

KALINA: *(Starting to apply it.)* Ohhh no, Kelly. Will not be too sexy. Just only for everyday sexy look.

CLAY: But. We're saying, she is a *child,* right?

KALINA: *(To Kayla.)* This is the lip liner which we use first.

CLAY: And there's really no reason for a child to look, uhh . . . is there?

CAROL: Oh, Kayla! You are going to look so *pretty*

KELLY: OK, I really want this to stop.

CLAY: Hey, Kalina?

KALINA: I tell you what. If she don't like it, we take it off! Is easy.

CLAY: Yeah, but. But given the world we're living in. You know? With what kids are exposed to. *(Continuous.)*

KALINA: *(Overlapping.) (To Kayla.)* After lining we will put in lip color.

CLAY: *(Continued.)* Wouldn't we rather protect them from certain premature experiences? Don't you think? Developmentally? Isn't that more or less obvious?

KELLY: Clay, a little less discussion, maybe.

CAROL: Even my first graders. This is interesting. They do experience arousal. The little boys in my class? When they lie down on the sleeping mats?

CLAY: Mom?

CAROL: No. I'm not judging. I think it's sweet. I mean, they're little *men,* after all. With their little penises poking up. And the little *girls.* You can tell, when they get on the teeter-totter —

CLAY: *Mom?* Really not helping.

CASH: Ever hear the one the pedophile at the circumcision?

CLAY: Right. That's funny.

KALINA: *(To Kayla.)* Now press the lips together like this.

CLAY: To make jokes, you know, when there are sick people in the world? Sick, abusive peo — ?

CASH: *(To Clay.)* Hey, I'm trying to remember. Remind me. When did you have that surgery?

CLAY: Wha — ?

CASH: Remember that? When they took out your sense of humor?
  (Carol cracks up.)
CLAY: Oh, right. I guess I'm crazy. Sure, everything's fine. I guess there are no more evil people in the world!!
CASH: *Evil??!!*
CAROL: *(Laughing, to Clay.)* Oh, that's funny! That is so true about you!
CLAY: Oh, OK! Everybody relax!! No more evil people!! No more predators! No more child abductors!
KALINA: *(To Kayla.)* Now strike pose like the supermodel!!
KELLY: *(To Clay, re: Kalina.)* Would you stop her, please?
CASH: *Evil.* What *evil?* Who are you, *Cotton Mather?*
CLAY: *(To Cash.)* Do you *know* the statistics? Do you *read* the paper? Or do you just prefer to talk out of your ass?
CAROL: *(Still laughing.) They took out his sense of humor!*
CLAY: One in every five adults, Cash. One in every five. Was victimized, OK? One in every five.
CAROL: Well . . . but . . . there are five adults *here.* And nothing bad ever happened to *me.*
CLAY: Kelly was abused.
CAROL: Oh, Kelly! Ohhhhh.
KELLY: True.
CAROL: I didn't know that! Oh, how awful.
KELLY: The family dynamic. Yeah. Textbook case.
CAROL: Ohh, how horrible. I hope that's not true!
CLAY: It *is* true. It absolutely is.
CAROL: Ohh, I hope you can talk to someone.
KELLY: No, I do. No, it's straight out of Alice Miller. Neglect alternating with sarcasm.
CAROL: *(Relieved.)* Ohhhhhh! Oh, *I see.* Oh, I thought . . . oh, *pffffft.*
CLAY: Don't be *dismissive!*
CAROL: Well, I thought she was talking about . . . *touching* things, and —
CLAY: It's *abuse,* Mom! Emotional *abuse.*
CASH: Oh, god. Not sarcasm.
CLAY: She should have been taken out of that household. *I* should have!!
CAROL: Should have *what?*
CLAY: I felt abused.
CAROL: Ohhhh, *never.* I don't believe you. By who?
CLAY: Dad was *abusive.*
CASH: By *whom.* Abused by *whom.*

CAROL: *(To Clay.)* Oh, *stop* it.

CLAY: Don't tell me to stop. I won't stop.

CAROL: *Abusive?*

CLAY: I won't stop. I won't. It's what I experienced.

CAROL: Nooo.

CLAY: Yes he was. Yes he was. Don't deny it.

CAROL: He was *irritable,* but I don't think *abusive.*

CLAY: And innocent people get hurt when *you* stick up for him and perpetu-
ate the pattern!

CASH: Do you mean innocent as in *not guilty?*

CAROL: Well, now, wait. Now, let me think.

CASH: Or do you mean innocent like *naïve?*

CAROL: No. Now, see, I would say that he was more abusive to *Cash.*

CLAY: *No he wasn't. It was me.*

CAROL: If it's between the two of you.

CLAY: It was *me!* This is so *unfair* of you!

CAROL: *(To Clay.)* I remember him being so friendly with you.

CLAY: *Because I was seeking his approval!* Oh, this is *so* perfect. So fucking *quin-
tessential.* Let him steal that from me, too. Just like you let him steal my
Hot Wheels.

CAROL: Oh, here we go again.

CLAY: You *knew* he did it!! Every single one of my Hot Wheels.

CAROL: This is so tiresome.

CASH: Mom, let Clay be abused if he wants to be.

CLAY: Remember? One day they're all *gone.* All my best ones. Disappeared!
And where are they? *Surprise!* They're all hidden under his bed!

CAROL: Kicking this *same old poor dead horse.*

CLAY: As long as he *denies* it, sure, let him do whatever he wants! Let him steal!
Just like the fucking president stole the election!! *Twice.* And I bet you a
thousand bucks last time he *voted* for the asshole. *(To Cash.)* Didn't you?
Huh? A thousand bucks. Admit it. You *thief.* Come on. *Admit it.*

CASH: That's none of your business.

CLAY: *(The ultimate triumph.) Ahhhhahaha!!* He voted for *Bush!! I knew it!
Look at him, Mom! For Bush!! Your son is a Republican!! Your beloved little
Cash is a fucking Republican!!! (He laughs and laughs.) Ahhhhahahaha-
haha!!!!!!*

(Pause. No one knows what to say.)

KALINA: *(Completely matter-of-fact.)* But you know, Kelly, you should put in
perceptive, these things. Because when I was raped, you know? As little

girl, when I was taken to the room and the soldiers, when they hold me down on the floor and they rape me over and over, when I was little girl? And then, after this, when having to have the bad abortion from doctor which makes it now so that I cannot ever have the children? And how I am now totally OK and everything despite these things? And when you think how you have family and big house and things and also the good job? I am saying maybe is good idea to put in perceptive.

(Pause.)

CASH: Perspective.

KALINA: *(Agreeing.)* Yes.

CASH: *Perspective.*

KALINA: This is what I say.

CASH: No. Per*spec*tive. The word is *perspective.*

KALINA: I *say* perceptive.

CASH: Per*speck* — tive.

CAROL: Well, *I,* for one, am getting hungry.

KALINA: Per*skep* — tive.

CASH: *Perspective!*

KALINA: Per —*skep* —

CASH: Jesus, whaddya *deaf?*

KALINA: I am trying to say the word.

CASH: *Per* — *speck* — *tive.*

KALINA: Don't yell at me.

CASH: Alright. *Speck.* Say *speck.*

KALINA: Why do you yell at me?

CASH: Speck. Speck. You can't say *speck?*

KALINA: I can say it how I want to say.

CASH: Say it.

KALINA: Perskeptive.

CASH: *(Exploding.) PERSPECTIVE!!!!! JESUS CHRIST, PERSPECTIVE!!! PUT IT IN PERSPECTIVE!!!*

KALINA: *(The same, overlapping.) DON'T YOU YELL AT ME YOU FUCK-ING FUCKER!!! YOU CANNOT YELL AT ME!!!!!!*

CASH: *THEN LEARN SOME GODDAMN ENGLISH, YOU DUMB-ASS!!! HOW LONG CAN IT TAKE TO LEARN THE GODDAMN ENGLISH LANGUAGE!!!?*

KALINA: *(Continuous.) I AM LEAVING!!! YOU STUPID ASS-MAN!!! THINK YOU CAN TALK ANY WAY YOU WANT TO ME IN FRONT OF FAM-ILY?!!!*

CASH: *(Overlapping.)* SO WHO'S STOPPING YOU, YOU LITTLE RE-TARD?!! GO BUY ANOTHER PAIR OF SIX HUNDRED DOLLAR BOOTS WITH YOUR BIG SALARY!!!

KALINA: *(Overlapping.)* I DON'T NEED THIS SHIT FROM YOU!!! I AM PERSON. I AM NOT TO BE TREATED LIKE THE GARBAGE!!!!

CASH: *(Overlapping.)* YEAH YEAH YEAH, GO LIVE IN A DUMPSTER, YOU FUCKING MORON!!!!!

KALINA: *(Overlapping.)* I HATE YOU I HATE YOU I HATE YOU !!!!!!
(She throws wine in Cash's face and storms up the stairs.)

CASH: *(Calmer.)* Idiot.
(Pause. Then, quite audibly, a noise overhead. All look up. We hear something move or roll from one side of the ceiling to the other. All follow with their eyes.)

CAROL: Now, *that* I heard.

CLAY: *(Possessed with fury.)* I knew it. I knew it. I knew it. Goddamm it goddamm it goddamm . . .
(He races off toward the kitchen. We hear slamming noises. Carol hands Cash a dishtowel, as Kayla tugs at her sleeve.)

CAROL: *(To Kayla.)* What, sweetheart?
(Carol bends down and Kayla whispers in her ear. Clay returns with flashlight on his way to the front.)

CLAY: . . . goddamm it goddamm it . . .

CAROL: *(To Kayla.)* Ohhh, well, of *course* I will. Why didn't you say so?
(Taking Kayla's hand, the two of them begin to exit as Kalina, in coat and scarf, comes stomping down the stairs, crying loudly. Mascara pours down her cheeks. She storms out the front door, leaving it wide open.)

CLAY: It's either on the roof or in the crawl space. Did you hear it again??!
(He grabs a golf club as he exits through the front door.)

CASH: So, this pedophile goes to a circumcision —

CLAY: *(Racing back in through the front door.)* I'm pretty sure I saw something run to the other side. I don't know what it is but I swear to god it was something!!
(He exits out to the back. Kayla and Carol are gone. Cash and Kelly are alone.)

KELLY: *(To Cash.)* Well, this has certainly been a real pleasure.

CASH: Thanks for having me.

KELLY: And now perhaps you could get the fuck out.

CASH: *(To the Baby as he rises to go.)* Wow. Hey, Junior. That's some bitter milk you're drinking there.

CLAY: *(From outside we hear Clay throwing rocks at the roof.)* Get outa here!!!! Get *away from my house!!! Yaaah!!!!*

KELLY: If you hurry maybe you can find yourself some more adolescent euro-trash beaver.

(A crash from upstairs. Breaking glass. A piercing burglar alarm starts to sound. Exterior floodlights turn on. Kelly remains seated. Clay races in, out of breath.)

CLAY: *(Shouting to be heard.)* I BROKE A WINDOW! I THOUGHT I SAW IT SO I THREW THE CLUB BUT I BROKE THE WINDOW!!! DO YOU HAVE THE ALARM KEY?!!!

KELLY: I GAVE IT TO YOU!!

CLAY: *(Searching through his keys.)* I THOUGHT I GAVE IT TO YOU!!!!

KELLY: YOU WERE THE LAST ONE TO HAVE IT!!!

CLAY: *(Searching his pockets.)* AT FIRST I THOUGHT IT MIGHT BE A RACCOON, BUT IT'S MOVING TOO FAST TO BE A RAC-COON!!!

CASH: MAYBE IT'S AN ADOLESCENT EUROTRASH BEAVER!!!

CLAY: *(To Kelly.)* I DON'T HAVE IT!!! WHAT AM I SUPPOSED TO DO!!?

KELLY: WELL, CLAY, THE ALARM ISN'T GOING TO SHUT OFF ALL BY ITSELF!!!!

(The alarm shuts off all by itself. Lights change. Mr. Hadid has a question.)

MR. HADID: Excuse me?

CLAY: *(Out of breath.)* Yeah?

MR. HADID: One more question.

CLAY: Uh-huh?

MR. HADID: This neighborhood?

CLAY: Right?

MR. HADID: In a neighborhood such as this one, what can one expect to pay for property tax?

(Clay stares.)

CLAY: I . . . in *what?*

MR. HADID: That is, with a house of this size and with the school district, upon what basis would the figure be calculated? The property tax?

CLAY: *(Growing frustrated.)* Um . . . yeah. I, uh, sorry. I have to say this. Not to be critical? But I kind of get the feeling that . . . that maybe you're not really listening to what we're trying to *say.*

MR. HADID: I am sorry.

CLAY: I mean, the *property ta — who cares?* That's not the point, alright? This isn't about . . . where did we get the table or . . . how much were my — I mean, *come on.* OK? Come on.

MR. HADID: I apologize.

CLAY: It's not what *we're about.*

MR. HADID: Then, if you wish, you may tell me what you are about.

(*Pause.*)

CLAY: Basically we're about the family.

MR. HADID: *Your* family.

CLAY: No.

MR. HADID: You are not for *my* family.

CLAY: No. I'm only talking about advantages. Giving your child every possible advantage.

MR. HADID: Advantage over *my* child.

CLAY: No, Jesus, *come on.* Don't make me talk in clichés. There is an intrinsic value, right, to . . . ? Look. Parents and children —

MR. HADID: Your children.

CLAY: No.

MR. HADID: You are for your children. And I am for my children.

CLAY: I disagree.

MR. HADID: Why would you be for my children? For my family? This makes no sense.

CLAY: (*The same.*) Because . . . wait a second . . . you're not looking at who we *are.*

MR. HADID: And this is the reason why you kill people.

(*Pause.*)

CLAY: No.

MR. HADID: You kill people.

CLAY: No.

MR. HADID: Yes. If it serves your family. You would kill them.

CLAY: No.

MR. HADID: As I would do for mine.

CLAY: You're looking at it all wrong.

MR. HADID: For your family. This is only how it is. And this is the reason why you kill my wife.

CAROL: Clay*?!*

(*The alarm resumes at full blast. The lights resume. Carol returns with Kayla in tow. Kelly stands and goes to the alarm box. Carol places Kayla on top of the coffee table. In one hand she holds Kayla's pull-up, and with the other she lifts Kayla's skirt to peer underneath. Kelly switches off the alarm.*)

KELLY: (*To Clay, key in hand.*) The key was sitting right on top of the box.

CAROL: Clay?

CLAY: Huh?

CAROL: I'm sorry, but . . . has anyone . . . ? I was changing her little thing here and . . . Oh dear. *(Re: Kayla.)* Has anybody else seen this?
(Clay looks at Kelly. Kelly looks at Cash. Cash looks at Clay.)

CASH: Maybe I oughta go.
(Blackout. End of Act One.)

ACT TWO

Later. Clay, Kelly, and Kayla sit around the table but no one seems to be eating much. Across the room, Kalina lies asleep on the sofa, under her coat, boots off. The remainder of a six-pack of beer dangles from her fingertips. Mr. Hadid stands away from the table, not far from Carol, who picks up where she left off.

CAROL: Anyway. So. *Genghis Khan and the Mongol Hordes.*

MR. HADID: Yes?

CAROL: The documentary? The one on PBS? The one I started to tell you about?

MR. HADID: Ah yes.

CAROL: So *good.* Oh, I wish you had seen it! Just for the music alone. When they go charging across the steppes with all the horses and the banners fluttering in the wind? And they establish this magnificent empire? Wonderful. But you didn't see it?

MR. HADID: I don't think so.

CAROL: And the narrator was that wonderful actor. That really fine actor. The British actor. And they had an interview with him afterwards and he was saying — this was interesting — he said that the secret to fine acting, that *acting* is actually all about *listening.* Isn't that interesting?

MR. HADID: Interesting.

CAROL: *(Laughs.)* I mean, maybe *you* should be an actor because you're such a wonderful *listener.*

MR. HADID: Thank you.

CAROL: Not like my husband, I don't mind telling you.

MR. HADID: I believe you mentioned your husband.

CAROL: Did I?

MR. HADID: That he was not a good listener.

CAROL: Is that right? Well, I guess maybe I did. *(Laughs.)* And see? You *remember*, too! You retain things. Not like me. I've gotten terrible. I'm like that woman in that joke. Where the woman goes to see her doctor?

MR. HADID: Yes. You have said this.

CAROL: And the doctor says I'm afraid I have some bad news?

MR. HADID: "I thought you were going to say I have cancer."

CAROL: Oh. Well, now that's the *punch line.*

MR. HADID: Yes, you said this.

CLAY: Mom?

CAROL: Oh, poop. I *did*, didn't I?

MR. HADID: Yes.

CLAY: Mom?

CAROL: Well, there you go. But no. My husband? No. In one ear and out the other.

CLAY: Mom?

CAROL: *(Turning back.)* Hmm?

CLAY: Can I have the Brussels sprouts, please?

CAROL: Oh, of course. *(Does so.)*

> *(Carol turns back to the table and the lights shift to Thanksgiving. Mr. Hadid sits to one side. Clay slowly serves himself, then:)*

CLAY: Anyone else? Brussels sprou — ? *(To Kelly, who stares at him.)* What?

KELLY: What?

CLAY: What?

KELLY: Nothing. What?

CLAY: What are you staring at?

KELLY: Who?

CLAY: You were staring.

KELLY: You're the one staring at *me.*

CLAY: *(To Carol.)* Mom? Brussels sprouts?

CAROL: Kay-Kay? I bet *you're* a Brussels sprout girl! All the special girls I know like a nummy Brussels sprout! And you're special, aren't you? Yes you are. And Brussels sprouts are the nummiest of the nummy! Aren't they, hmmm?

KELLY: *(Under her breath, re: Clay.) Staring.* Paranoid.

> *(Clay throws down his fork.)*

CLAY: OK. I give up.

KELLY: Go ahead and *eat*, Clay.

CLAY: Well, I'm *trying* to, aren't I? I seem to be the only one.

KELLY: You'll understand if I don't exactly have an *appetite* at the moment.

CLAY: Well, the interesting thing *is* that people actually can't *survive* without eating.

KELLY: No one's stopping you. Shovel it in.

CLAY: Exactly. So if I eat my dinner . . . *(Continued.)*

KELLY: *(Overlapping.)* You want a pleasant meal? Let's have a pleasant meal.

CLAY: *(Continuous.)* . . . somehow that demonstrates my *indifference to my child?* Is that it?

KELLY: Carol, would you pass the cranberries, please?

CAROL: *(Doing so.)* With *pleasure.*

KELLY: Thank you.
 (Pause.)

CAROL: *(To Kayla.)* Sweetheart, you know that sometimes grown-ups get sad, too, don't you? *Yes they do.* And you know, when that happens, you *know* that doesn't mean Mommy and Daddy are sad because of you, does it? It only means that —

KELLY: Please don't talk down to her like that.

CAROL: I didn't.

KELLY: In that baby voice.

CAROL: I . . . well. All right. You're right. It's not my place.

KELLY: *(To Kayla.)* Mommy and Daddy are fighting. You understand that.
 (Kayla nods. Kelly shrugs.)

CAROL: *(To Kayla, loud whisper.)* But they're not fighting because of you.
 (Kelly glares at Carol, then:)

CLAY: Good salad, Mom.

CAROL: Hm? Oh, well, you're very welcome.

CLAY: These nuts are great.

CAROL: Those are *soy nuts.* Aren't those good?

CLAY: Really good.

KELLY: *(To Kayla.)* Use your fork, please.
 (Pause. Clinking.)

CLAY: I was thinking. Maybe after dinner. If you want we could all play a game of —

KELLY: Clay? Let's just eat and get it over with.

CLAY: Well, you know what? We're all going to have to *go on living somehow,* I mean . . . *(Continued.)*

KELLY: *(Overlapping.)* A *game?* What, you feel like playing a *board game?*

CLAY: *(Continuous.)* . . . as far as I can tell . . . Wait. Let me check. Yes. The earth is *still revolving.*

CAROL: Kay-Kay? Are you done with your dinner now? Maybe you and I could watch a cartoon!

KELLY: A *game.* Yeah, let's all play *Yahtzee.*

CLAY: Fine. OK fine. I can't win. I can't. Why don't I just *move out?*

KELLY: Carol? Are you finished?

CLAY: Why don't I just go upstairs and *hang* myself?

CAROL: *(To Kelly.)* Not quite.

CLAY: Never mind that I'm the only person who seems to be capable of taking some *action.*

KELLY: But Clay.

CLAY: While everyone else stands around with their thumb up their ass.

KELLY: But think for a moment.

CLAY: I don't need to think. *(Continued.)*

KELLY: What good does it do to take an action when . . . *(Continued.)*

CLAY: *(Continuous, overlapping.)* What I *need* is to protect the health of my child!

KELLY: *(Continuous.)* . . . when you're not in possession of all the *facts?* And please stop using Kayla to justify yourself.

CLAY: OK. Clearly I'm worthless. Clearly I'm horrible.

CAROL: Oh, Clay, stop it.

CLAY: I'll get a rope or maybe a belt. And I'll just hang myself.

CAROL: You've been very judgmental. All evening.

CLAY: Right. Right. I see.

CAROL: And It's very *oppressive* to be judged.

KELLY: It would be one thing if you had all the facts. But you just get on the phone and blindly take the law into your own hands.

CLAY: *(To Kelly.)* Do you want me to call back? I'll call them back right now, if you want.

KELLY: It's too late *now.*

(Kalina begins muttering in her sleep.)

KALINA: *(Anguished.)* Nemojte! Molimvas, nemojte! Necu da udjem, necu! *(Phonetic: NEH-moy-tay! MOH-leem-vas, NEH-moy-tay! NEH-choo dah OOD-jem, NEH-choo!.)*

(All turn for a moment, then go on.)

CLAY: So what do you want me to do? You tell me.

KELLY: I want you to get all the *facts.*

CAROL: I'm not surprised Cash stays away.

CLAY: *(To Carol.)* Ohohohohoho. Don't *even.* I will *kill.* I will reach across this table and actively *kill.*

CAROL: Well, I'm *sorry.* But his holiday was ruined.

CLAY: *(Seething.)* Ohhhh, my *god.* Mother of *god.*

KELLY: There are a *number* of possible explanations.

CLAY: Mom? *(To Kelly.)* Excuse me. *(To Carol.)* Mom? I happen to discover that *(Lowers voice.) my daughter's health has been seriously compromised? And you say to me I ruined that prick's holiday!!!?*

CAROL: Cash didn't do anything to you.

CLAY: Oh right. Oh *never.* You know what? Just say to me *I prefer Cash in all things. I always have and I always will prefer Cash to you.*

KELLY: *(Rising.)* Carol? If you'll excuse me from the *festival of regurgitation?*

CLAY: Cash, who, apparently, can't even fulfill the basic requirement of the human *species. Reproduce!!*

CAROL: *(To Kelly, who has begun to clear.)* I didn't use my spoon.

KELLY: *(To Carol.)* It's all going in the dishwasher.

CLAY: And if you can't accomplish *that,* well, I'm sorry, but I'd have to say you're *disqualified* from the species! Case closed.

CAROL: Well, see? Now you're judging *Cash.*

CLAY: *(Pointing to Kayla.)* Look at that. Look at that child. *That* is the future, Mom. *We* live on. *We* succeed. Cash? No. Cash dies and his genes die with him! And guess what? Those are *your genes too!*

CAROL: You sound completely ridiculous.

CLAY: Ruined his *holiday.* Oh, what a *shame.* What a goddamn *shame.*
    (Phone begins to ring. Clay rises.)

CAROL: Cash is not the enemy.

CLAY: Let's go kill the fatted calf for *Cash's holiday.*

KELLY: *(To Kayla.)* Sweetie? Are you done?
    (Kelly helps Kayla down.)

CAROL: You have a *great* many blessings. There's no reason to take things out on —

CLAY: *(Stopping on his way to the phone.)* Sorry? What? What's that supposed to mean?

CAROL: Nothing.

CLAY: No no no. Don't try to back out of it.

CAROL: I meant nothing.

CLAY: I heard the inflection. "A *great* many." That's how you said it.

CAROL: Well, you do.

CLAY: And raising your eyebrows like that. Like with some kind of *disapproval?*

CAROL: I don't disapprove.

CLAY: Oh really?

CAROL: I only say that with such a *great* number of blessings —

CLAY: The eyebrows! You did it again.

CAROL: With such *great* blessings —

CLAY: Right there! You keep doing it! Just admit what you're doing.

CAROL: One oughtn't have to be judgmental.

(The phone is still ringing.)

CLAY: Oh oh. So you're calling us *rich.*

KELLY: *(Re: phone.)* Are you going to get that?

CLAY: *(To Carol.)* You people are *obsessed* with our money. Try to grasp this concept: We are *(Quietly.)* barely fucking scraping by. We are *so* not *rich.*

KELLY: Clay?

CLAY: Do you have any idea of the financing on a place like this?

CAROL: Well, what does that tell you?

CLAY: This isn't *liquid.* Jesus, it's an investment!

CAROL: Well, there are people in the world —

CLAY: That doesn't make us *rich.*

CAROL: Some people would *like* to be called rich.

CLAY: If it *applied.* And, in this case, it *doesn't.*

KELLY: Clay!

CLAY: *(Finally answering.)* Hello?

(We hear a car arriving.)

CAROL: I think you have some sort of *guilt complex.*

CLAY: *(Into phone.)* Yeah. No. No, she's here now. No, she's on the sofa.

CAROL: I wish someone would call *me* rich.

CLAY: *(Phone.)* No, *asleep* on the sofa. About half an hour ago. No, she couldn't because you have her credit cards. Well, where are you?

KELLY: *(To Carol as she exits to kitchen.)* I'm going to cover this with foil.

CAROL: Just use that plastic wrap.

CLAY: *(Phone.)* No, I won't. Because she's asleep. Well, maybe that's not our problem, OK?

(The front door opens and Cash walks in, cell phone to his ear — he has been talking to Clay.)

CAROL: Do you want to go help Mommy?

CLAY: *(Not yet noticing Cash.)* Maybe *you* have to *work that out for yourself.* Does that ring a bell? Huh? Where do you suppose you might have heard that particular turn of phrase before? Hmm? That stir up any memories for you?

CASH: Hey Mom.

(Clay turns. They both hang up.)

CAROL: Is that — ? Oh, *poop.* And we just *finished!* Poop poop *poop!*

CASH: *(Approaching Kalina.)* Doesn't matter.

CAROL: Sit sit. Let me fix you a plate.

CLAY: Hang on. No. Mom?

CAROL: Just a little plate.

CLAY: Right, but we're not in the eating stage now, are we? Now we're in the *cleaning-up* stage.

CAROL: But Cash didn't get any food.

CLAY: Well, unfortunately now the food is being *wrapped up.*

CAROL: *(To Cash.)* How about a little stuffing?

CLAY: And that applies to the stuffing.

CASH: Hey Mom? I'm not hungry.

CAROL: But you were out there driving around. You need something warm.

CASH: We're not gonna stay.

CAROL: Well, I'm making you a plate.

CLAY: *(Taking a seat.)* Guess I was wrong. Guess we're still eating, then.

CAROL: Clay, stop it

CLAY: *(Sitting.)* Right. OK, back to the table! Everybody sit down!
(Kelly re-enters.)

KELLY: *(Flat.)* Oh, look who's back.

CASH: *(Re: Kalina.)* I'm just gonna grab her and go.

KELLY: Stay. You and Clay play a board game.

CLAY: Is no one else sitting? *I'm* sitting.

KELLY: A quick round of *Stratego.*

CAROL: *(Dishing out a plate.)* What about this casserole? How about some of that?

CASH: Mom? Seriously. I'm not hungry, OK?

CAROL: Well at least some coffee.

CLAY: We don't have coffee.

CAROL: Oh, there's *plenty* of coffee.

CLAY: Not *made* there's not.

CAROL: Well it's easy enough to make *coffee.*

CLAY: Well, I didn't *want* to make coffee. *(To Kelly.)* Did you?

KELLY: Did I what?

CLAY: Want to make coffee.

KELLY: When? At what point?

CLAY: I mean *do* you.

KELLY: Strange way to ask.

CAROL: I mean, I personally don't want coffee, but maybe Cash — ?

CASH: You know what? We're not gonna stay.

CLAY: No, stay. Gonna have *coffee*.

CASH: No coffee for me.

CAROL: *(To Clay.)* Or maybe . . . *(Re: Kalina.)* . . . *she'd* like coffee because of — *(Mimes drinking.)* . . . ?

CASH: Mom? Never mind. They have a whole elaborate . . . process . . . so.

CLAY: *(As though considering this.)* Elaborate? Our coffee?

CASH: With the grinding and so forth.

CLAY: And that strikes you as *elaborate*.

CAROL: *(Raising her hand.)* Let's have a show of hands. Because I *don't* want coffee.

CASH: I dunno, Clay. However you guys make it.

CLAY: Wasn't aware you had all these thoughts about our *coffee*.

CASH: It's extraordinary coffee. It's superior coffee.

KELLY: *(Putting it to rest.)* So actually, *no one* wants coffee. Is that right?

CLAY: *Elaborate.* Huh. Fascinating.

> *(Kalina begins muttering again in her agitated way.)*

KALINA: *(Asleep.)* Stiscem me! Oww! Boli me ruka! Pustite me! Ocu kuci. Ne! Ne! (Phonetic: STEESH-chem meh! Oww! BOH-lee meh ROO-kah! POOS-tee-tay meh! OH-choo KOO-chee. NEH! NEH!.)*

> *(Pause. All stare. Cash jiggles Kalina's foot.)*

CASH: *(To Kalina.)* Hey.

CAROL: Oh, let her be. She looks so . . . *ohhh, oh look*. Is she *sucking her thumb*? Isn't that *adorable*. She looks like she could be *five years old*.

KELLY: *(To Cash.)* When does puberty usually hit?

CASH: *(To Kalina.)* C'mon.

CAROL: Cash, *don't*.

KALINA: *(Coming around.)* Why? What? What is happening?

CASH: Time to go.

KALINA: *(Bleary, but registering, and resenting, Cash.)* Don't do that to me. Stop it. *(Turns to Carol instead.)* What? What did I do? What time is it now?

CAROL: About nine thirty.

KALINA: Noooo, no. Now you are silly. Is *dark* outside.

CLAY: Nine thirty at *night*.

KALINA: No. I was sleeping.

CAROL: You just took a little *nap*.

KALINA: No. I was so *sleepy*. And also not feeling so good.

KELLY: Yeah, malt liquor'll do that to you.

CASH: Let's get outa here.

KALINA: *(Angry whisper.) Please do not be touching me. (Changing the subject.)* Ohhhh! *Heyyyy!* Look! It is Kayla!! It is Kayleetchka!! Hey, you come and sit with me now, yes? Huh? Because now we are going to be like sisters!! I will be the big sister!!

(Kayla does so.)

KELLY: Sweetie, time for bed.

KALINA: *(To Kayla.)* Hey, and look!! Look there is our mommy!! Our mommy the beauteous Kelly who is so perfect in all things and is also being the simultaneous *sex goddess,* huh? Are we so lucky, huh? To have the mommy who is the perfect *sex goddess?*

KELLY: Kayla?

KALINA: *(Still fairly drunk.)* Oh, Kelly, you know? Is all I ever wanted, is to be part of family like this!

CAROL: I assumed you *had* family.

KALINA: No, Carol. Is sad for me.

KELLY: We assumed they were circus people.

KALINA: *(Laughs.) Ohhhh, noo!!* Kelly is *crazy. (To Kayla.)* Our mommy is *crazy* to joke with me. *(To Kelly.)* You mean like the *gypsies?! (Laughs.)* Believe me, Kelly. I will tell you about the *gypsies. (Puts hand to head.)* Ow. I maybe am needing the Tylenols.

CAROL: *(Whispering to Cash as she goes.)* Just a *little plate,* is all.

(Carol exits to kitchen.)

KELLY: *(Taking Kayla by the hand and leading her upstairs.)* Come on. Time for bed.

KALINA: *(To Kayla as they go.)* Kayla Kayleetchka!! You know this, yes? That I cannot have the children? Due to the scar tissue the doctor put on my uterus? But if is not for the scar tissue on my uterus I would have *twenty* Kaylas just like *you!!*

(The Baby starts to cry upstairs. Kelly lifts Kayla and carries her up.)

CASH: *(To Kalina, as Kelly and Kayla exit.)* Hey.

KALINA: Hey? Hey, to *me,* you say? No. Not hey. Hey *you. You* hey. And here is other funny thing. Funny thing is how I am talking to *them* and not to *you.*

CASH: *(Sighing.)* I'm sorry if I raised my voi —

KALINA: Almost as funny as how I am a *nitwit,* but still have to take *orders* from *you? That* is funny. *(To Clay.)* And this also is something funny which you can tell him from me. How I am not just a little, uhh . . . *machine* for to give him the blow jobs, you know? He can buy for himself *machine* if he wants only to have the blow jobs on the regular base. *(Thinks.)* Regular *base?*

CLAY: Basis.

KALINA: Regular *basis*. For this, he can save money, get himself *machine*.

CASH: Where would I find such a machine?

KALINA: And for what am I to be this machine? So that I can have place to live? Ha. I think *fuck this*. I can go to hotel, maybe. And you will tell him this from me.

CASH: We had *assumed* you'd been hit by a truck.

KALINA: *(Shrugs.)* Would make you happy, maybe.

CASH: Little did we know. You just popped over to the mini-mart.

KALINA: What do you care? I am just a nitwit.

CASH: As I'm driving around out there for an hour and a half.

KALINA: So go away.

CASH: You do *know* they don't want you here? You do *know* this?

KALINA: How do you know?

CASH: Oh, I have a feeling.

KALINA: So you are expert now?

CASH: I just get a feeling.

KALINA: You don't even *talk* to them. I am *talking* to them. Because now we are friends, you know? *(To Clay.)* Is true, yes? How now we are friends?

CLAY: Sure.

KALINA: *(As a secret.)* Is because he is *jealous*. Is true, you know? Of you and Kelly. Even with all the problems. Still he is jealous.

CLAY: The problems.

KALINA: The problems with the marriage. Is no big deal.

CLAY: *(To Cash, calmly.)* *We* have problems. I see.

KALINA: Ooooch. My stomach is also not so good.

CLAY: *(To Cash.)* I mean, *problems?* OK, yeah. Problems *arise*. But you know what? The interesting thing about problems? You *work them out*. That's what adults *do*.

KALINA: I tell you, he is not happy person.

CLAY: *(To Kalina.)* But, of course, he wouldn't *know* that. Because *my* experience? My experience is, if you go to *Cash* with your problems? Cash's response is: *You guys work it out on your own.*

KALINA: *He* is the one who is like the gypsy, your brother.

CLAY: *(To Cash.)* I mean, seriously. Who's really the one with the *problems?*

KALINA: Is true. Because the gypsies, you see, they will always cheat you and steal from you and lie to you and they act like, *hey, so what? Is cool. Is no big deal!*

CLAY: Exactly.

KALINA: And I tell you something. If I was president of *my* country. This is true. If *I* was the president, I would get all of the gypsies, and take them to some place, and get rid of them.

(She breezily draws a finger across her throat and makes a slashing sound.)

KALINA: All of them. Is nothing else to do. Is nothing but to get rid of them. Is exactly the way it was with the Jews.

(Carol enters with a plate of food.)

CAROL: *(Quietly, to Cash.)* Now, I didn't give you any green beans because I know how you feel about green beans.

KELLY: *(From upstairs.)* Oh my god. Oh, god. Clay?

CASH: *(To Kalina.)* Let's go.

KALINA: I am not going with you.

(Kayla, in her pajamas enters from above. She carries a videotape.)

CAROL: *(To Kayla.)* Well look who's here. Are you all ready for sleepy sleep?

(Kelly appears behind Kayla, holding an avocado between tissues.)

KELLY: *(Quietly intense.)* It was in her *room*, Clay. That animal was in her *room*. Oh god, *look at this.*

CAROL: *(To Kayla.)* Look at this lonely empty lap. Is that your cartoon? Hmm?

KELLY: *(Quietly so as not to alarm Kayla.)* Wedged behind her My Little Pony House. *(Nauseous.)* Ohhhh god. Teeth marks. I'm gonna be sick.

CASH: *(Calling out to the room.)* Good night. I'm leaving.

KALINA: *(To Cash.)* Give me the credit cards.

CASH: *(Extracting his wallet.)* Why, certainly. Would that be the Mastercard you haven't paid for two years?

KELLY: How could it *carry* an *avocado*?

CASH: Or maybe you'd prefer the Amex with the balance of seventeen thousand dollars?

CLAY: *(Wheeling on Cash.)* Hey, would you stop hassling her?

CASH: *(Laughs.)* What?

CLAY: She's free to do what —

CASH: *Hassling* her?

CLAY: Just let her —

CASH: I shouldn't *hassle* her?

CLAY: Just leave her alone.

CASH: Whatever you say, *Billy Jack.*

KELLY: *(To Clay.)* Just let them go.

CASH: *(To Kalina.)* I could physically overpower you. I can *put* you in the car. Is that what you want?

CAROL: *(To Kayla, who now sits in her lap.)* Kay-kay, some people think that just because they're bigger and stronger they get to always have their way in the world. But we know that's not true.

CASH: Hey, Kayla? Do you know the phrase *sanitized for your protection?*

CLAY: *(To Kalina.)* You can sleep on the sofa.

KELLY: Wait wait wait wait wait.

CLAY: No. Let him go. He didn't want to be here in the first place. He has no interest in this family.

CASH: Clay, I'm *sorry.* I'm *sorry* your kid is sick, OK? I'm *sorry*

KALINA: Oh, Kayleetchka? You are not feeling so good?

KELLY: *(To Cash.)* Don't, OK? Not in front of —

CASH: We all *know.* Why do we have to act like — ?

CAROL: *(To Kalina.)* She has a little infection. *(To Kayla.)* Don't you, Miss Scratchy-Pants?

CASH: We're all sorry, Clay. All right? But the bullshit can get rather *exhausting.*

CLAY: So *our* life is *bullshit.*

CASH: Oh Jesus.

CAROL: *(To Kayla, underneath.)* We have nothing to be ashamed of. We're *innocent.*

KALINA: *(Standing unsteadily.)* Is bathroom this way?

CLAY: *(To Cash.)* So you are the great repository of the *truth.*

KELLY: Just *don't.* Just ask the two of them to *leave.*

CLAY: No no no. Let's hear the great *truth* that Cash has brought for us.

CAROL: *(To Kayla.)* You don't want to watch with me?

CLAY: Let us in on the *big picture.* Oh great guardian of the wisdom.

CASH: *(To Kelly.)* What do *you* want me to say? Do *you* have a suggestion?

KALINA: Kelly, do you have some of the Maalox?

CASH: *(To Kelly.)* Do you really want to have this conversation?

KELLY: *(To Cash.)* Shut up.

CAROL: *(To Kayla.)* Who's the specialest person for watching cartoons? Hm? You show me who!

CLAY: Who really has the problems, huh? Slandering us behind our backs.

KALINA: *(Exiting.)* Excuse me everbody, for my sickness!

CASH: Well, Clay. I don't know what you're going to do to me since *Daddy's* dead. Since you can't go *tattle* on me to someone who'll beat my ass with a *belt* for you. That's a real *quandary,* isn't it? You little sissy-ass *tattletale.*

CLAY: Lemme tell you something. *Golf is a very difficult and challenging game.* I'd like to see you *try* it.

KELLY: *(Overlap after "game.")* Clay. End it. Now.

CASH: *(Overlap after "to see.")* *(Falsetto.)* *Daddy!! Cash took my Hot Wheels!! Punish Cash, Daddy!!!*

CAROL: I *told* your father if he insisted on calling two boys Cassius and Clay that they were bound to fight.

(Kayla approaches Cash. She points at him.)

CASH: *(To Kayla.)* Hey. How you doin'?

KELLY: Kayla? *No.*

CAROL: Ohhh, I don't think *he* wants to watch.

KELLY: Come here, sweetie.

CAROL: I'm a better person for watching cartoons.

CASH: *(To Kayla.)* Hey. Look. Wanna see something?

CAROL: *(To Kayla.)* *I* like cartoons.

KELLY: Sweetie? Kayla?

CASH: Lemme show you something. Look at this.

(Cash makes his face into a pig face. Kayla starts to laugh.)

CAROL: Do you want to put in the tape? Let's do that.

CASH: *(Pig voice.)* I am Uncle Pig Face. Do you want to kiss my pig face?

KELLY: Kayla? *(To Cash.)* Leave her alone.

(Kayla is still laughing.)

CASH: *Greetings, little girl!! Come and kiss my Pig Face!!! Hahahaha!!!*

KELLY: *(To Cash.)* OK, *out.* I want you out.

CLAY: Kayla, go with Grandma.

KELLY: Now. Go. I'm sorry. I've had it. You can both leave now. You and your underage —

CASH: We're just goofing around.

KELLY: No no no. Waltzing into my home. Waltzing in and out of my *life?* I mean *who do you think you are?* I've had it, OK?

CASH: *Waltzing?*

KELLY: Waltzing in like you got the keys to the place? How *dare* you.

CASH: Thought I was doing the *fox-trot.*

KELLY: I've simply . . . oh god I fucking *HAAAATE YOU!!!* I would so gladly slice off your balls and cram them up your — *(Strangled shriek.)* *HAAAAATE YOU!!!!!!*

(A miserable silence. Finally:)

CAROL: *(To Kayla, taking her by the hand.)* I'm going to put on *my* jammies. Do you think you can help me do that? Hmmm?

(Carol and Kayla exit up the stairs. The silence returns. Then, from off, we hear Kalina retching. Cash stands.)

CASH: I . . . uhhh . . . I'm gonna . . . *(Indicates bathroom.)* . . . I'll see what's . . . yeah.

(Cash goes. Kelly begins to cry.)

CLAY: Shhh. C'mon. I know.

KELLY: No you don't.

CLAY: I can take care of it.

KELLY: No you can't.

CLAY: I'll take her to the right people. I swear.

KELLY: I . . . but . . . you don't —

CLAY: Listen to me. I can handle it.

KELLY: I just . . . why did you have to . . . I mean — ?

CLAY: What?

KELLY: Oh god, Clay. I'm just really *sad* right now. OK? I'm *sad*.

(He kneels close to her as she cries.)

CLAY: Hey. *Hey.* Shhhhh. Come on. I know. It's all scary. This is scary stuff and I'm scared, too. But I told them everything we know. And possibly it's *nothing*. But if not. If it's something bad. Something some person did. Some sick sort of . . . *(She cries more, he embraces her.)* . . . Hey. Ohhh, sweetie. Look at you. Look at your face. You're so beautiful. Don't you know how amazing you are? You're in the *dictionary* under amazing. Hey. We're still us. We're still the same two crazy . . . *people*. Hey, remember when I had that *beard?* Remember that? Why did I shave that off? I gotta grow another bea —

KELLY: *(Recoiling.)* Clay. Your *breath*.

CLAY: Whoops.

(Pause. He backs off.)

KELLY: And I hated that beard.

CLAY: Well.

KELLY: It was like kissing a vagina.

(Pause.)

CLAY: Tell you what, *Groucho*. As soon as everyone leaves. Mom goes to sleep. *I* am going to load up the *magic pipe*.

KELLY: I don't want to get *stoned*, Clay. I have a *career*. I don't want to spend *my* life getting *stoned* like some kind of deadbeat *loser*.

CLAY: I didn't mean —

KELLY: *"The same two crazy peo . . ."* What does that *mean?* Why do you have to use these *clichés*, these stultifying little predigested . . . god . . . why do you have to . . . *(Continued.)*

CLAY: OK.

KELLY: *(Continuous.)*. . . incessantly *do* that?

CLAY: OK. Oh . . . *kay.* Here's what I'm gonna do:

KELLY: I don't think I love you anymore.

> *(Pause.)*

KELLY: I don't think I've loved you for about four years.

CLAY: Huh.

KELLY: *(Sobbing again.)* Oh god. Oh god.

CLAY: Well, here's what *I* think. I *thought* that we'd worked through all this. That's what *I* thought.

KELLY: Apparently not.

CLAY: Apparently not. Apparently we didn't.

> *(We hear Carol from upstairs.)*

CAROL: *(To Kayla.) Grammy's in her jammies. Are we going to brush our teeth now?*

CLAY: So *apparently* when we said to the doctor, said that all of the problems seem to be resolved, water under the bridge and what was I thinking of course I love my husband *apparently* when we were sitting in that office saying all that *apparently* one of us wasn't exactly telling the truth, is that right?

KELLY: *(Pauses, then.)* I didn't say —

CLAY: Well, you know, the thing is, if you *pause* before you answer? When I ask these questions? Then I think it means you're about to lie to me. So: Were you telling the truth?

> *(Pause.)*

CLAY: *Pause* . . .

KELLY: Don't tell me how I'm supposed to answer.

CLAY: Well, what would you expect me to think? Wouldn't that be the natural assumption? In the space of the pause?

KELLY: No.

CLAY: That would be *my* assumption.

KELLY: Well, that's *you.*

CLAY: If *I* heard someone pause in that way.

KELLY: Well, you're not me.

CLAY: So were you?

> *(Pause. Clay nods.)*

CLAY: *Pause* . . .

KELLY: I'm *upset,* Clay! Can't you see how I *feel?*

> *(Cash has entered, holding a bath mat.)*

CASH: Whoops.

CLAY: No no. Stay. Please. This is good.

KELLY: Please don't.

CASH: *(Not sure whether to stay or go.)* Sorry.

CLAY: This is good. Now he can see what he missed.

KELLY: Not with him here.

CLAY: But we're *family*, right? This is my family. And when I call my family, four years or *whatever* ago and I say help me, can you help me out I think my wife may be in love with someone else and my family member says to me, says in this tone of voice, says "you guys work it out on your own," like that, see, then he never gets to see what it was really *like*. What it's like to pay some doctor a hundred and fifty bucks a week just so that *one* of us can make up stories about how, *now*, everything is just *fine*.

KELLY: *You* didn't pay.

CLAY: *(To Cash.)* True. I didn't pay. *She* paid so that *she* could make up stories.

KELLY: Right, because I'm such a *liar*.

CLAY: No. Hey. If you want to throw away your money making up little *stories*.

KELLY: *(As much for Cash's benefit as Clay's.)* I'm not the one with the giant closet full of *porn*. All right? I'm sick of it. I throw that shit out and two weeks later there's twice as much. I'm fucking *sick* of it. Sixteen-year-old girls in high heels with *come* dripping off their chins. It's fucking *disgusting*. I want it out of my house. It *disgusts* me.

KALINA: *(From the bathroom.)* Cash?

CASH: *(Re: the bath mat.)* I'm just gonna toss this.

KELLY: But somehow it's *me* that can't be believed.

CLAY: So —

KELLY: Is *that* what your notion of family is all about? Huh? If two people love each other wouldn't you at *least* expect one of them to believe what the other one says?

CLAY: *(Smug, to Cash.)* But see, she just got through telling me that she *doesn't* love me anymore.

(Kelly sighs, exhausted.)

KELLY: I still love you.

CLAY: That was persuasive.

KELLY: *Oh god would you STOP IT!!??*

(Kalina stumbles in, disheveled.)

KALINA: *(Like an orphaned child.)* Cash, I want to go home.

CASH: Me too.

KALINA: *(Holding him for support.)* I had too many beers.

CASH: I know.

KALINA: *(Climbing into his arms.)* And I think I ruin their bath mat.

CASH: They'll buy a new bath mat.

KELLY: *(Quietly, to Clay.)* Can't you at least put your arms around me?

CLAY: I don't think I will at the moment.

(Now Carol is entering from above.)

CAROL: *(Calling out to an unseen Kayla.) I'm putting the cartoon in now! But someone I know has to help me push the buttons!*

CASH: Let's put your boots on.

KALINA: Those boots, they give me such *blister.*

CASH: I know.

KALINA: For boots this expensive? Is total rip-off.

CASH: We'll get you some new boots.

CAROL: *(Calling upstairs.) Who's going to help me watch the cartoon?!!*

KALINA: *(Petulantly.)* Is hard word, you know?

CASH: What word?

KALINA: Per-skeptive.

CASH: I know.

KELLY: *(Quietly.)* Please, Clay. What do you possibly want me to say?

CLAY: Well, I have a suggestion. I don't know, I'll just toss this out. *Possibly* you could say this: See, you *might* say, I'm the person who made Clay kill his cat. How would that feel? So that I could have a couple of babies. Does that work for you? I made him kill his cat so that I could have some babies, and now, I'm thinking maybe I'd like to go off and fuck someone else. Try that if you want. Clay had a cat named Chester. *I* forced him to kill it. And now I think I want to —

(But Kelly has already exited.)

CAROL: *(Standing by the TV.)* Clay? I . . . I . . . I'm not sure I know how to work this.

(Everyone turns. Instead of cartoons, the TV screen is filled with graphic images from a porn video. A man and woman are getting it on. Much grunting and thrusting. No one knows what to do. Kalina busts out laughing.)

CAROL: I mean, it's not that I *disapprove.*

(Cash turns to Mr. Hadid. The TV fades out. The afternoon light returns, as does the snow. The others exit.)

CASH: So OK. So listen to this. So the other day this woman comes in my office. Says, to me, I think I want to get a nose job.

MR. HADID: I'm sorry. Is this a joke?

CASH: No. True story.

MR. HADID: It takes the form of a joke.

CASH: *(Thinks.)* Yeah, I guess it does. So she says Doc I want to get a nose job. The problem is: and get *this,* she says to me, the problem is, I don't *believe* in plastic surgery. I say wait a second. I'm sorry, what? She says, not believe like *it doesn't exist,* it's that my *belief* system tells me not to agree with it. So I say OK, *which* belief system is this? She says it's my *personal belief.* I think it's wrong. I don't think our lives should be determined by something so random as biology. I think that people should stop being hung up on the superficial. I have a wonderful personality. I'm a good friend. I'm funny. I'm lively. And still I don't have a boyfriend and I don't get the jobs I want. I'm at this enormous disadvantage all because I've got this *nose.* She says the world should *not be* that way. And that is what I *believe.* I *believe* it. And she says, so what can *you* say to me to put my mind at ease about the whole procedure? *(He thinks.)* Now, I'm trying to wrap my head around this. I'm trying to get this. I really am. I'm the doctor. Obviously I can't just act like . . . So I look at her. I put on a serious expression. And I say, well, let me ask you this: Which do think came first, your *beliefs,* or your nose? Because maybe, and I could be wrong, correct me if I am, but *maybe* if you hadn't been born with this giant . . . *with* this nose, you wouldn't have developed these beliefs. She says, yes, but my beliefs go deeper. My beliefs are who I really *am.* And I say, yes, right, understood, but see, the problem is, I can't *see* your beliefs. Whereas your *nose?* To put it mildly? *Readily* apparent. And she says you're acting like my beliefs aren't serious. And I say, as gently as I can, I say, well perhaps not serious *enough* since you're already here for the nose job. And she says I don't care for your attitude and I say OK. So she storms out. Goes to a friend of mine. He fixed her nose last week. Chin implant, too. My point is . . . well, you see what my point is.

MR. HADID: I see what your point is.

(Pause.)

CASH: So let me ask you something. You don't see the, uh, *irony* in all this?

MR. HADID: In this situation?

CASH: You drive a cab, right? Is that right?

MR. HADID: Yes.

CASH: It's a job.

MR. HADID: It is alright.

CASH: Make a decent living.

MR. HADID: I make a living.

CASH: Decent.

MR. HADID: I do not know what you think is decent.

CASH: You're not starving.

MR. HADID: No.

CASH: Maybe not *rolling in dough.*

MR. HADID: No.

CASH: But you're not starving.

MR. HADID: I am not starving.

CASH: But you got to pay the bills, right?

MR. HADID: Yes.

CASH: You're not a *hermit.* You're not some *saint.*

MR. HADID: No.

CASH: Some saintly . . . You're not *Gandhi.* You live in the world.

MR. HADID: I am not Gandhi.

CASH: Got your cab. Got your home. You got a kid, right? A boy, right?

MR. HADID: I have a son, yes.

CASH: Just saying. People aren't that complicated.

MR. HADID: I think you are probably right.

CASH: It's like actors, right? What actors say: *What's my motivation?*

MR. HADID: *My* motivation?

CASH: You know. What people want? Why you're here?

MR. HADID: You invited me here.

CASH: Not *here,* here. I mean in a broader sense. All you want is some of what *we* have. Right? That's all. Certain advantages. I don't blame you. Who wouldn't? Otherwise why would you have come here in the first place? But don't you see the rather comic dimension of it all? You don't? Look, *you* want to be more like *us . . . (Giggles to himself.) . . .* but we're a bunch of *assholes.*

(Kelly enters with a glass.)

KELLY: *(To Mr. Hadid.)* This might be the last of the apple juice.

MR. HADID: Thank you very much.

KELLY: It's not very cold.

MR. HADID: It will be fine.

(Carol follows with a plate of cookies.)

CAROL: *(To Mr. Hadid.)* I know you said you didn't want these. But just in case.

MR. HADID: Thank you.

(Carol sits next to Cash.)

CAROL: *(To Kelly.)* I mean, the funny thing is. I vaguely remembered that you and Clay had some problems. Way back when. I vaguely did. But, you know, I had I assumed that the problems had . . . well, sort of *resolved* themselves.

(Carol looks at Cash and Kelly. They both shake their heads. Kalina enters and joins them.)

CAROL: *(Turning to Mr. Hadid.)* What about *Charlie Rose?* Do you ever watch that program?

MR. HADID: I am aware of the program.

CAROL: Oh, isn't he *good?* He had that actor on the other night. The British actor? *(To Cash.)* Do you know the one I mean?

(Cash shrugs. Kalina joins them.)

CAROL: I wish that *I* could have a British accent. Don't you? It just sounds so *intelligent. (She tries it out.)* I *say.* Care for a *spot of tea? (She laughs.)* Chee-rio! *(Sighs.)* Anyway. He said, this actor said, that the secret to acting, aside from *listening,* the secret is that you should *like* your character. Have you heard that?

MR. HADID: I have not heard that.

(Clay enters and joins them, dressed as before.)

CAROL: And you know, I am just *addicted* to *Antiques Roadshow.*

(And now for the first time they are all gathered around Mr. Hadid. They stare uncomfortably.)

CLAY: Anyway.

KELLY: Anyway.

CAROL: So . . .

CASH: But enough about *me.*

CAROL: *(Laughs, embarrassed.)* Yes, look how we just keep *going on.*

CLAY: *(Explaining to Mr. Hadid, re: Cash.)* He's . . . uhh, that's a joke that peo-ple . . . If they've been talking all about themselves at length, you know, they say, "but enough about *me,* what do *you* think about me." Kind of a joke.

KALINA: *(Re: Cash.)* But we were not talking about him.

CLAY: No, I know, but —

KELLY: But it's emblematic right? Of the way we're perceived?

CAROL: Oh, *I* get it.

KELLY: As a nation that for some reason just can't seem to keep its big *trap* shut.

CAROL: "What do *you* think about" . . . that *is* funny.

KELLY: You know. Hopelessly in love with the sound of our own voices.

CLAY: Not all of us. Not *all.*

KELLY: I'm saying that's the *perception.*

CAROL: Oh I disagree.

CLAY: Then it's a *misperception.*

CAROL: I think other people *envy* us.

KELLY: But how would we know if they do?

CAROL: They do. We have a constitutional democracy.

CLAY: Not for long.

KELLY: No, we soundproof ourselves inside this self-satisfied *echo chamber,* while at the same time broadcasting to the world this empty Starbucks materialism posing as some kind of *dialogue?*

CLAY: But we're not all like that.

KALINA: Why do people make fun of Starbucks? I'm sorry. Is good coffee.

KELLY: And inevitably people are starting to wonder when exactly we intend to *shut up.* But we *don't* intend to shut up. Because we're basically not all that interested in what anyone else has to say.

MR. HADID: Excuse me?

CLAY: *(To Kelly.)* I refuse to accept that.

CAROL: We're *very* interested. That's just not true.

MR. HADID: Excuse me?

(Pause. All turn to Mr. Hadid.)

MR. HADID: Forgive me. But you did not finish the story.

KELLY: Uhhhh . . . no?

CLAY: Pretty much. Uhh . . . ?

MR. HADID: No no no. You have left something out.

CLAY: Uhhhh . . . *(To Carol.)* Did we?

CAROL: No. Not that *I* can think of.

KALINA: Oh yes! The animal! Is true! We are never to find out what kind of weasels it is that has been eating of the avocados!

CAROL: But other than that . . .

KELLY: I don't think so.

CLAY: I don't think we did.

MR. HADID: Oh, yes. Yes you did. Yes, the most important part. The central part.

CLAY: Well, let me think.

MR. HADID: The part in which you call the police.

(Pause.)

CLAY: Oh.

KELLY: Well, *technically* —

CLAY: That wasn't us.

KELLY: That was just the *system.*

CLAY: Not saying *blame the system* —

MR. HADID: Some person in this house called the police.

CLAY: *(A technicality.)* Technically, no.

KELLY: Technically not *us.*

MR. HADID: Oh, yes. I know that this is what happened.

CAROL: But that was much earlier.

CLAY: And not in the way you're thinking.

KELLY: Not like that.

CAROL: That was before the meal.

CLAY: But it wasn't like that.

KELLY: Not at all.

MR. HADID: Nevertheless. I would like to hear that part. If you would not mind going back. As a favor to me. That is the part which I would now like to hear.

(All exchange glances and confused gestures for a few moments. Then, the lights abruptly change. The piercing siren returns. They stand and resume positions from the end of the first act: Clay holds the flashlight. Cash holds his wine-stained shirt. Kelly is at the alarm box on the wall. Kayla stands on the table with her Huggie around her knees. Carol peers under Kayla's skirt. Kalina is gone. The dinner table is magically reset, complete with burning candles. Kelly turns the alarm off.)

KELLY: *(Exactly as before.)* The key was sitting right on top of the box.

CAROL: Clay?

CLAY: Huh?

CAROL: Has anybody else seen this?

(Clay looks at Kelly. Kelly looks at Cash. Cash looks at Clay.)

CASH: Maybe I oughta go.

CLAY: I . . . I know, Mom. I . . . uhh, Cash took a look at it. He's . . . giving her something.

CAROL: *(To Kelly.)* Did you see this?

KELLY: Um. No.

CAROL: It looks so itchy and scaly.

CLAY: It's an infection. It's a little problem.

CAROL: I wouldn't say little.

CLAY: *(To Kelly.)* I was just going to deal with it.

CAROL: It's all up and down the inside of her —

CLAY: Yeah, and we think. Cash and I. Or at least, *I* think it might be related to —

CAROL: Has she seen her doctor?

CLAY: Not yet.

CAROL: She needs to go to the doctor.

CLAY: I wanted to wait until I could isolate some of the potential —

CAROL: I don't think you should wait.

CLAY: *Mom! I'm not incompetent, OK?* All of you. Treating me like I'm this *failure.* Like some kind of *loser. I know what I'm doing.*

CAROL: I didn't —

CLAY: Yeah, I don't have a *job.* Is that your point? That I don't have a big desk and a big *swivel chair, like the two of them?* Well excuse me, but who here might just have the *most important job of all? Huh?* Standing there judging me.

CAROL: We weren't judg —

CLAY: *Three hours a week,* OK? So I can go play nine holes of golf and race back here again. That's the vacation *I* get. As if any of you could know the incredible amount of *work* involved.

CAROL: I raised two children.

CLAY: *And I'm trying to do a slightly less shitty job of it than you did, alright?!*
(Uncomfortable guilty pause. Carol is deeply hurt. She takes Kayla off of the table. Kayla wanders off.)

CAROL: *(To Cash, re: his shirt.)* I'll put some Spray 'N' Wash on that.

CASH: Thanks.
(Carol takes the shirt and exits to the kitchen. Cash, Clay, and Kelly are left alone. Pause.)

CASH: I oughta . . . she's out there walking around in the cold.

CLAY: I mean, let's *hope* it's an infection, OK? Because I don't even want to contemplate what the ramifications . . . I mean god almighty if someone was to hurt a *child.* Hurt *me.* Do what you want to *me.* But a *child.* An innocent . . . *(At Cash.) No evil in the world?* Let's hope you're right. That's all I have to say. Because otherwise . . . you know? Someone, *somewhere* is going to fucking *pay.*
(Cash looks at Kelly.)

CLAY: What?

KELLY: Oh, man.

CLAY: You think I fucked up? Is that it? I knew that's what you'd think. Go ahead. Say I fucked up. I don't care.

KELLY: *(Sadly.)* No. It seems like you were doing the right thing.
(Clay is confused. He had been expecting a rebuttal.)

CLAY: Well, I was trying to.

KELLY: I'm sure you were.

CLAY: OK.

CASH: Yeah, I don't know. Seems that way to me.
(Pause. Kelly and Cash stare at the floor.)

CLAY: OK but if the two of you just stand there and . . . If I'm the only one who goes on talking, see, while the two of you just continue to stand there staring then, inevitably, right? Then how would that look? Like I'm talking because I feel . . . OK, not *guilty,* but . . . like I'm hiding something. As I talk myself into a corner. Since I . . . I mean, that's how it would *look,* right?

CASH: Not necessarily.

CLAY: And OK, maybe I'm not the perfect father but I am *not* a sick evil twisted person.

KELLY: *(Calmly.)* You're a wonderful father.

CLAY: Since I'm the only one who . . . since no one else could've . . . *(To Cash.)* I mean, you said, right? Could be any number of things. You said that. Some reaction. I don't know . . . *(Continued.)*
(Phone begins to ring.)

CLAY: Something toxic in the . . . The Huggies, maybe. I don't know. Some kind of . . . *Jesus Christ why the fuck am I the only person talking!!! Huh??!! Why am I the only person that has anything to say!!!??*
(Carol has re-entered with half a loaf of bread in a plastic bag.)

CAROL: All right. Now, I admit that sometimes I get confused.

KELLY: Carol.

CAROL: But I did just hear you say you bought a *whole* loaf of this bread.

CASH: Oh, lord.

CAROL: Not a *half.*

CLAY: Oh, can we *not* go *back* to the *bread?*

CAROL: Well, I don't mean to contradict, *(To Kelly.)* but you did say a *whole* loaf, not —

CLAY: *Mom, I know you think you're helping.* But when you do this? You just . . . you just . . . you just —

CASH: Exacerbate.

CLAY: Exacerbate the situation!

KELLY: Someone must've cut it in half, Carol.

CAROL: Well, *I* didn't. Did any of *you?*
(Phone continues to ring.)

CAROL: Now, I know. It's just a loaf of *bread.*

KELLY: A *twelve-dollar* loaf of bread.

CAROL: But. If none of *us* took the missing bread. One has to assume.

CASH: Those giant rats again.

CLAY: *(Re: ringing phone.) Jesus, is that machine ever going to pick up?*
(Kelly goes for the phone.)

CAROL: All I did was open the bread box.

KELLY: *(Phone.)* Hello?

CAROL: Since we don't seem to be eating dinner.

CLAY: *Why,* Mom? Why would she do that to us?

CAROL: People lash out.

CLAY: She's a quiet, shy person. She cleans the house.

KELLY: *(Phone.)* No. Thank you. It's just a mistake.

CLAY: She looks after Kayla while I play golf. Why would she *steal* things?

CAROL: Maybe you should *ask* her why.

CLAY: *She can barely speak English!*

KELLY: *(Phone.)* No no. My husband broke a window, is all.

CAROL: *(To Clay.)* Well, then you have to make an effort.

CLAY: *(To Kelly.)* Who is it?

KELLY: The alarm system automatically called the police. *(Phone.)* Yes?
    (Kayla has entered with a surprise behind her back.)

CAROL: We don't know what people are capable of.

CLAY: So we should fire her. For taking a crust of bread.

CAROL: I didn't say that at all.

KELLY: *(Phone.)* No, he was trying to hit an animal.

CLAY: And what's more important at the moment? Protecting an innocent life?
    Or some idiotic — ?

KELLY: *(Phone.)* No, not *our animal.* We don't *own* an animal.

CASH: *Whose* innocence are we protecting here?

CAROL: *(To Kayla who tugs at her sleeve.)* No surprises right now, sweetheart.

CLAY: *(To Kayla.)* Sweetie? Go play with Kalina, OK? Go find Kalina.

KELLY: *(Phone.) No.* Not a pet. Arrrrgh!! *(To the room.)* I swear to god, people
    don't even speak *English.*

CAROL: I'm only saying that if we *don't* listen to these people, these poor un-
    derprivileged people, eventually they will rise up and lash out exactly as
    predicted by the Manifesto.

CASH: *(Hooting with laughter.)* Preach on, Comrade!

CLAY: And that is relevant *how?*

KELLY: *(Phone.)* Excuse me. Do you have a *supervisor?*

CAROL: It could be relevant.

KELLY: Clay? Will you deal with this please?

CAROL: *(Giving in to Kayla.)* Oh, alright, Little Miss. Let me see my surprise.

CLAY: *(Taking phone.)* Hello? Yeah.

CAROL: *Is it a special surprise? Hmmm? Could it be a . . . ?*
    (Kayla produces her hand from behind her back and Carol jumps and runs
    away, waving her hands in fear.)

CAROL: Oh no! No no no no no.

CLAY: What? What?

CAROL: Needle. It's a needle. No needles.

(Kayla is holding a small hypodermic syringe with needle. The others recoil.)

KELLY: *(To Carol.) Shhhhhh!!! (Then:)* Kayla. Look at Mommy. Put that down.

CLAY: Drop it, sweetie. Drop that right now.

(Kayla shakes her head.)

KELLY: *(To Clay.)* Where did she get a needle and a syringe?

CAROL: That is a nasty dirty thing.

CLAY: You drop that right this instant.

KELLY: Daddy's not kidding now.

CAROL: That is thing that will make you sick.

KELLY: Shhh! Listen to Mommy. Listen to me.

CLAY: *(Phone.)* Just a minute, please. *(To others.)* Whose is that? *(To Cash.)* Is that yours?

CASH: *Mine!?*

KELLY: That is not a toy. Needles are not toys.

CLAY: *(To Cash.)* From your *bag.* Your medical *bag.*

CASH: Who am I, *Marcus Welby?*

KELLY: Shhh!

CLAY: Well, it doesn't belong to us.

CAROL: Let's show your mommy where you found that.

KELLY: *No,* Carol. *(To Kayla.)* Kayla, *I mean it, now.* I'm counting to three. And then *you* are going to find yourself in some *very* big trouble.

CAROL: I know she's been getting into that back room.

KELLY: One . . .

CLAY: Mom. Please. Our cleaning person is not *dispersing biological weapons.*

KELLY: Two . . .

(Kayla holds the needle up like a spear and begins chasing them, shrieking with laughter. All scream.)

(Overlapping:)

CAROL: *Oh! Oh! Someone, take it from her! She's going to hurt herself or one of us! See what happens? She's lashing out! Now she's lashing out at us!!*

KELLY: *Jesus, Kayla! Stop that!! Clay, will you get that thing for her please, or do I have to do absolutely everything in this house?!!*

CLAY: *No no no no! The baby!! Watch out for the baby!!! Kayla, you are being very, very rude and inconsiderate!!*

CASH: *Hey hey. Don't get that thing near me. Whoa. Jesus, why don't you put a leash on this kid? Hang on. I got her.*

(Cash grabs Kayla from behind, Kelly takes the needle from her, then smacks her sharply on the bottom. Kayla glares.)

KELLY: What did Mommy say to you? Mommy said no. That is a dangerous, *dangerous* thing!!

CLAY: That is a *big* time-out for you, little lady.

KELLY: Next time you *listen* to Mommy.

CLAY: You just got a great big time-out. Right now.

KELLY: Go on. You heard what Daddy said. You go right now or we can make it *two.*

(Kayla turns and stomps up the stairs. Pause. All stare at the needle.)

CAROL: *(Quietly.)* Well, I don't mean to jump to conclusions. But we *know* she took the bread.

CLAY: Why? Why hurt our *child?* Why would she?

CASH: Hey Clay.

CAROL: We don't know. We don't know her reasons for *stealing* either.

KELLY: *(Handing the needle to Clay.)* I don't want to be touching this.

CAROL: But if your child is *sick.* And if she is *alone* with her.

CLAY: Look, obviously someone has done something to my child and it sure as hell wasn't *me*

CASH: Clay?

CLAY: What?

CASH: The phone.

(The lights change to isolate only Clay and Mr. Hadid.)

CLAY: And they put me on hold. For a minute. And you know, the mind devises these scenarios. You start to panic, and there you are on the phone with the people you've *paid* to protect you. Pay your taxes to protect you. And so maybe you say something stupid without thinking. To the police. About how someone who works in your home might've done something . . . deliberately given some *sickness* . . . to a child . . . So . . . I guess . . . so, yeah, so I guess . . . well, I guess the person who said that was *me.*

(Mr. Hadid nods.)

MR. HADID: *(Calmly, showing no emotion throughout.)* It is early evening. We are in the kitchen, myself and my wife. She has just given herself the medicine. We are about to eat. She says to me, here, look, have some of this bread. You remember this bread. We have had this before. You like this, with the figs and the nuts. I say to her, do you ask before you take this bread? Do they give you this bread, or do you simply take it? She says I do not ask. I take it. I say I am sure if you ask, they will give this to you.

She says I do not know how to ask. I say, then I will write it down for you. But she says, what difference will it make for them if I ask. I take it now. And they do not care. So I do not know what good it does to learn. *(As Mr. Hadid goes on talking, the others — minus Kayla — resume their places from before. Lights change. Snow begins to fall as before.)*

MR. HADID: Then there is a knocking on the door. I stand to open it, but before I do the policemen are inside the room. There are six of them. They are speaking very loudly, as though I cannot hear. I say what is it that you want? You may come in, you are welcome to come in, but tell me what it is that you want to see. Then my wife begins shouting, but not English. She says why do you come into our home? Please leave now. They say it is their right. And now my son runs out of his bedroom. He has heard the noise. And he is holding the stick of a broom. He is very angry. He says to them to get out of our house. Leave my father and mother alone and get out. They tell him to put down the stick. I say likewise to him, Farah, be quiet and put down the stick. But he does not, and so the policeman pushes my son. And suddenly everyone is shouting. I say to them my wife does not understand you. She does not speak plentiful English. Tell me what to say to her and I will say it. But still they shout, so my wife pushes the policeman who has pushed my son.

Now we are all pushed to the floor. The handcuffs are placed on us. We are taken down the stairs to the street. My son is wearing only his underwear. There are three police cars with the lights flashing. They are putting us each separate. Each in one. I say to them, please. My wife has the diabetes. She has taken the injection so now she must eat. We will cooperate with you, we are happy to do this, but please, the medicine requires this. My son is pushed into the one car. He says you cannot do this. You are breaking our rights. But they roll up the window. Then my wife is in the second car. Now I can no longer hold my temper. Now I shout at them. I say my wife must eat. Why do you not listen? And the policeman, he takes my arm. He says hey. Hey buddy. *You* listen. You listen to *me*. *You* will calm down first. I say listen please give her something to eat. He says listen buddy. We will not listen until *you* are more calm. We will now go somewhere and we will listen to what you have to say after we go there. But first, buddy, *you* must be calm. You will get nothing if you do not listen to us and be calm. But I cannot be calm. If only I could. But it is hard for me knowing that she has taken the injection and she now must eat and so I find that I cannot be calm.
(Pause.)

CAROL: And she died, then, on the way to the police station?

MR. HADID: She goes into a coma. And then some time later she dies.

CAROL: It's shocking.

KELLY: Sickening.

CAROL: It's just so wrong.

KALINA: But with the police, is always the way, you know?

CAROL: Thinking that they act on our behalf. But not like *that*.

KALINA: Because of having the guns as they do, and the power.

CAROL: And when you think that at that very moment we were right here in this room.

KELLY: Without a clue what was being carried out supposedly in our names.

CAROL: And if we had just had one little conversation —

KELLY: Which of course we should have had years earlier.

CAROL: Otherwise things get misconstrued.

KELLY: Things that are over and done with.

CAROL: Silly things, really.

KELLY: Ancient history.

CAROL: But of course we don't want to hurt each other. And that's why things get left unsaid.

KALINA: But still. Was wrong, you know, this way?

KELLY: *(Not wanting to use the word.)* Not *wrong*.

KALINA: *(Again, blithely unconcerned.)* Not to say the things. Not to say that these men, the soldiers who rape me? This is not to be ashamed. That when I was little girl and these men, they rape me, that they were to give me this sickness.

CASH: Which then —

KALINA: *(Shrugs.)* Is not going to *kill* me. I just have a sickness some of the times.

CASH: Which then . . . she gives to *me* while I . . . during the period, you know, while I . . . happen to be sleeping with my brother's pregnant wife —

(Pause.)

CAROL: But when you think of *all* the terrible diseases out there.

KELLY: And which I then —

CAROL: Thank god, really, with all of the things it *could* have been.

KELLY: Which I then pass along to my daughter.

KALINA: She will have the itching some of the time, is true. Some pain and some itching.

KELLY: And that's all, thankfully.

CAROL: *(Raising her hand.)* I had Chlamydia once!

KELLY: And as long as Clay . . . as long as one's *partner* makes sure to wear a condom —

KALINA: *(To Clay, gently.)* Yes. Always wear the condom.

CAROL: Yes.

(All nod and murmur assent. Pause. Mr. Hadid says nothing. Clay stares at the floor.)

CASH: *(Chuckles, then serious.)* I mean, not to be too . . . I mean. Think about it, isn't there something almost — That is if the whole thing wasn't so pathetic? Really, from a certain angle, *(Starting to chuckle again.)* From a *certain* perspective. . . ?

KELLY: *(Seeing him smile.)* No. Come on. Let's not. *(To Mr. Hadid.)* We're not. We don't —

CAROL: Well, yes, the truth is always a kind of *release*, isn't it?

CASH: *(Now laughing.)* I'm saying, c'mon. Isn't there an *element* to this that's . . . you know, just the *tiniest bit* — ?

CAROL: No no no no no. Now Cash? Now stop it. Now you're making me.

KELLY: *(Starting to lose it.)* No, seriously. Wait, seriously?

(Kelly, Cash, and Carol all stifle laughter.)

CAROL: *(To Mr. Hadid.)* Oh no, it's the discomfort. We're just *nervous*.

KELLY: Don't, because . . .

CAROL: Oh my goodness. It's just so *absurd*.

CASH: *(Laughing, to Clay.)* I mean, *how could you not know!?* Oh, Come *on!!! How could you not?!!*

CAROL: *(The same.)* Remember how you were running around with the *golf club*?

KELLY: *(The same.)* And then when you broke that window?

(Clay looks up, unsure. A smile comes over his face. Then, slowly, he starts to join in the laughter.)

CASH: *How could you not have known!!* It's *preposterous*.

CAROL: *(Wiping away tears, to Mr. Hadid.)* We're sorry. It's just that it's so *infectious*.

(The word "infectious" cracks them all up. Only Mr. Hadid and Kalina are not laughing.)

KALINA: *(Staring.)* I don't know. To me this is not being so funny.

(The Baby cries. Kayla enters.)

KELLY: *(To Kayla, trying to stop laughing.)* Come here, sweetie.

CAROL: *(The same.)* Kayla!! Oh look who's here!! Come here, darling.

KELLY: Come sit with us.

CAROL: We're just being silly.

    (Kayla joins them. Kelly quiets the Baby. Then, they all start to notice that Clay, who had been laughing, now silently cries. All stare.)

CAROL: What is he doing? I can't tell.

KELLY: Clay.

CAROL: Is he laughing? *(To Clay.)* Are you laughing?

KELLY: Clay, don't.

CAROL: Oh, really now.

KELLY: Please?

CAROL: I thought he was laughing.

KALINA: No. He is sad now, you see.

CAROL: *(To Mr. Hadid.)* He's just being silly. *(To Kayla.)* Your Daddy's *silly,* isn't he?

KELLY: It's not the time.

CAROL: Really, it isn't.

    (Kayla tugs at Clay's sleeve. He pulls away.)

CLAY: *(In tears, quietly to Kayla.)* Leave me the fuck alone.

CAROL: *(Admonishing.)* Clay.

CLAY: I hate you all. God I hate you all so much.

    (Long, long pause, while Clay recovers. Finally, Carol turns to Mr. Hadid.)

CAROL: Anyway. We all agree, I think. That it just seems so silly to have all of these *lawyers* involved.

KELLY: And what we hoped was, that by inviting you here —

CAROL: I mean, the money is just *symbolic.*

KELLY: That we could make it about something else.

CAROL: It's a symbol. It's not what's truly important.

KELLY: What's important is the *loss,* obviously, is the *coming to terms.*

CAROL: Money isn't the same as *healing.*

KELLY: And moving on past the loss to a place of —

CAROL: Of *recovery.*

KELLY: If that makes any sense at all.

    (Pause.)

KALINA: *(Confused.)* Wait, is it that you now say that you are *not* to give to him the money?

KELLY: *(Quietly silencing Kalina.)* Do you mind, please?

CAROL: No no no no no.

KELLY: *(To Kalina.)* We'll deal with this, OK?

CAROL: *(To Mr. Hadid.)* That wasn't what we meant.

KELLY: Not in the least.

CAROL: Not at all.

KELLY: Absolutely not.

CAROL: Although.

KELLY: Yes. Although.

CAROL: When you *think* about it —

KELLY: I mean, my partners and I, the people from my firm, when you look at the figures *your* people quoted . . .

CAROL: We're not here to talk about figures.

KELLY: Right. However *exorbitant* those figures may be We're talking about a *process.*

CAROL: About reaching out to one another, in this terrible terrible time, and finding a way. A simpler way . . . there's a Tibetan expression.

KELLY: We want to say we're sorry.

CAROL: Well, yes.

KALINA: But . . . I don't know why it is you don't just give to him the mon—?
    (Kelly harshly mouths the words "shut up" at Kalina, who stands and leaves the room. The rest all wait for Mr. Hadid to respond.)

KELLY: So, other things aside, money aside —

CAROL: Now I hope we can all hear what *you* have to say.
    (A smile comes over Mr. Hadid's face. He begins to chuckle.)

CAROL: Oh, *see . . . ?*

MR. HADID: *(Laughing.)* I am sorry.

CAROL: See? That you can laugh, *too.*

KELLY: No, seriously, though.

CAROL: After all the tension and sadness. The *relief.*

KELLY: Whatever would simplify the situation. Taking the focus off the money, for the moment.
    (Mr. Hadid starts to rise.)

MR. HADID: *(Still laughing.)* *I* am sorry.

CAROL: Oh. Oh wait. Oh no.

KELLY: Why don't you just tell us how best we can salvage the, or, well, not *salvage* —

CAROL: You can't go. We have *sandwiches.*

KELLY: Maybe I should use the word *rectify.*

CASH: *(To Kelly and Carol.)* Told you this would happen.

CAROL: Do you like grilled chicken? Or do you not eat chicken?

KELLY: Or let's use *your* terms, then. Whatever your terms are.

CASH: *(To Mr. Hadid.)* But you know what, *Hajji?* In some countries? When you come into a person's *home?*

CAROL: Or we could make you one with something else.

(*Mr. Hadid has put on a coat and made his way to the front door. He raises a hand to stop them.*)

MR. HADID: (*With finality.*) I am sorry.

(*He opens the door and exits.*)

CAROL: Oh no. This is awful. Oh no.

KELLY: (*As she follows him outside.*) Let's say this. Let's say you and I review the figures. Because maybe there's something I'm missing. Maybe I'm not seeing it in the correct light.

CASH: (*Calling after him.*) There is a thing known as *courtesy,* my friend!

(*Mr. Hadid is gone. Kelly sticks her head back in to berate Clay one last time.*)

KELLY: *Thank you,* Clay. *Thank you for your contribution.*

(*She is gone, leaving the front door open.*)

CAROL: Oh, how disappointing. After all that.

CASH: Smug little bastard.

CAROL: To have it end like that.

CASH: Sanctimonious little prick.

CAROL: After going to all this trouble. Ohh. That's very unsatisfying.

(*Pause. Kayla stares at Clay.*)

CASH: (*To Carol.*) Grilled chicken and what else?

CAROL: Pesto, I think?

CASH: I like pesto.

CAROL: Mm-hmm.

CASH: Is there cheese?

CAROL: Clay made them. You'll have to look.

(*Cash rises and exits.*)

CAROL: (*Shaking her head.*) Mm mm mm. Sometimes I wonder why we even *try.*

(*We hear a car start up and drive away. Carol looks at her watch.*)

CAROL: (*To Clay.*) What's your PBS station here? Is it Channel Eleven?

(*Clay nods. Carol rises and moves to the TV. Kelly returns to the door, talking on her cell phone.*)

KELLY: (*Phone.*) No, we tried. Total waste of time. No, He didn't go for it.

(*Carol is trying to use the remote.*)

KELLY: (*Phone.*) No, we said all the right things. At least, *I* thought we did.

(*Carol turns on the TV, but somehow instead of PBS, she has managed to turn on the porn.*)

CAROL: Oh no. No no no. Wait. Oh, poop, here we go again. Clay?

KELLY: *(Phone.)* No, I think we're screwed.

CAROL: *(Re: TV.)* Does anybody know how to stop this?

> *(Kayla tugs at Clay's sleeve. He turns to look at her. She reaches into a pocket and pulls out an avocado. Holding the avocado like an apple, she bites deeply into it and offers it to Clay. He takes it from her, and then — just as he realizes — the lights and TV fade to black.)*

END OF PLAY

VICTORIA MARTIN: MATH TEAM QUEEN

Kathryn Walat

PLAYWRIGHT'S BIOGRAPHY

Kathryn Walat's play *Victoria Martin: Math Team Queen* premiered in 2007 at the Women's Project, an Off-Broadway theater in New York, and received honorable mention from the Jane Chambers Award. Other plays include *Bleeding Kansas, Connecticut, Greenspace, Know Dog,* and *Johnny Hong Kong.* Her work has been produced at Actors Theatre of Louisville, Hangar Theatre, Salvage Vanguard Theater, and Perishable Theatre; and it has been developed at Manhattan Theatre Club, Playwrights Horizons, Ars Nova, Bay Area Playwrights Festival, Boston Theatre Works, Lark Play Development Center, and New Georges, where she is an affiliated playwright. Kate received her B.A. from Brown University and her M.F.A. from Yale Drama School. She lives in New York.

ORIGINAL PRODUCTION

Victoria Martin: Math Team Queen received its World Premiere at Women's Project in New York City in 2007. It was directed by Julie Crosby; the costume design was by Valerie Marcus Ramshur; the lighting design was by Sarah Sidman; the sound design was by Daniel Baker; and the production stage manager was Brian Meister. The cast was a follows:

VICTORIA	Jessi Campbell
FRANKLIN	Matthew Stadelmann
MAX	Tobias Segal
PETER	Zachary Booth
JIMMY	Adam Farabee

The World Premiere of Victoria Martin: Math Team Queen was produced in New York City in 2007 by Women's Project, Julie Crosby, Producing Director.

To my sister and brother.

CHARACTERS

(In order of speaking:)

VICTORIA: a sophomore

FRANKLIN: a junior

MAX: another junior

PETER: a senior

JIMMY: a freshman

TIME AND PLACE

January through June

Longwood High School

VICTORIA MARTIN: MATH TEAM QUEEN

ACT ONE

SCENE 1: THE PHONE

Tuesday evening. Victoria is in her bedroom, on the phone.

VICTORIA: I *know!* And then, when she said, I'll see you later — like, meaning she'll see me during third lunch, because you know how we're the
only ones who have third lunch on Tuesdays, I said — *maybe*. But that I
had some other things I had to do during —

Yeah, it was a total lie, but what was I supposed to say? That I would
save her a seat? Like was I going to save her a seat after I heard that she
said that I said —

I *know*. Oh wait. I'm getting another call — OK well I'll see you tomorrow in English. Later.

(She switches to the other line.)

VICTORIA: Hello? Oh, hey Jen. I was just on the other line with Jen.

Yeah, I totally missed you at lunch too. But I thought I told you
when I saw you on my way to Spanish that I had some other things I had
to —

Well, that sucks. But, I mean, third lunch, what are you going to do?
I know, my stomach is always digesting itself during Spanish, I was chewing on this piece of Big Red like my life depended on it, even though
Señor Johnson like totally outlawed gum last quarter because he said how
we could chew gum and speak Spanish at the same time — but that
doesn't make any sense, because if I can speak English while chewing
gum *no problemo*, then why wouldn't I be able to speak *Español* while I
chew, *comprendez?*

I *know*.

Of course I haven't read *Anne Frank* yet. I mean — "The diary of a
young girl?"

Totally.

Jen hasn't read it either. So even if we did what we did with *Scarlet
Letter* and I copied off of her, and you copied off of me, I feel like your
chances of getting more than a C+ are like approaching zero.

Totally.

Oh wait, I'm getting another —

Hang on.

(She switches to the other line.)

VICTORIA: Hello? Oh, hi.

Of course I'm applying myself.

Actually, Mom, I'm on the other line with Jen. No, the other Jen. They're both cheerleaders. But we're talking about *Anne Frank*. Fine.

VICTORIA: I sorta ate already.

It was fine.

Well, I'll see you — whenever *too-late-for-dinner* is.

(She switches back to the other line.)

VICTORIA: Jen? Sorry. That's Scott on the other — oh, shut up, I do not talk to him *every* single —

Look he's waiting, and do you want me to tell the star of varsity basketball, who just happens to be my boyfriend, that *you*, a mere *cheerleader*, are the reason that he's —

That's what I thought.

(Victoria hangs up the phone and looks at the audience. She talks to us.)

VICTORIA: In case you've forgotten? *This* is high school.

SCENE 2: MEET THE TEAM

After school Wednesday. Franklin and Max, both juniors, in an empty class-room. They play one-on-one basketball with a spongy ball.

FRANKLIN: And *then*.

MAX: It all came down to that one moment.

FRANKLIN: The clock was ticking.

MAX: His hands were sweating.

FRANKLIN: His *face* was sweating.

MAX: Like crazy! But that wouldn't slow him down.

FRANKLIN: Didn't even notice.

MAX: We didn't even notice, and you *know* the other kid has —

FRANKLIN: Total B.O.

MAX: But there was nothing stopping him.

FRANKLIN: The stands were going wild.

(Franklin acknowledges the stands.)

MAX: *We* were going wild. You were totally mad-dog, Franklin.

FRANKLIN: Mad-dog Franklin! Rabid and still he —

(Franklin slam-dunks the ball into a wastepaper basket.)

FRANKLIN: Scores!

MAX: You, like, injured my leg.

FRANKLIN: Max Werner, taking one for the team.

MAX: I had your fingernail marks on my thigh for three days.

FRANKLIN: Yeah, well, *you* were scared we were gonna lose.

MAX: I was focusing all my energy on making his pencil move faster.

FRANKLIN: And that's how we won that meet?

MAX: We won because we had the combined brainpower to blow that team out of the water.

FRANKLIN: We won because Sanjay Patel has the biggest brain in the state.

MAX: And it all came down to *him.*

FRANKLIN: To that one moment.

MAX: One tie-breaking problem.

FRANKLIN: One insane algebraic equation.

MAX: An algebraic equation of seismic proportions.

> *(Peter, a senior, enters the classroom.)*

FRANKLIN: A five on the Richter scale of algebraic equations.

MAX: The algebraic equation was prodigious, grandiose, Homeric —

FRANKLIN: Will you cut it out with the SAT vocab?

> *(Max stops, defensive.)*

MAX: What?

> *(Peter steals the ball from Max, just as Victoria enters the classroom, quickly closing the door behind her like she hopes nobody in the hallway saw her come in.)*

PETER: It was a multivariable, unrecognizably quadratic, irregular —

> *(After an elegant setup Peter goes for a three-point shot. Which misses.)*

FRANKLIN: And the buzzer buzzes —

MAX: *Aaaaaaaaant.*

PETER: Wicked hard math problem.

FRANKLIN: Which *you* could have solved using calculus.

PETER: True.

FRANKLIN: God, I can't *wait* to learn calculus!

> *(Victoria, still standing by the door, not used to being ignored.)*

VICTORIA: Ah, hello?

MAX: But Sanjay Patel just used his *brain.*

FRANKLIN: So what are we gonna do without him?

VICTORIA: Earth to math geeks . . . ?

MAX: *Today,* Peter.

FRANKLIN: At the meet *today* we —

PETER: I know, but don't worry, I figured something out.

VICTORIA: Come in, *math geeks* . . .

(They finally notice her.)

MAX: Oh. That would be us.

PETER: Hi.

FRANKLIN: Extra help is —

MAX: Next door.

VICTORIA: Yeah, OK, but I'm not here for . . . I'm —

PETER: Victoria Martin?

(Jimmy, a freshman, bursts through the door.)

JIMMY: Sorry, sorry, sorry, I know I'm late but someone unzipped my backpack, and my books fell out, all over the hallway, so I had to . . .

(He sees Victoria and stops.)

VICTORIA: It's *Vickie*.

PETER: I'm Peter. This is the team. Mr. Riley recommended that Vickie here
replace my-parents-are-moving-to-Arizona-in-the-middle-of-the-school-
year Sanjay Patel.

JIMMY: But she's — a girl.

VICTORIA: OK, I didn't say that I would totally do this.

FRANKLIN: No one can —

MAX: Replace —

FRANKLIN: Sanjay Patel.

VICTORIA: I just — came by, because Mr. Riley said I had to otherwise he was
totally going to give me detention for —

PETER: He told you there was a meet today.

VICTORIA: Yeah, but . . .

PETER: Because we need to leave now, to make it to the meet.

JIMMY: We have a girl on our team?

VICTORIA: OK, you know this isn't really *my scene*.

FRANKLIN: OK, but you are — a *sophomore?*

VICTORIA: And tonight I totally need to read *The Diary of Anne Frank*.

MAX: Bingo. Sophomore English.

PETER: You can read it in the van.

MAX: We'll tell you what happens.

FRANKLIN: Yeah. Like, that part near the end where Anne Frank starts inter-
cepting Morse code signals from Germany and almost gets brainwashed
into being a Nazi. Right Max?

MAX: Um. Yeah.

(Franklin and Max hoist their identical backpacks onto both shoulders.)

VICTORIA: OK, but if I go to this meet, this doesn't mean I'm like *doing this.* Maybe this once. But I'm not like a full-time — I mean, I am *so* not doing Math Team. OK?

PETER: The van is waiting.

(They start to file out of the classroom. Jimmy grabs Peter.)

JIMMY: There's going to be a *girl* in the *van?*

SCENE 3: THE NEXT DAY POST-PLAY

Victoria talks to the audience.

VICTORIA: I'm *popular.* Like totally, undisputedly popular. Like, I walk down the hallways, and even though I'm a sophomore, there are seniors — senior *guys,* with deep voices — who say: *Hey.* Sometimes they say: *Hey, Vickie, what's up?* Like, they know my name.

OK, so mostly they're on the basketball team so they know my boyfriend, who is totally varsity first string, even though he's only a junior, because this fall while the other guys were playing football all he did was practice his free throws, because he's a one-sport guy. Scott. He's totally into me. And that's why I'm a *sophomore* and those senior jocks know my *name,* but it's not like I'm one of those slutty girls whose names all the guys know, and plus I totally have girl friends too.

I'm friends with the *Jens.* Who are on the varsity cheerleading squad, even though they're sophomores, mostly because all the juniors who tried out this year had "weight issues" so forget trying to get *them* up in a pyramid — plus, the Jens are very, very peppy. They know how to do that thing where they toss their ponytails, and depending on the toss, it's either like: What*ever,* I am so walking away from *you.* Or, it's like: See this swish? That's right, this ponytail says: I will see *you* later.

I understand this distinction. I am not a cheerleader. But I *know* this. I have secured my place in the high school universe, after the very volatile freshman year, which the Jens and I refer to as: Versaille. Like, the Treaty of Versaille? You know — World War I, European power struggle, third-period history with Mr. Delano — that's where we met, our desks, in a row, across the back of the room: Jen-Me-Jen.

Yesterday at the math meet? All of that was suddenly meaningless. This one kid had an equation on his T-shirt. The quadratic formula, across his back. I *know!* I mean, nerd central, *all* math geeks, *and* I was the only girl. Except for these two on the other team, who would only speak to each other. In binary. For fun. And when I was in the girls' bathroom and I totally just got my period, and had to ask one of them for a pad, they just *giggled.* And so I had to stuff all of this scratchy schoolgrade toilet paper into my underwear and meanwhile, I almost missed the sophomore round of questions, because they put all the room numbers in Roman numerals. For fun. And when I finally got there, I was sitting next to this kid who kept clicking his retainer and it was driving me crazy, and I was like —

(Suddenly the rest of the team is there. She turns and speaks to them.)

VICTORIA: I don't *do* headgear, OK?

MAX: The kid with the retainer?

FRANKLIN: Rodney?

MAX: You're blaming this on Rodney from East Park High School?

VICTORIA: *And* we never even had problems like those yet in Mr. Riley's class.

PETER: Math meets are all about taking something you *should* know, or something you *might* know, and taking it one step further.

VICTORIA: That was *two* steps.

FRANKLIN: You messed up.

VICTORIA: In a direction I *don't want to go.*

MAX: You didn't even get partial credit.

FRANKLIN: You got your questions *all wrong.*

JIMMY: But that's OK — just this once . . . ?

PETER: So, Vickie, can you do this or not? Because we need to get this practice started.

VICTORIA: I thought practice was optional. Mr. Riley said that —

PETER: We like to practice as much as we can.

VICTORIA: Right, because you're nerds, and you have nothing better to —

JIMMY: Because we like math. That's why we practice.

FRANKLIN: Yeah. In case you didn't know? We really like math.

MAX: All of us.

FRANKLIN: OK?

VICTORIA: Oh. I mean. OK.

PETER: So?

VICTORIA: So — I get that. It's not like I actually *met* anyone who *said* they like math, but I can —

PETER: So you're staying?

VICTORIA: No, I — I think I should go. My ride is going to be waiting.

JIMMY: Peter could give you a ride home.

(They all look at Jimmy.)

JIMMY: What? Why doesn't anyone want her on the team?

VICTORIA: Yeah, my ride is totally waiting. And — actually, I just came by to say *thanks* for filling me in on what happens in *The Diary of Anne Frank*. About Anne's near-conversion to the dark side, and how the Stars Wars trilogy is totally based on that. I'm really glad I was prepared when Mrs. Snyder suddenly called on me. So, thanks. That was — really *shitty*.

(Victoria exits. Max looks at Franklin.)

FRANKLIN: What? You're the one who actually remembered what happened in *Anne Frank*. It's like we always say: two brains are better than —

MAX: That was *not* my brain's idea.

JIMMY: Everyone at the meet kept asking me what it was like having a girl on the team. I told them it was awesome. I like her. I really like her. Can we keep her?

PETER: Do we have a choice?

FRANKLIN: Because Vickie Martin is *nothing like* Sanjay Patel. I mean . . .

* * *

(Max talks to the audience.)

MAX: In case you didn't know?

FRANKLIN: This is The Legend . . .

MAX: Of Sanjay Patel.

FRANKLIN: Armed with his scientific calculator in one hand, his graphing calculator in the other . . .

(They make Wild West music. And then realize they're getting carried away.)

MAX: OK, he's not *that* kind of Indian.

FRANKLIN: Yeah, they moved to Arizona because his parents didn't like *the cold*.

(Max paints us a picture.)

MAX: Sanjay Patel is a legend — of a different sort.

FRANKLIN: It wasn't just him and his backpack riding on that ten-speed bike. It was *his brain*.

MAX: His mathematical ability was superlative, exemplary — monumental. Exorbitant. Astronomic. Incontrovertible. It was —

FRANKLIN: Huge, Max, it was *huge*. Look, the story is: Sanjay Patel was the reason we were going to win States this year. But now?

MAX: In case you didn't know, we need a *sophomore* on the team. Sanj was a sophomore.

FRANKLIN: We're juniors.

MAX: Actually, we function as a collective unit.

FRANKLIN: Like two brains are better than . . .

MAX: Like lab partners.

FRANKLIN: Except for *everything*.

MAX: But also lab partners.

FRANKLIN: In AP Physics.

MAX: In case you haven't noticed, Peter's a senior. He's going to M.I.T.

FRANKLIN: And he can *drive*.

MAX: And that leaves Jimmy, our over-achieving, socially retarded —

FRANKLIN: Freshman.

* * *

(Jimmy brings us back into the scene.)

JIMMY: Don't you *know* who she *is?*

MAX: Yeah, she's — popular.

JIMMY: I mean, her *ride?* Do you know who her ride is? Scott Sumner?

PETER: That tall guy on the basketball team — ?

JIMMY: That *I* keep statistics for. Yes, that varsity team, *that* Scott Sumner, who has the highest percentage of baskets-made in the entire league *and* keeps me from getting beat up in the locker room when I announce the stats. That's her ride.

FRANKLIN: Why don't we just get another sophomore, like that kid who plays bassoon?

PETER: Look, we don't just need a sophomore — we need a sophomore *girl.* OK? Now do any of you know any other sophomore *girls?*

(They all look at each other.)

PETER: I didn't think so.

MAX: You mean the only reason she's on the team is because she's a *girl?*

PETER: You thought it was because she was good at algebra? She's the one who sits in the back of Mr. Riley's class drawing with her pencil all over that desk.

FRANKLIN: All those games of hangman?

PETER: Mr. Riley said that Principal Nichols said that this is a co-ed team and so we need *a girl.*

MAX: But there's never been a girl on the Math Team before.

JIMMY: He's right. I checked the stats this morning before school.

FRANKLIN: God, that is so not fair!

MAX: So what are we going to do?

JIMMY: I like her.

FRANKLIN: Shut up, Jimmy.

MAX: So? Peter —

PETER: I don't know. I guess she's — on the team. But I do know one thing: There is no way in *hell* — sorry Jimmy, I know your mom doesn't like it when we swear. Let me just say: The probability of us making it to States with Vickie Martin on the Math Team? Is rapidly approaching *zero*.

SCENE 4: HER RIDE

Victoria is waiting for her ride. She reads from The Diary of Anne Frank.

VICTORIA: "Let me put it more clearly, since no one will believe that a girl of thirteen feels herself quite alone in the world. I know about thirty people whom one might call friends . . . but it's the same with all of them, just fun and joking, nothing more. I can never bring myself to talk of anything outside the common round . . . Hence, this diary."
(She flips ahead to the end of the book.)

VICTORIA: Wait — she *dies?*
(She looks out at the audience.)

VICTORIA: She dies — *and* they read her diary?
(She chucks the book.)

VICTORIA: That is — *so* not fair.
(She checks her watch. Out of the nothingness of the moment, she says this rhythmically to herself.)

VICTORIA: 3.14159265358979323846264643383 —

PETER: Pi.
(Peter is standing right there.)

VICTORIA: Oh. You. Yeah. Pi.

PETER: I thought your ride —

VICTORIA: My ride's practice schedule must have changed. And my other ride isn't home from work yet. But they'll be here. One of them. Or, I could totally walk, I just wanted to wait until everyone else was already home, so no one would see me walking home, like I was some kind of loser who didn't have a ride.

PETER: Isn't this yours?
(He holds out her copy of Anne Frank.)*

VICTORIA: I believe it's Property of Longwood High School.

(She does not take the book.)

PETER: Look, I'm — sorry about that.

VICTORIA: What?

PETER: How they told you —

VICTORIA: It wasn't you. Don't like apologize for living. It was those — those —

PETER: Gemini. Franklin and Max, that's what we call them. They've been like that since — third grade. But I let — I mean, I knew that Anne Frank wasn't conspiring with the Nazis.

VICTORIA: Right, everyone knows that. I'm so stupid.

PETER: That's not what I —

VICTORIA: You can only count on yourself.

PETER: What?

VICTORIA: You heard me, brainiac. Uno. That's what my mother says. If you want something done right — but I think she means at work, because she's pretty good at *paying* people to do things at home, like clean the house and shovel the driveway and fight with my dad about the divorce that neither of them really wants even though he's living in like California now — anyway, I should have counted *on myself.*

PETER: Your mom sounds . . .

VICTORIA: Like kind of a bitch. Yeah, thanks for clearing *that* up.

PETER: That's not what I was — forget it. Come on, I'll — give you a ride.

VICTORIA: I don't need a ride.

PETER: But I think you — do.

VICTORIA: What makes you think I want a ride *from you?*

PETER: I *think* you don't have any other choice.

VICTORIA: I could walk.

PETER: Except it's almost dark. And it's below freezing. And you're not wearing any . . . socks?

VICTORIA: *Socks* are so not cool this year.

PETER: So you'll probably be wanting this.

(He holds out Anne Frank.)

PETER: To pass the time, while you're sitting here, waiting for your ride.

(She looks at the book. Considers. Takes the book. Looks at its cover. Makes a face. Looks at Peter, still waiting.)

VICTORIA: I live on Glenview Road.

PETER: OK.

VICTORIA: OK.

PETER: Don't you need to get your other books?

VICTORIA: Don't you?

PETER: I already got into college. M.I.T. Early.

VICTORIA: I don't need my books either. I don't even need to study to pass my classes. I'm not stupid, you know. And you know something else? I am so not quitting.

Even if that's what all you nerds want me to do. You think you losers are the only ones who can do math? I can do *math*. I can *do* Math Team. I'm popular, but I'm also totally, totally smart.

SCENE 5: A MATH TEAM MONTAGE

Jimmy enters. He talks to the audience.

JIMMY: But we *didn't* lose.

PETER: Yet.

(Franklin and Max enter. Everyone tells the story to the audience.)

FRANKLIN: She stayed.

MAX: Vickie Martin.

FRANKLIN: A girl.

MAX: On the Math Team.

VICTORIA: In case you've forgotten what it's like when a girl decides she *wants* something?

PETER: It was — different.

JIMMY: It was totally awesome.

VICTORIA: I *applied* myself. Totally.

FRANKLIN: She wasn't even — *that* bad.

MAX: She was unambiguously good.

JIMMY: OK, at our next meet, against John F. Kennedy school, where we all expected to get crushed? We didn't. We lost. By one point.

VICTORIA: And that wasn't *my* lost point.

(They all look at Franklin.)

FRANKLIN: What? So I lost a point. We had an AP Physics test that day, right Max?

PETER: Max didn't lose a point.

MAX: Max . . . scored!

JIMMY: The next week, against Roosevelt High, we tied — *and* there was a personal victory, because I got this awesomely hard geometry proof that Peter just showed me —

VICTORIA: *Tie* isn't good enough.

(*Peter and Victoria have a moment with each other.*)

PETER: But Roosevelt is one of the best. We were up against them last year at Regionals.

VICTORIA: Are *you* satisfied with a tie, Peter?

(*Back to the audience.*)

MAX: Peter has never personally experienced a tie.

FRANKLIN: In case you didn't know, Peter *always* wins.

JIMMY: He's my Math Team hero . . .

PETER: OK, *tie* isn't good enough.

FRANKLIN AND MAX: See?

JIMMY: Meanwhile, the basketball team, lead by Scott Sumner, was on the road to sure victory!

VICTORIA: My boyfriend was kicking *butt.*

JIMMY: *And* still keeping my butt from getting kicked in the locker room when I announced the players' stats, if their stats weren't as good as they thought they were, and they were *never* as good as they were in their heads . . .

VICTORIA: I got my learner's permit and my mom said I could drive her car. When hell froze over.

* * *

(*They all sit in the van together.*)

JIMMY: When we would all be in the van, coming home from a meet? Sometimes Vickie Martin would be sitting right next to me, and I could smell her hair, and it smelled really nice, like fruit.

VICTORIA: And I would be thinking about avocados and California and how when the weather gets warmer here . . .

JIMMY: And it was kinda warm in the van, and I was kinda sleepy, thinking about the dinner my mom was making, and I wished I could get a little bit closer to smell her hair. *Vickie's* hair, not my mom's hair — and maybe even . . .

(*Jimmy reaches out to touch Vickie's hair.*)

VICTORIA: Like, in the spring, we'll be living in the same weather. Me and my dad.

(*He draws his hand back.*)

JIMMY: But then I remember who I am — just some *freshman* who will never, *ever* get to touch Vickie Martin's hair.

VICTORIA: And I want to call my dad up and tell him that, but then I remembered it's Wednesday, and he's supposed to call me Thursday — on Sundays and Thursdays — so I guess I'll just — wait until tomorrow.

JIMMY: She's probably sitting there thinking what a loser I am, and —

VICTORIA: Maybe my dad's thinking about Pi right now, like —

JIMMY: As soon as she gets home she'll call her popular friends and talk about what fruity shampoo they use. And I'll eat chicken pot pie with my mom.

VICTORIA: 3.14159265358979323846264338327950288419716939937510.

* * *

(Peter gets up from his place in the van. He talks to the audience.)

PETER: In case you need to review the facts. Number one: As unofficial Math Team captain and the senior on the team, I am the most mature member of the team. Number two: This is my *last chance* ever — *ever* — to prove our awesome collective mathematical brainpower at States!!!

(He collects himself, like the mature leader he is.)

PETER: Number three. As the leader of the Team, I have to accept this problem's given: We are without Sanjay Patel. And without Sanjay Patel, there is *no way* we're going to make it to States. And without one last chance for Math Team glory? High school for me is *over*.

I mean, I still go to class, even though I'm smarter than all my teachers. And this isn't me being conceited — my teachers *told* my parents this, on parents' night back in October. And I'm still senior class Treasurer, and go to all the student council meetings, and of course I'll crunch the numbers so the prom doesn't have to be in the cafeteria — but who cares about the *prom?* Or the class picnic or senior skip day — not me — but then . . .

She came. And said we couldn't take off our sneakers in the van because our feet smelled. And brought Cracker Jacks to practice, because she said they were *retro*, and then made us all give her our prizes. Except for the tattoos. Which she made us apply to our foreheads, because she said it would give us brainpower — which it *did*.

And at the meets, while she's working on her problem set, she always gets this funny look on her face, just when she *gets* a problem, and she *knows* she's got it, and I know she's got it, and we've totally got it — and that's when I think: This is awesome! Because the Longwood High School Math Team has started to *win* again. But this time?

Math Team is — different. Better. Like, it's more than just *math*.

* * *

(In the van, Max is resting his head on Franklin's shoulder. Franklin is asleep. Max sits up and looks at Franklin — in a different way. Victoria watches Max. Then she leans forwards and whispers.)

VICTORIA: You like him.

MAX: No, I don't! I mean, of course I like him. Duh.

VICTORIA: You know what I mean. I saw that. The way you were looking at him.

MAX: I didn't know it was illegal to look at my best friend.

VICTORIA: I'm not stupid. I know what it means when you look —

MAX: You didn't see anything.

VICTORIA: Don't worry. I'm not gonna blab your secret or anything —

MAX: Yeah, *right*. Like you don't *love* telling one Jen the other Jen's secrets, and then turning around and telling the other Jen —

VICTORIA: I'm not always like that, you know.

(Franklin wakes up.)

MAX: Yeah, right.

FRANKLIN: What?

(Max looks at Victoria, his life in her hands.)

VICTORIA: Nothing. Just, time to wake up, Franklin. From your *beauty sleep* — ooooh, Franklin needs his beauty sleep. Because . . . we're home. Right, Max?

MAX: Yeah. Right.

(The van has come to a stop. Peter and Jimmy file out.)

VICTORIA: So, you two can write up your physics lab and *I* can go home and make valuable use of my homework time calling all my popular friends. Because I totally have to apply myself to catching up on who has their period today, and which losers in third lunch totally had B.O. I mean . . . total AP cheerleading, wicked important stuff. Right, Max?

(Victoria takes off.)

* * *

FRANKLIN: What's she talking about?

MAX: I don't know. Girls. They're weird.

FRANKLIN: Yeah. This lab is gonna be a killer.

MAX: So, I copied down the data from your lab book.

FRANKLIN: What for?

MAX: So, actually, we don't need to get together tonight after dinner. We can just split up the sections, you know, check in over the phone.

FRANKLIN: You hate the phone. It gives your chin a rash.

MAX: I know, but —

FRANKLIN: Plus, we're lab partners —

MAX: It's not like we share one brain.

(Max rushes off. Franklin follows, confused.)

* * *

(Victoria is now home in her bedroom, talking on the phone.)

VICTORIA: I *know!* I totally saw that, in English, when Jen —
Oh, that was you?
Oh. Right.
No, I'm not a *space cadet*, I'm just —
I told you, my mom has been on this mother-daughter kick, all she wants to do is spend time with her amazing offspring. I mean that's totally why I haven't been able to hang out with all my friends, or make it to all the games . . .
Yes, I am still Vickie Martin, third-most-popular sophomore.
Oh wait, that's the other line, I'm sure it's Scott, I should . . .
(She switches to the other line.)

VICTORIA: Hi Mom. Yes, *actually*, I *am* applying myself.
(She talks to the audience.)

VICTORIA: Except in English, where . . .
(Back to the phone.)

VICTORIA: Mrs. Snyder said what? *Anne Frank*, right . . . well, English —
(To the audience.)

VICTORIA: Where I'm failing.
(Back to the phone.)

VICTORIA: Let's talk about English *later*. Like, when *you* get home. Whenever that is.

* * *

(She hangs up the phone and talks to the audience.)

VICTORIA: See, I *am* Vickie Martin, undisputedly popular *and* applying my-self to Math Team.
And because I am Vickie Martin, I can totally do this. I can *apply* myself anytime, anywhere I want, and I happen to *like* math. OK?

And that's not like a total news flash. I just never knew anyone else besides my dad who liked math too. So math — was just — Dad. But now he lives in California, where he's really, really busy with his new job, so sometimes he forgets if it's his night to call, so now I'm just like . . .

Vickie likes math.

Vickie Martin is good at math.

Vickie Martin, Math Team Queen.

Victoria Martin —

Call me *Victoria*, thank you very much. Because thanks to *me*, the Math Team? Is once more *victorious*.

And in case you're totally sitting there chewing your gum and wishing you were in the last row so you could get away with a little snooze, because you partied *way* too much last weekend?

In case *you* didn't notice . . .

* * *

(The Team is all there.)

JIMMY: The Longwood High School Math Team is on a *streak*.

FRANKLIN: We are kicking . . .

(Franklin looks to Max to finish his sentence.)

MAX: We're doing monumental, unequivocal, noncollateral damage.

FRANKLIN: Kicking *butt*, Max. You're supposed to say we're —

PETER: We're winning.

JIMMY: A lot.

PETER: And it's . . .

JIMMY: Totally awesome.

FRANKLIN: It's almost like with Sanjay Patel.

PETER: Except it's not. It's — Vickie Martin.

VICTORIA: That's Victoria.

MAX: For *victorious!*

FRANKLIN: We rule.

MAX: *She* rules.

VICTORIA: I rule.

FRANKLIN: You rule.

VICTORIA: I totally rule.

JIMMY: Victoria Martin, I just wanted to tell you that — that — that I think you're . . .

FRANKLIN: God, Jimmy, we all know about your stupid crush that has been going on for two *months*, you don't have to actually *say* it.

PETER: Actually, I think Jimmy was just going to say: You're really good at math, Victoria.

JIMMY: Yeah. That.

VICTORIA: Thanks.

> *(Victoria says this to Peter. They're looking at each other. It's sorta . . . different.)*

PETER: But . . .

SCENE 6: A LESSON TO DRIVE

> *The sound of tires screeching, a near accident. Then Victoria sits in the driver's seat of a parked car. Peter sits next to her. Fuming. They look straight ahead.*

PETER: You. You — are —

VICTORIA: I *know.*

PETER: No — you don't — you are a *hazard!*

VICTORIA: But I —

PETER: You almost — *we* almost —

VICTORIA: It won't happen again, I promise.

PETER: You don't have to! Because you will never, ever —

VICTORIA: It was an accident.

PETER: No, the point is — it was *almost* an accident. A really bad —

VICTORIA: But it's not that bad considering it was my first time ever driving.

PETER: What?! But the other week you said —

VICTORIA: I said my mom finally said she was going take me, but then she — didn't.

PETER: So, you don't —

VICTORIA: So I haven't exactly . . .

PETER: So. You don't know how to drive.

VICTORIA: I showed you my learner's permit! I took driver's ed. Well. The classroom part.

PETER: You don't know how to drive!

VICTORIA: Why do you think I asked you if I could practice on your car?

PETER: I thought you just needed a little *practice*, Vickie.

VICTORIA: Victoria.

PETER: If I knew you had *never driven,* we would not have gone *on the road.*

VICTORIA: I thought I'd jump right in.

PETER: We would have gone to a *parking lot* or — no, we wouldn't — I would have said *no.*

VICTORIA: We're not *dead.*

PETER: No, we're not *dead.*

VICTORIA: You're just not used to it.

PETER: Being almost dead?

VICTORIA: Being a little bit out of control.

PETER: I think I should drive you home now.

VICTORIA: Like, your hands shaking like that.

PETER: They are — *not.*

VICTORIA: I know your hands are sweaty.

(Peter casually wipes his sweaty hands on his jeans.)

VICTORIA: Mine are too.

PETER: Just — a little bit.

VICTORIA: My dad was supposed to teach me how to drive. But he's in California right now. He got this awesome computer-programming job. He used to work from home, designing software, but my mother says he wasn't any good because he never thought about the *people* who would be *using* the software. He's the smartest man my mom ever met. But at the end of the day, which is like my mom's favorite expression: "At the end of the day . . . " his *brain* wasn't enough.

He moved away on this really hot day at the end of last summer, and all of a sudden I was like a sophomore at this big opening game party, which I only went to because the Jens said we should totally go and my mom said I should get out of the house, and I felt kinda stupid and I drank this nasty punch and then I felt really weird and I was sitting outside on the curb, and Scott Sumner said he would give me a ride home — I think he was feeling left out or something because he doesn't play a fall sport — and we made out in his car and then he called me the next day because I left my jacket in his car, and then by Monday Jen — or Jen — I forget which one, said that we were dating.

So we would hang out together after school, me and Scott, those last warm afternoons in October, while the other guys were at football or soccer practice and the Jens were doing cheerleading squad. We would drive down by Weber Pond — it's so pretty there — and make out in his car, or just sit there and watch the yellow leaves floating on the water and everything would just — slow down.

We didn't really talk about my dad. I mean, he knew my parents were separated and stuff. He hates his dad. They get in fights like after every basketball game. Basketball is really important to Scott. He would always talk about how he just wanted his game to get better and better.

I just wanted to survive. To make it through the school year to the summer, when I could go to California, where no one would know who I was. Except my dad. Who knows what I like without even asking, like pizza with sausage and broccoli, and reruns of *The Honeymooners,* and numbers. I guess what I really like are numbers. But then I would think *numbers* are stupid to like. Because, in high school, what can you do with numbers?

PETER: Do you still think that now?

VICTORIA: Now it's sorta different.

PETER: Because now you're on Math Team?

VICTORIA: Like, at the meet on Wednesday? I was in the middle of that totally nasty multivariable algebraic equation, and I was almost freaking out —

PETER: And your hands were — sweaty?

VICTORIA: Totally, so I'm like wiping my palms on my jeans just so I can hold my pencil. And all I can hear is the breathing of that red-haired kid with asthma. In and out. In and out — and it's like I can't *stop* listening because I swear any second he's gonna *stop breathing,* and I totally cut gym class the day we did that CPR stuff.

But then I just start moving my pencil. Fast. I pretend it's like the brush of that guy on that painting show — do you ever watch that after school? Scratch, scratch, scratch, and I don't know where I'm headed, I'm just *doing* it — substituting in, distributing — stabbing at it through the mist, like when that artist guy makes a stroke of color across the white canvas, and you think: How the heck is he gonna make a mountain scene out of *that?*

PETER: But there's no time to think, because the clock is ticking, and so you just make your pencil *move.*

VICTORIA: And suddenly, the equation starts to look like something else, right?

PETER: Something different.

VICTORIA: Something new, in terms of *y,* and then I know *exactly* where I'm going.

PETER: And that's when you get that funny look on your face!

VICTORIA: What look?

PETER: Right when you . . . never mind.

VICTORIA: It's like, I can see the steps in front of me, and I just keep stepping and stepping and . . .

PETER: And your heart is pounding.

VICTORIA: And I have no idea if the kid with asthma is breathing or what, and I don't care.

PETER: You just want to get to the answer before they say *pencils down.*

VICTORIA: Yeah. And you know what? That whole time I didn't once think about my dad in California, or the Jens at cheerleading practice, or failing English class. In my head it's like yellow leaves floating on Weber Pond. Like the numbers have — stopped. I think that's what it must feel like, when Pi ends.

PETER: Pi never ends. It just keeps going and going —

VICTORIA: With no pattern at all.

PETER: None that anyone has figured out.

VICTORIA: But *if* it ends — and it *might end* — I think that's what it would feel like.

(For a moment they look straight ahead, contemplating Pi.)

SCENE 7: SATURDAY NIGHT

Jimmy stands outside the high school gym, holding an extra-large fountain soda. He talks to the audience.

JIMMY: OK, *this* is the big game. In case you don't remember, every school year, there is *the game.* And this is that game — bigger than homecoming, bigger than the Thanksgiving game or any other football thing. It's bigger than Sanjay Patel's totally, unbelievably awesome final Math Team meet before he moved to Arizona. Bigger than any of the Chess Team matches — I know, I'm on the team — bigger than the swim meet when Bruce Owen was standing on the starting block with a total boner — *bigger* than Bruce Owen's boner — this is the basketball State Championship game. And we were in it. And I was doing the stats. And Scott Sumner — even though he is only a *junior* and no one even *knew* his name last year — is totally, totally awesome.

And really nice to me too. Like, whenever Scott Sumner sees me, he says: Hey Jimmy. And he means me. And he *really* means it. And that makes me feel like when my mom wakes me up on Saturday morning sometimes — like she did this morning, because it was a big day because I was going to do the stats for the big game — and says: Guess who's getting blueberry muffins with maple syrup? And she means *me.*

The guys on the team were so nervous in the locker room that some of them started praying. And the cheerleaders must have been nervous too because someone said they were all throwing up in the girl's locker room. And the whole team shaved their heads.

Even second-string. But I think some of them wished they didn't now, like one of the point guards, who has really bad acne in his hairline, except now there's no hairline, so it's just a line of zits.

And the cheerleaders were all going to get their legs waxed. I don't really know why they'd do that, but I guess it's something that hurts, and the second-string forward said he thought that showed solidarity. Well, he didn't use that word, solidarity, but I was listening to the whole conversation, sitting there at my little card table next to the bench, and I know that's what he meant.

Victoria Martin is sitting in the stands right in the middle of our section, right where she always sits. She looks *so beautiful*. And when Scott Sumner runs in right at the front of the tunnel run, while they play that music that makes everyone get up and shake their butts — he always looks up to the stands, right to that spot, and I know he's looking for her. And their eyes meet. And every game I think: Wow, that's love.

OK, halftime's almost over. I really, really hope that I can make it through the second half without having to pee again, because I don't want to miss a *second* of this game.

(Jimmy runs into the game.)

* * *

(Meanwhile, in an alternate social universe, Franklin and Max are studying on the floor in Max's bedroom.)

FRANKLIN: God, why do the SATs have to be so stupid?

MAX: My brother said they're nothing, compared to all the other stuff with college applications next year.

FRANKLIN: Yeah, but I really don't want to have to take these again when I'm taking BC Calc next year, because all I want to be doing is *that*, so I better do good this time.

MAX: Do *well*.

FRANKLIN: What?

MAX: Never mind.

FRANKLIN: All these stupid *words*.

MAX: At least the math sections are easy.

FRANKLIN: Yeah. But not everyone's a vocab god like you.

MAX: You'll totally get 800 on the math.

FRANKLIN: I know, but every time I start reading one of those stupid stories, my brain cells start to vaporize and then I'm at the end of the passage, but I have no idea what I just read.

Does that happen to you?

MAX: What?

FRANKLIN: Are you even listening to me? See you're doing that —

MAX: I'm listening. You were talking, and I was just —

FRANKLIN: Earth to Maxwell.

MAX: I could help you with them.

FRANKLIN: I wouldn't want to disrupt your space flight.

MAX: Sorry. I was just — thinking about something else.

FRANKLIN: Did you make flashcards?

MAX: I have my brother's old ones. I mostly know them all now. You can have them.

FRANKLIN: Forget it. You're mom will get mad, she —

MAX: Whatever, like my mom would ever get mad at *you*.

FRANKLIN: She probably wants you to save them for your younger brother.

MAX: You could just borrow them.

FRANKLIN: OK. Maybe. Thanks. Do you want to do another section?

MAX: Didn't we practice enough?

FRANKLIN: I did come over to study SAT.

MAX: But it's Saturday night.

FRANKLIN: I know, we always study SAT on Saturday nights.

MAX: I know, but I just thought, maybe we could talk about something else for once.

FRANKLIN: Like what?

MAX: I don't know. Don't you ever think about anything else besides school?

FRANKLIN: Did you *really* want to go to the basketball championship?

MAX: No. Not if you weren't going. Even though *everyone else* from Longwood High School is there at the game *right now*. I mean, I wanted to hang out with you.

FRANKLIN: OK, so we are.

MAX: Hang out means *not* do homework. We're always doing homework.

FRANKLIN: It's junior year, and *now* you decide you don't want to be a nerd?

MAX: I don't care about being a nerd! It's just . . .

FRANKLIN: What?

MAX: Now that I have my license we could actually *do something*.

FRANKLIN: Like what?

MAX: I don't know. Go to the movies or something.

FRANKLIN: Your parents would never let you take the car on a Saturday night.

MAX: Maybe if *you* asked.

FRANKLIN: If *I* ask *your* parents if *you* could take their car?

MAX: My mom *loves* you.

FRANKLIN: OK, whatever Max. Set the timer, we'll do one more stupid verbal section.

(Max sets the timer.)

MAX: I just think it might be nice. For us to do something besides homework together.

(They start a practice section in their SAT books.)

* * *

(Meanwhile, Victoria runs out of the gym, in a fury, letting this one rip.)

VICTORIA: 3.14159265358979323846264338327950 —

(Peter enters, just arriving at the game.)

PETER: Have they started the second half?

VICTORIA: She is such a *bitch!*

PETER: My car wouldn't start, I just got here.

VICTORIA: I mean — how could she say that?

PETER: What? Don't you need to get back to your special seat?

VICTORIA: I'm going to *scream.*

PETER: I don't think they'll hear you, it's sounds like they just . . .

VICTORIA: I don't care!

PETER: But isn't Scott —

VICTORIA: I hate her.

PETER: Jen? Or —

VICTORIA: Forget it.

PETER: Jen?

VICTORIA: She is so . . . *shitty.* Peter, you have no idea.

PETER: OK. Then — tell me.

* * *

(Franklin and Max are doing their practice SAT section. Franklin works feverishly, as the timer ticks. Max does a problem and then stops. Looks at Franklin.)

FRANKLIN: You're done already? God, how can you be done, I have —

MAX: No, I was just — nothing.

> (*Max goes back to his test book. Franklin turns the page frantically. They work. Max does a couple problems efficiently and turns the page. Stops. Looks at Franklin.*)

FRANKLIN: What?

MAX: Nothing.

FRANKLIN: Then why are you looking at me?

MAX: I'm not *looking* at you.

FRANKLIN: You're not doing your test.

MAX: Yeah, I am. I'm almost done.

FRANKLIN: Well, good for you. I'm not.

* * *

> (*Back at the game. Victoria and Peter are mid-conversation.*)

PETER: So then what did you say?

VICTORIA: Nothing. I said — nothing. I mean, she doesn't know *anything* about what's going on with my dad or whatever because I never even said anything to her about it anyway, and then she goes and says that about my parents' divorce and I was standing right there and she *knew* I was standing there because then she like flips her ponytail and looks over her shoulder at me and — I mean, what was I supposed to say?

PETER: Nothing.

VICTORIA: I mean — I — I don't know. What.

PETER: It's OK. You did the right thing.

VICTORIA: I did?

PETER: She's just — a bitch.

VICTORIA: Totally.

PETER: A total bitch.

VICTORIA: I know.

PETER: I'm really sorry, Vickie. Victoria, I mean.

VICTORIA: It's OK, I just. I feel shitty.

PETER: I would feel shitty too. Actually, I do. I feel shitty — for you. I'm sorry.

VICTORIA: Don't keep saying you're sorry.

PETER: But I —

VICTORIA: Don't apologize for living, Peter. You're not the one who did it.

PETER: But I feel bad for you.

VICTORIA: I don't want you *feeling bad* for me.

PETER: Then. What do you want me to do?

* * *

(Meanwhile, in Max's bedroom.)

MAX: What?

FRANKLIN: You're doing it again!

MAX: What?

FRANKLIN: Looking at me, like — like I'm an idiot or something. Look, this verbal stuff — I'm bad at this, OK? I suck.

MAX: You don't suck.

FRANKLIN: And all you can do is sit there and watch me eat my eraser because I don't know *any* of these words, meanwhile you can do this stuff in *pen* because you know every —

MAX: I could help you.

FRANKLIN: Thanks, but I don't need your *extra help*. And it doesn't *help* you're sitting there looking at me like —

MAX: I like to look at you.

FRANKLIN: Oh, so you like making me mess up even more? Thanks, Max.

MAX: You don't know what I'm thinking, OK?

* * *

(Back to the game.)

VICTORIA: I want you to do what *you* want to do.

PETER: You don't know what I want to do right now.

VICTORIA: I know what *I* want you to be wanting to do right now. And if what I'm wanting you to be wanting is anything like what you might be wanting, then I want you to do that.

PETER: You do?

VICTORIA: Yeah. I mean — thanks for listening, Peter.

PETER: Is that all you want to say to me?

VICTORIA: No — I mean, yes, I want to thank you for that, because I really needed to talk to someone, and when I ran out here, I think you might be the only person in the world who might have understood me just now, or who I could tell all that to —

PETER: So you're saying that I'm — good at listening. Like, a really good friend?

VICTORIA: I'm saying that I think there was a reason that you walked through that door.

PETER: You think that's why my car didn't start? Like it was some kind of —

FRANKLIN: No, I guess I don't know what you're thinking. Because we're *not* one brain. Which for some stupid reason you keep reminding me, as if I really thought our cerebral cortex was like fused —

MAX: I like you.

FRANKLIN: Well, I didn't think you hated your lab partner.

MAX: I mean, I feel *different.*

* * *

VICTORIA: Are you making fun of me?

PETER: No! No, I wasn't. I swear. I was . . .

* * *

FRANKLIN: Whatever, Max.

MAX: No, listen to me!

FRANKLIN AND VICTORIA: What?

MAX: Different — like, I want to kiss you. On the lips.
  (*Peter kisses Victoria, on the lips. The SAT timer rings as the final basketball buzzer goes off. Jimmy runs out of the gym, totally having to pee, and sees them kissing.*)

JIMMY: WHAT?!?
  (*Max grabs the timer and turns it off. Jimmy points to Victoria.*)

JIMMY: Scott Sumner is in there scoring the — and you're . . .
  (*Jimmy points to Peter.*)

JIMMY: And you. Peter. With *her.* My — after I —

PETER: Jimmy —

JIMMY: No, there's nothing —

PETER: No, Jimmy, you — wet your . . .
  (*Peter points to the growing dark spot on Jimmy's pants. Jimmy has wet himself.*)

JIMMY: In case you even care? We *won.*
  (*The sound of the cheering basketball crowd.*)

END OF ACT ONE

ACT TWO

SCENE 8: THE MONDAY AFTER SATURDAY NIGHT

An empty classroom. From another place, we hear a phone ringing. No one picks up. Max enters, looks around the empty room. Elsewhere, an answering machine picks up.

ANSWERING MACHINE: Hi, you have reached the Sumner residence. We're sorry that no one is here right now to take your call. Please wait for the sound of the beep and leave us a message. Have nice day!

(Beeeeeep. We hear the sound of Victoria's voice leaving a message as Franklin enters the classroom. It's been a rough day.)

VICTORIA'S VOICE: Uh. Hi Scott. It's Victoria — I mean, Vickie. Hey. What's up?

(Max won't look at Franklin.)

VICTORIA'S VOICE: It's Sunday night, so I thought you would be home. But maybe you're out to dinner at Luigi's with your parents, celebrating your victory. Anyway, I just wanted to call to say that — that . . .

(Peter enters the classroom and looks anxiously who's there.)

VICTORIA'S VOICE: It's really great about the State Championship, and that you were just — so awesome. During the first half. Which I saw. And . . .

(Jimmy enters. He makes a face at Peter behind his back and sits down, scowling.)

VICTORIA'S VOICE: I'm really, *really* sorry that I — missed the second half. And the free throw you made to tie the score. And the basket you made with three seconds left on the clock. That's really awesome. But I guess you know that. And I guess you probably know something else too, that other people have told you about me, and I just want to say that I'm — sorry.

(Peter keeps looking at the clock and then at the door.)

VICTORIA'S VOICE: So. That's it. I'll see ya tomorrow at school, I guess. And — hi Mr. and Mrs. Sumner. Please don't erase this message before Scott gets it, OK?

(They all sit there, not looking at or talking to each other. Peter checks the clock and the door once more, and then begins.)

PETER: So. We have —

(Victoria enters. She slips in and closes the door immediately after her. She's wearing a baseball hat and sunglasses, incognito. They all look at her.)

VICTORIA: What?

PETER: Nothing.

FRANKLIN: *None* of this would have happened if Sanjay Patel were still here.

PETER: We're just — I was just starting.

VICTORIA: Then start. Because I can't stay.

JIMMY: Because you don't want to keep your *ride* waiting?

VICTORIA: No, because, since when do we have Monday practice? Like don't you geeks have orchestra practice or something on —

MAX: This a Math Team *emergency meeting*.

PETER: I said that in the message I left on your machine. And I guess you *did* get my message, because you're *here*, even though you decided *not* to call me back.

VICTORIA: Maybe I had other things I had to do, because in case you didn't know, I do have a life outside Math Team, and I went through a lot to come here — *and* I can't stay. So.

PETER: OK, fine.

JIMMY: See, your *boyfriend* understands.

VICTORIA: I don't have a —

PETER: Look team, there's been a serious shake-up in the Math League. Over the weekend, some very shocking news has been revealed, and it's going to affect each and every one of us sitting in this classroom. That's why I called this emergency meeting, because we need to *talk* about this. Together. OK?

(They all look at each other.)

PETER: Springdale High School, which you all know is in number-one position, has been caught cheating, and they've been eliminated entirely from Math League this year.

FRANKLIN: What?

PETER: Their geometry teacher Mr. Simons was *somehow* involved with one of the teachers who makes up the questions for the meets, and was getting copies of the questions before the meets and giving them to the Springdale team, and they were practicing the problems before the meets, and *that's* how they were getting every one right, which is why the League got suspicious in the first place.

JIMMY: So?

PETER: So — it's shocking!

JIMMY: To *lie* and *do things behind someone's back* like that, you mean?

MAX: Shut up, Jimmy.

JIMMY: Don't tell me to shut up!

FRANKLIN: Yeah, Maxwell.

VICTORIA: Make your point, Peter.

PETER: The point is, now with Springdale out of the way, if we win this Wednesday's meet against Roosevelt, then . . . We. Are going. To. States. *(No one reacts.)*

PETER: Isn't that awesome?

JIMMY: *If* we win Wednesday's meet. Which is a big *if.*

VICTORIA: Yeah, I'm not sure I can *do* a meet Wednesday.

PETER: What do you mean you're not sure?

FRANKLIN: Who even said we wanted to go to States anyway?

PETER: Of course we want to go to States!

FRANKLIN: That's like an overnight thing. And sitting in a van is one thing, but whoever said I wanted to be *overnight* with any of you.

VICTORIA: I don't *do* weekends.

MAX: Don't worry, Franklin, you won't have to share a *pillow* with me —

FRANKLIN: I'm not *worried* about anything.

MAX: You can sleep with the bed wetter.

JIMMY: Shut up, shut up, shut up!

PETER: Come on, team! This is exactly what we've been practicing for. This is why we've been spending all this time —

VICTORIA: And that's the only reason for all these hours of practice. This is *all about math.* Just — numbers. Is that . . . really true, Peter?

PETER: There was never any *complication* or *confusion* about that.

VICTORIA: Right. Because otherwise why would I be spending time with all you losers? In fact, the time that I'm spending with you math geeks is just about over. I am so *over* Math Team.

JIMMY: That's fine, because we never wanted you on the team anyway. Right, Peter?

PETER: What?

JIMMY: And don't tell me to shut up! Any of you. OK, Vickie, now that you're *quitting* —

VICTORIA: I didn't say I was —

JIMMY: We can tell you the whole entire truth, which is: The only reason you're even on the Math Team is because we needed *girl.* And you're — a girl. And we don't know any other sophomore girls. It had nothing to even *do* with math. Isn't that right, team?
(No one answers.)

JIMMY: You were just *totally popular* Vickie Martin, who happened to show up five minutes before the van left, so that she wouldn't get detention from Mr. Riley.

VICTORIA: Shut up.

JIMMY: Why? It's true. Ask Peter. He's the one who said that with Vickie Martin on our team, there was no way in *hell* we were going to make it to States.

VICTORIA: Peter? You didn't — say that — did you?

PETER: This emergency meeting of the Longwood High Math Team is officially over.

(Peter runs out of the classroom.)

VICTORIA: Jimmy.

JIMMY: Yeah?

VICTORIA: You're a *freshman.*

JIMMY: So?

VICTORIA: So go home to your *mother.* Because you don't understand *any* of this.

JIMMY: I know what I hear! I know what I *see*, when I come out of the gym and —

FRANKLIN: Come on, Jimmy. Let's leave these two *girls* alone with their hormones.

(Franklin and Jimmy exit together.)

SCENE 9: SECRETS

Victoria and Max are left in the classroom.

VICTORIA: So.

MAX: So.

VICTORIA: Peter didn't really say . . . ?

(Max starts heading for the door.)

MAX: I should go too. Now that I have to do this physics homework *alone* it takes —

VICTORIA: He figured it out, didn't he? Franklin.

(This stops Max.)

MAX: No.

VICTORIA: Your secret. He totally —

MAX: I told him.

VICTORIA: You did?

MAX: Yeah. I did.

VICTORIA: Wait — you *told* him and — what happened?

MAX: Nothing. We were practicing SATs.

(*Max turns to the audience.*)

MAX: In case you don't remember . . .

* * *

(*Franklin is there with his SAT book. They replay the scene from Saturday night.*)

FRANKLIN: . . . and then I'm at the end of the passage, but I have no idea what I just read.

(*Franklin is in suspended animation, while Max talks to the audience.*)

MAX: And I'm watching his lips move, but I'm not hearing any of the words. Or like I'm hearing his voice, but the words aren't making sense to me — because for once, I don't care about the *words*. I care about his lips. Watching them move. And I —

FRANKLIN: Does that happen to you?

MAX: What?

FRANKLIN: Are you even listening to me? See you're doing that —

(*Max back to the audience.*)

MAX: Actually I was thinking about the hair on his arms. And how it looks different than it did last year. And how I want to touch it. To touch his arms with my fingertips, really, really softly —

FRANKLIN: Earth to Maxwell.

MAX: Sorry. I was just — thinking about something else.

(*To the audience.*)

MAX: Like, how nice it would be to just sit close and not talk. To just *be* together, somewhere else in the time-space continuum — or like, in my parent's car? Where we could be *alone*, and I don't just mean with no other people, I mean like, no books, no school, nothing we had to think about or do, to just be able to —

FRANKLIN: What?

MAX: Nothing.

FRANKLIN: Then why are you looking at me?

* * *

(*Max talks to Victoria.*)

VICTORIA: And then you told him?

MAX: I was just so *tired* of having this thing — Franklin has been my best friend since he moved in two houses down from mine when we were seven, and my mom made me go over and ride bikes with him, and this was the first time ever that I had something that I couldn't tell him about.

VICTORIA: But you told him.

MAX: I couldn't keep pretending that everything was the same, because it wasn't.

VICTORIA: So — what did he say?

MAX: Nothing.

VICTORIA: Max, I'm not going to tell anyone about this, *ever*, I swear I'm —

MAX: He said *nothing*, OK? I said I wanted to *kiss him* — Franklin, my best friend — and he just closes his SAT book, and puts it in his backpack — actually, he started to put it in my backpack — we have the same exact backpacks . . .

* * *

(We see Franklin stuffing his book into Max's bag. Max talks to him, quietly.)

MAX: That's mine.

FRANKLIN: What?!

MAX: My bag, that's my — yours is . . .

(Franklin throws off Max's bag, grabs his own, and exits.)

MAX: Franklin — !

* * *

(Max continues to Victoria.)

MAX: He ran downstairs and I heard him tell my mom that I had a stomachache, so he was just going to go home now. And my mom asked him if he wanted a snack after all his hard SAT work and he said: No thanks, Mrs. Werner, I'm just gonna go. And he left.

And he hasn't said anything to me since. And now I have *no idea* why I felt like it was *so important* for those words to come out of my mouth.

(Victoria takes out a copy of The Catcher in the Rye *and removes a much-folded piece of paper from it. She hands it to Max.)*

VICTORIA: Here.

MAX: What is this?

VICTORIA: It's origami for: A note. Open it.

(He unfolds the piece of paper. This is an involved task.)

MAX: It's addressed to you.

VICTORIA: Read it.

(Max starts to read it to himself.)

VICTORIA: Out *loud?*

(He reads from the note.)

MAX: For the eyes of Vickie Martin. *Only.* So don't even *think* about —

(He looks at Victoria with concern.)

VICTORIA: Whatever.

MAX: I know that you know my handwriting, but this is a note from me *and* the other Jen. We have discussed it, and we feel *exactly* the same way about this. And that is totally strongly. About everything we're going to say here.

(As he reads, Max finds the voice of the note. Like he's channeling the Jens.)

MAX: OK. Just because we're inside the gym, cheering our butts off for our team and *your* boyfriend, don't think for a *second* that we don't know about everything else that is going on inside Longwood High School.

We know *exactly* who you were kissing while your boyfriend — I mean, ex-boyfriend (Ha!) — was scoring the winning basket. One of those nerds. The sorta cute, sorta normal one, who is a senior — BUT, who is totally NOT cool enough for anyone that we sit with at lunch to be kissing (ew!), committing like a totally taboo act with *during* the State Championship game!!!

And I *know* that what Jen said about your parents divorce and whatever during halftime was a bit harsh, but who knew you would totally *freak* and like *walk out* of the game?

I mean, call Jerry Springer . . .

OK and another thing: We *know* about you and the Math Team. Like how you've been lying to us like the whole third quarter of the school year, saying that you were with your mom or babysitting when really you were practically *making out* with the whole entire Math Team in the back of that loser van.

That is *so* not cool. And so you better cut it out. Pronto. It's either MATH TEAM *or* ever having a normal life in high school AGAIN.

MAX: And believe *us*, if you choose a bunch of losers over Jen and me (Jen) then you are totally, totally *screwed.*

And we mean all that sincerely.

Sincerely yours,

Jen & Jen

P.S. One of us *will* be dating Scott Sumner by the time we all get our next period.

(Max hands the note to Victoria, who begins refolding it.)

MAX: OK, that was . . .

VICTORIA: Yeah. Jen put it inside my copy of *The Catcher in the Rye* when she was passing out books for Mrs. Snyder in English today. Total espionage. So. I know your secret. And now you know why I can't be on the Math Team anymore.

MAX: Wait, so, this whole time they didn't *know* you were on Math Team?

VICTORIA: Are you kidding?

MAX: But it's not a secret who's on the team.

VICTORIA: The Math Team doesn't even *register* on the Longwood High School social radar. It's like — the black hole of the popular universe.

MAX: I wasn't the only one with a secret.

VICTORIA: Yeah. But. Max. I mean, you had a — real secret.

MAX: Yeah, it's pretty real.

VICTORIA: And I . . .

MAX: And I came clean. I *told* him, Victoria. Do you think that was easy? And you — you lied about — all of us. You lied about *math*. Until you got caught.

VICTORIA: I didn't mean to —

MAX: What — get caught? You know, I thought you actually *liked* being on the Math Team.

VICTORIA: I do, I guess. I mean —

MAX: So. What's the problem?

VICTORIA: The problem is that I sit right in between them. Jen and Jen. One on each side. In English class, *which* I'm going to have to repeat in summer school if I skip one more —

MAX: So don't skip. Go to class, and sit there, right in between them. Do your homework. Because English class might actually require you to open a book and read it. And when you get to class, raise your hand. Open your mouth, and I don't mean to pop in a stick of Big Red. In case no one told you, Victoria, you have to *show up*. Just like the rest of us in this school. *(Victoria puts the folded-up note inside the pages of* The Catcher in the Rye.)

MAX: Really — you should read that. It's my favorite book.

SCENE 10: MONDAY NIGHT

Victoria is in her bedroom. She talks on the phone

VICTORIA: 3.14159265358979323846264338327950288419716939937510.

Maybe this summer when I come to California we can memorize more digits, because there's always more numbers to add to it, as long as you don't get one of those answering machines that cuts the person off when they're talking too much.

That is *if* I'm coming to California. I might have to redo sophomore English in summer school, which would take practically the whole summer. I just thought you might like to know. I was going to tell you that last night, and I kept waiting and waiting for you to call, and I kept thinking that you just hadn't called yet because of the different time zones, and then you just — didn't.

Yesterday was Sunday night. In case you forgot. Did you forget, Dad?

(Victoria hangs up the phone. She picks up The Catcher in the Rye *and continues her reading. She puts a piece of gum in her mouth, never lifting her eyes from the page. Chews. Reads. The phone rings, and she immediately picks it up.)*

VICTORIA: Dad?

Oh.

Uh-huh.

Soon, like, in *three hours*, because if you mean three hours, I think my stomach will —

Wait, Jade Garden *tonight?* Like, not take-out, but we can eat *there*, in one of the booths that we have to cross the green bamboo bridge to get to?

Yeah, that sounds . . . But, how soon is soon, really, like — OK. But, actually, could we make it like thirteen minutes instead of ten? I just want to finish this chapter.

Well, if *you're* late, I'm not sharing any of my chicken fingers with you either, Mrs. Poo-Poo Platter . . .

(Victoria is smiling.)

VICTORIA: I'll be ready-set.

SCENE 11: THE TEAM GOES ON

Jimmy enters. This is a changed boy from Act One. He talks to the audience.

JIMMY: In case you're like totally retarded and don't remember? Tuesday comes after Monday. Even if it's the worst Monday of your *life*. I'm talking about two days after the Saturday night of the big game, where you *wet your pants* and then because of some *major cognitive malfunction*, instead of running *out* of the building and continuing to run away, into the night, not stopping until you reached the safety of your mother's kitchen, you instead thought it was more important to go *back into the gym*, right up to Scott Sumner — who hadn't even wiped off the sweat of victory yet — to tell the Longwood High School basketball superstar that his girlfriend is *kissing* another guy, right outside the gym.

And for some reason I thought everyone would *thank me* for this? That Scott Sumner would finally recognize me as the *special fan* that I am, instead of just that nerdy freshman keeping stats for the team?

Of course what actually happened is that Scott Summer's moment of high school glory turned instantly *shitty*. And everyone else looking at me could only see *one thing:* the dark piss spot on the front my pants.

But, I am very happy to remind you that *Tuesday* does come, even after the darkest Monday of your very limited high school life. And after Tuesday, it was Wednesday. And I don't think I need to tell you that Wednesday is the day of the Math Team meet that's going to decide if we're going to States.

(Victoria talks to the audience.)

VICTORIA: In case I've made it seem like my mom is a total bitch? She's not. Actually, sometimes she's pretty cool — *sometimes*, like when she's *not* trying to do the right thing for a mom to do, and instead just does what she feels like. Like Chinese food on a Monday night.

Jade Garden is my favorite restaurant. When we were leaving, the owner Mr. Lin handed me a fortune cookie, but I was driving home — with my learner's permit — and so I forgot all about it until yesterday, when I put on my jacket and found it in the pocket.

(She takes out the fortune and holds it against her forehead with her fingers.)

VICTORIA: It says: YOU WILL DO GREAT THINGS, BUT YOU HAVE TO DO THEM. Also, my lucky numbers are all prime, so that's cool. I totally listen to cookies.

(As the team enters, Victoria puts away her fortune and passes out T-shirts. She takes off her jacket, and we see she's wearing the same shirt. They say: Longwood High Math Team. WE WILL ROCK U.)

VICTORIA: I was going to put: Longwood Math Team Kicks Butt!!! But then I thought Mr. Riley might like disapprove of the whole butt thing.

(The boys take off their shirts to put on the T-shirts. Franklin self-consciously looks over at Max.)

FRANKLIN: Hey, don't look!

MAX: Don't worry Franklin, no one wants to see your undershirt.

VICTORIA: And then I was going to put a math joke across the back, but then I was like: OK I *do* have to *wear* this.

(They all have the Math Team T-shirts on.)

MAX: We all showed up Wednesday.

PETER: And we won!

JIMMY: Kicked *ass.*

VICTORIA: It was totally the shirts.

FRANKLIN: So now we're headed for States.

MAX: But that doesn't mean everything's OK.

PETER: You can say that again.

FRANKLIN: Everything was *not* OK.

JIMMY: In the van Wednesday? We had to arrange it so that Franklin wasn't next to Max, who suddenly seemed to have cooties, and Peter and Victoria weren't sitting together, because —

PETER: How could it be OK? Because when she *finally* called me back, she called during student council, so she *knew* I wouldn't be home.

MAX: And Jimmy still felt like totally betrayed by the now-legendary kiss between Victoria and Peter —

PETER: So, *clearly* she doesn't really want to talk to me.

MAX: Even though it wasn't like Victoria was Jimmy's girlfriend, or Peter was his — boyfriend.

(Max looks at Franklin, who looks uncomfortable.)

FRANKLIN: The point *is* Jimmy couldn't sit next to either of them.

VICTORIA: Plus, Jimmy needs to be by a window because he gets *carsick.*

PETER: It was all of us, in the van, moving along a trajectory at an accelerating velocity —

VICTORIA: It was a word problem.

MAX: Meanwhile, in case you're *that* much older than high school, you might have forgotten what the fourth quarter of the school year was like?

JIMMY: Spring! *Finally* . . .

VICTORIA: The teachers were all *so over* us. I mean, like, what's *their* problem?

MAX: I signed up for AP English next year.

FRANKLIN: I spelled spring S-A-T.

MAX: And Creative Writing.

VICTORIA: And everyone was hooking up left and right — like it was a total mack-down, school-wide make-out session, like you couldn't even walk down the hallway without . . .

(She can't help looking over at Peter, who doesn't know what to say.)

PETER: Right, but — who would want to be doing *that?*

VICTORIA: Right. Like, ew.

(Peter converses privately with the audience, while Victoria tries to distract him.)

PETER: Clearly there was no reason I should even be *thinking* about that.

VICTORIA: Clearly, ewwww.

PETER: And of course I wasn't thinking about going to the beach on senior skip day or renting a tux for the prom, because —

VICTORIA: Ew!

PETER: It's not like I cared about any of *that.*

VICTORIA: Ew-ew-ew-ew-ew.

PETER: I mean, I should be thinking about getting a perfect score on my calculus AP so that I'll place into the accelerated math sequence next year. But —

VICTORIA: Ewwwwwwwwwwwwwww . . .

PETER: That's not on my mind either.

VICTORIA: Whatever, Peter.

(Victoria gives up. As she walks away, Peter steals a look at her.)

PETER: Because, for the first time in my life — I don't even *know* my mind! It's like this vast, unknown, lumpy territory inside my skull that I needed a lunar module to explore.

And that feels — different. And totally, totally *weird.*

And then suddenly . . .

JIMMY: We're at States.

SCENE 12: STATES

Peter bends forward, hands on his knees, like a winded athlete. Victoria runs up and holds out a pencil.

VICTORIA: Look alive, mathlete.

PETER: I don't feel so good.

VICTORIA: Here. Number two. Unchewed.

(She waves the pencil.)

PETER: I feel weird.

VICTORIA: You're just nervous, Peter. Take the pencil — don't worry, I didn't *lick* it.

PETER: Maybe I'm sick.

VICTORIA: You're not sick — you're just scared. Come on.

PETER: But I think I might —

VICTORIA: Vomit. I know. Me too. But — don't you . . . kind of like that feeling?

PETER: No!

VICTORIA: Don't be such a sissy, it's time for the next event.

PETER: I could have food poisoning, from that breakfast buffet?

VICTORIA: Except you *don't*. You're really just terrified, because you didn't know there were so many kids *almost* as smart as you are living in the same state, and I'm terrified because: A. There are so many geeks here that I think I might just be one of them. B. I'm starting to understand Klingon. C. We might actually *not* win. Or place. And I really, really, really want to win.

    Or maybe, just because — we're here. Together. Both wearing our math shirts. And . . .

PETER: And *what*, Victoria, we get to share a pencil?

(Jimmy enters, reading the manual for States, trailed by Franklin and Max.)

JIMMY: OK, team, the next event is: Group work. Group work? We *suck* at group work.

(Jimmy, Franklin, Max, Peter, Victoria all turn to the audience.)

ALL: We do.

                      *   *   *

(Jimmy hands Victoria the manual as the group splits up: Peter and Jimmy sit together, working on one problem set, while Franklin and Max work on another. Victoria refers to the manual as she explains.)

VICTORIA: OK, one person tackles the first problem, and then when they're done, they pass off the answer to the second person, who takes that answer and substitutes it for one of the variables in the next problem. And if that answer is clearly wrong, because it won't work in the next problem? Then you can pass it *back* to the first person, and tell them their answer can't be right because it won't work in the next problem. Like —

JIMMY: Wrong.

   (*Jimmy pushes the problem back across the table to Peter.*)

PETER: What?

JIMMY: Wrong. It's wrong, Peter.

PETER: No, it's not. That's the answer. I just —

JIMMY: It's *wrong*. It can't be a negative number and substitute into the second problem.

PETER: OK. Well. Let me just — check my work.

* * *

   (*Victoria has joined group two, where Franklin works on the first problem and Max looks on anxiously, checking his watch.*)

MAX: Aren't you done yet?

FRANKLIN: No.

MAX: We should be on the next problem already.

FRANKLIN: Move your hand.

MAX: What?

VICTORIA: Let him work, Max.

FRANKLIN: Your *hand*. Stop touching my paper.

MAX: It's not *your* paper.

VICTORIA: Cut it out, you guys!

FRANKLIN: I'm not doing another thing to this problem until *he* stops touching my —

MAX: Whatever, Franklin.

VICTORIA: Do I have to sit between you two?

FRANKLIN: Don't whatever-me, Maxwell! Stop grabbing —

VICTORIA: Max, you're changing seats with me right now —

MAX: No, I'm not moving. I'll put my hand anywhere I feel like it!

   (*Max puts his hand right in the middle of Franklin's paper. Franklin shoves Max, who lands on the ground.*)

VICTORIA: Franklin!?!

FRANKLIN: What?

VICTORIA: Are you trying to get us disqualified?

   (*To Max, still on the ground.*)

FRANKLIN: Your turn. I'm finished.

   (*Franklin pushes the paper away from him. Max grabs it and begins working on the floor.*)

* * *

(Meanwhile: Jimmy pushes the paper back to Peter.)

JIMMY: *Wrong* — still, Peter!

PETER: What?

JIMMY: Why can't you get this right?

PETER: I don't know, I checked my work, I know I need to distribute and then integrate, or maybe I need to . . .

JIMMY: I thought you always knew the answer.

PETER: Well, I guess *I don't.*

JIMMY: Until I opened my eyes and saw that you could be a total idiot.

PETER: What's that supposed to mean?

JIMMY: I mean, *look at her*, Peter.

(Peter steals a glance at Victoria, as he works on the problem.)

JIMMY: She's perfect.

PETER: No, she's not.

JIMMY: OK, so maybe she kind of messed everything up, but — *look at her.* Have you ever seen or heard or smelled *anything* like her at a math meet? I mean, the way you have to look up from your calculator when she walks into the classroom — and I'm not talking about that thing she does with her ponytail — I mean, because you don't know what she's gonna say or do next, but whatever it is, you don't want to miss it. Not one second of it. Not one heartbeat. Because you know it's going to make you feel —

PETER: I'm the one messing everything up.

(Peter stops working on the problem.)

JIMMY: You're being an idiot, Peter.

PETER: I think I'm going to throw up.

JIMMY: You have *everything*, and all you have to do is —

PETER: Here, try this.

(Peter slides over the test paper.)

JIMMY: You do know she *likes* you, don't you?

PETER: She does?

(Peter looks over at Victoria. Jimmy starts to work on the next problem.)

JIMMY: OK, this answer works. *Finally.*

* * *

(Max works on his problem on the ground. Franklin talks to the audience.)

FRANKLIN: So. In case you didn't stop to think about me. How I feel, during all this. Do you even know what this is like?

To wake up one morning — after going to bed every night for nine years knowing that my best friend is two houses away, turning on his night-light and climbing into bed — the one person in the galaxy who I thought — who I *knew* — thought and felt the same way I did. About everything.

But I was wrong. Because I wake up, and it's Sunday morning like every other Sunday morning, except I look over at my backpack in the corner of my room where I threw it the night before after I ran the whole entire way from his house to mine. And I remember those *words*. That he said. He just — said them. While we were sitting there, studying, like we've done ten million times before — and now everything is — wrong. Different and wrong, and I want my best friend back.

So what about that? How I feel — doesn't anyone care about —

(A buzzer buzzes.)

VICTORIA: Time?

(Franklin yells at Max.)

FRANKLIN: I mean — what did you expect me to say!?!

(Max stands up and passes Victoria the test.)

VICTORIA: Because, I haven't even started my problem . . .

FRANKLIN: Tell me, Max, I want to know. Since we're not *one brain*, I don't —

MAX: No, we're not. We're not *the same*. But I'm not a complete loser Franklin, I mean, I'd have to be a major idiot to think that you'd —

FRANKLIN: What?!

MAX: I mean, don't worry, you're not a — it's not like I expected — you were *never* going to say you felt the same way.

FRANKLIN: Then why did you even tell me?

MAX: Because it's how I feel, OK? It's who I am, and you've been my best friend since third grade, Franklin, and more than anyone else in the world, I need you to know who I am —

FRANKLIN: Who you are *now*.

MAX: It's *who I am*.

FRANKLIN: God, do you even know how not fair that is?

MAX: Not fair is making me lie and pretend.

FRANKLIN: Why do things have to change? Tell me that, because I just don't understand when that even happened — like, while we were studying for SATs? While we were writing up one of our lab reports? I don't understand —

MAX: Neither do I, but —

FRANKLIN: Why did things ever have to change?

MAX: They just did.

(Franklin runs off.)

MAX: Franklin — !

(This time, Max follows him. Silence. Victoria looks around, taking in the room. Everyone is watching. She talks to everyone.)

VICTORIA: OK, so — I guess all you math geeks heard that, right? That's why you're all just standing there with your mouths hanging open, holding on to your test papers while your retainers dry out. So what's the matter, can't stomach the —

(Peter exits pronto, like he's gonna vomit.)

VICTORIA: Peter — ?

(Victoria watches him go. Then turns to the crowd, holds up her test paper.)

VICTORIA: OK, *this* is math. Numbers, variables, equations — we can all *do* this. We solve things, and yes, it's pretty awesome, but it's just *math.* Just some pencil marks on a piece of paper, right Jimmy?

(Jimmy picks up the test paper that Peter dropped.)

VICTORIA: And since when are we ruled by a piece of paper? A piece of paper that isn't even like — the Treaty of Versaille or the "diary of a young girl" or whatever, and no matter what you write on it, or how many times you fold it up like top-secret origami, it's just *paper.* So, go on Jimmy, show them what you can do with paper.

(Jimmy holds the test paper above his head. He tears it in two. This surprises and thrills Victoria, who continues with even more conviction.)

VICTORIA: That's right. Just paper. Just math. But what you were all listening to before? Between those two kids, Franklin and Max — *my teammates.* That's real, and it's hard, and it's life.

So come on, you math gods — if you really *are* Klingon warriors, if you really *do* know Bernulli's equation — then raise your hands, brave the paper cuts, and show us all what you can do with a little piece of group work. Something like . . .

(Victoria raises the test paper she's holding, and then tears it in two. This feels amazing. She and Jimmy tear their test papers again and again.)

VICTORIA: That's right, mathletes! Rip! Rip!!!

(The entire room is filled with the sound of students tearing up their group work test papers. It's a magical moment.)

VICTORIA: And *this*, I am proud to say, is my other teammate Jimmy. He's totally almost a sophomore. We're the Longwood High School Math Team. And last time I checked, this competition was *not* over.

So — come on, Jimmy. Time to kick some math butt.
(Victoria saunters off, and Jimmy follows, too-cool-for-school.)

SCENE 13: ANOTHER LESSON

Peter's parked car. Victoria sits in the driver's seat. Peter sits next to her.

VICTORIA: What, are you kidding? I thought I was going to *die*. Why are you — you think that's amusing? I'm serious, Peter, I almost stopped breathing and dropped *dead*, on the spot.

PETER: But you didn't.

VICTORIA: But then I was like, ew, who's gonna try to give me mouth-to-mouth when I pass out, so then I started breathing again. And then I . . . looked over at Jen. Sitting there sideways in her desk, pretending to be looking at the *parking lot* when really I knew she was listening to me and totally thinking: Since when does *she* do her English homework?

And *then* I looked over at the other Jen, who *was* looking up at me, but I knew she wasn't listening to a word I was saying about *Catcher in the Rye*. Instead she was memorizing every inch of my outfit, so that she could pick it apart tonight on the phone.

PETER: And that made you *not* be nervous anymore?

VICTORIA: No, that made me want to be sick, but then I thought: I really don't care what they think. Or, at least for that one English class period, I cared more about Holden Caulfield. You know, Holden was a really messed-up kid. Or maybe just a little lonely and confused, I don't know — that's what Max thinks. He let me practice my oral report with him. I wanted to make it really — awesome. And not just to show the Jens, or to impress Mrs. Snyder so she won't fail me in English, but like, awesome for *me*. Because that's how I want to be now.

Or, that's *who I am*, and it just took a little time for me to figure that out. But now I don't care what the Jens or anyone else at this school thinks — I'm just going to *do it*.

PETER: Do — school?

VICTORIA: Do anything! And, like, be who I am, and say how I feel — even if I feel like I'm going to —

PETER: Vomit.

VICTORIA: Yeah — actually, Peter — I'm really — sorry — about that.

PETER: Don't apologize for living, Victoria. It's not your fault I got food poisoning.

VICTORIA: I know, but you said you were sick, and I said you were just *afraid* and —

PETER: I *was* afraid.

VICTORIA: And I just wanted to *show you*, after you said that stupid thing about how with me on the Math Team there was no way in —

PETER: But that was before I even knew —

VICTORIA: But you *said* it, and that means you must have thought it. And when Jimmy said that you had said that, I — felt this pit in my stomach because I hated the way that sounded.

And I hated most of all knowing that if I were you, I probably would have thought that about me too. So when we actually made it to States, I knew that I needed to *do this*, to *show you* that —

PETER: You didn't need to show me anything.

VICTORIA: Whatever, Peter, what does that even *mean* —

PETER: I was being an idiot —

VICTORIA: Especially since you've been acting all weird ever since —

PETER: Every time you were near, I felt weird, like I might —

VICTORIA: OK, I'm sorry I make you feel like *vomiting*.

PETER: No, it's not like —

VICTORIA: You didn't call me back.

PETER: What?

VICTORIA: You never called me back.

PETER: But you're the one who didn't call *me* back —

VICTORIA: But then I did!

PETER: During the student council meeting, when you *knew* I wouldn't be able to —

VICTORIA: How am I supposed to know when stupid student council meets —

PETER: Every Tuesday night.

VICTORIA: I'm not like the senior class Treasurer!

PETER: You've been at this school for *two years*.

VICTORIA: OK, student council is *not* as cool as you might think, Peter.

PETER: I wasn't going to call you back when I thought you clearly didn't even want to talk to me.

VICTORIA: OK, *that* is really — flawed reasoning. And totally *not clear*. And by the way, I really don't need to practice driving your car around this parking lot, so maybe I should just walk home.

PETER: You're walking home?

VICTORIA: I said *maybe*. God, aren't you even listening to me?

PETER: But I thought we were going to have a driving lesson.

VICTORIA: Actually, my mom's been letting me drive. On real roads. Actually, I drove on the highway last week. So clearly I *don't* need to be sitting here.

PETER: So then why did you say *yes* when I asked if you wanted to practice driving my car around the school parking lot?

VICTORIA: Peter, are you *really* such an idiot?

(They sit there. She makes a move to leave.)

PETER: Victoria, will you go to the prom with me?

VICTORIA: What?!

PETER: Does that mean yes?

VICTORIA: It means — like — I thought you didn't care about any of that *normal* high school stuff?

PETER: I thought I didn't either, but now I think — maybe I do. I don't know anymore. It's like an alien sucked out my brain, and I hardly know how to tie my sneakers, and it's not even the prom, it's more just like — me thinking about you.

VICTORIA: And did you ever think I might need time to get a dress? The prom is in like three days!

PETER: The only thing I know is, I want to be with you, Victoria. Like, all the time. Or, like even for five seconds. Because, five seconds with you — in the hallway or across the cafeteria, trying to get behind you in the hot-lunch line even when I'm not getting hot lunch, or trying to see you before you walk into Spanish when I'm on my way to calculus —

VICTORIA: Second period Thursday.

PETER: And when I look over at you, and you're looking at me, and I think maybe you're thinking what I might be thinking it's like —

VICTORIA: Two brains, both thinking the same thing.

(He says this with difficulty.)

PETER: 3.141592653589793238462643. That's — all I know now. And I know it's only the first twenty-four decimal places, but — wait, how many do you know?

VICTORIA: Fifty-two.

PETER: That's — amazing. Victoria Martin, you *amaze* me.

VICTORIA: But I would like you even if you only knew a quarter of that.

PETER: Just six digits?

VICTORIA: Or three.

PETER: 3.14. But everyone knows —

VICTORIA: But it's — different. When you say it, it's like . . .
   (Victoria kisses Peter. It's sweet.)
VICTORIA: *Pi.*
PETER: Pi.
   (They kiss some more.)

SCENE 14: THE WRAP-UP

Jimmy enters, sees them kissing, and turns to audience.

JIMMY: Kids . . .
   (He chuckles and shakes his head like the older and wiser almost-sophomore he is.)
JIMMY: In case you haven't noticed? In high school, nothing's changed. Except — *everything.*
   We totally came in third at States. Which sucks — but is also *awesome,* especially since our senior was in the infirmary throwing up four years of math knowledge.
   Luckily, the group work round was thrown out entirely by the judges. I mean, how could they score all those torn up test papers?
   (He smiles innocently.)

* * *

(Max practices his three-point shot with the spongy basketball. Until the ball is suddenly intercepted by Franklin.)
FRANKLIN: So . . . ?
MAX: So.
FRANKLIN: Did you get them?
MAX: Yeah.
   (From their back pockets, both pull out score reports from the College Board like a Wild West quick draw. They exchange reports.)
MAX: What?! You got the same verbal score I did.
FRANKLIN: I scored!
MAX: But — I don't understand!
FRANKLIN: Neither do I.

MAX: I mean, you're *terrible* in verbal, and we got the same exact SAT scores. So —

FRANKLIN: So, I guess — I mean — I just wanted to say . . .

MAX: You don't have to say anything, Franklin.

FRANKLIN: But I want to say —

(Jimmy comes rushing into the classroom.)

JIMMY: Sorry, sorry, sorry, I know I'm . . .

FRANKLIN: *Thanks.* For letting me share your brain.

MAX: Sure thing.

JIMMY: Wait, I thought there was an emergency meeting about next year's Math Team?

(Victoria and Peter enter.)

VICTORIA: There is.

FRANKLIN: So, if this is about *next year's* team . . . ?

MAX: What's *he* doing here?

(They look at Peter.)

VICTORIA: He's with me.

PETER: She has my keys.

(Victoria tosses Peter his car keys.)

JIMMY: OK, I met this girl? She'll be a freshman next year, and I think she might be perfect. For the team, I mean. Especially if I do a lot of practice problems with her this summer . . .

PETER: Nice work, Jimmy.

FRANKLIN: Yeah, nice work, Romeo, but — *that's* the math emergency?

VICTORIA: Actually, there is no emergency. I just wanted to call this emergency meeting because — I could. As the Math Team's new unofficial captain. If I *am* unofficial captain . . . ?

MAX: Wait, are you going to make us tear up our test papers?

VICTORIA: Only if its group work.

FRANKLIN: Actually, I was thinking maybe we could *work* on group work.

VICTORIA: As your unofficial captain, I think that's an excellent idea. I mean — I *am* captain, right?

PETER: I think that's a given.

FRANKLIN: Yeah, Victoria Martin . . .

MAX: Math Team Queen.

JIMMY: Totally.

SCENE 15: THE END

Victoria's phone is ringing. She rushes in with her school bag full of books, answers.

VICTORIA: Hello?

Oh, hi Dad.

I just — didn't know you'd be calling today, I mean, it's not your night to —

Yes, today *was* a good second-to-last-Tuesday of my sophomore year, thank you very much. You know, final exams aren't that bad if you study for them. Señor Johnson said I was *excelente* — *and* you were right, Mrs. Snyder totally liked my essay about what would happen if Anne Frank and Holden Caulfield were locked together in an attic, so my final grade in English is a C+ which is not like awesome, but it's like *adios* summer school.

So it's a good thing I've been checking the temperature in California every day and creating a scatter plot of the values, right? I'll totally be set climate-wise when I get there.

Yeah. I can't wait too.

(*She talks to the audience.*)

VICTORIA: Because summer is going to be really awesome, in California *and* right here. Like — coast to coast, day after day after day, all the way to — OK, maybe not infinity, but at least until my junior year.

Because in case you didn't already know? I make Pi totally, totally cool.

END OF PLAY